THE GIFT OF PROPHECY IN 1 CORINTHIANS

Wayne A. Grudem
Assistant Professor of New Testament
Trinity Evangelical Divinity School
Deerfield, Illinois

Wipf and Stock Publishers
150 West Broadway • Eugene OR 97401
1999

The Gift of Prophecy in 1 Corinthians

By Grudem, Wayne A.
Copyright©1999 by Grudem, Wayne A.

ISBN: 1-57910-325-1

Reprinted by *Wipf and Stock Publishers* 1999
150 West Broadway • Eugene OR 97401

Previously Published by University Press of America, 1982.

To my parents,
Arden and Jean Grudem,

without whose encouragement and help
this book would not have been possible.

Acknowledgements

I am grateful for permission from the following publishers and journals to reprint parts of my previously published articles in the following sections: pages 185-201, the Westminster Theological Journal; pages 234-239, Paraclete (Springfield, Missouri); pages 239-255; The Standard (Arlington Heights, Illinois); pages 263-288; Biblische Zeitschrift; and parts of pages 12-20 and 50-53, the Zondervan Corporation (for material to be published in a forthcoming book, Scripture and Truth, edited by D. A. Carson and J. D. Woodbridge). I am also grateful to the Division of Christian Education of the National Council of Churches of Christ in the U.S.A. for permission to cite frequently from the Revised Standard Version of the Bible, copyrighted 1946, 1952 © 1971, 1973.

TABLE OF CONTENTS

	Page
ACKNOWLEDGEMENTS	v
TABLE OF CONTENTS	vii
PREFACE	xv
ABBREVIATIONS	xvii
INTRODUCTION	1
CHAPTER ONE: THE AUTHORITY OF PROPHECY IN 1 CORINTHIANS	7

  I. DIFFERENT TYPES OF DIVINE AUTHORITY . . . 7

    A. Divine Authority as Perceived by Speaker or by Audience? 7

    B. Divine Authority for General Content or Exact Words? 9

    C. The Problem of False Prophecy 10

    D. Summary 11

  II. DIVINE AUTHORITY OF ACTUAL WORDS: SOME OLD TESTAMENT EXAMPLES 11

    A. The Prophets as Messengers of God . . 12

    B. The Prophet's Words as Words of God 15

    C. Implications of Divine Authority in Prophetic Words 18

      1. The people think that to disbelieve or disobey a prophet's words is to disbelieve or disobey God 18
      2. The words of a true prophet are thought to be beyond challenge or question 19

		Page
III.	DIVINE AUTHORITY OF GENERAL CONTENT: SOME EXAMPLES FROM EXTRA-BIBLICAL JEWISH LITERATURE	21
	A. The Belief that Prophecy with a Divine Authority of Actual Words had Ceased	21
	B. The Acknowledgement that Revelatory Activity Continued	24
IV.	THE NEUTRALITY OF THE נָבִיא AND ΠΡΟΦΗΤΗΣ WORD GROUPS WITH REGARD TO VARIOUS TYPES OF DIVINE AUTHORITY	33
V.	OLD TESTAMENT PROPHETS AND NEW TESTAMENT APOSTLES	43
	A. New Testament Apostles are Seen as Messengers of Christ	43
	B. The Apostles as Prophets	53
VI.	PROPHETIC AUTHORITY IN 1 CORINTHIANS	54
	A. The Structure of 1 Cor. 12-14	54
	B. 1 Cor. 14.29: Evaluating Prophecies	58
	1. Is this verse connected to διακρίσεις πνευμάτων in 1 Cor. 12.10?	58
	2. Does οἱ ἄλλοι in 1 Cor. 14.29 refer to the other prophets?	60
	3. Conclusion: οἱ ἄλλοι refers to the entire congregation	62
	4. How is the prophecy judged?	62
	C. 1 Cor. 14.30: Revelation Which is Lightly Esteemed	67
	1. Prophecies which could be lost	67
	2. Does "revelation" imply divine authority?	69
	D. 1 Cor. 14.36: No Rules for Worship from Corinthian Prophets	71

			Page
	E.	1 Cor. 14.37-38: Prophets Who are Subject to Paul's Authority	72
	F.	1 Cor. 11.5: Prophetesses Who Remain Subordinate	72
	G.	Conclusion	73
VII.	PROPHETIC AUTHORITY ELSEWHERE IN THE NEW TESTAMENT		74
	A.	The Scope of This Investigation	74
	B.	Mt. 10.19-20	75
	C.	Ac. 11.28	76
	D.	Ac. 13.2	77
	E.	Ac. 19.6	77
	F.	Ac. 21.4	78
	G.	Ac. 21.9	78
	H.	Ac. 21.10-11	79
	I.	Eph. 2.20 and 3.5	82
	J.	1 Th. 5.19-21	105
	K.	The Book of Revelation	106
	L.	Did. 11	109
	M.	Conclusion	110
	N.	Additional Note on Prophecy in Early Church History	111
VIII.	SUMMARY OF CHAPTER ONE		112
CHAPTER TWO: THE PSYCHOLOGICAL STATE OF THE PROPHET			115
I.	1 CORINTHIANS 14.30: THE RELATIONSHIP BETWEEN PROPHECY AND "REVELATION"		115
	A.	The Situation	115

		Page
	B. An Analysis of the "Revelation" to the Prophet	116
	1. Spontaneity	117
	2. Individuality	117
	3. Origin	118
	a. The Use of Ἀποκαλύπτω	119
	b. 1 Cor. 14.32: The Spirits of the Prophets	120
	4. Perspective	129
	5. Perceptibility	131
	C. Related Verses in 1 Corinthians	136
	1. 1 Cor. 12.8-11: Is Prophecy "Miraculous"?	136
	2. 1 Cor. 14.6	138
	D. The Essential Characteristics of Prophecy: The Difference Between Prophecy and Teaching	139
II.	1 CORINTHIANS 13.8-12: CERTAINTY AND CLARITY OF PERCPETION	144
III.	1 CORINTHIANS 14.29-33: THE QUESTION OF PROPHETIC ECSTASY	150
	A. The Problem Defined	150
	B. 1 Cor. 14.29-33	152
	C. Related Verses in 1 Corinthians	155
	1. 1 Cor. 14.3-4	155
	2. 1 Cor. 14.23-25	155
	3. 1 Cor. 14.40	155
	D. Objections	
	1. The Problem at Corinth	155
	2. 1 Cor. 12.1-3	156
	E. Related Verses in the NT	173
	1. Ac. 19.6	174
	2. 2 Cor. 12.1ff	174
	3. 2 Pet. 1.21	175
	F. Conclusion	176

		Page
IV.	1 CORINTHIANS 13.2: UNDERSTANDING MYSTERIES AND KNOWLEDGE: THE EFFECT OF LOVE	177
	A. Mysteries and Knowledge	177
	B. Love	178
V.	SUMMARY OF CHAPTER TWO	179

CHAPTER THREE: THE FUNCTION, CONTENT AND FORM OF PROPHECY 181

I.	THE FUNCTIONS OF PROPHECY	181
	A. 1 Cor. 14.3: Upbuilding, Encouragement, Consolation	181
	B. 1 Cor. 14.31: Teaching?	185
	C. 1 Cor. 14.20-25: A Sign of God's Attitude	185
	1. Is. 28.9-13	186
	2. Paul's Use of Is. 28.11	190
	3. Prophecy and Tongues as Signs	192
	D. Functions Outside 1 Corinthians	201
	1. Ac. 15.32	201
	2. Ac. 11.27 and 21.11	202
	3. 1 Tim. 1.18	202
	4. 1 Tim. 4.14	203
	5. The Book of Revelation	205
	6. Other Possible Functions	206
	E. Prophets as "Charismatic Leaders"?	207
	F. 1 Cor. 13.8-13: The Time of the Cessation of Prophecy	210
	1. The Purpose of 1 Cor. 13.8-13	210
	2. 1 Cor. 13.10: The Cessation of Prophecy at the Parousia	211
	3. Objections	214
	4. Conclusion	219
II.	THE CONTENT OF PROPHECY	219

		Page
III.	THE FORM OF PROPHECY	222
IV.	ADDITIONAL NOTE: PROPHETIC CONTRIBUTIONS TO THE GOSPEL TRADITION	224
V.	SUMMARY OF CHAPTER THREE	229

CHAPTER FOUR: THE QUALIFICATIONS FOR BEING A PROPHET 231

- I. INFORMAL RECOGNITION: THOSE WHO PROPHESY ARE PROPHETS 231
- II. CAN ALL BELIEVERS PROPHESY? 234
  - A. Permission to Prophesy 235
  - B. Potential Ability 235
  - C. Actual Ability 236
  - D. Ability to Prophesy at Will 238
  - E. Summary 239
- III. 1 COR. 14.33b-35: COULD WOMEN PROPHESY IN CHURCH? 239
  - A. Statement of the Problem 239
  - B. The Possibility of a Post-Pauline Interpolation 240
  - C. Contextual Limitations on Σιγάω and Λαλέω 242
  - D. The Structure of 1 Cor. 14.26-36 . . 245
  - E. Reasons Why Vs. 34 Refers to the Evaluation of Prophecies 251
  - F. Conclusion 255
- IV. THE ABILITY TO PROPHESY 256
  - A. Was prophecy a Temporary or a Permanent Gift? 256
  - B. Degrees of Prophetic Ability 257

		Page
C. Seeking the Prophetic Gift		259
V. SUMMARY OF CHAPTER FOUR		261
CONCLUSION		261
APPENDIX: GERHARD DAUTZENBERG ON 1 COR. 12.10		263
BIBLIOGRAPHY		289
INDEX OF AUTHORS CITED		311
INDEX OF SUBJECTS		317
INDEX OF HEBREW AND GREEK WORDS DISCUSSED		323
INDEX OF BIBLICAL AND EXTRA-BIBLICAL PASSAGES DISCUSSED		327
ABOUT THE AUTHOR		333

PREFACE

This book attempts to define in detail the nature of the New Testament gift of prophecy as it was practiced in the church at Corinth at the time of Paul's First Epistle to the Corinthians, and then to compare that type of prophecy with the prophecy in other New Testament churches, and with Old Testament prophecy. The manuscript is identical to my 1978 doctoral dissertation for the University of Cambridge, England, except that I have added two brief sections (pp. 43-53 on New Testament apostles and pp. 82-105 on Eph. 2.20) which were originally written for the dissertation but which could not be included in it because of the 80,000-word limit on dissertations at Cambridge.

Although this study itself remains primarily exegetical and makes no attempt to evaluate any of the current phenomena of prophecy found, for example, within the modern charismatic movement, I think that many contemporary applications of this study will be evident to all present-day readers who, like myself, consider the Bible to be the Word of God as well as the word of man, and, as such, an eminently trustworthy guide for life today.

I found that a detailed study of the biblical text led me to a definition of New Testament prophecy which was somewhat different from the teachings of many within the charismatic movement, but also different from the views of those, especially within Reformed and Dispensationalist circles, who have expressed objections to or skepticism about claims to prophecy found in charismatic groups today. But even though I do not agree fully with either group, I hope that in my somewhat new definition of the nature of Christian prophecy both pro-charismatics and anti-charismatics may be able to find a "middle ground" with a considerable potential for reconciling their current differences.

Yet most Christians today probably find themselves in neither a pro-charismatic nor an anti-charismatic camp. I hope this book will provide for them a great encouragement in the realization that this gift, which Paul says we should "earnestly desire" (1 Cor. 14.39), has already been occurring from time to time in the ordinary functions of their small prayer fellowships, Bible studies, Sunday School classes, and (perhaps?) even in an occasional church business meeting, where the Holy Spirit has seemed to be present in a remarkable way, guiding the conversation in unexpected and wonderfully rewarding ways. Perhaps for them this study will prompt a better understanding of the gift of prophecy when it occurs, and will even encourage its more frequent use, within biblical guidelines, for the edification of the church.

Since I completed this manuscript two important books have appeared: <u>New Testament Prophecy</u> by Dr. David Hill (Atlanta: John Knox Press, 1979) and <u>Perspectives on Pentecost</u> by Dr. Richard Gaffin (Phillipsburg, N.J.: Presbyterian and Reformed, 1979). Although I have not altered the present manuscript to interact with either book, I have profited from these and other writings of both men, and from their own personal comments on the first draft of my dissertation (which each of them graciously read and commented on in 1976 and 1977). (I have also written a review of Dr. Hill's book which will appear in a forthcoming issue of <u>Themelios</u>).

I am very grateful to my supervisor, Professor C. F. D. Moule, for his unfailing friendship, encouragement, and wise guidance throughout the preparation of this study, and to Dr. A. J. M. Wedderburn and the late Professor G. W. H. Lampe for many helpful comments on an earlier draft of the manuscript. I am also grateful to my friend, Dr. Vern Poythress, who read and made many valuable comments on this work as it was in progress.

I am deeply appreciative to my parents, Mr. and Mrs. Arden Grudem, who generously provided financial assistance without which I could not have pursued this research.

I wish to thank Miss Jean Lindblom of Bethel College, who has now twice typed this manuscript quickly and well, and Mrs. Sharon Provo and Mrs. Janice Seifrid, who helped in the typing. Four friends also were a great help: Alan Steier and Morris Johnson in proofreading, and C. Michael Johnson and Grayson Paschke in compiling the indices.

Finally, my wife Margaret and sons Elliot, Oliver, and Alexander, each in a unique way, have been a constant and very special source of encouragement and support, and have helped me in this work much more than they realize.

If this work in some small way can contribute to our understanding of the New Testament and ultimately to the edification of the church, then I shall be grateful above all to the Lord, for "from him and through him and to him are all things. To him be the glory forever" (Rom. 11.36).

Wayne Grudem
September, 1981

ABBREVIATIONS

General notes: Commentaries are cited by the author's last name only. Foreign works are cited from an English translation when available. New Testament citations are from the United Bible Societies' text (third edition), and Biblical quotations in English are generally from the RSV, although at many points I have retranslated to bring out certain emphases. In all cases, the responsibility for the translation is my own.

Quotations from the Apostolic Fathers, Philo, Josephus, and Classical authors are from the Loeb Classical Library editions unless otherwise specified. The Dead Sea Scrolls are quoted from E. Lohse, ed., Die Texte aus Qumran (Munich, 1971^2), and G. Vermes, The Dead Sea Scrolls in English (Harmondsworth, 1968^3). For the Mishnah I have used H. Danby, The Mishnah (Oxford, 1933), and for the Babylonian Talmud and Midrash Rabbah, the Soncino Press translations (although I have at points made a more literal translation, always then including the Hebrew or Aramaic original in parentheses).

Abbreviations for Philo are those in the Loeb Classical Library edition, Vol. X, xxxv-xxxvi. Abbreviations of tractates in the Mishnah, Talmud and Tosefta are those given in H. Danby, The Mishnah, 806.

AG	Walter Bauer, Wm. Arndt and F. Gingrich, A Greek-English Lexicon of the NT (ET Chicago, 1957)
AHG	Apostolic History and the Gospel (Fs. F. F. Bruce), ed. W. Gasque and R. P. Martin (Exeter, 1970)
ANET	Ancient Near Eastern Texts Relating to the OT, ed. James B. Pritchard (Princeton, 1950)
Aq.	Aquila
Asn. Mos.	Assumption of Moses (Charles, Pseudepigrapha, 407ff)
b.	Babylonian Talmud

2 Bar.	2 Baruch (Charles, *Pseudepigrapha*, 470ff)
3 Bar.	3 Baruch (Charles, *Pseudepigrapha*, 527ff)
Barn.	Epistle of Barnabas
BASOR	Bulletin of the American Schools of Oriental Research
BDB	Francis Brown, S. R. Driver, C. A. Briggs, Hebrew and English Lexicon of the OT (Oxford, 1907)
BETS	Bulletin of the Evangelical Theological Society
BibSac	Bibliotheca Sacra
BJRL	Bulletin of the John Rylands Library
Bl.-D.	F. Blass and F. Debrunner, A Greek Grammar of the NT (ET Chicago, 1961)
BNTC	Black's New Testament Commentary
BTB	Biblical Theology Bulletin
BWANT	Beiträge zur Wissenschaft vom Alten und Neuen Testament
BZ	Biblische Zeitschrift
BZNW	Beihefte zur Zeitschrift für die neutestamentliche Wissenschaft
CBQ	Catholic Biblical Quarterly
CGT	Cambridge Greek Testament
CHI	Christian History and Interpretation (Fs. John Knox), ed. W. R. Farmer, C. F. D. Moule and R. R. Niebuhr (Cambridge, 1967)
CJT	Canadian Journal of Theology
1 Cl.	1 Clement
2 Cl.	2 Clement
CNT	Commentaire du Nouveau Testament

CSNT	Christ and Spirit in the New Testament (Fs. C. F. D. Moule), ed. B. Lindars and S. Smalley (Cambridge, 1973)
DBS	Dictionnaire de la Bible, Supplément
Did.	Didache
DJD	Discoveries in the Judean Desert, ed. D. Barthelemy et al. (Oxford, 1955ff)
1 En.	1 Enoch (Charles, Pseudepigrapha, 163ff)
2 En.	2 Enoch (Charles, Pseudepigrapha, 425ff)
Ep. Arist.	The Epistle of Aristeas (Charles, Pseudepigrapha, 83ff)
Ep. Pol.	Epistle of Polycarp to the Philippians
EQ	The Evangelical Quarterly
ET	English translation
EvTh	Evangelische Theologie
4 Ezr.	4 Ezra (Charles, Pseudepigrapha, 542ff)
Fs.	Festschrift
F.T.	Fragmentary Targum
HDB	Hastings's Dictionary of the Bible

Herm.	Hermas, The Shepherd
	    Mand.: Mandate
	    Sim. : Similitude
	    Vis. : Vision

HNT	Handbuch zum Neuen Testament
HTKNT	Herders theologischer Kommentar zum Neuen Testament
HTR	Harvard Theological Review
HUCA	Hebrew Union College Annual
ICC	International Critical Commentary
IF	introductory formula

Ign.	Ignatius		
	Eph.	:	*Epistle to the Ephesians*
	Mg.	:	*Epistle to the Magnesians*
	Phld.	:	*Epistle to the Philadelphians*
	Pol.	:	*Epistle to Polycarp*
	Rom.	:	*Epistle to the Romans*
	Sm.	:	*Epistle to the Smyrnaens*
	Tr.	:	*Epistle to the Trallians*

j.   Jerusalem Talmud

Jastrow   Marcus Jastrow, *A Dictionary of the Targumim, the Talmud Babli and Yerushalmi, and the Midrashic Literature* (New York, 1961)

JBL   *Journal of Biblical Literature*

JE   *The Jewish Encyclopedia* (ed. I. Singer et al.; New York and London, 1901-06)

JETS   *Journal of the Evangelical Theological Society* (continuation of *BETS*)

JJS   *Journal of Jewish Studies*

Jos.	Josephus		
	A.	:	*Antiquitates Judaica*
	Ap.	:	*Contra Apionem*
	B.	:	*Bellum Judaicum*
	V.	:	*Vita*

JQR   *Jewish Quarterly Review*

JSS   *Journal of Semitic Studies*

KD   *Kerygma und Dogma*

Lampe   G. W. H. Lampe, ed., *A Patristic Greek Lexicon* (Oxford, 1961-68)

LS   H. G. Liddell and R. Scott, *A Greek-English Lexicon* (Oxford, 1940^9)

LXX   Septuagint (ed. A. Rahlfs; Stuttgart, 1935)

M.   Mishnah

Mart. Is.   Martyrdom of Isaiah (Charles, *Pseudepigrapha*, 155ff)

Mart. Pol.	Martyrdom of Polycarp
MM	J. H. Moulton and G. Milligan, The Vocabulary of the Greek Testament (repr. Grand Rapids, 1972)
MNTC	Moffatt New Testament Commentary
Moule	C. F. D. Moule, An Idiom-Book of NT Greek (Cambridge, 1963^2)
NASB	New American Standard Bible
NCB	New Century Bible
NClB	New Clarendon Bible
NEB	New English Bible
NIC	New International Commentary
NIV	New International Version
NPNF	Nicene and Post-Nicene Fathers
NTD	Das Neue Testament Deutsch
NTS	New Testament Studies
OTL	The Old Testament Library
R.	Midrash Rabbah (The R. follows the title of the Biblical book, as Gen. R. for Midrash Rabbah on Genesis)
Relig St	Religious Studies
repr.	reprint
Robertson, Grammar	A. T. Robertson, A Grammar of the Greek NT in the Light of Historical Research
RP	A. Robertson and A. Plummer, 1 Corinthians
RScR	Recherches de Science Religieuse
RSV	Revised Standard Version
RTR	Reformed Theological Review
SANT	Studien zum Alten und Neuen Testament

SBET	Studia Biblica et Theologica (Pasadena, Cal.)
SBLDS	Society of Biblical Literature Dissertation Series
SBM	Stuttgarter Biblische Monographien
SBT	Studies in Biblical Theology
SEÅ	Svensk exegetisk årsbok
Sib.Or.	Sibylline Oracles (Charles, Pseudepigrapha, 368ff)
SJT	Scottish Journal of Theology
SNovT	Supplements to Novum Testamentum
SNTSMS	Society for New Testament Studies Monograph Series
ST	Studia Theologica
Str.-B.	H. Strack and P. Billerbeck, Kommentar zum Neuen Testament aus Talmud und Midrasch (Munich, 1926ff)
SUNT	Studien zur Umwelt des Neuen Testaments
Symm.	Symmachus
T. Abr.	Testament of Abraham (tr. Michael E. Stone; Missoula, Mt., 1972)
T. Asher	Testament of Asher
TDNT	Theological Dictionary of the New Testament, ed. G. Kittel and G. Friedrich, trans. G. Bromiley (9 vols., ET Grand Rapids, 1964-74)
Th.	Theodotion
THNT	Theologischer Handkommentar zum Neuen Testament
ThZ	Theologische Zeitschrift
TLZ	Theologische Literaturzeitung

T.N.	Targum Neofiti
T.Naph.	Testament of Naphtali
TNTC	Tyndale New Testament Commentaries
T.O.	Targum Onkelos
Tos.	Tosefta
T. Ps.-Jon.	Targum Pseudo-Jonathan
T.Sol.	Testament of Solomon
TU	Texte und Untersuchungen
VT	Vetus Testamentum
WC	Westminster Commentaries
WTJ	Westminster Theological Journal
ZNW	Zeitschrift für die neutestamentliche Wissenschaft

INTRODUCTION

The gift of prophecy in the New Testament has been the subject of a number of recent studies.[1] The most generally accepted conclusions among these studies are that New Testament prophets spoke "words

---

[1]The two most useful longer studies are T. M. Crone, Early Christian Prophecy: A Study of Its Origin and Function (Baltimore, Md., 1973) and E. Cothenet, "Prophétisme dans le Nouveau Testament," DBS, 8, cols. 1222-1337, (largely summarized in his "Prophétisme et ministère d'après le Nouveau Testament," La Maison-Dieu 107 [1971], 29-50). Both of these are much wider in scope than this investigation, and both include much useful material. Some of the other important longer studies which are partly or completely devoted to the question of NT prophecy are M. A. Chevallier, Esprit de Dieu, paroles d'hommes (Neuchatel, 1966); G. Dautzenberg, Urchristliche Prophetie (Stuttgart, 1975); J. D. G. Dunn, Jesus and the Spirit (London, 1975); G. Friedrich, "προφήτης: D. Prophets and Prophecies in the New Testament," TDNT VI, 282-61; H. A. Guy, New Testament Prophecy (London, 1947); K. Maly, Mündige Gemeinde (Stuttgart, 1967).
The most perceptive short study is probably Ernest Best, "Prophets and Preachers," SJT 12 (1959), 129-50. Other brief studies include J. D. G. Dunn, "New Wine in Old Wine-Skins: VI. Prophet," ExpT 85 (1973-74), 4-8; H. Greeven, "Propheten, Lehrer, Vorsteher bei Paulus," ZNW 44 (1952-53), 1-43; C. M. Robeck, Jr., "The Gift of Prophecy in Acts and Paul," SBET 4 (1974), 15-35 and 5 (1975), 37-54; J. Lindblom, "Altchristlicher Prophetismus," in Gesichte und Offenbarung (Lund, 1968), 162-205; H. Sasse, "Apostles, Prophets, Teachers," RTR 27:1 Jan.-Apr., 1968), 11-21.
Still other studies have treated more specialized questions. On attempts to discover and analyze "prophetic" sayings in the NT text the literature in this century alone is vast, beginning with the early work of E. C. Selwyn, The Christian Prophets and the Prophetic Apocalypse (London, 1900), and continuing to the very recent work by U. Müller, Prophetie und Predigt im Neuen Testament (Gütersloh, 1975). On the history of the προφήτης word group the standard work is still E. Fascher, ΠΡΟΦΗΤΗΣ (Giessen, 1927), and on OT prophecy and its relationship to prophecy in other

of the Lord"[2] in a manner similar to that of the Old
Testament prophets (Ac. 21.11, Rev. 2-3),[3] provided
some kind of "charismatic leadership" for the early
church (Ac. 13.1, 15.22; Rev., passim),[4] perhaps had a
role in the development of the Gospel tradition,[5] and,
at times, had among their number false prophets who
proclaimed false doctrine while claiming divine

---

religions, the well-known work by A. Guillaume,
Prophecy and Divination among the Hebrews and Other
Semites (London, 1938), is now superseded by the monumental study of J. Lindblom, Prophecy in Ancient Israel
(Oxford, 1962).

[2] At the beginning of Chapter 1 I discuss in some
detail the various senses in which the claim to speak
"words of the Lord" might be understood.

[3] So Dunn, JS, 237; Friedrich, TDNT VI, 848-50;
Müller, Prophetie und Predigt, 234; Guy, NT Prophecy,
118; Sasse, "Apostles Prophets, Teachers," 14; Lindblom,
"Altchristlicher Prophetismus," 162-64; J. Reiling,
Hermes and Christian Prophecy: A Study of the Eleventh
Mandate (Leiden, 1973), 13. However, there have also
been those who tended to equate prophecy with preaching
or teaching: note the references in Dunn, JS, 418, n.
147 (to p. 228).

[4] See, for example, Dunn, JS, 180-82, 285-300;
E. Ellis, "The Role of the Christian Prophet in Acts,"
AHG, 55-67; E. Käsemann, "Ministry and Community in the
New Testament," in Essays on New Testament Themes (ET
London, 1964), 63-94; however, cf. Cothenet, DBS 8,
cols. 1284, 1288, 1291, 1301-03, 1312, and the discussion in Chapter 3, below (pp. 211ff).

[5] R. Bultmann, The History of the Synoptic
Tradition (ET Oxford, 1972; from second German edn.,
1931), 127-28; F. W. Beare, "Sayings of the Risen Jesus
in the Synoptic Tradition," CHI, 161-81; M. Eugene
Boring, "How May We Identify Oracles of Christian
Prophets in the Synoptic Tradition?" JBL 91 (1972),
501-22; however, cf. D. Hill, "On the Creative Role
of Christian Prophets," NTS 20 (1973-74), 262-74, and
the discussion in Chapter 3, below (pp. 224ff).

inspiration (Mt. 7.15, 24.11, 24, Mk. 13.22, 1 Jn. 4.1).[6] Examples of such early Christian prophets include John in Revelation, Paul at certain points in his epistles, the prophets spoken of in Mt. 10.19-20 and parallels, the prophets mentioned in Did. 11-15 and in Herm. Mand. 11, and, in Acts, perhaps Agabus (Ac. 11.28, 21.10-11) and Judas and Silas (Ac. 15.32). Somewhat earlier, John the Baptist and Jesus himself also seem to have fit this general prophetic pattern. Investigations into these aspects of NT prophecy have been quite thorough.

However, several scholars have called attention to the fact that NT prophecy does not appear to have been a homogeneous phenomenon. There seem to have been at least two types of Christian prophecy, or perhaps even several slightly different types. Vielhauer, for example, sees some differences between prophecy in Pauline churches and prophecy in Palestinian Christian circles.[7] Cothenet sees a particular kind of "apocalyptic prophecy" in Thessalonica.[8] Müller distinguishes (i) prophetic missionary preachers, (ii) itinerant prophets (Ac. 11, 21 and the Didache), and (iii) community prophets (Pauline epistles and Revelation).[9] Lindblom contrasts those prophets who had a lasting gift ("professional" prophets) with those who prophesied only occasionally.[10] Lampe writes, "Within the New Testament period there seems to have been a definite, though to us obscure, distinction between occasional prophesying by 'ordinary' church members, on the one hand, and the exercise of a ministry by 'specialist' prophets, on the other."[11] So several types of distinctions have been made,

---

[6]G. W. H. Lampe, "'Grievous Wolves' (Acts 20:29)," CSNT, 253-68; Cothenet, DBS 8, cols. 1311-1316.

[7]P. Vielhauer, "Prophecy," in New Testament Aprocrypha, ed. E. Hennecke, W. Schneemelcher, R. McL. Wilson (2 vols.; ET London, 1963-65), II, 605-07.

[8]DBS 8, cols. 1289f.

[9]Prophetie und Predigt, pp. 19ff.

[10]"Altchristlicher Prophetismus," 179. Similarly, see Ellis, "Role," 62f.

[11]Lampe, "Grievous Wolves," 257.

distinctions, for instance, in content, form, purpose, frequency, and type of activity.

Another important distinction has been noticed occasionally, a possible distinction in authority. Best thinks that there were some NT prophets to whom the early church attributed less authority than it did to the writings of the canonical OT prophets.[12] And Friedrich concludes that, in contrast to the prophet of Revelation, some NT prophets did not "enjoy such unlimited authority" as the OT Jewish prophets.[13]

Keeping the valuable background of these studies in mind, I propose in this investigation to examine in more detail the data in 1 Corinthians relating to prophecy in Corinth, and first to determine whether the evidence indicates the existence at Corinth of a secondary type of prophecy, perhaps less authoritative and more widely distributed than the primary type of prophecy which is represented, for instance, by John in Revelation. Then I shall examine more briefly NT verses outside 1 Corinthians relating to prophecy, attempting to ascertain whether there are other indications of a secondary kind of prophecy which is distinguished by its lesser claims of authority. These investigations will comprise the first chapter of the book.

In the remaining three chapters, I shall return to 1 Corinthians to examine the psychological state of the prophet (Chapter 2), the form, content and function of prophecy (Chapter 3), and the qualifications for being a prophet (Chapter 4). In each chapter the conclusions reached are compared briefly with revelant NT verses outside of 1 Corinthians. Because of this focus on prophecy in 1 Corinthians, I have not dealt in detail with several other related questions, such as prophecy in the history of religions, John the Baptist and Jesus as prophets, or prophecy in early church history outside the NT.[14]

---

[12] Best, "Prophets and Preachers," 145.

[13] TDNT VI, 849f.

[14] Excellent surveys of these topics, with extensive bibliographical information, are found in Crone, Early Christian Prophecy, and Cothenet, "Prophetisme," DBS 8.

Focussing on 1 Corinthians in this way has several advantages. First, it helps avoid the danger of blurring any possible distinctions among various types of prophecy in various parts of the NT church.[15] Second, there is in 1 Corinthians 12-14 enough material on prophecy to make an extended study quite rewarding. The chapters include longer and more specific discussions of the nature, function and purpose of prophecy than are found anywhere else in the NT. Moreover, these are not isolated verses, but are set against the very helpful background of a discussion of the use of all of the gifts of the Spirit in the church. Third, none of the recent studies of prophecy has produced a fully detailed, exegetically-based definition of the gift of prophecy in 1 Corinthians. This has either been because the studies were quite short, or because the scope of the particular study was so broad that considerations of space and time simply did not allow a thorough treatment of the data in 1 Corinthians.[16]

So the goal of this study is to define in detail the type of prophecy represented in 1 Corinthians, and then briefly to compare the conclusions with the texts which speak of other, possibly different types of prophecy in the rest of the NT. This kind of study, if successful, will (i) define clearly a distinctive type of prophecy which has too often been overlooked or just vaguely hinted at in New Testament research, and (ii) analyze that type of prophecy in much greater detail than has previously been done. If the goal of the study is attained, it will significantly increase our understanding of Christian prophecy at the time of the New Testament.

---

[15] Although Greeven, "Propheten," 8, suggests that even in 1 Corinthians we have a glimpse of a church in transition between the period when all could prophesy and a period when prophecy was restricted to a certain group (followed by Best, "Prophets and Preachers,") 142. I discuss this particular question in Chapter 4, pp. 237ff.

[16] I have listed the more important studies, both short and long, in note 1, above.

CHAPTER ONE

THE AUTHORITY OF PROPHECY IN

1 CORINTHIANS

I. DIFFERENT TYPES OF DIVINE AUTHORITY

After a detailed study of prophetic experience in several religions and cultures, Johannes Lindblom notices that one feature which characterized all prophecy was a belief in some kind of revelation: "Common to all representatives of the prophetic type here depicted is the consciousness of having access to information from the world above and experiences originating in the divine world."[1] This means that a study of prophecy inevitably involves us in a question about divine authority. If a prophet is someone who thinks he has been given a message from God, he will often claim for his prophecies some kind of divine authority.

But the phrase "divine authority" may mean several different things. For our purposes it is useful at least to make two types of distinctions, according to the person perceiving the authority and according to the nature of the authority which is claimed.

A. Divine Authority as Perceived by Speaker or by Audience?

It is important to distinguish between a prophet's own subjective evaluation of his authority and the evaluations of his authority which are made by others. If these evaluations differ, a conflict of authority can result: a prophet may claim to be speaking for God, while his hearers may reject that claim. Or the audience itself may be divided, some thinking the prophet to be an authentic divine spokesman and others thinking him to be an impostor, or self-deceived.

---

[1]Lindblom, Prophecy, 32.

The case of Micaiah in 1 Kgs. 22.1-28 is an interesting example. On one side we find about 400 prophets claiming to speak for the Lord (vss. 6, 11-12) and prophesying victory for Ahab and Jehoshaphat. Ahab wants to believe their claims to divine authority, for the message is favorable, but his words and actions betray some doubt (vss. 16, 30). On the other side is Micaiah, also claiming to speak for the Lord (vss. 19, 23, 28), and prophesying a message opposite to that of the 400 prophets (vss. 17, 20, 23, 28). Jehoshaphat is even more suspicious of the 400 prophets than Ahab is (vss. 7, 8), but does not seem to be persuaded by Micaiah either, since he agrees to go to battle in spite of Micaiah's warning (vss. 28-29). Both Micaiah and the 400 prophets (especially Zedekiah the son of Chanaanah) react with outrage at a challenge to their authority by the other party (vss. 24, 25, 28). So here a prophet's own estimate of his possession of divine authority is seen to differ sometimes from the evaluation made of his authority by other prophets, and sometimes from the evaluation of his authority made by his audience.[2]

Related to this is the fact that the prophet himself may feel varying degrees of certainty or doubt concerning the divine authority of his message. When Jeremiah's prophecies of destruction continued to be unfulfilled, and he was being mocked and punished for his prophesying, he cried out, "O Lord, thou has deceived me, and I was deceived" (Jer. 20.7). Yet if he tried to stop prophesying there was an inward compulsion to continue: "There is in my heart as it were a burning fire shut up in my bones, and I am weary with holding it in, and I cannot" (Jer. 20.9). So within the speaker's perception of his own authority, as well as that of his audience, one can distinguish varying degrees of certainty.

Investigating the type of prophetic authority in 1 Cor. 12-14 we primarily have access to Paul's evaluation of the type of authority possessed by Corinthian prophets. This could be seen as one aspect of "audience" perception of the type of divine authority possessed by Corinthian prophets, although other members of the prophet's audience at Corinth, and

---

[2]Cf. the similar conflict in Jer. 28 between Jeremiah and Hananiah.

the prophet himself, may have had different evaluations.
Of course, we only have indirect access to the prophet's
own evaluations of his authority, and the evaluations
made by others at Corinth, through inferences drawn
from Paul's epistle.

B. Divine Authority for General Content or Exact Words?

It is also possible to distinguish different
aspects of a speech for which divine authority might
be claimed. One prophet might only claim that the
general content of his prophecy was of divine origin,
while another might claim that the very words he used
in his prophecy had been revealed to him by God. We
could call these two types "authority of general content" and "authority of actual words."

This distinction often manifests itself in the
form taken by a prophecy. If a prophet thinks that
the very words of his prophecy have been given by God,
then he will often speak for God in the first person:
"Thus says the Lord, 'For three transgressions of
Damascus, and for four, I will not revoke the punishment'" (Am. 1.3). But a prophet who thinks he has
received no specific verbal message which God wants
him to deliver, but only a general sense of the need
to demand repentance or pure worship or social justice,
for instance, would not be likely to presume to give
a direct quotation of something which God had said,
or to use forms of speech which in the Ancient Near
East would have suggested that he had been given
absolute authority to act as an exact spokesman or even
a mouthpiece for God.

The distinction between claims to "authority of
general content" and claims to "authority of actual
words" would also affect the evaluation of the
prophet's words by others. If a prophet only claimed
a divine authority of general content, then the hearers
might not be very concerned about smaller details of
the prophecy: although they might think that the main
point of the prophecy was to be believed and obeyed
because it came from God, they would be prepared to
allow for the possibility of disagreement and charges
of error in smaller details or finer points of interpretation, since these details and fine points stemmed
from the prophet himself and not from God. In fact,
since the audience would have no way of knowing for

sure which parts of the prophecy were from God and which were not, the prophet who claims only a divine authority of general content must be prepared for challenges, questions and doubts at every point of his prophecy. Any single part of it might be thought by the audience to be in error, or to reflect the prophet's own misunderstanding of what had been revealed to him by God.[3]

But if a prophet claimed a kind of divine authority which encompassed all the actual words of his prophecy, and if the audience accepted that claim as genuine, then a different kind of audience reaction would occur. Then if someone were to disbelieve or disobey even a minor detail of the prophecy--or indeed, even one word--he would think himself to be disbelieving or disobeying God. The words of someone accepted as a true prophet would in such a case be beyond challenge or question; they would possess an "absolute" divine authority.

C. The Problem of False Prophecy

Both of the preceding distinctions affect the way in which false prophecy is understood. To begin, it should be clear that the title "false prophet" is simply the report of one audience's evaluation (and rejection) of a prophet's claim to divine authority. No prophet in the Bible ever applies the title "false prophet" to himself. Rather, even those who are judged by the Biblical narrator to be "false," continually claim for themselves legitimate divine authority (cf. 1 Kgs. 22.11-12, 24; Jer. 28.10-11).

Furthermore, the tests applied to a prophet will differ somewhat according to the kind of authority he

---

[3] For this reason, it might be somewhat misleading to call this type of authority a _divine_ authority of general content, because the prophecy can be so freely challenged. Nevertheless, I retain the word "divine" in order to indicate that there is still thought to be some kind of divine revelation to the prophet which gave rise to the prophecy.
(I am not now trying to decide whether any specific prophecies fit these categories; I am only setting forth the different types which could be imagined.)

claims. If he claims a divine authority of actual words, he will be held accountable for every single item of his prophecy, even the minor details. But if he only claims a divine authority of general content, then his audience will not brand him as "false" simply because occasional details of his prophecies turn out to be wrong.

D. Summary

I have suggested some of the different things which might be meant by the phrase "divine authority" when applied to prophecy. It might mean that the prophet claims divine authority, or that someone else attributes to him divine authority. It might also mean that the prophet's very words are thought to be from God (authority of actual words), or simply that one (or some) of the main ideas of the prophecy is thought to have a divine origin (authority of general content). In subsequent discussion I shall attempt to specify at each point the particular sense in which I am speaking of "divine authority" in prophetic speeches.

II. DIVINE AUTHORITY OF ACTUAL WORDS: SOME OLD TESTAMENT EXAMPLES

The Old Testament provides many specific examples of prophets who claimed that divine authority extended to their actual words. In some cases we are told of the response to those claims by one audience or another. We also find that the OT narrative itself evaluates some of those claims as true, and others as false. It is useful for us to examine this diverse picture of prophetic phenomena in some detail at this point, in order that we might begin to build a background against which to evaluate the data in 1 Corinthians. After looking at this OT picture, I shall also examine several examples of "divine authority of general content," primarily in extra-biblical Jewish literature.

A. The Prophets as Messengers of God

The OT prophets are frequently pictured as messengers sent by God to speak God's words to men.[4] James F. Ross lists several discernible characteristics of a "messenger speech" (Botenspruch) in the OT narratives:[5] An introductory formula (כֹּה אָמַר יהוה), a standard conclusion (נְאֻם יהוה), the frequent use of the verb שָׁלַח to indicate that the prophet is sent by God,[6] and a commissioning narrative in which Yahweh tells the prophet, "Go and say to N, 'Thus says Yahweh . . .'" Ancient Near Eastern parallels, especially those found in the Mari and Ras Shamra texts, provide additional examples of prophets as messengers of a god. (However, the evidence from such sources is not completely unambiguous.)[7]

Furthermore, the prophet is seen as a specific kind of messenger; he is a messenger of the covenant.

---

[4] James F. Ross, "The Prophet as Yahweh's Messenger," in Israel's Prophetic Heritage, ed. Bernhard W. Anderson and Walter Harrelson (London, 1962), 98-107; J. Lindblom, Prophecy in Ancient Israel (Oxford, 1962), 104; Claus Westermann, Basic Forms of Prophetic Speech (ET London, 1967), 98-128; Jörg Jeremias, "Die Vollmacht des Propheten im Alten Testament," EvTh 31 (1971), 308; Rolf Rendtorff, TDNT VI, 810; Th. C. Vriezen, An Outline of OT Theology (ET Oxford, 1970²), 231f; R. E. Clements, Prophecy and Covenant (London, 1965), 24f.

[5] Ross, "Messenger," 99.

[6] Ross, "Messenger," 99, n. 9, includes a long list of such שָׁלַח-verses. By contrast, to prophesy without being "sent" was to be a false prophet (Jer. 14.14, 15, 28.15, 29.9, 23, Neh. 6.12).

[7] Ross, Messenger," 100f, and John S. Holladay, Jr., "Assyrian Statecraft and the Prophets of Israel," HTR 63 (1970), 29-51, show positive parallels where the messengers are spokesmen either for a god or for a human king. A thorough summary of the research to 1975 is in John F. Craghan, "Mari and Its Prophets," BTB 5 (1975), 32-55. The year 1968 was a turning point in the study of Mari prophecy, since newly published tablets showed that not all the Mari prophets were messengers. It is safe to conclude that at times the

His function is to remind Israel of the terms of her
covenant with Yahweh, calling the disobedient to
repentance and warning that the curse sanctions of the
covenant will soon be applied (Jer. 7.25, 2 Chr. 24.
19, Neh. 9.26, 30, Mal. 4.4-6).[8]

It is characteristic of this kind of messenger
that his words are thought to possess not merely his
own personal authority but the authority of the one
who sent him. So it is with the OT prophets: their
words purport to carry the authority of Yahweh himself,
because they are convinced that he has called them to
speak for him.[9]

Mari prophets were messengers of a god, and at other
times not, since the texts show different kinds of
functions (liturgical or cultic, political, private,
public, etc.).

[8] Herbert B. Huffmon, "The Covenant Lawsuit in
the Prophets," JBL 78 (1959), 285-95, sees only a few
pure covenant lawsuits in the OT. But although this
lawsuit form per se may not be dominant in the prophetic literature, the prophetic summons to repentance
and conformity to the terms of the covenant are found
throughout the OT. See Meredith Kline, The Structure
of Biblical Authority (Grand Rapids, 1972), 58-62. However, R. E. Clements, Prophecy and Tradition (Oxford,
1975), 8-23, challenges attempts to see OT prophets as
covenant spokesmen on the basis of Ancient Near Eastern
parallels.

[9] Ross, "Messenger," 101-05; Jeremias, "Vollmacht,"
315; Sheldon H. Blank, "'Of a Truth the Lord Hath Sent
Me'" An Inquiry into the Source of the Prophet's
Authority," in Interpreting the Prophetic Tradition,
(Cincinatti, 1969). J. B. Pritchard, ANET 103f, gives
a translation of a 14th c. B.C. Egyptian text in which
the god Nergal fails to show proper respect to the
messenger of Ereshkigal, and therefore Ereshkigal
seeks to kill Nergal. For later Jewish and Christian
views on the importance of a messenger, see M. Ber.
5.5, Jn. 3.34, Ign. Eph. 6.1, and Str.-B. III, 2-4.
On the question of the possible relationship
between the Jewish שליח and the New Testament ἀπόστολος,
see K. Rengstorf, TDNT I, 413-20; J. A. Kirk, "Apostleship Since Rengstorf: Towards a Synthesis," NTS 21
(1974-75), 250-52; W. Schmithals, The Office of
Apostle in the Early Church (ET London, 1971), 98-110;

Lindblom is no doubt correct when he points to the council (סוֹד) of Yahweh as one way of speaking of the source of a prophet's speech: "That the prophets are in possession of the divine word depends on the fact that they are admitted to the sōd of Yahweh.... The words of the prophets are words which they have heard directly from Yahweh."[10] But more basic even than this council to OT thought is the simple hearing-speaking pattern Lindblom describes: "Yahweh speaks to the prophet, the prophet hears what Yahweh says, and then he pronounces what he has heard to the listening people."[11]

B. Gerhardsson, "Die Boten Gottes und die Apostel Christi," SEÅ 27 (1963), 89-131.

[10] Lindblom, Prophecy, 112f; cf. Ross, "Messenger," 102f, and Jer. 23.18, 22; Am. 3.7.

[11] Lindblom, Prophecy, 110; cf. 113f. Otto Eissfeldt, The Old Testament: An Introduction (ET Oxford, 1965), 78 says that not all prophetic sayings go back to special moments of inspiration--some owe their origin to the "lasting prophetic consciousness of being the messenger of Yahweh and . . . can therefore with equal right as the others be set out as direct divine speech in the first person." However, I doubt whether the OT attributes as much independence to the prophetic messenger as Eissfeldt suggests. In fact, to speak a word which Yahweh has not given makes one a false prophet (Dt. 18.20; Jer. 23.16, 18, 21, 22; Ezk. 13.1-7). The true prophet, as Yahweh's messenger, must confine his message to what Yahweh has told him.

There is also a danger in overemphasizing the סוֹד of Yahweh when we have so few Biblical data (only Jer. 23.18, 22, Am. 3.7, and without the term used, 1 Kgs. 22:19, in connection with prophets). We are on safer ground if we think primarily in terms of the hearing-speaking pattern mentioned by Lindblom and repeated consistently throughout the prophetic literature (Ex. 7.1-2 with 4.15-16, which Lindblom takes as a paradigm of OT prophecy (pp. 113ff); 1 Sam. 3.10ff, 2 Sam. 7.14-17, 24.11-13, 1 Kgs. 14.5, 22.14, 2 Kgs. 20.4ff, Is. 6.9, 7.4, Jer. 1.4ff, Ezk. 2.1-3.37, Am. 3.8, Jon. 3.2, etc.).

B. The Prophet's Words as Words of God

The distinguishing characteristic of a true prophet was said to be this: he did not speak his own words or "words of his own heart," but words which God had sent (שלח) him to deliver (Dt. 18.18-20, Jer. 14.14, 23.16ff, 29.31-32, Ezk. 13.1ff; cf. Num. 16.28).[12] So throughout various parts of the OT we find an emphasis not simply on the general content of prophetic speech as coming from God, but on the very words themselves. "I will be with your mouth and teach you what you shall speak" (Ex. 4.12, cf. 24.3). "I will put my words in his mouth" (Dt.18.18, cf. vss. 21-22). "I have put my words in your mouth" (Jer. 1.9). "The word that God puts in my mouth, that I must speak" (Num. 22.38, cf. 23.5, 16). "You shall speak my words to them" (Ezk. 2.7, cf. 3.17).

It is not surprising then that we find the OT prophets very frequently speaking for God in the first person (2 Sam. 7.4ff, 1 Kgs. 20.13, 42, 2 Kgs. 17.13, 19.25-28, 34, 21.12-15, 22.16-20, 2 Chr. 12.5, and the Latter Prophets, passim). The manner in which the prophet's words were so completely identified with Yahweh's words is seen when the prophet says things like "You shall know that I am the Lord" (1 Kgs. 20.13) or "I am the Lord, and there is no other, beside me there is no God" (Is. 45.5). Clearly no Israelite would have thought that the prophet was claiming to speak his own words in such cases; he was simply thought to be repeating the words of the one who had sent him.[13]

---

[12] Lindblom, Prophecy, 110; H. H. Rowley, "The Nature of OT Prophecy in the Light of Recent Study," in The Servant of the Lord and Other Essays on the Old Testament (London, 1952), 123f; Geerhardus Vos, Biblical Theology (Grand Rapids, 1948), 235.

[13] Nevertheless the prophets who claim a divine authority of actual words do not always speak for God in the first person. Note, for instance, the alternation between first and third person speech in 2 Kgs. 19.20ff, Jer. 23.13-21, etc. It is enough to say that they generally do so, and that to speak for God in the first person is tantamount to claiming a divine authority of actual words.

The frequent use of the introductory formula
פֹּה אָמַד יהדה or its equivalent is a further indication
that the prophet's words were meant to be thought of as
God's words.[14] An interesting extra-Biblical parallel
is seen by J. S. Holladay in the Neo-Assyrian phrase.
Amāt šarri ana PN" ("word of the king to PN"). This
phrase is "almost invariable in the letters of the
king to his subjects," says Holladay. "That amāt šarri
is an especially authoritative, compelling mode of
address (equivalent to 'edict of the king') is shown
(a) by the fact that it appears as an introductory
formula only in the king's letters. . . . (b) by the
fact that, when the king addresses his letters to
presumed equals . . . he invariably uses the introductory formula normally reserved for more personal or
familial communications."[15]

One final indication of a belief in the divine
origin of prophetic words is seen in the frequency with
which God is referred to as the speaker of something a
prophet said. In 1 Kgs. 13.26, "the word which the
Lord spoke to him" is the word which the prophet spoke
in vs. 21. Similarly, Elijah's words in 1 Kgs. 21.19
are quoted in 2 Kgs. 9.25f as a burden which the Lord
put on Ahab, and Elijah is not even referred to. (Cf.

---

[14]Walter Eichrodt, Theology of the Old Testament,
(2 vols.; ET London, 1961-67), I, 340.

[15]Holladay, "Assyrian Statecraft," 43, n. 54.
Note the conflict between Yahweh the king of Israel and
Sennacherib the king of Assyria in Is. 36-37, where the
Rabshakeh's פֹּה אָמַד הַמֶּלֶךְ הַגָּדוֹל מֶלֶךְ אַשּׁוּר is set against
Isaiah's פֹּה אָמַר יהוה אֱלֹהֵי יִשְׂרָאֵל (36.4, cf. vss. 13-14,
16; 37.21, cf. 37.6). The "messenger verb" שָׁלַח is used
several times (36.2, 12; 37.14 of Rabshakeh; cf. 37.21).
On another level, Hezekiah is the king who sends
(וַיִּשְׁלַח, 37.2) messengers to Isaiah saying פֹּה אָמַר חִזְקִיָּהוּ
(37.3).
Royal messengers from Ben-hadad also use the IF
in 1 Kgs. 20.2 (3) and 5: פֹּה אָמַר בֶּן־הֲדַד. There is a
response in kind to Ahab from the prophet (1 Kgs. 20.
13, 14, 28). However, once Ben-hadad has been
defeated, he cannot use the royal messenger formula,
but instead sends messengers who say, "Your servant
Ben-hadad says . . . (עַבְדְּךָ בֶן־הֲדַד אָמַר)" (vs. 32)!
In Jer. 28.2, 11 a false prophet uses the messenger formula, but with disastrous consequences (vs. 17).

Hag. 1.12, 1 Sam. 15.3, 18). It is common to read of "the word of the Lord, which he spoke by (בְּיַד) his servant the prophet" (1 Kgs. 14.18, 16.12, 2 Kgs. 9.36, 14.25, 17.23, 24.2, 2 Chr. 29.25, Ezr. 9.10-11, Neh. 9.30, Jer. 37.2, Zech. 7.7, 12, etc.).

To summarize the discussion so far: (1) The prophet who claims divine authority for his actual words often presents himself as Yahweh's messenger, claiming to speak to men words which he has heard from Yahweh. (2) The prophet, in order to be accepted as a true prophet, must convince his audience that he does not speak his own words, but God's. (3) He speaks in the first person for God, often prefacing his speech with "Thus says Yahweh," and often saying things which his hearers could only be expected to understand as God's words, not the prophets's own. (4) He uses an especially authoritative kind of royal messenger formula. (5) God is often said to be the one who speaks "through" his prophets, according to the narrator of various OT events.

Such a view of a claim to the divine authority of actual words was often neglected by scholars of the previous generation,[16] so much so that James Barr in 1963 said in protest:

> Direct verbal communication between God and particular men on particular occasions. . . . is, I believe, an inescapable fact of the Bible and of the OT in particular. God can speak specific verbal messages, when he wills, to the man of his choice. . . . If we persist in saying that this direct, specific communication must be subsumed under revelation through events in history and taken as subsidiary interpretation of the latter, I shall say that we are abandoning the Bible's own representation of the matter for another which is apologetically more comfortable. . . .

---

[16]Cf. H. Knight, The Hebrew Prophetic Consciousness (London, 1947), 116; S. Mowinckel, The OT as the Word of God (ET Oxford, 1960; first pub. Oslo, 1938), 24-26; C. H. Dodd, The Authority of the Bible (London, 1928), 16; more recently, G. von Rad, OT Theology (2 vols.; ET London, 1962-65), II, 72 (a mixture of divine and human words).

> Modern theology has really failed to give us any lead along lines that come near to the biblical representation of [OT prophecy, because it claims that the words of the prophets]. . . . are the thoughts of the prophets, meditating on history, and not words given them by God as the biblical tradition states them. . . .[17]

In fact, many more recent studies of OT prophecy have expressed positions more in accord with Barr's statement. It has become quite common now to understand many of the OT prophets as claiming to speak not just an expression of ideas which God approves, and not just true words about God, but words which God himself is speaking through the prophet.[18]

C. Implications of Divine Authority in Prophetic Words

If the prophet's words were thought of by his audience as God's words, it is not surprising that we find in the OT the following implications of this concept:

1. <u>The people think that to disbelieve or or disobey a prophet's words is to disbelieve or disobey God.</u> This is the most significant consequence of the fact that the prophet's words are seen as God's words. Once a prophet's hearers are convinced that the prophet's very words have absolute divine authority, they will not risk disobeying or disbelieving even the slightest part of them, for fear of being punished by God himself for disobedience or disbelief. One can easily observe how common this idea is throughout the OT: Dt. 18.19, 1 Sam. 8.7, 15.3 with vss. 18

---

[17] J. Barr, "The Interpretation of Scripture II; Revelation through History in the OT and in Modern Theology," <u>Interp.</u> 17 (1963), 201f.

[18] Lindblom, <u>Prophecy</u>, 109f, 114; Westermann, <u>Forms</u>, 94f; W. F. Albright, <u>From the Stone Age to Christianity</u> (New York, 1957^2), 308, n. 44; A. R. Johnson, <u>The Cultic Prophet in Ancient Israel</u> (Cardiff, 1962^2), 37; Holladay, "Assyrian Statecraft," 30; A. Heschel, <u>The Prophets</u> (New York, 1962), 427ff; O. Procksch, <u>TDNT</u> IV, 97; Vos, <u>BT</u>, 233, 239; E. J. Young, <u>My Servants the Prophets</u> (Grand Rapids, 1952), 176.

and 23, 1 Kgs. 20.36, 2 Chr. 20.20 and Is. 7.9 (note parallelism), 2 Chr. 25.16, Is. 30.12-14, Jer. 6.10-11, 16-19, 36.29-31, etc.[19]

2. The words of a true prophet are thought to be beyond challenge or question. They are held to be true and good and pure by definition, because they come from God. Thus, we do not find in the OT any instance where the prophecy of someone who is acknowledged to be a true prophet is evaluated so that the good might be sorted from the bad, the true from the false. Rather, when Samuel was established as a prophet, "the Lord was with him and let none of his words fall to the ground" (1 Sam. 3.19). Because Samuel was a man of God (that is, a prophet), Saul's servant could say, "All that he says comes true" (1 Sam. 9.6).

The prediction of a prophet like Moses in Dt. 18.15-22 is instructive in this respect. When a prophet spoke in the name of the Lord, if his prophecy did not come true, he was a false prophet (Dt. 18.22). The authority attaching to the prophetic office was so great, and thus the effect on the people resulting from the emergence of a false prophet was so disastrous, that the penalty for false prophecy was death (Dt. 18.20, 13.5).

So what we find in the OT is that every prophet is judged or evaluated, but not the various parts of every prophecy. The people ask, "Is this a true prophet or not? Is he speaking of God's words or not?" They never ask, "Which parts of this prophecy are true and which are false? Which parts are good and which are bad?" For one bit of falsehood would disqualify the whole prophecy and would show the prophet to be a false prophet. A true prophet who claimed a divine authority of actual words could never speak in his prophecy some of his own words and some of God's--they were to be all God's words, or he was a false prophet.

Thus, once it was plain that the Lord was with Samuel and let none of his words fall to the ground (1 Sam. 3.19), then "all Israel . . . knew that Samuel

---

[19]Lindblom, Prophecy, 110, says, "Yahweh sends his words through the prophet, and then the people are willing to obey 'the voice of Yahweh,' their God (Is. 42.6)."

was established as a prophet of the Lord" (vs. 20). Then it was thought that to disobey Samuel or to second-guess even seemingly arbitrary commands was wrong and would lead to punishment from God (1 Sam. 13.13 with 10.18, 15.23 with vs. 3). Micaiah was willing to stake his entire reputation as a prophet on the fulfillment of one prophecy (1 Kgs. 22.28). Because God was thought to be the speaker of all that a prophet spoke in his name, ("in the name of the Lord," Dt. 18.22), it was unthinkable that a true prophet should deliver some oracle which was a mixture of good and bad or true and false elements. It was believed that what the prophet received from the Lord, he spoke. What the Lord thus spoke through the prophet was thought to have absolute divine authority, extending even to the very words the prophet used.[20]

---

[20]Of course, this does not mean that a true prophet would never apostatize (1 Kgs. 13.18). The distinction I am trying to make concerns the type of evaluation which the people were expected to perform. If a prophet were thought to be speaking merely human words, his own words and not those of Yahweh, then every sentence he pronounced would be subject to evaluation and question. The hearers would ask of each statement, "Is this true or not? Is this right or not?" This kind of word from the prophet would be a word of men among other words of men, and would possess no more authority than any other word. This would be true of all his words in general, even if he claimed a "divine authority of general content," for minor mistakes might occur at any point, so long as the main point was relatively clear.

But if the prophet claims to be speaking God's words, another sort of evaluation takes place. There are only two possibilities, and there is no middle ground. The question becomes, "Are these God's words or not? If so, I must obey. If not, the prophet is misrepresenting God and must be put to death" (so Dt. 18.20). Once his words are accepted (by whatever means) as God's words, they have a different status and are beyond challenge or question.

III. DIVINE AUTHORITY OF GENERAL CONTENT: SOME
     EXAMPLES FROM EXTRA-BIBLICAL JEWISH LITERATURE

   A. The Belief that Prophecy with a Divine
      Authority of Actual Words Had Ceased

Space does not allow us to develop the views of OT prophetic authority represented by the various strands of later Jewish tradition, but they were in general very similar to the views we have seen expressed in the OT itself.[21] Yet there was an additional element. It was thought that the kind of prophecy found in the OT, prophecy with a divine authority of actual words, had come to an end. This belief is a theme which runs through several different types of Jewish literature at different periods.[22]

In 1 Maccabees (ca. 100 B.C.) the author writes of the defiled altar, "So they tore down the altar, and stored the stones in a convenient place on the temple hill until there should come a prophet to tell what to do with them" (1 Macc. 4.45-46). Then after the death of Judas he says, "Thus there was great distress in Israel, such as had not been since the time that prophets ceased to appear among them"

---

[21] See, for example, b. Sanh. 99a; T. O. on Ex. 14.31, F. T. on Ex. 19.9; Jos. A. 9.145, 10.126, Ap. 1.37-38, 42; Philo (with extreme emphasis on the divine influence, however) Fug. 197, Spec. Leg. 1.65, 2.189, 4.49, Quis Her. 259, Q.G. 4.140 (cf. p. 422, note "a" in Loeb edn.), Q.G. 4.196; Str.-B. IV, i, 443-51; G. F. Moore, Judaism in the First Centuries of the Christian Era (3 vols.; Cambridge, Mass., 1927-30), I, 239; H. A. Wolfson, Philo (2 vols,; Cambridge, Mass., 1947), I, 140; G. Delling, "Die biblische Prophetie bei Josephus," in Josephus-Studien, ed. O. Betz et al. (Göttingen, 1974), 120.

[22] See esp. R. Leivestad, "Das Dogma von der prophetenlosen Zeit," NTS 19 (1972-73), 288-99; also W. D. Davies, Paul and Rabbinic Judaism (London, 1970³), 208-16; I. Abrahams, Studies in Pharisaism and the Gospels: Second Series (Cambridge, 1924), 121; J. Dunn, Jesus and the Spirit (London, 1975), 382, n. 81; and n. 31 below.

(9.27).[23] Third it is said of Simon, "The Jews and their priests decided that Simon should be their leader and high priest forever, until a trustworthy prophet should arise" (14.41).[24] A prophet who can speak with divine authority in his actual words, or "absolute" divine authority, is simply not known to the writer during this period: this kind of prophet belongs to the distant past or the unknown future.

The Prayer of Azariah 15 (1st or 2nd c. B.C.) laments, "At this time there is no prince, or prophet, or leader, no burnt offering, or sacrifice . . ." In the pseudpigrapha, 2 Bar. 85.3 (130-200 A.D.) says, "The prophets have fallen asleep."

The rabbinic literature reflects a similar conviction. "After the latter prophets Haggai, Zechariah and Malachi had died, the Holy Spirit departed from Israel, but they still availed themselves of the bath qol" (b. Yom. 9b, repeated b. Sot. 48b. Sanh. 11a, Song R. 8.9.3).[25] That "the Holy Spirit" is primarily a reference to prophecy is clear both from the fact that the bath qol (a voice from heaven) is seen as a substitute for it, and from the frequent use of רוח הקדש elsewhere to refer to prophecy.[26]

---

[23] Opinions on the exact date of this cessation varied somewhat. Cf. Davies, PRJ, 208ff.

[24] E. Fascher, ΠΡΟΦΗΤΗΣ (Giessen, 1927), 145, notes the qualitatively different authority accorded to a prophet by this verse: "Die Schätzung des Propheten ist so gross, dass er als Mund Gottes dem selbstgewählten menschlichen Führer übergeordnet werden würde."

[25] Str.-B. I, 127 (b) also note Tos. Sot. 13.2 and j. Sot. 9.13 (24b, 1.21). Leivestad, "Dogma," 289, dates this as a pre-Christian saying because of its close connection with Hillel (30 B.C.-10 A.D.) in Tos. Sot. 13.2. (The connection also exists in b. Sot. 48b, b. Sanh. 11a and Song R. 8.9.3.)

[26] Str.-B. I, 127-34, esp. 129 (a). For a general study of prophecy in rabbinic literature, see J. Bowman, "Prophets and Prophecy in Talmud and Midrash," EQ 22 (1950), 107-14, 205-14, 205-20, 255-75.

Josephus[27] (born 37/8 A.D.) explains, "From Artaxerxes to our own time the complete history has been written, but has not been deemed worthy of equal credit with the earlier records, because of the failure of the exact succession of the prophets" (διὰ τὸ μὴ γενέσθαι τὴν τῶν προφητῶν ἀκριβῆ διαδοχήν, AP. 1.41).

In Philo we lack any such clear statement, but H. A. Wolfson thinks that Philo's silence indicates agreement with Palestinian Jews about the cessation of "the type of prophecy which gave Scripture its special character."[28]

The Qumran Manual of Discipline states that the "men of holiness . . . shall be ruled by the primitive precepts in which the men of the Community were first instructed until there shall come the Prophet (or 'a prophet') and the Messiahs of Aaron and Israel" (עַד בּוֹא נָבִיא וּמְשִׁיחֵי אַהֲרוֹן וְיִשְׂרָאֵל, 1 QS 9.11). Here also a prophet is awaited whose words will have authority to supersede any existing regulations.[29]

---

[27] For a general study see J. Blenkinsopp, "Prophecy and Priesthood in Josephus," JJS 25 (1974), 239-62. I also wish to express appreciation to Dr. Carl Holladay, who, with the kind permission of the editors of the forthcoming volumes of A Complete Concordance to Flavius Josephus, ed. K. Rengstorf (Leiden, 1973ff), made available to me a complete list of the occurrences of the words in the προφήτης word group.

[28] Wolfson, Philo, II, 54. However, Philo's account of the translation of the Septuagint (Mos, 2.37-40) should perhaps be taken as an exception.

[29] It is sometimes argued that the Teacher of Righteousness is himself a prophet (so Gert Jeremias, Der Lehrer der Gerechtigkeit (Göttingen, 1963), 141, 295-99 (with bibliography), 324f; A. Dupont-Sommer, The Essene Writings from Qumran (ET Oxford, 1961), 360-64; Peter R. Jones, The Apostle Paul: A Second Moses According to 2 Cor. 2.14-7 (Ph.D. dissertation, Princeton, N.J., 1973), 179ff; effectively answered by Leivestad, "Dogma," 297f, and Crone, ECP, 101-14). Of course, if one defines the term "prophet" broadly enough, it is possible to make the Teacher a prophet. He does have God-given abilities to understand and interpret the (OT) prophetic writings (1 QpHab. 7.4-5).

B. <u>The Acknowledgement that Revelatory Activity
    Continued</u>

Nevertheless, alongside of these statements about
the cessation of prophecy, and in the very same literature, there are frequent accounts of revelatory
phenomena of a supernatural sort.[30] These accounts are
presented without any attempt on the part of the
authors to reconcile them with the prevailing doctrine
of the cessation of prophecy. So the historian faces a
problem of interpretation, and there are three major
options.

First, one could say that the cessation doctrine
is in error. These statements represent the "orthodox"
position of the Jewish religious authorities, but in
spite of such opposition, the continuing revelatory
phenomena show that "far from being extinct, prophecy
was in luxuriant bloom, and also that prophets were
numerous, and secured both adherents and readers."[31]

However, he never creates new prophecies of equal
authority to the OT prophets. So he is more appropriately called in the Qumram literature a "teacher,"
never a prophet.
    Knowing God's סוד in 1 QH 12.12 is not unique to
the author of the hymns; cf. 1 QH 11.9. The text of
1 QpHab. 2.2-3 is so corrupt that it cannot be given
much weight:

כי לו [   ] מורה [צ.ק.ה̇ .פיא אל
("for not . . . the Teacher of Righteousness from the
mouth of God"); cf. M. Burrows, ed., <u>The Dead Sea
Scrolls of St. Mark's Monastary</u>, Vol. I (New Haven,
1950), Plate LV, and the suggested reconstruction in
Lohse, <u>Texte</u>, 228, and Vermes, <u>DSS</u>, 236.

[30]See below, pp. 27ff.

[31]A. Harnack, <u>The Mission and Expansion of
Christianity in the First Three Centuries</u> (2 vols.; ET
London, 1908²) I, 332; more reservedly, R. Meyer, <u>Der
Prophet aus Galiläa</u> (Darmstadt, 1970²), 45-60; <u>idem</u>,
<u>TDNT</u> VI, 812-28; O. Michel, "Spätjüdisches Propheten-
tum," in Neutestamentliche Studien für Rudolf Bultmann,
ed. W. Eltester (Berlin, 1957), 60-66; P. Vielhauer,
"Prophecy," in <u>New Testament Apocrypha</u>, ed. E. Hennecke,
W. Schneemelcher and R. McL. Wilson (2 vols.; ET
London, 1963-65), II, 601-04.

However, this position is unacceptable because: (i) It cannot adequately account for the fact that examples of revelations are not confined to literature outside of orthodox Judaism, but also occur in Josephus and the rabbinic traditions (see examples below). Nor is this cessation doctrine only found in "orthodox" literature (cf. 1 QS 9.11). Rather, the same literature can present both the doctrine of the cessation of prophecy and examples of continuing revelations. (ii) It is inaccurate to suppose that the Jewish leaders were united in wanting to prevent the recurrence of prophecy.[32] Wherever the cessation of prophecy is mentioned, it is lamented.[33] The renewal of prophecy is hoped for and is viewed as a future sign of blessing from God.[34] (iii) Very few if any of the examples of contemporary revelation are accorded an authority equal to that of the OT prophets.[35] So while these revelations were like OT prophecy in some respects, they were unlike it in others, and a careful evaluation of the differences, not a blurring of all distinctions, is required for an accurate historical investigation.

Second, one could take the opposite approach and attempt to minimize or deny the reported occurrences of

---

[32]Contra Leivestad, "Dogma," 290; however, his other criticisms of this first position, especially as it was expressed by R. Meyer, are very good.

[33]Note the contexts of the "cessation" passages quoted above. Also in the OT the withdrawal of prophecy is seen as an indication of God's judgment: 1 Sam. 28.6, 1 Kgs. 22.20-33, 2 Kgs. 3.14, Ps. 74.9, Is. 29.10, Lam. 2.9, Mic. 3.6; cf. also Num. R. 20.1 (on 22.2).

[34]Cf. Num. R. 15.25 (on 11.17). Prophecy is seen as a reward for righteous living in, for example, the Mekilta, Pisha 1.59-60, and 165-66 (J. Lauterbach, Mekilta de Rabbi Ishmael (3 vols.; Philadelphia, 1933-35), I, 5 and 15) and in Philo, Quis Her. 249. Cf. J. Abelson, The Immanence of God in Rabbinical Literature (London, 1912), 243, 248f.

[35]Note the absence of any such claims in the many examples on the following pages, and cf. Davies, PRJ, 212: "It surely is significant that even the 'prophetic spirits' of Rabbinic Judaism did not declare 'Thus saith the Lord' but appealed to a past revelation, 'It is written.'"

revelatory phenomena.36 But the examples are so numerous and widespread that such an argument seems forced and unconvincing.

Third, it is possible to reconcile the two strands of tradition by concluding that the Jews understood contemporary revelatory phenomena to be something different than OT prophecy. This solution, it seems to me, best accounts for all the data. There was thought to be no more prophecy of the OT type, which possessed an absolute divine authority extending to the very words of the prophet; at the same time, the occurrence of occasional revelatory phenomena was readily acknowledged. This secondary type of phenomenon may sometimes have been called "prophecy" and sometimes other names, and it may have been thought to possess some kind of "divine authority of general content," but it was always understood that it did not possess the kind of absolute divine authority which would make it equal in authority to the acknowledged prophecies of the OT. Therefore, its continued existence posed no problems at all for the belief in the cessation of the kind of prophecy found in the OT. So long as this distinction in types of prophecy is made clear, it does not really matter whether we call the second type "prophecy" or something like "quasi-prophetic activity."

C. K. Barrett says that the rabbis "have supernatural knowledge, but they do not utter inspired speech."37 Similarly, J. Abelson says that the rabbis distinguished between OT canonical prophecy and "a sort of prophetic sense" by which people were given special foreknowledge even after the close of the canon.38 And H. A. Wolfson writes:

> When we speak of a cessation of prophecy we must first determine what type of prophecy is meant by such a cessation . . . according to Palestinian tradition . . . the kind of prophecy

---

[36] So W. D. Davies, PRJ, 208-15.

[37] C. J. Barrett, The Holy Spirit and the Gospel Tradition (London, 1966²), 123.

[38] Abelson, Immanence, 260.

which inspired the teachings contained in the Hebrew Scripture came to an end, so that henceforth no other teachings will have been inspired by the same kind of prophecy . . . however . . . prophecy in the sense of prediction and in the sense of knowing things beyond sense perception and reason never ceased to exist.[39]

In a similar vein, A. Guttmann says, "The Talmud recognizes the continuance of revelation in its own time. It emphasizes, however, the inferior quality of post-prophetic revelation."[40]

It now remains to list some examples.[41]

Revelatory experiences are recorded quite frequently in the rabbinic literature. Rabbi Meir (140-164 A.D.) saw some women coming to visit him. "As soon as R. Meir saw them, he saw by means of the Holy Spirit"[42] and knew the substance of a quarrel one of the women had just had with her husband (Lev. R. 9.9; cf. 13.5).[43] Rabbi Gamaliel II (80-120 A.D.) had a similar experience. He was walking on the road when he met a Gentile who was a total stranger and immediately called the Gentile by name. "He saw by the Holy Spirit that the man's name was Mabgai" (Lev. R. 37.3; cf. b. Erub. 64b).[44] Rabbi Akiba (died 132 A.D.) also

---

[39] Wolfson, Philo, II, 52f. Blenkinsopp, "Prophecy and Priesthood," 253, distinguishes a second kind of "oracular priestly" prophecy in Josephus, but makes his definition so restrictive that he must say this kind ended with the death of John Hyrcanus.

[40] A. Guttmann, "The Significance of Miracles for Talmudic Judaism," HUCA 20 (1947), 367.

[41] Cf. Str.-B. II, 133 (q); Meyer, Der Prophet, 45-60, and TDNT VI, 812-28.

[42] While the Holy Spirit was thought to have been withdrawn in the sense that there was no more prophecy like that of the OT, the Holy Spirit could still be said to be present to bring about lesser phenomena.

[43] Str.-B. I, 216-17 list further parallels: j. Sot. 1.16d, 1.37, Num. R. 9 (153b), Dt. R. 5 (202d).

[44] Cf. Tos. Pes. 1.27, j. A. Zar. 1.40a, 1.44 (Str.-B. I, 127).

had this ability, according to Lev. R. 21.8. There we read that R. Hanina was studying at R. Akiba's college when he received a letter from his wife imploring him to come home and get his daughter married, for she was of marriageable age. But R. Hanina did not tell R. Akiba about the letter. "Nevertheless R. Akiba saw it by means of the Holy Spirit and said to him, 'If any one has a marriageable daughter he may go and get her married'" (Lev. R. 21.8).

R. Hanina b. Dosa (80-120 A.D.) would pray over the sick and then be able to predict whether they would recover (M. Ber. 5.5). He also predicted the rescue of a girl who had fallen in a well (b. Yeb. 121b).[45] R. Eliezer b. Hyrcanus (80-120 A.D.), on his death bed, predicted the violent death of R. Akiba (b. Sanh. 68a; cf. b. Ber. 61b). Samuel the Little (80-120 A.D.), before his death, predicted the manner of death of four other rabbis (b. Sanh. 11a; cf. b. Sot. 48b, Song R. 8.9.3).[46] R. Johanan b. Zakkai predicted that Vespasian would become emperor (69 A.D.), and shortly afterward a messenger came from Rome announcing this fact (b. Git. 56a-b).[47] Furthermore, meditation which led to visions was sometimes part of Pharisaic training, and, according to John Bowker, may even have been part of the training received by the Apostle Paul.[48]

There are also many accounts of revelation by means of a bath qol.[49] The evidence is quite convincing that at least after 90 A.D. this was not thought

---

[45] However, he refused to accept the title "prophet" at this point, apparently because it was clear to him that at least at that moment the people intended the term in the narrower OT sense, or might have understood it that way.

[46] Cf. Tos. Sot. 13.4 (p. 319), j. Sot. 9.24b, 1.27 (Str.-B, II, 133 [q]).

[47] Crone, ECP, 318, n. 30, has a good summary of the historical problems connected with this account.

[48] J. Bowker, "'Merkabah' Visions and the Visions of Paul," JSS 16 (1971), 157-73.

[49] A large number of occurrences are listed in JE II, 588-92 and Str.-B. I, 125-34.

to be the unmediated voice of God, but was rather understood as an "echo" of God's voice; hence the name "daughter of a voice."⁵⁰ However, between 70 and 90 A.D. its authority was strong enough to decide a dispute between the schools of Hillel and Shammai. After three years of dispute, "a bath qol issued announcing, '(The utterance of) both (lit., "these and these") are the words of the living God (אלו ואלו דברי אלהים חיים) but the halachah is in agreement with the rulings of Beth Hillel. Since, however, 'both are the words of the living God'⁵¹ what was it that entitled Beth Hillel to have the halachah fixed in agreement with their rulings? --Because they were kindly and modest . . ." (b. Erub. 13b; repeated almost verbatim, j. Ber. 3b, line 3 from bottom). But sometime after 90 A.D. a bath qol which sided with R. Eliezer against the majority of rabbis was completely disregarded (b. B.M. 58b-59a). Guttmann attributes this shift in attitude to the increasing threat of Christianity, which emphasized miracles to confirm its message.⁵² However we evaluate the earlier Jewish view of the bath qol (and for this the evidence is scarce), it is clear that after about 90 A.D. it too was viewed as a sort of revelation without absolute divine authority.

---

⁵⁰Str.-B. I, 127 (a); Moore, Judaism, I, 422; Davies, PRJ, 212-15, 374f; contra L. Blau, "Bat Ḳol," JE II, 588-92.

⁵¹The phrase "words of the living God" is apparently intended here in some weakened sense, such as "teaching approved of by God," or "teachings which accord with the words of God." This would be consistent with the expressed basis on which a decision was made between them, which had nothing to do with the content or authority of their words. On the other hand, these two reports might be freely embellished attempts at self-justification later inserted into the tradition by the triumphant Hillel school. However this phrase is understood, neither the rabbinic teachings nor the bath qol are ever explicitly said to equal the OT prophets in authority or to provide a counterexample to the doctrine of the cessation of prophecy. If something as momentous as the resumption of prophecy had occurred, we would have expected at least some comment about it.

⁵²Guttmann, "Miracles," 384-86.

Josephus reports several revelatory incidents in some detail. John Hyrcanus (ruled 135-105 B.C.) heard a voice in the temple which allowed him to predict the outcome of a battle many miles away (A. 13.282-83). He was able "to foresee and foretell the future" with some regularity (A. 13.300, B. 1.68-69). The high priest Jaddus received special instructions from God in a dream (A. 11.327-29), and the Pharisees in general "were believed to have foreknowledge of things through God's appearances to them" (A. 17.43).

Judas the Essene gave his disciples instruction in foretelling the future (A. 13.311), and his own predictions "never once proved erroneous or false" (B. 1.79). He correctly predicted the day and place of the death of Antigonus (B. 1.79). Menahem the Essene predicted Herod's reign, including several details, when Herod was still a boy and an ordinary private citizen (A. 15.373-78). Other Essenes could also predict the future or interpret predictive dreams (A. 17.346-48 [= B. 2.113]; B. 2.159).

Josephus himself says that he had nightly dreams "in which God had foretold (προεσήμανεν) to him the impending fate of the Jews and the destinies of the Roman sovereigns" (B. 3.351). He also predicted Vespasian's accession as emperor, the capture of Jotapata after 47 days, and his own fate of being taken alive by the Romans (B. 3.401-08).

Philo admits the possibility that in deep sleep the mind will discern "absolutely true prophecies (μαντείας) concerning things to come" (Mig. 190), and says of himself that a voice in his own soul often "divines (μαντεύεσθαι) what it cannot know" (Cher. 27).

In the Dead Sea Scrolls themselves there are no detailed and explicit statements about contemporary revelation, but we do read that the author of the Hymns has knowledge by the Spirit of God (1 QH 13.18-19; cf. 11.9 and 12.11-13), and that to the Teacher of Righteousness "God made known all the mysteries of the words of His servants the Prophets" (1 QpHab. 7.4-5). There also seems to be some kind of prediction implied in the fragmentary 1 Q Book of Mysteries, line 8: "This word shall surely come to pass; this burden (משא) is true."[53]

---

[53] DJD I, 103; Vermes, DSS, 210.

Finally, we must take note of the large body of Jewish apocalyptic literature.⁵⁴ Although these works are pseudepigraphal, the revelatory experiences claimed for the alleged authors often may reflect actual revelations experienced by the real authors.⁵⁵ Whether these authors thought of their works as equal in authority to the OT prophecies, but hid that pretension in a pseudepigraphal guise to avoid the displeasure of Jewish religious officials,⁵⁶ or whether they thought of their work as revelation of an important but nevertheless inferior sort,⁵⁷ can perhaps not be determined with certainty. On the one hand there is a notable absence of claims to inspiration by the Holy Spirit⁵⁸ and (in much of the literature) of "Thus says the Lord"

---

⁵⁴Two fairly recent (and differing) surveys of views regarding the relation of apocalyptic to prophecy are P. Vielhauer, "Apocalyptic," in NT Apocrypha II, ed. E. Hennecke et al., 581-60, and K. Koch, The Rediscovery of Apocalyptic (London, 1972), esp. pp. 36-56. A detailed examination of this question is outside the scope of this study.

⁵⁵D. S. Russell, The Method and Message of Jewish Apocalyptic (London, 1964), 158ff. Yet Russell is also careful to notice "a certain artificiality about the literature as a whole" (p. 158).

⁵⁶R. H. Charles, Religious Development Between the Old and New Testaments (London, 1914), 40ff; idem, Eschatology (London, 1913²), 200ff; criticized by Russell, Method, 131ff (but with a substitute explanation which is even less convincing), and by Koch, Rediscovery, 134, n. 21.

⁵⁷A difference in the kind of authority claimed is seen, for instance, by E. Cothenet, "Prophétisme dans le Nouveau Testament," DBS 8, col. 1226, and L. Morris, Apocalyptic (London, 1973), 36. On the general inferiority of apocalyptic to classical prophecy, cf. Russell, Message, 92; Davies, PRJ, 205; Y. Kaufmann, The Religion of Israel, (ET London, 1961), 349.

⁵⁸Russell, Method, 160, finds only nine passages in which the Spirit is said to have a role in inspiration, but even then in only one of them (4 Ezr. 14.22) is the Spirit said to have an immediate influence on the speech of the author in the manner of the OT prophets.

forms of introduction.[59] On the other hand, there is
reflected a strong consciousness of the privileged
reception of divine revelations (cf. Asn. Mos. 1.13-18,
2 En. 33.5-6, 36.1, 3 Bar. 1.3-8, 4 Ezr. 14.7-8, etc.).

Yet whether we evaluate apocalyptic as the suppressed revival of full-fledged OT prophecy or as some lesser type of quasi-prophetic phenomenon, its importance for our present purpose is not great, because the other literature we have examined seems quite adequately to demonstrate both the doctrine of the cessation of the type of prophecy found in the OT and many attestations of continuing revelations.

Now the primary concern of this chapter is not to decide whether or not any of these revelatory phenomena actually occurred, or even whether every Jew during the period in question believed that the OT type of prophecy had ceased. (Indeed it would be very surprising to find absolute unity of opinion on any one doctrine in any group so diverse as the Jews from about 200 B.C. to 200 A.D.) My only concern in this section is to show the existence of a conceptual framework in which one could think that the fact of continuing revelations was entirely consistent with a belief in the cessation of prophecy with a divine authority of actual words, because the two were thought of as related but nevertheless distinct. In order to show that, it is only necessary to demonstrate that the same writers or traditions who believe in the one also accept the other. For the rabbis, for Josephus, probably for the Qumran community and Philo, and perhaps (but not necessarily) for the apocalyptists the evidence seems very clear that such a belief in cessation was in fact coupled with an acceptance of further

---

[59]The Similitudes of Enoch (1 En. 37-71) are a clear exception (cf. 1 En. 37.2, 39.2, 45.3-6, 50.5, 51.3, etc.), but may be quite uncharacteristic of apocalyptic in this regard, and perhaps constitute a thinly veiled late claim to canonicity for 1 Enoch (these chapters were not found at Qumran). Cf. J. C. Hindley, "Towards a Date for the Similitudes of Enoch," NTS 14 (1967-68), 551-65.
Other exceptions are somewhat less clear, but see for example Sib. Or. 3.1-7 and 809ff, 4 Ezr. 14.37-48, 2 En. 39.2, 40.1, 2 Bar. 1.1, 2.1, 6.6, 8, 10.1-2, etc. Nevertheless, such claims are as a whole less frequent and less strong than in the OT prophets.

revelations of a less authoritative sort.

The existence in Jewish literature of such a concept of revelation with only a "divine authority of general content" will become important when we turn to examine prophecy in the NT church. Of course this background material in Jewish literature does not prove that NT prophecy must have belonged to such a secondary category or that NT prophecy must resemble one or another of these revelatory phenomena in every respect. Nevertheless, it does demonstrate the distinct possibility that at least some NT prophecy could have been understood in this way. Especially for a former rabbi such as the Apostle Paul, the conceptual framework was already available and would have seemed quite natural. But before we examine the NT evidence to see if prophecy was in fact understood in this way, it is necessary to ask whether the Hebrew and Greek words for "prophecy" and "prophet" had a range of meanings broad enough to enable them to be used of phenomena other than prophecy with a divine authority of actual words, perhaps revelatory phenomena like those we have seen in extra-Biblical Jewish literature.

IV. THE NEUTRALITY OF THE נָבִיא AND ΠΡΟΦΗΤΗΣ WORD GROUPS WITH REGARD TO VARIOUS TYPES OF DIVINE AUTHORITY

It is clear from our earlier study that the term "prophet" was often used to designate the messengers of God in the OT who claimed a divine authority of actual words. But the question now is whether, by the time of the NT, the Hebrew word נָבִיא and the Greek word προφήτης, along with the other members of their respective word groups, could only refer to such a person, so that in the minds of first century Christians the word "prophet" always meant, "one who claims to speak with a divine authority of actual words." It is the purpose of this section to show that this was not the case. Rather, the terms for "prophet" also had several broader and more general senses, such as "one who speaks as a result of an external spiritual influence" (emphasis on energizing force) in some cases, "one who predicts the future" or "one who has knowledge beyond sense perception" (emphasis on content of message) in others, and simply, "spokesman, announcer" (emphasis on function) in still others. Thus, although the term "prophet" was very often used in one particular sense to apply to the prophets of

the OT, these other uses show that the idea of a
divine authority of actual words was not essential to
every use of the term "prophet," but would apply to
its use only in certain contexts.

In the LXX προφήτης is the regular translation of
נָבִיא and προφητεύω of נָבָא, so we shall examine both
word groups at the same time.[60] In 1 Sam. 18.10-11 we
read that "an evil spirit from God rushed upon Saul and
he prophesied (וַיִּתְנַבֵּא, προεφήτευσεν (A)) within his
house, whole David was playing the lyre . . . and Saul
cast the spear, for he thought, "I will pin David to
the wall." Here the meaning "to speak words with
absolute divine authority" is impossible, but "to
utter sounds as the result of an external spiritual
influence" is a more general meaning which is appropriate.

1 Sam. 19.20-24 provides several more examples.
When Saul's messengers came to Ramah to capture David,
and saw Samuel standing as head over a company of
prophets who were prophesying, "the Spirit of God came
upon the messengers of Saul, and they also prophesied"
(וַיִּתְנַבְּאוּ, προφητεύουσιν, vs. 20). Saul sent other
messengers "and they also prophesied" (וַיִּתְנַבְּאוּ,
ἐπροφήτευσαν, vs. 21). Saul sent a third group, "and
they also prophesied" (וַיִּתְנַבְּאוּ, ἐπροφήτευσαν, vs. 21).
Finally Saul himself went, and on his way "the Spirit
of God came upon him also, and as he went he prophesied
(וַיִּתְנַבֵּא, προφητεύων) until he came to Naioth in Ramah.
And he too stripped off his clothes, and he too
prophesied (וַיִּתְנַבֵּא, ἐπροφήτευσεν) before Samuel, and
lay naked all that day and all that night. Hence it
is said, 'Is Saul also among the prophets?'" (vss. 23-
24). The narrative portrays some kind of involuntary
activity which subdued the would-be captors. In this
context there is no thought of speech with divinely
authoritative actual words which would have prompted
the writer to choose the term הִתְנַבֵּא. But the idea of
speech prompted by an external spiritual influence
(here, a divine one) is evident, and if that is an

---

[60]We must realize of course that προφήτης could
have taken on new nuances as a standard translation
word used by the LXX translators. Cf. Fascher,
ΠΡΟΦΗΤΗΣ, 148.

acceptable sense of הִתְנַבֵּא then the choice of words is very suitable.⁶¹

It is also interesting that the text attaches the proverb, "Is Saul also among the prophets?" (בַּנְּבִיאִם, ἐν προφήταις) to this incident. If to be a "prophet" always meant "to be one who speaks the very words God has given him," this incident would hardly have prompted anyone to attach the title "prophet" to Saul. But if "prophet" could mean "one who spoke under external spiritual influence," then Saul would easily have been counted among them.⁶²

1 Chr. 25:1-7 speaks of 288 men trained in singing to the Lord (vs. 7). They were under their leaders who prophesied (vs. 1: הַנִּבְּאִים Qerê; הַנְּבִיאִים, Kethîb; LXX: ἀποφθεγγομένους; Aq.: τῶν προφητῶν; Symm.: τῶν προφητευσάντων διὰ λύρας) with lyres, with harps, and with cymbals. In this manner Asaph is said to be one who prophesied (vs. 2: הַנִּבָּא, τοῦ προφήτου (Lucian;

---

⁶¹הִתְנַבֵּא is not restricted to ecstatic or unintelligible speech. I count 13 examples of "intelligible" speech out of 28 OT occurrences (1 Kgs. 22.8, 10, 18, 2 Chr. 18.7, 9, 17, 20.37, Jer. 14.14b, 23.13, 26.20, 29.27, Ezk. 13.17, 37.10; cf. Ezr. 5.1 (Aram.), perhaps 1 Kgs. 18.29). הִתְנַבֵּא seems to be interchangeable with נִבָּא in 1 Sam. 10.10 with 11, 19.20a with 20b, 1 Kgs. 22.10 with 12, 2 Chr. 18.9 with 11, Jer. 14.142 with 14b, 26.20b, Ezk. 13.17 with vss. 2 and 6, 37.7 with 10. However, the Hithpael is perhaps given slight preference in referring to prophecy which is less voluntary and more spontaneous.
A. Jepsen, Nabi (Munich, 1934), 8, gives a chart of a suggested historical development in the meanings of the verbs, but his suggestion does not adequately account for all the cases of interchange which I list here.

⁶²Young, My Servants, 56-65, sees broader uses for the verb forms but not for the noun. But passages such as this one show that broader meanings did attach to the noun as well.
Young briefly summarizes the many proposed etymologies for נָבִיא (pp. 56f) and concludes that it is impossible to arrive at a certain decision. However, it is significant that none of the meanings of the proposed Semitic cognates ("to speak," "to announce," "to be called," "to give ecstatic cries," "to bubble forth") includes in itself any idea of divine authority.

untrans. B, A]). Jeduthun is also said to be one who prophesied with a harp (vs. 3: הַנִּבָּא, LXX: ἀνακρουόμενοι [pl. ptcpl. includes the sons of Jeduthun], Aq.: προφητεύω, Symm.: προφητεύοντος) to give praise and thanks to the Lord. Again, the contrast between this passage and those which speak of prophecy by a divinely-commissioned messenger prophet is striking. Here there is no hint of anyone being commissioned to go and say to someone, "Thus says Yahweh." Indeed, it is not God-to-man communication but man-to-God communication (vss. 3, 7). The meaning "messenger who speaks words with absolute divine authority" is unsuitable. But the text could well imply songs of praise prompted by the Spirit of God (cf. the description of the glory of the Lord in 2 Chr. 5:14). If so, the idea of speech prompted by an external spiritual influence would once more make the use of the נָבִיא word group appropriate.[63]

Similar conclusions can be drawn about 1 Sam. 10:5-13: Saul will see a band of prophets (נְבִיאִים, προφητῶν) prophesying (vs. 5: מִתְנַבְּאִים, προφητεύοντες) with harp, tambourine, flute and lyre. The Spirit of the Lord will come upon him and he will prophesy (vs. 6: וְהִתְנַבִּיתָ, προφητεύσεις [dialogue in 2nd person]) with them. When the prophets did meet him, he prophesied among them (vs. 10), and people began to say, "Is Saul also among the prophets?" (vss. 11-12). Additional instances of נָבִיא and προφήτης are in vss. 10, 11 (twice) and 12 הִתְנַבֵּא and προφητεύω in vss. 10 and 13 and נִבָּא in vs. 11.

To this list of examples should probably be added Num 11:24-30, where the 70 elders with Moses prophesy. Seventy men speaking at once can hardly have been thought to belong to the divinely authoritative messenger category we noticed earlier: they do not deliver a message from God to anyone. Rather,

---

[63] Johnson, Cultic Prophet, 72-75, sees these verses as an indication that, from the Chronicler's viewpoint, prophets have become members of musical guilds or the Temple choir. It is doubtful where there is sufficient evidence to make such a historical generalization. At any rate our concern is again simply with the linguistic sense of the terms as they stand in the present context.

they simply utter some form of speech (perhaps praise)[64] which is prompted by an external spiritual influence (vss. 25, 29). Yet הִתְנַבֵּא (= προφητεύω) occurs three times and נָבִיא (= προφήτης) once.

Finally, it must not be overlooked that the OT writers use נָבִיא to refer to those whom they evaluate as "false" prophets 96 times in the OT, and it is translated by προφήτης in all but 10 of those cases. נָבָא is used of allegedly "false" prophets 27 times and הִתְנַבֵּא 6 times,[65] and all are translated by προφητεύω.

If the OT writers thought that these terms could refer only to those who uttered God's very words, then this choice of terminology would have been quite surprising. One might say that it referred to those who themselves purported to speak God's words, but then one must still account for the prophets of Baal, who are not thought by the OT writers either to speak Yahweh's words or even to purport to do so. For these "prophets" the meaning "one who speaks with a divine authority of actual words" is manifestly inappropriate, but "one who speaks as a result of some external spiritual influence" is quite acceptable.[66]

Of course these examples fall short of making up a majority of the uses of נָבִיא and προφήτης and related words. The words are used roughly 60% of the time[67] to refer to allegedly "true" messenger prophets in the OT (with a claimed divine authority of actual words). But the other uses, where the terms do not

---

[64] Young, My Servants, 69, suggests that the speech was similar to speaking in tongues.

[65] These numbers are the result of my count. The verses are too numerous to list.

[66] I have not included here other possible examples which seemed too ambiguous: Gen. 20.7, Ex 7.1, 15.20, 1 Sam. 9.9, Is. 8.2, Jer. 29.26, and the passages about the "sons of the prophets" (2 Kgs. 2.3, 5, 7, 15, 4.1, 38, etc.).

[67] I count 187 out of 306 uses of the noun and 61 out of 113 uses of the verbs to refer to allegedly "true" prophets who speak with a divine authority of actual words. For the nouns and verbs combined this makes 248 out of 419 occurrences, or 59%.

mean that, would be quite obvious to any Jew reading the OT in Hebrew or in Greek. Not only are the examples quite numerous; they also occur mostly in prominent and easily-remembered sections of the historical books, sections where an understanding of the nature of prophecy would be an important issue. So these examples should caution us against saying, for instance, that נָבָא means "to speak with a divine authority of actual words" in every case. A more general sense such as "to speak as a result of an external spiritual influence" is often preferable.[68]

We can now examine more briefly the use of these words in extra-Biblical literature. In the rabbinic literature members of the נָבִיא word group are sometimes used of a person who has knowledge of things beyond sense perception and can refer, for example, to people who predicted the future but who were never thought to speak with a divine authority of actual words or to have the status of divine messenger. Some examples are Rebekah (b. Sot. 13a refers to "her prophecy" (נבואתה) and the context shows that the idea of prediction, not that of authority, is what motivated the choice of this word), Miriam (b. Meg. 14a, with נביאה, נבואה and התנבא all used because of something she predicted), and Hannah (a prediction is said to justify the application of the term נביאה to her in b. Meg. 14a).

There also seems to be an emphasis on prophecy in the sense of revealed knowledge in b. Ber. 55b and 57b: "R. Johanan said, 'If one rises early and a Scriptural verse comes to his mind, this is a small prophecy'" (זה נבואה קטנה). Similarly, R. Hanina b. Isaac said, "The incomplete form (נוֹבֶלֶת)[69] of prophecy (נבואה) is the dream" (Gen. R. 17.5; again, 44.7). That the term "prophecy" can be applied to such phenomena is not due to the fact that the recipient would authoritatively deliver the message to someone else, or would claim a divine authority of actual words, but rather to the suggestion in each case of some kind of

---

[68] In fact, this general sense would account for the more specialized use, "to speak with a divine authority of actual words," for that is a particular type of speaking under spiritual influence, but the more specialized use could hardly explain the more general one.

[69] Or "inferior variety"; Jastrow, 883.

special impartation of knowledge to the prophet from
without. The examples indicate that a broad range of
meanings attached to the word נבואה.[70]

In the Apocrypha we note Wisd. 7.27 (late 1st c.
B.C.): speaking of wisdom, it says, "In every generation she passes into holy souls and makes them
friends of God, and prophets (προφήτας).[71]

Josephus quite clearly designates John Hyrcanus
as a prophet: he "was accounted by God worthy of three
of the greatest privileges, the rule of the nation,
the office of high priest, and the gift of prophecy
(προφητείας), for (γάρ) the Deity was with him and
enabled him to foresee and foretell the future; so, for
example, he foretold of his two elder sons that they
would not remain masters of the state" (A. 13.299-300;
both προφητεία and προφητεύω are used in the parallel
account in B. 1.68-69). The passage is significant
because in it Josephus makes explicit what it was that
qualified John for the title "prophet": not the ability
to speak with a divine authority of actual words, but
the ability to predict the future. Since this ability
was thought to come from God, his predictions might
have been attributed a kind of divine authority of
general content, but one of actual words is not
claimed.[72]

In Philo we read that the mind in dreams prophesies (προφητεύω) future events (Spec. Leg. 1.219),
that Isaac and Jacob are said to have prophesied
(προφητεύω) because they predicted the future to their
children (Quis Her. 261), and that a conjecture in
which Moses anticipated the next day was closely akin
to a prophecy (προφητεία, Mos. 2.265). Then Philo also
uses προφήτης to mean simply "spokesman," in a sense
more often found in pagan Greek literature. In Quod
Deus 138 reason is the προφήτης of God. Speech is said
to act as prophet for understanding in Det. 40

---

[70]Cf. also b. B.B. 12a-b.

[71]Possible similar uses are in Sir. 24.32 (does
Ben Sira think of his present words as some kind of
"prophecy"?) and in the pseudepigraphal T. Levi 8.15,
where John Hyrcanus may be called a prophet.

[72]Cf. p. 22 above.

(προφήτης) and <u>Mig</u>. 169 (προφητεύω).[73]

A detailed survey of the προφήτης word group in pagan Greek literature is beyond the scope of our present research, and the subject has already received extensive treatment in Erich Fascher's book, ΠΡΟΦΗΤΗΣ.[74] After an extensive survey, Fascher concludes (pp. 51-54) that προφήτης itself is a "frameword" (<u>Rahmenwort</u>) without a narrowly defined meaning of its own. Rather, it is used in the widest number of circumstances and takes its precise meaning from the context. One general definition which fits almost every case, however, is "proclaimer" or "announcer" (<u>Verkünder</u>). Thus, a poet is a prophet of the muses, a philosopher is a prophet of nature, and when a μάντις announces a message he is a προφήτης. There are prophets of Apollo, of Bacchus, of the truth, etc. Προφήτης alone almost never has the sense of "predictor, foreteller" (<u>Weissager</u>), but must receive this meaning from other qualifying words in the context. Similarly with the verb προφητεύω: it never means "to predict, foretell, divine" (for which μαντεύομαι is used), but can mean "to speak in the name of a god," or "to reveal something hidden," or "to hold the office of a prophet."

Helmut Krämer[75] also mentions several broader uses of προφήτης. It may refer to the members of an upper priestly class in Egypt, the advocates of some particular philosophy, the "specialist" in botany, or (ironically) to the "quack" in medicine. Even the heralds who declared the victor at games were called προφῆται.

---

[73] Even though some of these are metaphors, they are metaphors for the role of spokesman in general, not for the role of absolutely authoritative or commissioned messenger who could speak words which could be attributed to the one sent him.

[74] Cf. n. 24.

[75] <u>TDNT</u> VI, 793-95. Another good summary of pagan Greek usage is found in Crone, <u>ECP</u>, 12-39.

With respect to the specific question of the Delphic oracle,[76] it should be noted that the role of the prophet at the oracle differs from that of the OT prophets. The woman who receives the inspired utterance, the Pythia, may be called a πρόμαντις (with respect to her disclosure of the future) or a προφῆτις (with respect to her role as a mouthpiece of the god). But the προφήτης, the prophet, was one who heard her words and then interpreted and proclaimed them to the inquirers who were seated in another room. He himself is not inspired by the god in any way.[77] So here the προφήτης word group is "neutral in the question whether the person who bears the name is divinely inspired or not."[78] It may mean simply one who translated the Pythia's semi-coherent babbling into an intelligible response.[79]

When we turn to the NT we must take into account this large diversity in usage. NT Christians will have their linguistic stock influenced by the OT, by intertestamental Judaism, and by the everyday Koine Greek usage of the pagan culture in which they lived. When these influences combine, it is inevitable that the προφήτης word group will have a range of meanings much broader than simply "a messenger for God who speaks with a divine authority of actual words." Of course, when the NT writers have occasion to use the words προφήτης, προφητεία, and προφητεύω, it will mostly be in contexts dealing with the great writing prophets of the OT, whose writings they saw fulfilled in Christ. In these contexts, the προφήτης word group will quite often refer to men with, in their opinion, a divine authority of actual words. But that does not tell us what προφήτης will mean when it is applied to men other than these OT prophets. It may take any one of the

---

[76] Cf. H. Krämer, TDNT VI, 784-92; H. W. Parke and D. E. W. Wormell, The Delphic Oracle (2 vols.; London, 1956²), I, 17-45.

[77] Philo is careful to point out to his non-Jewish readers that an OT prophet, in contrast to an oracle prophet, both receives the oracles and is the spokesman ("interpreter") who reports them: cf. Mos. 2.191 and Wolfson, Philo, II, 42.

[78] Krämer, TDNT VI, 788.

[79] Parke and Wormell, Oracle, I, 39.

various meanings current in Koine Greek.

In fact, that is what happens. In Tit. 1:12 we find προφήτης in the sense of "one who predicts the future." Referring to Epimenides (Cretan religious teacher ca. 6th c. B.C.), the verse reads: "One of themselves, a prophet of their own, said, 'Cretans are always liars, evil beasts, lazy gluttons.'"[80] In Lk. 22:64 the high priest's assistants who had blindfolded Jesus demand,"Prophesy! Who is it that struck you?" The meaning is not "Speak words with absolute divine authority" but "Show that you have knowledge by supernatural means."[81] In the narrative about the woman at the well, as soon as Jesus tells the woman the secrets of her past life, she says, "Sir, I perceive that you are a prophet" (Jn. 4.19). Now Jesus had not yet convinced her that he could speak with a divine authority in his actual words; he had just demonstrated that he had knowledge which had not come by ordinary means. These last two examples are especially important because they give us a glimpse of the sense attached to προφήτης and προφητεύω by ordinary people of first century Palestine, who had nevertheless had some contact with the OT through their religious background.

Similar indications come from Christian writings outside the NT. In T. Sol. 15.8[82] (ca. 100 A.D.) a demon prophesies (προφητεύω) to Solomon that his kingdom will be broken, and in Mart. Pol. 12.3 we read that Polycarp had said prophetically (προφητικῶς), "I must be burnt alive." In both cases prediction as a

---

[80] Epimenides was thought to be able to predict the future: cf. M. Dibelius and H. Conzelmann, The Pastoral Epistles, 136; TDNT VI, 828.

[81] Cf. the parallels in Mt. 26.68, Mk. 14.65. The passage from b. Sanh. 93b mentioned by W. Lane, Mark, 540, n. 148, is not really relevant here because it has nothing to do with prophesying, but rather refers to legal judgments (which are not in view in the Gospel passages).

[82] Text in C. McCown, The Testament of Solomon, (Leipzig, 1922) 47*; ET in F. C. Conybeare "The Testament of Solomon," JQR 9 (1898-99), 32. The passage is clearly Christian: note the following lines, esp. 15. 10-11. (For date, see Conybeare, p. 12.)

result of some supernatural knowledge, not absolute divine authority, is in view.

The result of this study then is the realization that when the NT writers apply members of the προφήτης word group to someone other than an OT prophet, it is impossible to decide in advance what sense the term will have. The precise meaning will have to be determined from the context. In themselves, προφήτης and its related words will have to be viewed as neutral with respect to the question of the type of divine authority possessed.

V. OLD TESTAMENT PROPHETS AND NEW TESTAMENT APOSTLES

A casual reader of the NT might quite naturally assume that NT prophets would be similar to OT prophets[83] in many respects, including, perhaps, the matter of authority. However, the purpose of this section is to suggest that those who are viewed as divinely authoritative messengers in the NT are most often called not "prophets" but "apostles." This is significant for our investigation because if the NT apostles are frequently seen as the counterparts to the OT prophets, then NT prophets might often be something quite different.

A. New Testament Apostles are Seen as Messengers of Christ[84]

One marked parallel between the OT prophet and the NT apostle is that an apostle was commissioned by

---

[83] I shall subsequently use the designation "OT prophets" to refer to the divinely authoritative prophets in the OT, unless otherwise specified.

[84] One can hardly say that there is scholarly agreement today about issues such as the requirements for apostleship, the origin and development of the term ἀπόστολος, the nature of the apostolic office, and the number of the apostles. Considerations of space do not allow detailed discussions of these issues here, except as they relate to the specific question of the status of apostles as divinely authoritative messengers. Some of the more important studies on these general questions are: J. B. Lightfoot, "The

Christ, "sent" by him on a specific apostolic mission (Rom. 1.5, 1 Cor. 9.17, 2 Cor. 1.1, 5.20, Gal. 1.1, Eph. 1.1, Col. 1.1, 25, Ac. 26.17; cf. Mt. 10.1ff and pars.).[85] In fact, just as the OT prophets were covenant messengers, so in 2 Cor. 3.6 Paul calls himself a minister of the New Covenant.[86]

Name and Office of an Apostle," in St. Paul's Epistle to the Galatians (London, 1896[10]), 92-101; A. Harnack, Mission and Expansion, I, 319-52; K. H. Rengstorf, "ἀπόστολος," TDNT I, 398-447; H. Mosbech, "Apostolos in the New Testament," ST 3 (1950), 96-110; J. N. Geldenhuys, Supreme Authority (London, 1953); C. K. Barrett, "The Apostles in and after the NT," SEÅ 21 (1956), 30-49; idem, The Signs of an Apostle (London 1970); H. von Campenhausen, Ecclesiastical Authority and Spiritual Power in the Church of the First Three Centuries (ET London, 1969), 12-54; W. Schmithals, The Office of Apostle in the Early Church (ET London, 1971); B. Gerhardsson, "Die Boten Gottes und die Apostel Christi," SEÅ 27 (1963), 89-131; R. Schnackenburg, "Apostles Before and During Paul's Time," ET in Apostolic History and the Gospel, ed. W. Gasque and R. P. Martin (Exeter, 1970), 287-303; F. Hahn, "Der Apostolat im Urchristentum," KD 20 (1974), 54-77; J. A. Kirk, "Apostleship Since Rengstorf: Towards a Synthesis," NTS 21 (1974-75), 249-64; J. Schütz, Paul and the Anatomy of Apostolic Authority (Cambridge, 1975).

I still find Rengstorf's position most convincing, that an apostle was one who (a) was an eyewitness of the risen Lord, and (b) was specially commissioned by Christ as an apostle (TDNT I, 431; cf. Lightfoot, Galatians, 97f). Even if one held a differing view on this or some of the other questions listed above, however, it would not significantly affect the following discussions so long as one is willing at least to compare the statements made about NT apostles with data about OT prophets and NT prophets.

The following discussion specifically concerns apostles of Jesus Christ, and therefore does not consider the non-technical use of the term in Jn. 13.16, 2 Cor. 8.23 and Phil. 2.25.

[85]Cf. Gerhardsson, "Boten," 105-16; V. P. Furnish, "Prophets, Apostles, and Preachers," Interp. 17 (1963), 48-51, 54f; Hahn, "Apostolat," 66-69.

[86]Cf. Kline, SBA 70ff. Jones, "Second Moses," 37, argues that ἐκ θεοῦ in 2 Cor. 2.17 is another way in which Paul claims divine authority for himself.

It is not surprising, then, that in the NT the apostles are several times connected with the divinely authoritative OT prophets, but NT prophets, by contrast, are never connected with OT prophets in the same way. First, this is true of Jesus when the term "apostle" is applied to him. Heb. 1 begins, "In many and various ways God spoke of old to the fathers by the prophets, but in these last days he has spoken to us by a son." But then in 3.1, instead of calling Jesus a "prophet" on the basis of this speaking, the author says, "Therefore . . . consider Jesus, the apostle and high priest of our confession," and goes on to contrast him with Moses, the archetypal OT prophet according to Jewish tradition.[87] Similarly, when Paul is defending his ministry to the Corinthians, he contrasts it with that of Moses: as Moses was a minister of the Old Covenant, so Paul is a minister of the New (2 Cor. 2.14-4.6).[88] In 2 Pet. 3.2, the readers are urged to remember "the words spoken beforehand by the holy prophets and the commandment of the Lord and Savior through your apostles."[89] Lk. 11.49, admittedly a difficult passage, is probably best explained by Plummer: "It is of the Divine Providence (Prov. 8.22-31), sending Prophets to the Jewish Church and Apostles to the Christian Church, that Jesus here speaks: 'God in His wisdom said'. . . . Jesus here speaks with confident knowledge of the Divine counsels."[90]

---

[87] Moule, Colossians, 158, n. 2, says, "It is highly significant that Heb. 3.1 corresponds to the well-attested fact that Jesus spoke of himself as 'sent' by the Father."

[88] Paul's conception of his apostleship in fulfilling the role of a second Moses is defended at length by Jones, "Second Moses."

[89] That OT prophets are meant is evident (a) from 1.20f and 2.1, 16, where OT prophets are in mind; (b) because the prophets are not connected with Christ or his words, as are the apostles; (c) because 2 Pet. 3.1 makes it clear that a reference to 1 Pet. is intended, and there the OT prophets are in view (1.10-12); and (d) because in exhorting his readers to call certain words to mind, the author probably is thinking of written collections of words, of which there are many attributed to OT prophets, but few or none attributed to NT prophets.

[90] Plummer, Luke, 313; so Creed, 167; Leaney, 194; contra Ellis, 170ff. O. J. F. Seitz, "The Commission

In the early church also, the apostles are several times connected with OT prophets, but I am aware of no instance where NT prophets are associated with OT prophets.[91]

J. M. Myers and Edwin D. Freed examine eight parallels between Paul and the OT prophets and conclude, "There may be, in the final analysis, not very much difference between Old Testament prophet and New Testament apostle."[92]

Yet by the time of the NT the term προφήτης would have been inadequate to designate the authoritative messengers of Christ, for two reasons. (a) The term did not adequately emphasize the status of divinely authoritative messenger, because in everyday use it often simply meant "one who predicts the future or has supernatural knowledge" or "spokesman" (without any necessary connotations of authority). (b) Since Joel (2.28) had predicted the outpouring of God's Spirit on all flesh, resulting in prophecy and related phenomena, and since there was an expectation of widespread prophetic experience in the age to come (Num. R. 15.25: "In the world to come all Israel will be made prophets"; cf. Num. 11.29: "Would that all the Lord's people were prophets"),[93] προφῆται would have

---

of Prophets and 'Apostles': A Re-examination of Mt. 23. 34 with Lk. 11.49," in Studia Evangelica IV, ed. F. L. Cross (Berlin, 1968), 236-40, suggests that Jesus conflated several OT passages about prophets and introduced the resultant summary with "the wisdom of God has said."

[91] Ign. Phld. 5.1-2, 9.1-2, Ep. Pol. 6, Herm. Sim. 9.15.4; cf. Justin, Dial. Trypho 75. On Eph. 2.20 see below, pp. 82ff. In the Didache, however, ἀπόστολος seems to mean just "missionary" (Did. 11.3, 4, 6; note a probable explanation in Burton, Galatians, 383f.)

[92] J. M. Myers and E. D. Freed, "Is Paul Also Among the Prophets?" Interp. 20 (1966), 40-53. Kaufmann, Religion, 212ff, describes the OT prophets as "apostolic prophets" because their being sent by God to bring his word to the people is what distinguished them from pagan prophets. Cf. Cothenet, DBS 8, col. 2188; idem, "Prophétisme et ministère," 35-39; contra Schmithals, Apostle, 56.

[93] Cf. Str.-B. II, 615-17 for parallels.

been too broad a term to apply to a special, limited group of men such as the apostles.

Thus, a better term than προφήτης was needed, and ἀπόστολος was well suited to the task. (a) What distinguished those who spoke with divine authority in the OT from those who did not was the status of "messenger." An OT prophet who was sent by God to speak to the people was the only kind of prophet who spoke God's words. Now the obvious relation of ἀπόστολος to the verb ἀποστέλλω gave it immediate connections with the divinely authoritative OT prophet who had been sent (שׁלח = ἀποστέλλω) by God.[94] Thus, ἀπόστολος could become a more restricted term for one specific aspect of the broad range of meaning possessed by the προφήτης word group. It could refer to men who were the NT counterpart of the messengers of God in the OT, and who spoke with divine authority. And even though the NT apostle was in many ways unlike the Jewish messenger (the שׁליח), the idea of a delegate who bore the authority of the one who sent him was common in Jewish thought,[95] and a Greek term which meant "one who is sent" would have been well suited to take on similar connotations.[96] (b) Since ἀπόστολος in this sense was a new term,[97] it could be used of a limited group of

---

[94] Westermann, Basic Forms, 116.

[95] Str.-B., III, pp. 2-4, show that the idea of an authoritative שׁליח is widely attested in Rabbinic literature; see esp. M. Ber. 5.5.

[96] Kirk, "Apostleship Since Rengstorf," 250-52, summarizes the debate over Shaliach theories, and concludes. "Neither the word nor the function of an ἀπόστολος Χριστοῦ Ἰησοῦ can strictly be derived from שׁליח, nor can its meaning be constrained by the sense in which it might have been used in first-century Judaism. As Rengstorf himself suggests, though the idea may have come from rabbinic Judaism its characteristic use in the New Testament has a peculiarly Christian origin and emphasis" (p. 252). Schmithals, Apostle, 98-110 summarizes and attacks the Shaliach theory; answered by Gerhardsson, "Boten," 105-16.

[97] Mosbech, "Apostolos," 168, doubts whether pre-Christian Jews used the term ἀπόστολος in the NT sense: Josephus uses the term once, and in a non-religious sense (A. 17.300), and Philo uses ἱεροπομπός

men without seeming to conflict with any OT or rabbinic expectations of a wide diffusion of prophetic abilities.⁹⁸

It is not possible at this point to define in detail the kind of authority attributed to the words of the apostles in the NT. However, we should note briefly that again there are several similarities to the OT prophets. Myers and Freed cite many instances in which Paul's experience parallels that of the OT prophets who received their messages by standing in the council of the Lord: 1 Cor. 9.1, 11.23, Acts 20. 24, 23.11, 27.23, Gal. 1.12, 2.1f; cf. Acts 16.6-7, 20.22-23.⁹⁹ Paul adamantly insists that his message has not come from men, but from Jesus Christ himself: "The gospel which was preached by me is not man's gospel (κατὰ ἄνθρωπον). For I did not receive it from

---

not ἀπόστολος to refer to the Jewish שָׁלִיחַ (Leg. 312, Spec. Leg. 1.78). In the LXX the one occurrence at 3 Kgs. 14.6 (A, also Aq.; cf. Symm. Is. 18.2) is obscure enough to be of little significance. In pagan Greek literature the term was applied to military expeditions or naval vessels, but, as Rengstorf says, "It could not become the usual term for an emissary in the Greek world, since the Greeks had many other words which they could use for this purpose (ἄγγελος, κῆρυξ, πρεσβευτής etc.)" (TDNT I, 407f). Thus, the Christian usage of the term ἀπόστολος gave it a new meaning, unparalleled in other literature.

⁹⁸It is also interesting at this point to note the appropriateness of the term προφήτης to apply to a man who did not speak with divine authority but nevertheless received "revelations" from God and reported them in the church assembly. Many of the other words available to the NT authors were somehow deficient: βλέπων, "seer," would have emphasized too much the revelatory side of the man's experience, to the exclusion of his speaking function; μάντις, "diviner," would have carried too many secular and exclusively ecstatic connotations; θεσπιστής "prophet, oracular speaker" (LS, p. 795; the verb θεσπίζω is much more common) would have placed too much emphasis on the supernatural, oracular character of the utterance. Προφήτης, on the other hand, also had the advantage of OT and rabbinic expectations of a distribution of prophetic abilities to all the people.

⁹⁹Myers and Freed, "Paul Also?," 48ff. They note

man, nor was I taught it, but it came through a revelation of Jesus Christ" (Gal. 1.11-12). Here the οὐδὲ γὰρ ἐγὼ παρὰ ἀνθρώπου παρέλαβον αὐτό, plus the οὔτε ἐδιδάχθην, make it very unlikely that Paul is talking about any human mediation of the central message of his gospel (although the sentence could certainly allow for later additions of factual details about Christ through contact with traditions circulating in the early church). Such insistence on the divine origin of his message is clearly in the tradition of the OT prophets (Dt. 18.20, Jer. 23.16ff, Ezk. 13.1ff, 1 Kgs. 22.14, 28).

In addition to these parallels, we can simply note here the many instances, especially in Paul, where NT apostles seem to be making claims for their authority which sound similar to the claims of the OT prophets: Rom. 2.16, 1 Cor. 2.13, 2 Cor. 13.3, Gal. 1. 8-9, 1 Th. 2.13, 4.8, 4.15, 5.27, 2 Th. 3.6, 14, and claims made in statements about the apostles: Ac. 5. 3-4, 2 Pet. 3.2, 16.[100]

---

in addition Paul's frequent visions: 2 Cor. 12, Ac. 26.19, 1 Cor. 15.8, Ac. 16.9-10, 18.9.

[100]Ellis, Paul's Use of the Old Testament (Edinburgh, 1957), 111, suggests that the sporadic λέγει Κύριος citations in the NT may have originated with early Christian prophets, "including not only leaders such as Paul but also many minor figures." Since Ellis's case is primarily drawn from Pauline examples we could equally well suggest that the citations originated with NT apostles, especially Paul himself.

Finally, we should also notice at this point that the NT gives us no warrant for thinking that the apostles always spoke divinely authoritative words: They could discuss (πολλῆς δὲ ζητήσεως γενομένης, Ac. 15.7), disagree (Ac. 15.39), and even be wrong (Gal. 2.11ff, Ac. 27.10, 22).

How the early church (or the apostles themselves) distinguished between those words which they considered divinely authoritative and those they did not, is a difficult question and one beyond the scope of this study. It is clear from the examples given in this section, however, that there were many times that the apostles, and especially Paul, claimed to be speaking with divine authority. It is the purpose of this section to point out those instances and to contrast them with what is said of the NT prophets.

For our purposes one of the most significant Pauline passages on this topic is 1 Cor. 14.37-38, because here Paul is writing to a community where several prophets were active, and he still asserts his authority over the entire community, even over the prophets. Paul writes, Εἴ τις δοκεῖ προφήτης εἶναι ἢ πνευματικός, ἐπιγινωσκέτω ἃ γράφω ὑμῖν ὅτι Κυρίου ἐστὶν ἐντολή· εἰ δέ τις ἀγνοεῖ, ἀγνοεῖται.[101]

---

[101] The reading ἐστὶν ἐντολή is to be preferred in vs. 37. Ἐστίν alone, although shorter, is very unlikely because, with the exception of Origen, it is supported only by Western witnesses (D* G [it d, e, g] Origen [gr, lat] Ambrosiaster Hilary Pelagius), most of which are unreliable in other parts of this passage (D G it d,e,g and Ambrosiaster transpose vss. 34-35 to follow vs. 40; Origen in the following verse gives three different readings). Also, the ἐντολή could have been dropped to eliminate the awkward singular predicate nominative (ἐντολή) following a plural subject (ἅ). The readings with ἐντολαί are best viewed as later attempts to conform to the plural ἅ. This leaves two alternatives, ἐντολή ἐστιν (ℵ*) and ἐστὶν ἐντολή, which has significant and diverse support (p[46] AB 048 1739 syr[pal] cop[bo] eth Augustine), and is thus the one I have chosen. Contra G. Zuntz, The Text of The Epistles (London, 1953), 139f.

In vs. 38 the decision is more difficult. Ἀγνοείτω, "let him be ignorant," has early and strong Alexandrian support (p[46] B Ψ 81, 104, 326), and is adopted in the Byzantine text tradition (K Byz eth; arm?). It also has some Western support (88, 181, 614; perhaps D[b,c], syr[p,h]; arm?). But ἀγνοεῖται, "he is not recognized," also has Alexandrian (ℵ* A*vid 048 1739 cop[sa, boh, fay]) and Western (it[d,e]) support. In addition, ἀγνοεῖτε (D[gr*]) arises by an itacism for ἀγνοεῖται (Bruce Metzger, A Textual Commentary on the Greek New Testament [London and N.Y., 1971], 566) and ignorabitur (it[ar(vid),f,g,x,z],vg), "he shall not be recognized," would most easily have come from ἀγνοεῖται. These are also Western witnesses.

On the basis of external evidence neither reading can be strongly preferred. But several internal considerations combine to favor the indicative ἀγνοεῖται: (a) Paul uses ἀγνοέω in the passive two other times (2 Cor. 6.9, Gal. 1.22), in both cases

So Paul claims here that what he writes to the
Corinthians is itself a command of the Lord. How much
of the preceding discourse is comprehended by the
ἃ γράφω ὑμῖν is perhaps impossible to determine with
certainty, but we can note that it comes exactly at the
end of the discussion of spiritual gifts (12-14) and
would seem most naturally to apply to the entire
section.[102] It might be argued that this statement
refers only to the preceding sentence, or to the
directive about women (33-35). However, the statement
is so general ("the things that I am writing to you"),
and is made so indefinite by the use of the plural
(ἅ), that such a restriction would seem highly arti-
ficial. Paul's purpose is to conclude the discussion
and at the same time to bar the way for any prophet at
Corinth to propound "ἐν πνεύματι" new rules which would
contradict those given by Paul. Certainly this concern
would apply to the whole range of directives for worship, reaching back to chapters 12 and 13, and perhaps even to chapter 11.

But this means that we have in 1 Cor. 14.37 a
very strong statement of Paul's authority. For it is

---

meaning "to be unknown, unrecognized." In 2 Cor. 6.9,
as in 1 Cor. 14.37, ἐπιγινώσκω is placed in contrast
to ἀγνοέω. (b) Ἀγνοείτω could have arisen if a
scribe, not understanding the meaning of ἀγνοεῖται,
gave ἀγνοέω the more common Pauline sense, "to be
ignorant," which is especially likely in view of the
introduction to this section in 12.1: Περὶ δὲ τῶν
πνευματικῶν, ἀδελφοί, οὐ θέλω ὑμᾶς ἀγνοεῖν (cf. Rom. 1.
13, 6.3, 7.1, 11.25, 1 Cor. 10.1, 2 Cor. 1.8, 1 Th.
4.13). (c) On the other hand, ἀγνοείτω is such a
difficult reading to understand in context that it becomes almost impossible: to condemn someone to ignorance simply because of previous ignorance is a rather
cruel and un-Pauline thought; neither would this provide a good transition to the following ὥστε clause.
(d) The alternation between active and passive forms
of the same verb in "judgement" sentences is a Pauline
characteristic. (Cf. Ernst Käsemann, "Sentences of
Holy Law in the NT," in New Testament Questions of Today (ET London, 1969), 66ff. Käsemann, however, takes
Paul's statements as typical not specifically of NT
apostolic speech, but of NT prophetic speech in general.)

[102]RP, 327; Lietzmann, 77; Meyer, 334.

inconceivable that all the instructions in 1 Cor. 12-14 are based on words of the earthly Jesus handed down to Paul through oral or written tradition (otherwise we would certainly have echoes of such a large group of "χαρίσματα - logia" elsewhere in the NT). Rather, Paul has here instituted a number of new rules for church worship at Corinth and has claimed for them the status of ἐντολαὶ Κυρίου.[103] Furthermore, the penalty is severe (if we adopt the reading ἀγνοεῖται): the man who refused to acknowledge Paul's divine authority will himself not be known or recognized by the Lord.[104] Edwards summarizes 14.38: "He that refuses to hear Christ's Apostles refuses to hear Christ Himself and incurs His displeasure" (p. 384).

So we have here a very close parallel to OT prophetic authority. Anyone who disobeyed Paul's instructions would be disobeying a "command of the Lord," and would be punished not by Paul but by God himself. On the other hand, nothing even approaching this kind of claim is made for NT prophets. Indeed, even the prophets at Corinth were expected to be subject to Paul's apostolic authority. G. W. H. Lampe notes that Paul "was driven flatly to refuse to admit

---

[103] Similarly, Héring: "The orders given by the Apostle should be considered as orders from the Lord—not as referring to 'logia' handed down, but because the Lord has guided him by His Spirit" (p. 155). Dautzenberg, UP, 290-98, sees all of 14.33b-37 as a postapostolic interpolation. B. A. Person, The Pneumatikos-Psychikos Terminology in 1 Corinthians (Missoula, Mt., 1973), 44, thinks that 14.37 indicates that some Corinthians referred to all ecstatic speech as "prophecy."

[104] So Ellicott, 285; Conzelmann, 246; Lietzmann, 77; Weiss, 343; cf. Mt. 25.12. Barrett, 334, Héring, 155, and Bruce, 136, prefer "will not be recognized as an inspired spokesman." But the use of the passive with an unnamed subject is a common Semitic circumlocution for God's activity (Käsemann, "Sentences," 69; cf. ἐπεγνώσθην in 1 Cor. 13.12). If Paul were thinking of community recognition, he would have given an imperative: "let him not be recognized." Or if he had meant, "I, Paul do not recognize him," he would have used the active voice and the first person. The present passive indicative, as Käsemann has rightly seen, here bespeaks a pronouncement of divine judgement.

the possibility that a prophet might be right and he
himself be wrong (1 Cor. 14.37-38)."[105]

B. The Apostles as Prophets

It is important to recognize, in addition to what
has been said in the previous section, that the NT can
sometimes view the apostles as "prophets."[106] Paul,
for instance, spoke of prophesying when he came to
Corinth (1 Cor. 14.6). He also seems to include himself in 1 Cor. 13.9, "we prophesy in part."[107] In Ac.
15.32 Judas and Silas are called "prophets," yet their
function as apostolic delegates suggests that they
held the office of apostle or of elder.[108]

---

[105] G. W. H. Lampe, "'Grievous Wolves' (Ac. 20.
29)," in CSNT, 258.

[106] Cf. Best, "Prophets and Preachers," 145;
P. Minear, "False Prophecy and Hypocrisy in the Gospel
of Matthew," in Neues Testament und Kirche, ed. J.
Gnilka (Freiburg, 1974), 76-78; W. Mare, "Prophet and
Teacher in the NT Period," BETS 9 (1966), 147; Guy, NT
Prophecy, 98, 115.

[107] Godet, Romans, II, 416f, understands Rom. 16.
26 to mean "the prophetical writings of the apostles."
If this interpretation were correct, it would simply
provide another example of the way in which the NT can
see the apostles as having a prophetic function. However, I cannot accept Godet's suggestion because (a) he
too readily discounts the possibility that the διά
indicates that the OT prophecies are the means by which
the NT apostles proclaim the mystery which was formerly
hidden; (b) the parallel in both wording and content
with Rom. 1.2 is very strong, and there OT prophets
are meant; (c) γραφή is always used by Paul of OT
Scripture; and (d) evangelistic proclamation at the
time of the writing of Romans was primarily or perhaps
exclusively oral, not written.

[108] In Ac. 15.22 ἐξ αὐτῶν is best understood to
mean "from the apostles and elders"; cf. vs. 25 with a
repetition of the construction in a place where, as vs.
23 shows, the reference is only to the apostles and
elders who sent the letter. The σύν in Ac. 15.22 gives
the following phrase a parenthetical sense: "(with the
consent of the whole church)."

This overlap of terminology with respect to apostles is common with other terms for NT functions or offices as well. 1 Tim. 2.7 and 2 Tim. 1.11 speak of Paul as a "preacher" and "apostle" and "teacher." 1 Pet. 5.1 speaks of Peter as a "fellow elder."[109]

In each case, some particular function receives special emphasis. As I argue in Chap. 2, the distinctive characteristic of a NT prophet is that he receives a revelation and reports it in the church. So when an apostle wished to emphasize his role of receiving and reporting revelations, it would be possible for him to refer to himself as a "prophet." Yet it is significant that Paul never appeals to a gift of prophecy to establish his authority, something which would have been very natural and very easy if NT prophets had been commonly thought to speak words with absolute divine authority. Rather, when Paul wants to establish his authority he appeals to his status as an ἀπόστολος. This is a further indication that for the NT authors the title which signified authority similar to that of the OT prophets was not "prophet" but "apostle."

My broader concern in this chapter, however, is to investigate the possibility that at Corinth there were NT prophets who were <u>not</u> also apostles. We now must examine specific texts in 1 Corinthians to determine whether the evidence there supports such a possibility.

VI. PROPHETIC AUTHORITY IN 1 CORINTHIANS

A. The Structure of 1 Cor. 12-14[110]

Among the many problems Paul was forced to deal with at Corinth were the problems of pride on the part

---

[109] Also, Paul is seven times called a διάκονος (1 Cor. 3.5, Col. 1.25, etc.).

[110] Rather than entering into a detailed treatment of the background to 1 Corinthians at this point, I have included discussions of those questions which are relevant to an understanding of prophecy at appropriate places in the following chapters. For general studies of matters relating to the situation at Corinth see

of those who had noticeable spiritual gifts (1.31, 3.3, 4.7, 5.6, 8.1, 10.12, 11.21ff, 12.21ff, 13.4-5) and resultant jealousy or feelings of unimportance on the part of those who were less noticeably gifted (10.10, 12.7, 12.14ff, 13.4). Paul deals with both problems at once in 1 Cor. 12.28 when he says, "God has put in the church first apostles, second prophets, third teachers . . ." On the one hand, by pointing out that such ministries are from God, he reminds the Corinthians that they should not be proud but humble (cf. 4.7). On the other hand, since God has distributed gifts as he thought best (cf. ὁ θεὸς ἔθετο, vs. 18, and ἔθετο ὁ θεός, vs. 28; also vs. 11), the Corinthians should neither be jealous of one another nor grumble about God's decisions, but should be content. Furthermore, since each believer had been given some kind of gift (12.6, 7, 11), and since every gift is needed (12.7, 15, 17, 21, 23, 26), no one need feel unimportant.

Yet in solving these problems Paul might have created another one if he had stopped there. The

---

esp. W. G. Kümmel, Introduction to the NT (ET London, 1975), 269-79; J. Munck, Paul and the Salvation of Mankind (ET London, 1959), 135-67; T. W. Manson, "The Corinthian Correspondence (1)," in Studies in the Gospels and Epistles (Manchester, 1962), 190-209; N. A. Dahl, "Paul and the Church at Corinth according to 1 Corinthians 1.10-4.21," in CHI, 313-35; W. Schmithals, Gnosticism in Corinth (ET Nashville, 1971); R. McL. Wilson, "How Gnostic were the Corinthians?," NTS 19 (1972-73), 65-74; J. M. Ford, "The First Epistle to the Corinthians or the First Epistle to the Hebrews?," CBQ 28 (1966), 402-16; J. C. Hurd, The Origin of 1 Corinthians (London, 1965); C. K. Barrett, "Christianity at Corinth," BJRL 46:2 (Mar., 1964), 269-97; idem, "Cephas and Corinth," in Abraham unser Vater, ed. O. Betz et al. (Leiden, 1963), 1-12; J. P. M. Sweet, "A Sign for Unbelievers: Paul's Attitude to Glossolalia," NTS 13 (1966-67), 249-54 (a critique of Hurd on 1 Cor. 12-13); and the commentaries by Barrett, 1-27, and Conzelmann, 2-16. (My own conclusions are that 1 Cor. is a unified letter written by Paul from Ephesus in the spring of ca. 55 A.D. to a mixed Jewish-Greek congregation beset with pride, jealousy, selfishness and bickering. I do not find convincing evidence for developed Gnosticism or for clearly defined factions.)

Corinthians might have become fatalistic through an unbalanced emphasis on God's sovereignty in the distribution of gifts. They might have made no further progress toward attaining those gifts which would most help the church. So Paul adds a corrective exhortation set off by the adversative δέ: although God has placed gifts in the church as he wanted (vss. 28-30), you should nevertheless continue to seek after the greater gifts (vs. 31).[111]

However, even the greater gifts could be misused if the Corinthians had wrong attitudes. So Paul goes on to something even better than seeking the greater gifts ("a still more excellent way," vs. 31b), namely, using the gifts they had or wanted in love (13.1-13). In the use of gifts, love means speaking in an intelligible and orderly way so that the church might be built up (14.1-35).

Returning to 12.28, we are now in a position to ask what kind of ranking is implied by Paul's πρῶτον . . . δεύτερον . . . τρίτον. It is certainly not chronological, for tongues are last here but came at the very beginning of the church (Acts 2.4). Is it a ranking of "dignity" or "spiritual eminence"?[112] This is unlikely, since Paul is trying to combat spiritual pride, and rather than claiming dignity for himself sees the apostles as "exhibited last of all . . . a spectacle to the world, to angels, and to men" (4.9). The correct answer is partly provided by v. 31a. Paul's readers would most naturally assume that the "greater (μείζων) gifts" are those which Paul has just finished ranking "first, second, third." Paul's thought is then made explicit in 14.5b, where in a probably intentional use of the same word, he says that he who prophesies is greater (μείζων) because through him the church is edified. Thus, greatness in this context measures usefulness to the church.[113] So in 12.28, apostles are first because they are most

---

[111]The hortatory character of the entire passage, and the parallel in 14.1, require that ζηλοῦτε here be an imperative, not an indicative. (So Orr and Walther, 288.)

[112]RP, 279; Ellicott, 245; Godet, II, 222f.

[113]So T. Holtz, "Das Kennzeichen des Geistes (1 Kor. 12.1-3)," NTS 18 (1971-72), 366f; Barrett, 296; Orr and Walther, 289.

useful in building up the church. Prophets are second and teachers are third, because they also contribute greatly to the church's edification. This interpretation fits with Paul's overall purpose of encouraging gifts and attitudes which build up the church (note this emphasis at crucial summary points: 12.7, 25-26; 14.5b, 12, 26b).

Even though some of the details presuppose later conclusions from this study, it is helpful here to paraphrase all of 12-14: "Concerning spiritual gifts (v. 1): you all have useful gifts (12.2-30) and it is good to seek the greater gifts (12.31a), but it is even better (12.31b) to use the gifts you have or want in love (13.1-13), that is, speaking intelligibly and worshipping in an orderly way so that the church may be built up (14.1-36). You must obey my words, for they are the Lord's command (14.37-38). Now with regard to the specific matters of prophecy and tongues, desire prophecy, don't forbid tongues, but do all in order (14.39-40)."[114]

So 1 Cor. 14.29-33a is, on this understanding of chapters 12-14, part of a larger section of the epistle (14.1-36), in which Paul is giving instructions to the Corinthians on how to conduct themselves in a worship service. Vss. 29ff express Paul's views about the proper use of the gift of prophecy in particular.

---

[114]Understanding the structure of chaps. 12-13 in this way, I view ch. 13 as necessary to Paul's purpose before he can introduce ch. 14 (so Greeven, "Propheten," 3, n. 6; Barrett, 297-99; Bruce, 124; RP, 285). In ch. 14 Paul urges the Corinthians to use the gifts in a way that will most edify the church. But why should they do this? Because this is the way of love, which "is patient and kind . . . not jealous or boastful . . . (and) does not insist on its own way."
Whether Paul is using material written before, or whether this chapter was composed specifically for the Corinthian epistle, is impossible to determine with certainty. It is unlikely to be a later insertion, however (argued by J. Sanders, "First Corinthians 13: Its Interpretation Since the First World War," Interp. 20 (1966), 181-87; Héring, 134, 145; Weiss, 309-21; cf. Conzelmann, 217-20 (with bibliography on the chapter), since Paul's emphasis on edification in ch. 14 would not have been very convincing without ch. 13 preceding it.

B. 1 Cor. 14.29: Evaluating Prophecies

Paul says, "Let two or three prophets speak, and the others evaluate" (προφῆται δὲ δύο ἢ τρεῖς λαλείτωσαν, καὶ οἱ ἄλλοι διακρινέτωσαν).

1. Is this verse connected to διακρίσεις πνευμάτων in 1 Cor. 12.10? It is assumed by a few, though not many, NT commentators that οἱ ἄλλοι who are mentioned here are those with the gift of "distinguishing between spirits" in 1 Cor. 12.10.[115] The major reason in favor of this view is the similarity between the noun διάκρισις in 12.10 and the verb διακρίνω in 14.29. (Another argument is advanced by Gerhard Dautzenberg,[116] namely, that the gifts of prophecy and διάκρισις πνευμάτων are intentionally placed together in 12.10. I discuss this argument in the excursus below.)

Concerning the use of διάκρισις in 12.10 and διακρίνω in 14.29, it must be noted that both the noun and the verb have an extremely wide range of meaning.[117]

---

[115] Allo, 370; apparently Meyer, 331.

[116] Dautzenberg uses these two verses as a starting point for his view that διακρίσεις πνευμάτων means "interpreting the utterances of the Spirit" (UP 122-48, 284-88; also his "Zum religionsgeschichtlichen Hintergrund der διάκρισις πνευμάτων (1 Kor. 12.10)," BZ 15 [1971], 93-104). I have treated this position in an extended appendix: see below, pp. 263ff.
Dunn, JS, 233f also claims that 1 Cor. 12.10 refers to the testing of prophecies, but the evidence is not sufficient to draw that conclusion. It is preferable to let 12.10 have a more general, unrestricted sense, "distinguishing between the Holy Spirit and various other spirits at work in people claiming to be under the influence of the Spirit." This could include evaluating supposed prophets, and also the evaluation of miracle-workers, tongue-speakers, teachers, healers, etc. The plural διακρίσεις would support this view, indicating the ability to make discriminating judgments in various types of situations (cf. χαρίσματα, vs. 9, ἐνεργήματα and γένη, vs. 10; RP, 267).

[117] Barrett, 274, says, "It is impossible to find a consistent rendering of the word distinguish (διακρίνειν), because Paul did not use it consistently."

It is not at all unlikely that Paul would have used διάκρισις in 12.10 to mean "distinguishing" (among different kinds of spirits) while using διακρίνω in 14.29 to mean something quite different, such as "evaluate" or "judge" (prophetic utterances). In fact, in 1 Corinthians alone Paul uses διακρίνω in several senses. In 11.31 he uses it to mean "evaluate"; in 11.29, to mean "distinguish" (or "evaluate"); in 6.5, to mean "give a legal judgment"; and in 4.7, to mean "distinguish." In Rom. 14.1 he apparently means "arguments" or "disputes" by διακρίσεις. In view of this wide range of Pauline meaning, it would be overly bold to assume that διάκρισις in 12.10 must have the same sense as διακρίνω in 14.29, and must refer to the same activity or gift.

Moreover, it is not legitimate to presuppose that 12.10 is restricted to the testing of prophets and prophecies. Bittlinger, for instance, mentions as examples of διακρίσεις πνευμάτων some of the exorcisms of Jesus where he knew there was a demon present, and the cases of Elymas (Ac. 13.8ff) and the soothsaying girl (Ac. 16.16-18).[118] Robertson and Plummer define the ability as, "The gift of discerning in various cases (hence the plur.) whether extraordinary spiritual manifestations were from above or not."[119] If we resist the temptation to read into the text a limitation to the testing of prophecies, then a more general definition, like the one just mentioned by Robertson and Plummer, is in order. Something like "the ability to recognize the influence of the Holy Spirit or of demonic spirits in a person," might be suggested.

This means that any situation in which first century Christians would have seen demonic influence was a potential opportunity for the use of the gift of

---

[118] Bittlinger, Gifts and Graces, 46. Other commentators who see "distinguishing between spirits" as applying to more than just prophecy include Calvin, 263; Grosheide, 287f; Findlay, 889; and Lenski, 503f. Those who do restrict it to prophecy generally refer to 1 Jn. 4.1-6 and Did. 11, but give no further arguments.

[119] RP, 267. They soon say, "Perhaps the expression chiefly refers to the prophetic gift," but they do not restrict it to that.

διάκρισις πνευμάτων. Was some sickness the result of demonic influence (cf. Mt. 12.22, Mt. 9.32-34)? Then the person with this gift could recognize it, and the demon could be cast out. Was an evil spirit causing someone to interrupt preaching or teaching or worship services (cf. Ac. 16.16-18)? Then the person with this gift could recognize the source of the trouble. Was someone prophesying by the power of an evil spirit (1 Jn. 4.1-6)? Then the person with this gift could call attention to it. Since it was thought that demons were involved in pagan worship in Corinth (cf. 1 Cor. 10.20f), one can imagine a large number of cases where this gift would have been thought useful.

But if 1 Cor. 12.10 is understood in this way, then οἱ ἄλλοι in 1 Cor. 14.29 need not be restricted to those who possess the gift of distinguishing between spirits. For that gift would include a much broader range of activity than simply judging prophets. Furthermore, if Paul had meant to restrict his instructions in 14.29 to those with this gift, he would not have used such a general term as οἱ ἄλλοι and left it without further specification. Such a restricted meaning would not have been clear to his readers.

2. <u>Does οἱ ἄλλοι in 1 Cor. 14.29 refer to the other prophets?</u> A more common view of 1 Cor. 14.29 is that by οἱ ἄλλοι Paul means "the other prophets."[120] Once again appeal is usually made to 12.10, where it is clear that not all had the gift of distinguishing between spirits. Then two unwarranted assumptions are made: first, that the limited group possessing the gift of "discernment" includes mostly prophets, and second, that this gift is used in the evaluation in 14.29. But in 12.10, Paul distinguishes one with the gift of prophecy from one who had this gift (ἄλλῳ, 12.10). He certainly does not say that all prophets had the gift of discerning between spirits. And several other considerations make this view very unlikely.

---

[120]So K. Maly, <u>Mündige Gemeinde</u> (Stuttgart, 1967), 218; Greeven, "<u>Propheten</u>," 6; Chevallier, <u>Esprit</u>, 190f; Calvin, 302; Ellicott, 279; Grosheide, 338; Hodge, 169; Lenski, 611; <u>RP</u>, 322; Weiss, 340.

(a) In other places in Paul where judging congregational speech is discussed, it seems that all the congregation is involved. 1 Cor. 12.3 gives a test anyone could apply, and 1 Thes. 5.21 is addressed to a whole church (cf. 1 Jn. 4.1-6, Acts 17.11). Now this does not mean that all would play an equal role in the public evaluation of what was said. We would expect the mature (cf. Heb. 5.14), the wise (cf. 1 Cor. 6.5), those perhaps with the gift of distinguishing between spirits (1 Cor. 12.10) to speak more often and with more authority. But nowhere do we find judging limited to those with one particular office or gift.[121]

(b) If Paul had meant to say, "Let the rest of the prophets judge," he would probably have used other words than οἱ ἄλλοι.[122] Godet (II, 303) points out that οἱ λοιποί, "the rest of the prophets" would have been most appropriate if this had been Paul's meaning.

(c) If we understand οἱ ἄλλοι to be restricted to a special group of prophets, we have much difficulty picturing what the rest of the congregation would do during the prophecy and the judging. Would they sit "neutrally," waiting for the prophecy to end and be judged before knowing whether to believe any of it? This can hardly be true. They would sit and immediately evaluate in their own minds what was being said. But this mental process would be well described by διακρινέτωσαν, and so it is difficult to exclude anyone from what Paul says. Especially hard to believe is the idea that teachers, administrators and other church leaders without special gifts of prophecy would sit passively awaiting the verdict of an elite group before they knew whether to accept a prophecy as genuine. Much to be preferred is the view which pictures such leaders as taking a prominent role in

---

[121]This argument also applies against those who would limit οἱ ἄλλοι to those with the gift of distinguishing between spirits.

[122]Robertson, Grammar 775, says, "The article is frequent with ἄλλος but never in the sense of 'the rest of,' like ancient Greek." Then, apparently presupposing the interpretation "the rest of the prophets" in this verse, he says "But οἱ ἄλλοι (1 Cor. 14.29) is close to it."

the judging of prophecies.¹²³

   3. Conclusion: Οἱ ἄλλοι refers to the entire congregation. The preceding arguments have shown several serious difficulties in attempting to place any restriction on οἱ ἄλλοι, and have provided reasons for letting the phrase have reference to the whole church.¹²⁴ As a prophet was speaking, each member of the congregation would listen carefully, evaluating the prophecy in light of the Scripture and the authoritative teaching he already knew to be true. Soon there would be an opportunity to speak in response, with the wise and mature no doubt making the most contribution. But no member of the body would have needed to feel useless (cf. 12.22), for every member at least silently would weigh and evaluate what was said.

   4. How is the prophecy judged? Paul's statement, "Let the others evaluate" (οἱ ἄλλοι διακρινέτωσαν),¹²⁵ indicates that Paul had in mind the kind of evaluation whereby each person would "weigh what is said" (RSV) in his own mind, accepting some of the prophecy as good and helpful, and rejecting some of it as erroneous or misleading. This is evident both from the general context and from the sense which attaches to the term διακρίνω.

   (a) The argument from context. At first one might suppose that οἱ ἄλλοι διακρινέτωσαν meant that others were to judge whether the speaker was a true or false prophet. This would fit the picture given in the Didache, for instance, where criteria are given by which the congregation could decide whether a prophet who came was true or false (Did. 11.3-12). Similarly, Matthew has a warning about false prophets "who come

─────────

   ¹²³This argument also applies against those who would limit οἱ ἄλλοι to those with the gift of distinguishing between spirits.

   ¹²⁴Barrett, 328; Bruce, 134; Godet, II, 303f; Leitzmann, 74; Cothenet, DBS 8, col. 1296.

   ¹²⁵D F G read ἀνακρινέτωσαν, a Western reading inexplicably adopted by Héring, 153.

to you in sheep's clothing but inwardly are ravenous wolves": these will be known by their fruits (Mt. 7.-15-20, cf. Mt. 24.11, 24). 1 Jn. 4.1-6 also has a warning about false prophets, and a test for distinguishing them.

Yet on closer inspection it turns out that 1 Cor. 14.29 is unlike these other passages. The other passages give warnings of strangers coming to the church from outside (Mt. 7.15; Did. 11.5, 6; (?) 1 Jn. 4.1, 3), and provide criteria by which they could be tested. But in 1 Cor. 14, Paul is talking about a meeting of those who are already accepted in the fellowship of the church (ὅταν συνέρχησθε, vs. 26; ζηλοῦτε τὸ προφητεύειν vs. 39). When he says, "Let two or three prophets speak," he certainly does not mean that at every worship service there would be two or three more prophets newly arrived at Corinth, waiting their turn to be tested and (so they hoped) approved by the congregation. Rather, the picture is one of several prophets who are known and accepted by the congregation, each speaking in turn. In such a case, it would be very unlikely that they would be "judged" and declared "true" prophets again and again, every time they spoke, month after month.

A better parallel to 1 Cor. 14.29 than Mt. 7, 1 Jn. 4 or Did. 11 could be found in another Pauline passage, 1 Th. 5.19-21. There it is the prophecies (vs. 20) that are evaluated or judged, not the prophets. This Pauline passage is much closer to 1 Cor. 14.29 than the other non-Pauline passages, which may be speaking to situations which are quite dissimilar. In fact, in both 1 Th. 5.19-21 and 1 Cor. 14.29ff there is an absence of any warning about false prophets, a lack of any criteria for judging them and an absence of any hint of strangers coming from outside and pretending to be prophets. While the other passages speak of tests to reveal false prophets, 1 Cor. 14.29 and 1 Th. 5. 19-21 seem to speak rather of a different sort of evaluation of the utterances of those who are already accepted by the congregation.

Finally, the idea that the prophet would be judged "true" or "false" simply does not fit the picture which Paul gives of a congregational meeting. The only way an entire congregation could pass judgment and make a declaration of "true" or "false" would be by some kind of vote, a complex process indeed. On such an important matter, no doubt several members would wish to express their opinions. In Mt. 7 and

Did. 11, the judging would take several days of watching and evaluating a prophet, and perhaps longer. Yet Paul's οἱ ἄλλοι διακρινέτωσαν seems to indicate an activity which would take place during the meeting, while the prophets are speaking, or just when they finish (cf. vs. 27, on tongues and interpretation). In fact, the prophets can speak so closely in succession that one could interrupt another (vs. 30).

In conclusion, the context of 1 Cor. 14.29 indicates that the members of the congregation all listen to the prophet's <u>speech</u> and evaluate it in some way, but they do not <u>judge</u> the prophet <u>himself</u> "true" or "false."

(b) <u>The meaning of διακρίνω</u>. Paul's use of the term διακρίνω helps us further define the kind of evaluation which would be done. Although the word has quite a wide range of meanings, it very frequently carries a sense of separating, distinguishing, or making careful distinctions among related things or ideas. It can be used, for instance, of sifting wheat (Philo, <u>Mut</u>. 249, <u>Jos</u>. 113), of distinguishing clean from unclean animals (Jos. <u>A</u>. 3.259), or of separating persons who were guilty of wrongdoing from the rest of the crowd (Jos. <u>B</u>. 4.118, 543). It is used of distinguishing good from evil (T. Asher 1.5; cf. διάκρισις in Heb. 5.14) and of sorting true words from false (Philo, <u>Congr</u>, 18; cf. Job 12.11: νοῦς μὲν γὰρ ῥήματα διακρίνει).

In the NT, διακρίνω can be used of distinguishing between Jewish and Gentile believers (Ac. 15.9, probably also 11.12). Paul says in 1 Cor. 4.7, "Who distinguishes (διακρίνει) you?" (from other people and thereby regards you as more important). Then in 1 Cor. 11.31 we read, "If we (correctly) evaluated ourselves, we should not be judged" (εἰ δὲ ἑαυτοὺς διεκρίνομεν, οὐκ ἂν ἐκρινόμεθα). The idea is one of conscientiously weighing one's own attitudes and actions, and determining which are right and which are not.

This sense of "making distinctions" or "carefully evaluating" makes διακρίνω an appropriate word in 1 Cor. 14.29 if Paul had meant to speak of a process whereby every member of the congregation would listen carefully and evaluate each statement, distinguishing what he felt to be good from the less good, what he to be helpful from the unhelpful, what he felt to be true from the false.[126]

Now since this is not the only possible meaning for διακρίνω, one cannot say on lexical grounds alone that it absolutely requires this sense in 1 Cor. 14.29. But it fits very well in the context and is a common meaning for διακρίνω. Furthermore, if Paul had meant that the Corinthians were to judge whether each speaker was a true prophet or a false prophet, he probably would have used some other word, probably κρίνω.[127] This is the term the NT prefers when speaking of judgments where there are only two possibilities, such as "guilty" or "not guilty," "right" or "wrong," or "true" or "false" (cf. Mt. 7.1, 19.28, Jn. 7.51, 18.31, Ac. 16.15, 25.10, Rom. 2.1, 14.3, 4, 10, 13, 1 Cor. 4.5, 5.3, 12, 6.1, 2, 3, 6, 10.15, 11.13, Col. 2.16, Heb. 10.30, 13.4, Jas. 4.11, etc.).[128] In fact, in 1 Cor.

---

[126] Whether this evaluation would be completely silent or whether some members of the congregation would respond orally cannot be determined from the term διακρίνω alone. The emphasis of the verb is on the deliberative process itself, but spoken response to prophecies by leaders in the congregation no doubt would sometimes have been appropriate, and would have contributed to "edification" (14.26).

The criterion for evaluation of public speech in the NT seems always to have been conformity to Scripture or received teaching (Gal. 1.8, 1 Cor. 14.37-38, 1 Jn. 4.2-3, 6, Ac. 17.11).

Paul is talking here about true prophets within the church, but the possibility of false prophets coming and speaking under the influence of some demonic spirit nevertheless existed (cf. 1 Jn. 4.1, 3). They would presumably have been detected by those with the ability to distinguish between spirits (1 Cor. 12.10), and they would have betrayed themselves by their blatantly aberrant doctrine (1 Cor. 12.3, 1 Jn. 4.2-3).

[127] Although κρίνω and διακρίνω were roughly synonymous in Classical Greek, by the time of the NT they appear to have become distinct enough so that there are no instances where κρίνω means "separate," "distinguish" (AG, 452; Lampe, 778).

[128] Another possible word would have been δοκιμάζω, "to test, prove," but it would have been ambiguous unless followed by an accusative object. "Let the others test (δοκιμαζέτωσαν) the words spoken" would

6.2-6, Paul may consciously be distinguishing formal legal judgments outside the church (for which he uses κρίνω) from more informal decisions inside the church (for which he uses διακρίνω). Within the church, it is less likely that one party will be declared "guilty" or the other "not guilty," and more likely that a careful evaluation will find some fault on both sides.

(c) <u>Conclusion</u>. Taking into consideration both the context and the sense usually attached to διακρίνω, one can conclude that 1 Cor. 14.29 indicates that the whole congregation would listen and evaluate what was said by the prophet, forming opinions about it, and some would perhaps discuss it publicly. Each prophecy might have both true and false elements in it. The RSV captures this meaning very well: "Let two or three prophets speak, and let the others weigh what is said."

It is interesting to compare this process with the judging of prophets found in the OT.[129] There, a false prophet was to die (Dt. 18.20). In order to qualify as a false prophet, one only needed to claim to be speaking for God and then to speak something which God had not commanded (Dt. 18.20, cf. Jer. 23.16). In Dt. 18.22, one false prediction would mean that the prophet had spoken "presumptuously"; his word was something the Lord had not spoken. So he would die for speaking falsely in the name of the Lord and thereby misrepresenting the Lord. We may surmise that herein lay the cause for the severity of the penalty. The prophet was to be speaking God's words ("I will put my words in his mouth," vs. 18; "my words which he shall speak in my name," vs. 19). To disobey the words of a true prophet would bring punishment from

---

have implied roughly the same process as is now implicit in 1 Cor. 14.29 (cf. 1 Th. 5.21), whereas a command to test (δοκιμαζέτωσαν) the prophet would have implied more of an all-or-nothing judgment, a verdict of "true prophet" or "false prophet" (cf. 1 Jn. 4.1, Did. 12.1). 1 Jn. seems to be written to a situation where there were false religious leaders, whom the author of 1 Jn. would have considered to be unbelievers, in the church, and the testing is with a view to purging the church of their false teaching. In 1 Cor. 14, however, Paul is giving instructions for evaluating the words of true prophets within the church.

[129] Cf. pp. 19f above.

God (vs. 19). Since such a prophet would have exercised tremendous authority, it would have been important to safeguard the prophetic office with stiff penalties for impostors.

There is no such picture in 1 Cor. Rather, as we have seen, the congregation would simply evaluate the prophecy and form opinions about it. Some of it might be very valuable and some of it not. Now this process is understandable only if there is a difference in the kind of speech envisioned by the OT and that in 1 Cor. The OT prophets claimed to be speaking God's very words. But it is inconceivable that Paul or the Corinthians thought that God's words needed to be evaluated to see whether or not they were true or useful. So the prophets at Corinth must not have been thought to speak with a divine authority of actual words, but rather with just a divine authority of general content, which made the prophecies subject to evaluation and questioning at every point.[130]

C. 1 Cor. 14.30: Revelation Which Is Lightly Esteemed

After giving instructions that two or three prophets could speak, Paul guarantees that an orderly pattern will be followed: "If a revelation is made to another sitting by, let the first be silent" (ἐὰν δὲ ἄλλῳ ἀποκαλυφθῇ καθημένῳ, ὁ πρῶτος σιγάτω). In order to discuss the bearing of this verse on the question of prophetic authority, I must anticipate some of the conclusions reached in Chap. 2. Briefly, the verse pictures the following situation: while one prophet is speaking, another suddenly has something "revealed" (ἀποκαλύπτω) to him. He signals this in some way, perhaps by standing. The first prophet does not finish his prophecy but immediately sits down and is silent, allowing the second one to speak.

1. **Prophecies which could be lost.** This verse raises two issues with respect to prophetic authority. First we notice that Paul seems to be totally unconcerned by the fact that the first prophecy might be lost forever and never heard by the church. While

---

[130] Cf. H. B. Swete, The Holy Spirit in the NT (London, 1910²), 189f.

this is by no means a decisive consideration, it does fit the picture of NT prophecy which we have seen in 1 Cor. 14.29. For if prophets had been thought to speak with a divine authority of actual words, we would have expected Paul to show more concern for the preservation of these words and their proclamation to the church. If God actually were speaking his words through a prophet to the church, it would be important for the church to hear those words! (Compare, for example, Jer. 36, where Jehoiakim shows callous disregard for the prophetic words written for him to read [vss. 23-25], and is sentenced to greater punishment as a result [vs. 30]). Yet Paul in 1 Cor. 14.30 advocates a system whereby some of the words the first prophet was to say would never be heard by the church. If NT prophets had been thought to speak with a divine authority of actual words, this verse would be very hard to understand. However, if the NT prophets were only thought to be speaking with some kind of divine authority of general content, Paul's instructions would be quite reasonable: many Christians had things to contribute to the worship service (1 Cor. 14.26), and there was only a limited amount of time. Therefore, as many people as possible should be allowed to contribute, in order that through the diversity of contributions everyone present would be edified in some way (vs. 31). Of course, there would be times when someone would come with "a hymn, a teaching, a revelation, a tongue, an interpretation" (or a prophecy) which, because of time, could not be used. But that did not matter. What was important was that all things were done for edification (vs. 26).

At this point one might object that the words of the first prophet need not be lost: he would simply hold his peace until the second prophet had finished, and then he would resume his speech. But this objection does not adequately account for Paul's words. For why then would Paul command the _first_ prophet to be silent? If he could retain his revelation and speak later, then so could the second prophet. And in that case it would make much more sense for the second prophet to wait, instead of rudely interrupting the first prophet and making him give his speech in two parts. In order for Paul's instruction to be understandable, we have to suppose that he assumed that the first prophet would not resume speaking after the second prophet had stopped.[131]

2. Does "revelation" imply divine authority?
The second point of interest for us in this verse is
the term ἀποκαλυφθῇ. As I argue in Chap. 2, this
term, along with vss. 32-33, indicates that it is a
specific revelatory activity of the Holy Spirit which
gives rise to any prophecy by a NT prophet: Paul
pictures some kind of process whereby the prophet is
spontaneously made aware of something which he feels
God has caused him to think about. Now the fact that
NT prophecy is based on "revelation," one might argue,
necessarily implies that the prophet was speaking with
divine authority.

In a certain sense, this is true. There is a
kind of divine authority which would be thought to
attach to a report of a "revelation" from God. But the
question is whether it would need to be thought of as
the same type of divine authority which we earlier
called a "divine authority of actual words," and for
which several examples were found in the OT. Several
instances of the terms ἀποκαλύπτω and ἀποκάλυψις in
the NT show that this need not have been the case.
Rather, the report of a "revelation" can often be
thought to have only a divine authority of general content: the main point of the report is thought to have
come from God, but the words in which it is expressed
to others are not thought to possess an absolute divine
authority or to be actual words from God.

---

[131]One might answer this argument by saying that
the second prophet had a "revelation" while the first
prophet did not. But this would be special pleading
indeed. There is no hint anywhere in the NT that a
"prophet" speaks by anything but by revelation: were
he giving an ordinary speech he would no longer be
termed a prophet but a "teacher," or simply a member of
the congregation. Clearly, Paul has the specific gift
of prophecy in view of the entire section (vss. 29-33).
Also, how could Paul ever have known that it was always
the first speaker who would be without a "revelation"?
Furthermore, in vss. 31-33, Paul uses the revelatory
activity of the Holy Spirit within the first prophet
as a basis for arguing that the first prophet should
be silent. (See Chap. 2 for an analysis of these
verses.)

In Phil. 3.15, Paul encourages his readers to be zealous for continual growth and effective service for Christ, and then says, "If in anything you are otherwise minded, God will reveal (ἀποκαλύψει) that also to you." If any of the Philippians strayed from their high calling, God would make known to them their error. But we cannot suppose that whenever some Philippian Christian told his neighbor that God had revealed some sin in his life, Paul would have thought that that conversation would have a divine authority of actual words.

Similarly, in Rom. 1.18 Paul writes that "the wrath of God is revealed (ἀποκαλύπτεται) from heaven against all ungodliness and wickedness of men." This revelation of God's wrath was plain for all men to see, but certainly, when men discussed what God had revealed to them, Paul would not have claimed for these discussions the special category of divinely authoritative actual words. And in Eph. 1.17 we read a prayer that God would give the readers "a spirit of wisdom and revelation (ἀποκαλύψεως) in the knowledge of him," so that they would know more of the benefits which were theirs as Christians. Once more, it would not be possible to think that every time a NT believer gained new insight into his privileges as a Christian and reported it to a friend, the actual words of that speech would have been thought divinely authoritative. Finally, in Mt. 11.27, Jesus says that if anyone knows the Father, it is because the Son has revealed (ἀποκαλύπτω) the Father to him. If one wanted to argue that a report of an ἀποκάλυψις is always couched in divinely authoritative actual words, then this statement would require one to say that any believer reporting how he came to know God would be speaking with a divine authority of actual words--clearly an impossible situation.

So the term ἀποκαλύπτω alone by no means indicates that prophets in 1 Cor. 14 were thought to speak with a divine authority of actual words.

D. 1 Cor. 14.36: No Rules for Worship from Corinthian Prophets

After a brief section about women speaking in the church, Paul says, "Or from you did the word of God go forth (ἐξῆλθεν), or unto you only has it come?" This verse has Paul taking the offensive against the Corinthian church and denying them the right to establish norms for church worship contrary to the one Paul has just laid down, namely, that women should in some sense keep silent in the churches.[132]

'Εξῆλθεν is probably an inceptive aorist, and therefore Paul is speaking of the original proclamation of the Gospel (RSV: "What! Did the word of God originate with you, or are you the only ones it has reached?").[133] This would be a direct challenge to the assumed autonomy of the Corinthian church. They were not the source and definition of Christian truth; rather, they should conform to what was done "in all the churches of the saints." (v. 33).

But there is another implication in this question. Let us assume for a moment that prophets in Corinth were able to speak with a divine authority of actual words, perhaps not even for the whole Christian world, but simply words which would have absolute divine authority for the Corinthian church alone. If this were the case, then we would certainly assume that they would be able to speak this kind of a "word of the Lord" on such a secondary issue as the role of women in worship. But Paul denies them even this ability; they are unable to do what they want concerning the speaking of women in worship; they must obey Paul and others who are able to speak with greater authority. They are unable to challenge Paul's rules or propose new ones. So vs. 36 makes it very unlikely that anyone at Corinth, even any prophet, was thought to speak with absolute divine authority.

---

[132]Cf. Chap. 4 below. It is possible that 14.36 applies to all of chaps. 12-14, but at least it applies to the immediately preceding verses. If 14.33b-35 be taken as a post-Pauline interpolation, the argument I propose here would still apply, except that vs. 36 would refer to the rules for worsip in vss. 26-33a. If vs. 36 also be thought an interpolation, then this argument only indicates the interpolator's attitude toward prophecy.

[133]Cf. 1 Th. 1.8 for "the word of the Lord" in a similar sense; also "the word of God" in Tit. 2.5, Phil. 1.14 (AB, etc.).

E. 1 Cor. 14.37-38: Prophets Who Are Subject to Paul's Authority

In 1 Cor. 14.37-38, Paul is writing to a community where several prophets were active, and he still asserts his authority over the entire community, even over the prophets. These verses are thus the positive counterpart to vs. 36. Paul writes, "If anyone thinks himself to be a prophet, or spiritual, let him acknowledge that what I am writing to you is a command of the Lord. If anyone does not recognize this, he is not recognized."

As the previous discussion of this verse indicated,[134] Paul is here claiming something more than the correctness of his own opinion: he is also claiming that anyone who disobeyed him would be disobeying a "command of the Lord" and would be punished not by Paul but by God himself. Whether everyone at Corinth would have accepted Paul's words as having the status of a "command of the Lord," is difficult to say without further evidence. But for our purposes it is sufficient to notice that Paul's claim sounds very much like a claim that what he has written to Corinth has a divine authority of actual words. And this authority is set over against the authority of everyone at Corinth, including the prophets: according to Paul, the words of the prophets at Corinth were not and could not have been sufficiently authoritative to show Paul to be wrong. If he is claiming for himself a divine authority of actual words, he is attributing to the Corinthian prophets something far less than that.[135]

F. 1 Cor. 11.5: Prophetesses Who Remain Subordinate

Before leaving 1 Cor. we note briefly that Paul assumes women could prophesy in church: "Any woman who prays or prophesies with her head uncovered dishonors her head" (1 Cor. 11.5). Yet in 1 Cor. 14.34 he says

---

[134] See above, pp. 50ff.

[135] It is also significant that here as elsewhere Paul refrains from appealing to his status as a "prophet" to establish his authority. This may be because, in his view, there could be "prophets" with less authority than he had.

that "women are not permitted to speak, but should be subordinate."[136] Anticipating the discussion in Chap. 4, it is possible to say briefly that the type of speech in view in 14.34 is not all speech but only speech which assumes authority over the men of the congregation, speech which is not "subordinate." (Note the strong contrast implied by ἀλλά: "to speak" in the sense forbidden by Paul is to act in a way which is exactly the opposite of being subordinate.) If this interpretation is correct, then 1 Cor. 11.5 can easily be reconciled with 14.34, provided that the type of prophecy done by women at Corinth did not involve authoritative speech, that is, speech which assumed the right to enforce obedience or belief. Now speech which purported to have a divine authority of actual words would have assumed that right, but the same would not be true of speech which assumed only a divine authority of general content, for that kind of speech could have been questioned or challenged at any point. So it seems that the prophecy uttered by women at Corinth could not have claimed the extremely high authority of speech with a "divine authority of actual words." Thus, 1 Cor. 11.5 is one more indication that prophets at Corinth were not thought by Paul to speak with a divine authority of actual words.

G. Conclusion

We have now examined five different short passages in 1 Corinthians. In each one there are indications that, in Paul's view at least, the prophets at Corinth did not speak with a divine authority of actual words, and were not accorded an absolute divine authority by others. In 14.29, it seems that the prophet's words could be challenged and questioned, and that the prophet could at times be wrong. Yet there is no indication that an occasional mistake would

---

[136] The view that 1 Cor. 14.34-35 is a post-Pauline interpolation must not be lightly dismissed in an investigation of this sort. This view is based primarily on a conviction that these verses irreconcilably conflict with 1 Cor. 11.5. I have attempted to show in Chapter 4 how these two passages can be reconciled; however, for those for whom that argument is not persuasive, this final section will not be thought relevant to the case I am presenting, and may be disregarded.

make him a "false" prophet. In 14.30, Paul seems unconcerned that some of a prophet's words could be lost forever and never heard by the church. In 14.36, he refuses to the prophets the right to make rules for worship other than the ones he has given, and in 14.37-38 he seems to indicate that, in his opinion, no Corinthian prophet had a kind of divine authority equal to his own. Finally, in 11.5 and 14.34-35 (if this be accepted as Pauline, and if my argument in Chapter 4 be accepted), Paul allows women to prophesy while denying to them the right to enforce obedience or belief on the congregation, and this would be consistent with a view that prophets spoke with something less than "absolute" divine authority.

These five passages, then, indicate that Paul thought of prophecy at Corinth as something different than the prophecy we see, for instance, in Revelation or in many parts of the OT. There, a divine authority of actual words is claimed by or on behalf of the prophets. But the prophecy we find in 1 Corinthians is more like the phenomena we saw in extra-Biblical Jewish literature: it is based on some type of supernatural "revelation," but that revelation only gives it a kind of divine authority of general content. The prophet could err, could misinterpret, and could be questioned or challenged at any point. He had a minor kind of "divine" authority, but it certainly was not absolute.

It now remains to examine briefly the accounts of prophecy elsewhere in the NT, and to compare these accounts with our conclusion from 1 Corinthians.

VII. PROPHETIC AUTHORITY ELSEWHERE IN THE NEW TESTAMENT

A. The Scope of This Investigation

It is clearly not possible to treat in great detail every one of the NT verses which might bear some relation to prophecy. If one attempted to analyze all the verses pertaining to revelations, visions, dreams, and other types of communications from the Spirit, the size of the resultant study would be unmanageable. I have therefore had to be quite selective in the following section, and have only included passages where prophets or prophecy are specifically mentioned. This means that I have omitted verses such as Ac. 16.6-7, 20.23, 2 Th. 2.2 and 1 Tim. 4.1. I have also omitted verses which seemed to me to have little direct bearing on the question of prophetic authority, such as Ac. 2.17-18 and 1 Jn. 4.1. With regard to 1 Pet. 4.11 it is only necessary to point out that it is not speaking about authority but about the solemnity of purpose and care with which all congregational speech should be uttered.

I have not discussed any verses which upon examination seemed to refer to OT prophecy, such as Lk. 11.49,[137] 1 Pet. 1.10,[138] 2 Pet. 3.2,[139] and Rom. 16.26.[140]

In the verses which are discussed, the depth of treatment varies greatly depending both on the complexity of the problems encountered and the degree of importance for this investigation.

B. Mt. 10.19-20

In this passage Jesus says, "When they deliver you up, do not be anxious how you are to speak or what you are to say; for what you are to say will be given to you in that hour; for it is not you who speak, but the Spirit of your Father speaking through you." If this passage be understood to refer to NT prophecy, then it clearly belongs in the first category, that of prophecy which is thought to have a divine authority of actual words. Verse 20 ("for it is not you who speak . . .") makes this claim especially clear. (Cf. the parallels in Mk. 13.11, Lk. 12.11.)[141]

---

[137] See above, p. 45.

[138] Selwyn, 259-68, argues for NT prophets; effectively answered by Best, 83f.

[139] See above, p. 45, n. 89.

[140] See above, p. 53, n. 107.

[141] The possibility that these three passages should be understood to refer primarily to the apostles cannot be easily dismissed. In Mt., the statement is primarily addressed to the Twelve ("apostles," Mt. 10.2; cf. Filson, 131; Hill, 188f), and the other two are also set in the context of an address to members of the Twelve (Mk. 13.3, Lk. 12.1;

C. Ac. 11.28[142]

Here Agabus "signifies a famine by means of the Spirit" (ἐσήμανεν διὰ τοῦ πνεύματος). It is interesting that Luke has NT prophets speaking διὰ τοῦ πνεύματος, a phrase which is not used in the LXX to refer to prophetic inspiration. The διά seems to signify "the originator of an action" (so AG 179, III, 2.b. δ.), and would be well suited to express a rather loose relationship between the Holy Spirit and the prophet, since it allows room for a large degree of personal influence by the speaker himself (cf. Ac. 1.2, 21.4, Rom. 8.37, 2 Cor. 1.20, 2 Tim. 1.14). A degree of imprecision is also suggested by σημαίνω, which is elsewhere used of prophetic speech "that simply gives a vague indication of what is to happen" (AG, 755). Although the evidence here is too slim to draw any certain conclusions, Luke's language is entirely compatible with a kind of NT prophecy similar to that in 1 Corinthians, prophecy which was based on a "revelation" but not reported in divinely authoritative actual words.

---

on Mark 13.11, cf. Carrington, 227 and Grundmann, 264). It is sometimes argued that these passages were inserted in the Gospels in order to encourage Christians who were undergoing persecution and were being brought to trial (so, e.g., Nineham, Mark, 349; Anderson, Mark, 294). But this view does not fully account for the fact that in all three Gospel traditions the words are set in a context of address not to Jesus' followers generally but to members of the Twelve. Furthermore, one could argue that the evangelists in inserting this narrative in the Gospels were attempting to justify bold disobedience to the Jewish authorities by the apostolic leadership of the early church in situations such as that recorded in Ac. 4.5-22 and Ac. 5.27-42.

[142]For a general study of the contrast between prophets and apostles in Acts, see E. Ellis, "The Role of the Christian Prophet in Acts," AHG, 55-67.

D. Ac. 13.2

While the prophets and teachers (named in vs. 1)[143] were worshipping the Lord and fasting, the Holy Spirit said (εἶπεν τὸ πνεῦμα τὸ ἅγιον), "Set apart for me Barnabas and Saul for the work to which I have called them." It is often assumed that this is the quotation of a prophecy given by one of the prophets mentioned in v. 1 and if this verse is speaking of prophecy, the first person speech by the Holy Spirit would indicate that this prophecy is thought by Luke to be of the first type, with a divine authority of actual words. However, it is not certain whether this passage does speak of prophecy. The fact that prophets and teachers are mentioned in vs. 1 need only show that they were the leading men of the Antioch church, to whom such a revelation, whatever its form, would appropriately come.

More significant is Luke's attribution of these words not to a prophet but to "the Holy Spirit." An examination of similar expressions in Acts shows that where no human spokesman is named prophecy is not in view: Ac. 8.29 (εἶπεν δὲ τὸ πνεῦμα), 10.19 (εἶπεν τὸ πνεῦμα), 18.9 (εἶπεν δὲ ὁ κύριος).[144] Just as in these other examples, it is likely that in Ac. 13.2 Luke is speaking of a (perhaps inaudible) voice which was "heard" mentally by one or more members of the group. Luke's failure to attribute the speech to any one of the prophets, coupled with his clear pattern of attributing non-prophetic speech to the Holy Spirit, make it somewhat doubtful that prophecy is in view here.

E. Ac. 19.6

In this passage, about twelve disciples at Ephesus speak with tongues and prophesy when Paul lays

---

[143] The second τε in vs. 1 does not group Manaen and Saul together in any special way: cf. Jackson-Lake, Beginnings, IV, 141f, and the merely stylistic use of τε in Ac. 2.9-11, 26.20.

[144] Cf. also Ac. 19.1 (p^{38} D) (the Spirit to Paul), Ac. 23.9 (a spirit or angel to Paul), and perhaps Ac. 15.28. Ac. 16.6-7 and 20.23 are ambiguous, and in 21.11 a human agent is specifically named.

hands on them. Here the verb προφητεύω is used to describe some group speech activity which reminds us somewhat of the bands of prophets in the OT. It might be that we have here an additional example of προφητεύω in the broad sense, "to speak as a result of a spiritual influence," or on the other hand the passage might represent an unrestrained use of a kind of prophecy similar to what was found in churches like that of Corinth. In either case, the incident bears no resemblance to the messenger speeches in the OT which were thought to possess a divine authority of actual words, for in such a confused situation no one's speech would have been heard distinctly. Whatever kind of "prophesying" is referred to here at Ephesus, it does not seem to have been of the type which was thought to possess a divine authority of actual words.

F. Ac. 21.4

Some disciples at Tyre, "by means of the Spirit,"[145] tell Paul not to go on to Jerusalem (ἔλεγον διὰ τοῦ πνεύματος μὴ ἐπιβαίνειν εἰς Ἱεροσόλυμα). This verse does not mention prophecy directly, but the parallel with Ac. 11.28, where speech διὰ τοῦ πνεύματος is explicitly attributed to a prophet, suggests that these disciples were in fact prophesying. (In contrast to 13.2, human spokesmen are here explicitly credited with the warning.) This is significant because Paul simply disobeyed their words, something he would not have done if he had thought that they spoke words with absolute divine authority. But if the disciples at Tyre had had some kind of revelation about the suffering which Paul would face at Jerusalem, it would have been very natural for them to couple their subsequent prophecy with their own (erroneous) interpretation, and thus to warn Paul not to go. So this passage indicates a type of prophecy most like that at Corinth, which was not thought by Paul (or perhaps in this case by Luke) to possess a divine authority of actual words.

G. Ac. 21.9

The mention of prophecy by Philip's four unmarried daughters simply gives some slight confirmation

---

[145]The plural ἔλεγον with the singular τοῦ πνεύματος excludes the possibility of translating "by means of their own (human spirits."

to our earlier discussion of 1 Cor. 11.5.[146]

H. **Ac. 21.10-11**

In this passage Agabus comes from Judea to Caesarea, binds his own hands and feet, and says, "Thus says the Holy Spirit (τάδε λέγει τὸ πνεῦμα τὸ ἅγιον), 'So shall the Jews at Jerusalem bind the man who owns this girdle and deliver him into the hands of the Gentiles.'" Τάδε λέγει Κύριος is a common LXX equivalent for כֹּה אָמַר יהוה, the divine messenger formula used by OT prophets. The similar phrase here, with only the substitution of τὸ πνεῦμα τὸ ἅγιον, leads one to think that Agabus is claiming to speak with a divine authority of actual words.

However, using OT standards, Agabus would have been condemned as a false prophet, because in Acts 21. 27-35 neither of his predictions are fulfilled. Paul was not bound (δέω) by the Jews but by the Romans (δέω, 21.33 and 22.29), and far from delivering Paul over (παραδίδωμι, v. 11; essential to the word is the notion of active or intentional giving on the part of the subject of the verb) to the Romans, they tried to kill him (vs. 31), and he had to be delivered <u>from</u> the Jews by the soldiers (vss. 32-33); even then the violence of the crowd was so great that the soldiers had to carry Paul (vs. 35).

Now it might be argued that Luke has no intention of showing that Agabus gave an inaccurate prophecy. Jackson and Lake say that "the discrepancy is merely superficial" and point to similarly loose Lukan language in Acts 2.23 (the Jews are said to have crucified Christ) and 28.17 (Paul says he was delivered out of Jerusalem into the hands of the Romans).[147] But this solution is not entirely satisfactory, because the difficulty in 21.11 is much more acute than in the other verses mentioned. In 2.23 Luke is careful to use διὰ χειρὸς ἀνόμων to specify the agents (the Romans actually carried out the crucifixion) while fixing ultimate moral blame on the Jews with the phrase προσπήξαντες ἀνείλατε (since the Jews were the ultimate cause of the crucifixion, Luke can say that

---

[146] See pp. 72ff.

[147] Jackson-Lake, <u>Beginnings</u>, IV, 268.

they "crucified and killed" Christ). And in 28.17 ἐξ Ἰεροσολύμων can hardly be taken to refer to Paul's initial capture by the tribune <u>in</u> Jerusalem (21.32-33), but makes much more sense as a reference to his transfer <u>out of</u> Jerusalem to Caesarea (23.23ff). Τῶν Ῥωμαίων then, as Meyer rightly states, "refers to the procurator in Caesarea, who represented the Romans ruling over Palestine."[148] So in both Acts 2.23 and 28.17 Luke uses language which is in fact quite precise, and not nearly as loose as that which would be required on Jackson and Lake's view of 21.11. Especially in this case of prophetic pronouncement, where accuracy of detail was traditionally an essential mark of authenticity (cf. 1 Kgs. 17.14 with 17.16; Josh. 6.26 with 1 Kgs. 16.34; 1 Kgs. 21.19 with 2 Kgs. 9.6; 1 Kgs. 13.2 with 2 Kgs. 23.16; 2 Kgs. 7.1 with 16, etc.), such a solution is very unlikely. Furthermore, Luke is aware of the legitimacy of making prophetic fulfillment explicit where it occurs (Lk. 4.21; 24.44; Ac. 1.16; 3.18; 11.28; 13.27). But here his silence is telling: not only do we have an unfulfilled prophecy, but a prophecy whose two elements, binding and giving over, are explicitly falsified by the whole thrust of the subsequent narrative.[149]

Now it is not necessary to suppose that Luke is intentionally trying to portray Agabus as a false prophet. It is more likely that he simply intends to show Agabus's prophecy "with the blemishes," not trying to conceal even a clear error.

Two other considerations support this interpretation. First, the nature of the error itself: it is not that Agabus has spoken in a totally false or misleading way; it is just that he has the details wrong. But this kind of minor inaccuracy is exactly compatible with the type of prophecy we found earlier in 1 Corinthians, in which the prophet receives some kind of revelation and then reports it in his own words. He would have a "divine authority of general content"

---

[148]<u>Acts</u> II, 319. This explanation makes the statement contribute to Paul's purpose of explaining why he is still in custody.

[149]Cothenet, <u>DBS</u> 8, col. 1283, and Crone, <u>ECP</u>, 198, see in the discrepancy between the prophecy and its fulfillment an indication that Luke has preserved the oracle exactly.

(Paul would be imprisoned at Jerusalem), but with the details wrong. In this case, for instance, the text could be perfectly well explained by supposing that Agabus had had a vision of Paul as a prisoner of the Romans in Jerusalem, surrounded by an angry mob of Jews. His natural interpretation would be that the Jews had bound Paul and handed him over to the Romans, and that is what he would (erroneously) prophesy.[150]

Second, such a solution makes the Agabus narrative fit Luke's larger purpose in the section, which is no doubt to show the contrast between Paul's sure knowledge of God's will and resolute purpose to obey it in spite of personal danger (cf. 20.22-24, 21.13), and the uncertain grasp of God's will possessed by the prophets and other disciples whom Paul meets (21.4, 12-14).[151] The close connection with the misleading instructions in 21.4 is especially significant.

Although this solution fits the narrative as we have it, the problem with τὸ πνεῦμα τὸ ἅγιον remains as a difficulty. There are four solutions which might be proposed:

(1) Luke has confused either the prophecy, or the introductory formula, or the subsequent narrative about the capture of Paul. In this case we can draw no certain conclusions about Agabus from this narrative, and, since one can hardly believe that Luke would have made such a mistake intentionally, it would also be difficult to draw any conclusions about Luke's own view of prophecy.

(2) Agabus claimed a divine authority of actual words for his prophecy and the minor discrepancies are not sufficient to nullify that claim, for he was generally correct. In this case Agabus will simply be an example of a prophet who is different from the

---

[150] How easy it would have been for Agabus to add very slight interpretative details and thus make Paul's destiny seem so much like that of Jesus, who was bound by the Jews and delivered over to the Romans (Mt. 27.2, Mk. 15.1, with δέω and παραδίδωμι). Cf. Jos. B. 1.79 for a similar example of misinterpreted prophecy.

[151] Cf. H. Patsch, "Die Prophetie des Agabus," ThZ 28 (1972), 231.

prophets in 1 Corinthians. He will be more like the first type of prophet, such as John in Revelation, who claims an absolute divine authority, My own problem with this view is that I find it hard to reconcile with the OT pattern of precise fulfillment of prophecies (strictly speaking, Agabus predicted two events which "did not come to pass," Dt. 18.22) and with the fact that Luke so clearly describes the non-fulfillment of the two parts of the prophecy in the immediately subsequent narrative.

(3) Τάδε λέγει meant here not that the words of the prophecy were to be thought of as words of the Holy Spirit, but only that the general content had been revealed by the Spirit. In this case Ac 21. 10-11 would fit the pattern of prophecy in 1 Corinthians. However, τάδε λέγει Κύριος is used too frequently in the LXX as a messenger formula for those who claimed a divine authority of actual words to make this solution likely.

(4) Agabus, perhaps in trying to imitate the OT prophets or other NT prophets who claimed a divine authority of actual words, wrongly used an introductory formula which was inappropriate to his status as a prophet with lesser authority. Since we know very little else about him, it would be dangerous to conclude that such a misunderstanding of his role would have been impossible. In this case his prophecy would be like those pictured in 1 Corinthians.

None of these solutions is without problems, yet I tend at present to prefer the fourth one. Others, however, may find one of the first three more acceptable. In any case, this passage is one of the more difficult to classify in one category or the other.

I. Eph. 2.20 and 3.5

Eph. 2.19-20 reads: ἄρα οὖν οὐκέτι ἐστὲ ξένοι καὶ πάροικοι ἀλλὰ ἐστὲ συμπολῖται τῶω ἁγίων καὶ οἰκεῖοι τοῦ θεοῦ, ἐποικοδομηθέντες ἐπὶ τῷ θεμελίῳ τῶν ἀποστόλων καὶ προφητῶν, ὄντος ἀκρογωνιαίου αὐτοῦ Χριστοῦ Ἰησοῦ.

Several different interpretations have been proposed for the term θεμέλιος, "foundation," in vs. 20, and because of the complexity of issues involved it will be necessary to examine the four major interpretations in greater detail than was required for the verses in Acts.¹⁵²

(a) Θεμέλιος is primarily non-personal.¹⁵³ It refers not to the apostles and prophets themselves, but to their preaching and teaching, or to their activity of receiving and proclaiming the gospel, or to their ruling and guiding activity in the NT church.¹⁵⁴ In this case τῶν ἀποστόλων καὶ προφητῶν is a subjective genitive, "the foundation laid by the apostles and prophets."

(b) Θεμέλιος refers to the apostles and the OT prophets.¹⁵⁵ (In this and the following cases τῶν ἀποστόλων καὶ προφητῶν is taken as a genitive of apposition, "the foundation which is the apostles and prophets.")

(c) Θεμέλιος refers to the apostles and NT prophets.¹⁵⁶

---

¹⁵²There are some other possible interpretations in addition to the main ones I list here, but none of them is widely adopted. To say that the foundation is Christ, who was preached by the apostles and prophets (cf. 1 Cor. 3.11), confuses the metaphor because Christ must also be the cornerstone in Eph. 2.20. Nor does this view have any advantages over interpretation (a).
   The foundation could be the first converts of the apostles and prophets, but this would make the metaphor unable to represent the presence of the apostles in the church: they were members of the church before their converts and would certainly be more "foundational."

¹⁵³J. J. Meuzelaar, Der Leib des Messias (Aasen, 1961), 127-30; M. Barth, I, 314-17 (but not unambigously); Calvin, 242; Ellicott, 53; Meyer, 142-44.

¹⁵⁴This distinction between personal and non-personal interpretations is useful for purposes of analysis but of course the personal interpretations also include functional elements, such as the apostles in the role of teachers, etc. These will be made more explicit below.

¹⁵⁵K. H. Rengstorf, TDNT I, 441 (with little argument); R. J. McKelvey, The New Temple, (Oxford, 1969), 113f (but only as a possibility).

¹⁵⁶See esp. J. A. Robinson, 67-69, 163 and T. K. Abbott, 69-72; also J. Gnilka, 156f; P. Vielhauer, Oikodome (Wiesbaden, 1940), 124-27; Hodge, 148-51; Hendriksen, 50f, 142; C. Masson, 169f; Conzelmann, 70; M. Dibelius, 72f; H. Schlier, 142f; and apparently B. F. Westcott, 40. Cf. also G. B. Caird, Paul's

(d) θεμέλιος refers to "the apostles who are also prophets."¹⁵⁷

One consideration in favor of (a) is 1 Cor. 3. 10-15, where θεμέλιος refers to Paul's work of founding the Corinthian church (vs. 10), and especially to his preaching and teaching about Christ (vs. 11). Similarly, in Rom. 15.20, θεμέλιος refers to the work of establishing new churches. But these verses are not decisive for Eph. 2.20, both because the author of Ephesians (whether Paul or not)¹⁵⁸ could well have used the same metaphor in a related but slightly different way,¹⁵⁹ and because even in the two passages cited it is difficult to dismiss the idea that Paul was also thinking of the result of an apostle's work (the people who are converted), not just the work itself. So in Eph. 2.20 the meaning of the foundation metaphor must be decided primarily on the basis of the immediate context. And in Eph. 2 there are several considerations which make interpretation (a) very unlikely:

Letters from Prison (Oxford, 1976), 61, who chooses interpretation (c) but admits (d) as a possibility.

¹⁵⁷F. J. A. Hort, The Christian Ecclesia (London, 189), 165-68; also his Prolegomena to St. Paul's Epistles to the Romans and the Ephesians (London, 1895), 143-48; J. Pfammatter, Die Kirche als Bau, Analecta Gregoriana 110 (Rome, 1960), 92-97; Paul Joüon, "Notes de Philologie Paulinienne," RScR 15 (1925), 532-34 (Jouon and Pfammatter take "prophet" to mean one who proclaims God's word, however); G. C. A. von Harless, 258-60 (howbeit with θεμέλιος as the preaching of the apostles); A. Monod, 139f; Cothenet, DBS 8, cols. 1306-09. Meyer, 143 n. 2, lists other older commentators who favor this view but rejects it himself.

¹⁵⁸Except at one point noted explicitly below my argument in this section does not depend upon the Pauline authorship of Ephesians, so I shall simply speak of "the author." Pauline authorship was challenged strongly by C. L. Mitton, The Epistle to the Ephesians (Oxford, 1951), and was most recently defended in great detail by A. van Roon, The Authenticity of Ephesians, SNovT 39, (Leiden, 1974).

¹⁵⁹Also, in Eph. 2.20 the building must represent the universal church (the letter is a general one to be read by several churches; there is one foundation composed (apparently) of all the apostles). But in

(1) The context requires that the "building" pictured be one made entirely of persons. Ἐποικοδομη-θέντες as a plural participle refers not to the house which is built but to the ὑμεῖς implied by ἐστὲ in vs. 19, that is, to the Gentile recipients of the letter. The Gentile converts are added on (ἐποικοδομέω ἐπί) to the foundation of the apostles and prophets.[160] The purpose for saying this is to emphasize the fact that the Gentiles are full-fledged citizens of equal standing with Jews in the house of God ("no longer strangers and aliens . . . but fellow citizens . . . and household members," vs. 19; cf. vss. 12-18). Now if the foundation be one of activity or doctrine, this part of the metaphor does not contribute to showing Jew-Gentile equality. But if the foundation be the Jewish apostles and prophets themselves, then it becomes clear that the Gentiles are no longer a separate or excluded class, but are made members of the same building of which the apostles and prophets are members (cf. σύσσωμα in 3.6). In order to serve its purpose in the argument, therefore, the foundation is best seen as consisting of persons.

Then also, Christ as the chief cornerstone, the primary stone of the foundation (ἀκρογωνιαῖος),[161] is

---

1 Cor. 3 and Rom. 15 individual local churches are signified. So the examples are not exactly parallel in any case. Furthermore, in 2 Tim. 2.19 the foundation seems to consist of God's own people. Cf. J. A. Robinson, 67f, and Abbott, 70f. The foundation metaphor is used variously at Qumran to speak of a pattern of true actions (1 Q S 5.5), the lower ranks in the assembled congregation (1 Q Sa 1.12), and the people of the community themselves (1 Q S 8.4-10). Cf. Franz Mussner, "Contributions made by Qumran to the understanding of the Epistle to the Ephesians," in Paul and Qumran, ed. J. Murphy - O'Connor (London, 1968), 168-73.
   In Herm. Sim. 9.4.2-3, 9.12.2, the foundation and the building consist of people.

[160]More precisely, both Jewish and Gentile converts are added together on to the foundation (cf. n.163).

[161]J. Jeremias argued that ἀκρογωνιαῖος here meant "capstone," the prominent last stone put on a building, usually over the door (ΑΓΓΕΛΟΣ 1 (1925),

best understood to mean Christ himself, not teachings about Christ. Because the term ἀκρογωνιαῖος is very unusual, it is unlikely that the author of Eph. 2.20 could have learned it from any source other than the LXX of Is. 28.16.[162] So the idea of Christ as a cornerstone in Eph. 2.20 is best thought to derive from a common early Christian interpretation of Is. 28.16 in which Christ himself is the foundation stone there mentioned (cf. Rom. 9.33, 10.11 with 13,

---

65-70, 85; ZNW 29 (1930), 264-80 (the fullest treatment); ZNW 36 (1937), 154-57; TDNT I, 792 (a summary of all his essential material). His case is unconvincing because (a) the only clear examples of ἀκρογωνιαῖος to mean a high cornerstone are in the Testament of Solomon, which is of uncertain date (it is a Jewish work with clear Christian additions); (b) he does not take sufficient account of the fact that a broad term which simply means "end of a corner" or "extreme corner" will no doubt be used to represent several different types of corners (of foundations, roofs, etc.), and no one usage can be seized upon as representing the definitive meaning; (c) Is. 28.16, the most certain source for the term in Eph. 2.20 (see following note), along with Barn. 6.2 and probably 1 Pet. 2.6, clearly understand it to mean cornerstone of the foundation (cf. ZNW 29 [1930], 278), and these are much more relevant for Eph. 2.20 than T. Sol. 22.7, 17 or any non-Greek works; and (d) the context of Eph. 2.20 must finally be decisive, and here "cornerstone of the foundation" makes much better sense, since Christ was the first member of the New Covenant community (cf. the convincing arguments of R. J. McKelvey, "Christ the Cornerstone," NTS 8 (1961-62), 352-59, and The New Temple, 114-16 and 195-204; cf. also J. A. Robinson, 164, and M. Barth, 317-19 (who accepts Jeremias's "parallels" too uncritically and blurs this building metaphor with the head-body metaphor in Eph. 4.15-16).

[162]Is. 28.16 is the only example known to me of ἀκρογωνιαῖος in Greek literature which clearly predates Ephesians. The other instances are 1 Pet. 2.6, Barn. 6.2 (ca. 70-100 AD), Symm. Ps. 117 (118).22, 4 K. 25.17 (2nd c.AD), and T. Sol. (McCown) 22.7, 17, and D 6.10 (? 1 c.AD, with clear Christian additions). The T. Sol. references are in C. C. McCown, The Testament of Solomon (Leipzig, 1922), pp. 66*, 68* and 95*, and (ET) F. C. Conybeare, "The Testament of Solomon," JQR 9 (1898-99), 41-42.

1 Pet. 2.4-6; Barn. 6.2). In Eph. 2.20 itself the
αὐτοῦ before Χριστοῦ Ἰησοῦ implies that "Christ Jesus
himself," not teachings about Christ is meant. In
addition, the repeated ἐν ᾧ in vss. 21-22 echoes
earlier statements in the epistle about incorporation
into Christ (1.3, 4, 7, 10, 11, 13, 2.6, 10, 13, 15)
and thus gives a dynamic and personal picture if it
means "in Christ," but is highly incongruous if it
means "in teachings about Christ."

So the metaphor in Eph. 2.20 shows three components of the dwelling place of God (vs. 22): the
Gentiles, the (Jewish) apostles and prophets, and
Christ. All three elements are represented as persons
who are joined together in this new house.[163] This
cumulative picture is a final argument in favor of
understanding θεμέλιος as representative of persons.
If any one component represents persons, an interpretation which sees the other two components as persons
gives a consistency to the metaphor which, though perhaps not absolutely necessary, is certainly preferable.[164]

(2) If we understand θεμέλιος to represent
apostolic teaching about Christ, what does the cornerstone represent? Presumably that must also be teaching
about Christ. But then why does the writer distinguish
one from the other? The metaphor becomes too complicated for a normal reader to understand, and does not
thereby contribute to the demonstration of Jew-Gentile
equality in the church. On the other hand, if θεμέλιος
represents teaching (or the activity of teaching) about
Christ and the cornerstone is then taken to be Christ
himself, the metaphor becomes hopelessly confused.
Two personal elements (Christ and the Gentiles) are
united in one building with a non-personal element
(the teaching of the apostles and prophets). So

---

[163]To be more specific, the superstructure is
apparently seen as including Jews as well as Gentiles:
the Jews are the "saints" of vs. 19 with whom the Gentiles have become συμπολῖται. So in one sense there
are actually four components to the building, and all are
personal. Cf. R. J. McKelvey, The New Temple, 111 n. 2.

[164]It is not even a question here of mixing metaphors, but of consistency within one metaphor.

θεμέλιος as an image for persons best accounts for the three elements of the metaphor.

(3) The entire context focuses attention not on the human activity involved in building churches but on the divine activity of uniting Jew and Gentile in the church. The whole of 1.3-2.10 is a description of the blessings the readers have received from God (1.3, 4, 5, 7, 9, 12, etc.). The redemptive work of Christ in uniting Jew and Gentile is described in 2.14-18. Then vss. 19-22 are introduced by an inferential ἄρα οὖν, "so then, consequently." It is as a result of the aforementioned activity of God and Christ that "you (Gentiles) have been built up on the foundation of the apostles and prophets." There is no mention of any human activity, for the passage speaks only of a divine plan and the divine activity in carrying it out.[165] So God is seen as the builder who placed both Jews and Gentiles in his one new building, and that picture is entirely consistent with "the foundation which consists of the apostles and prophets," but not with "the foundation laid by the apostles and prophets."[166]

(4) The metaphor of a living, growing house (vs. 21) in which God dwells (vs. 22) fits well with a picture of a house which consists of persons, but poorly with a picture of a house some of whose components are impersonal teachings or activities.[167]

(5) Taking θεμέλιος as impersonal requires one to import into the text speculative factors which are not there. No explicit mention is made in Eph. 2.20

---

[165]Human preaching activity might be implied by vs. 17, but even here it is remarkable that the emphasis is all on divine activity, and human agents are not even mentioned.

[166]This observation helps to account for the different use of the metaphor in 1 Cor. 3.10ff, for there Paul is speaking about the human activity of founding churches.

[167]Cf. the explicit mention of "living stones" in 1 Pet. 2.4-8, a passage in many ways similar to this one.

of teaching acitivity or Christian doctrine or any
other impersonal factors like these. To say that
θεμέλιος equals one of these requires a speculative
step which is unnecessary if one understands the
foundation to equal what is explicitly mentioned in
the text, the apostles and prophets themselves.

(6) The aorist passive participle ἐποικοδομηθέντες ("you have been built up on" . . .) refers to a
completed activity in the past. Had it been a present
participle (followed by perhaps ἐν or ὑπό) we might
more easily have pictured people who "are being built
up" on (or by) apostolic doctrine. This would refer
to a continual process throughout the readers' lives.
But here the completed past activity spoken of here is
not likely to be a building up on apostolic teaching.
Rather, it speaks of the once-for-all incorporation
of the Gentile readers into the church.

For all of these reasons I feel that it is not
possible to adopt interpretation (a). Eph. 2.20 must
mean instead, "the foundation which consists of the
apostles and prophets."

Interpretation (b), that the foundation consists
of the apostles and OT prophets, has in its favor the
fact which I noted above, that NT apostles are often
connected with OT prophets and perform similar functions. Furthermore, the metaphor would show that the
Gentiles are joined into the same building as the OT
Jews, and therefore have equal citizenship in God's
kingdom. A similar idea is seen in the olive tree
metaphor in Rom. 11.17-24.

But again these considerations are not decisive.
The parallel between OT prophets and NT apostles is
certainly not seen in every NT mention of apostles
(cf. e.g., 1 Cor. 12.28, 14.6, Eph. 4.11). The olive
tree image does show the continuity between the Old
Covenant and New Covenant people of God, but because
of its limitations as a metaphor it cannot at the same
time represent what Paul also taught, that there is
also a discontinuity between the covenants which is so
great that it can be seen in terms of a totally new
creation (Rom. 8.29, 1 Cor. 12.13, 15.20, 2 Cor. 3.
14-16, 5.17, Gal. 2.20, 3.28-29, Col. 1.13, 9-11). So
the identity of these prophets cannot be determined
solely on the basis of parallels external to Ephesians,
but must be decided from the immediate context. In
that context, there are weighty considerations which

make this proposal unacceptable.

(1) Eph. 2.14-18 is one of the strongest passages in the entire NT on the total newness of the creation made by Christ out of Jews and Gentiles. He abolished the law of commandments and ordinances ἕνα τοὺς δύο (Jew and Gentile) κτίσῃ . . . εἰς καινὸν ἄνθρωπον (vs. 15). There is no thought of adding a new part which consists exclusively of Gentiles onto a pre-Christian Jewish part, for both parts are newly reconciled to God in one body (vs. 16), both needed to have peace preached to them by Christ (vs. 17), and both have gained access through Christ in one Spirit to the Father (vs. 18).[168] So a metaphor which suggested the addition of the Gentile readers to a building which had an Old Covenant base would be out of place in this context. The picture is rather one of a base which consists of "the apostles and prophets" onto which are added all other New Covenant believers, both Jew and Gentiles alike (the phrase συμπολῖται τῶν ἁγίων requires that the Jews--the ἅγιοι--are also seen as part of the superstructure, along with the Gentiles). This is what gives the illustration so much force: both Jews and Gentiles are united as equal members in the same building, the building is based on the (Jewish) apostles and prophets, and the entire building (cornerstone, foundation, super-structure) is a new creation in Christ.

(2) The metaphor of laying a foundation and building onto it suggests a chronological order which makes the OT prophets very unlikely candidates for the role of a θεμέλιος. For they were neither the first nor the only members of the OT covenant community. If chronological priority qualified one to be a foundation, we would have expected Abraham, Isaac, Jacob and the other Patriarchs. On the other hand, if the author means to say that the Gentiles are added on top of all

---

[168]Vss. 12 and 19 do speak of the fact that the Gentiles were once excluded from the Jewish covenant community and are now included, but it is still the NT covenant community which is primarily in view and to which the Gentiles are united. The terms οἰκεῖος and οἱ ἅγιοι in vs. 19 are used elsewhere of NT believers (Gal. 6.10; Ac. 9.13, Rom. 15.25, Eph. 3.8, Heb. 6.10, etc.).

the OT people of God, it is strange that he only mentions the prophets and neglects all the other righteous men who by grace were true children of Abraham (cf. Rom. 4.12). In both cases, the OT prophets are inappropriate or confusing symbols for all the OT Jews.

(3) If the OT prophets stand here as representatives of the OT people of God, and if these OT Jews constitute the foundation of a building which represents all of God's people, then it is difficult to account for the presence of the apostles in the foundation as well. There are three possibilities here: (i) If the foundation consists of OT believers then the apostles should be part of the superstructure, not the foundation. (ii) If the foundation consists of Jews, then other Jewish NT believers should be part of it, not just the apostles. (iii) If the foundation consists of representative leaders of the Old and New Covenants, then the prophets are an inadequate choice (why not Patriarchs, as in Rev. 21.12-14, or righteous kings?).[169]

(4) On this interpretation it is difficult to account for the presence of Christ as the cornerstone, the first stone laid in the foundation. It is Christ in the role of New Covenant mediator who is in view in vss. 14-18, and he came as such long after the OT prophets. Yet the cornerstone is laid before the other stones of the foundation. (In this and the two preceding points it might be objected that consistency within any one metaphor is not always to be expected in the NT. Nevertheless, an explanation of the metaphor which is internally consistent is to be preferred if one can be found.)

(5) The word order τῶν ἀποστόλων καὶ προφητῶν would not suggest OT prophets to any reader unless the

---

[169] One might argue that in the eyes of NT Christians OT prophets were, like NT apostles, proclaimers of Christ (cf. 1 Pet. 1.11). However, the metaphor of a foundation would certainly be an unusual one to represent this proclamation activity (we would have expected perhaps the metaphor of a builder who lays a foundation, as in 1 Cor. 3.10).

context clearly demanded it for other reasons. OT prophets would be signified instead by τῶν προφητῶν καί (τῶν) ἀποστόλων.

(6) In Eph. 3.5, ὡς νῦν ἀπεκαλύφθη and αὐτοῦ (referring to Χριφτοῦ in vs. 4) make it certain that OT prophets are not referred to there: the mystery of the Gentile inclusions has now been revealed to Christ's holy apostles and prophets. This verse is such a close parallel to 2.20, and lies so near, that unless the reader has clear indications to the contrary he is justified in thinking that the same people are spoken of in both verses.

(7) The picture of the whole building[170] growing to maturity (αὔξει, vs. 21)[171] better represents a group of people who are still alive than a mixed group also consisting of those long since dead and making no further progress toward spiritual maturity.[172]

These seven objections seem to give more than sufficient reason to reject interpretation (b).

---

[170] In vs. 21, πᾶσα οἰκοδομή is somewhat better attested (ℵ* B D G Byz) but πᾶσα ἡ οἰκοδομή (ℵ^a A C P 81 88 syr^{p,h} cop$^{sa, bo}$ arm eth) is much more suitable in the context. In either case the readers are pictured as a building growing to maturity.

[171] Αὐξάνω (αὔξω) always in the NT (22X) means "grow to a larger size or to maturity" rather than "increase in number" (cf. Mt. 6.28, 13.32, Lk. 2.40, 2 Cor. 10.15, Eph. 15, Col. 1.10, 2.19, etc; the only possible exceptions are Ac. 7.17 and 1 Cor. 3.6-7). The close parallel in Col. 2.19 is especially revelant. If the verse had meant "increase in numbers" we would have expected πληθύνω. (The passage does not of course exclude the possibility of growth in number of members; it simply does not discuss it.)

[172] It should not be objected that the picture would be invalid once the apostles had died, for this was not the concern of the author of Ephesians in presenting the metaphor: he is speaking to a contemporary situation.

In favor of interpretation (c), "the apostles and NT prophets," is the fact that προφήτης in the NT is used frequently to refer to a separate category of people who were able to prophesy but were distinct from the apostles. In fact, Eph. 4.11 is a clear example. It might be argued that the readers could scarcely have been expected to understand anything other than this meaning of προφήτης, especially if interpretations (a) and (b) are excluded. Also, the καί of τῶν ἀποστόλων καὶ προφητῶν might be said to imply two distinct groups of people.

However, as I argue more fully below, the absence of an article in front of προφητῶν shows that two groups are not necessarily implied by the καί, and "the apostles who are also prophets" is a possible translation. The term προφήτης is not decisive either, for a "prophet" in the NT is not necessarily someone who belongs to a formally distinct group or who holds a particular ecclesiastical office (cf. Chap. 4). Rather, anyone who prophesies can be called a NT prophet, and prophecy simply consists of receiving a "revelation" from God and reporting that revelation in public (cf. Chap. 2, pp. 139ff). So just as an apostle could be called a teacher or preacher when he engaged in teaching or preaching activities (1 Tim. 2.7, 2 Tim. 1.11), he could also be called a prophet when he received a revelation and reported it to others. This does not mean that all apostles were necessarily prophets (perhaps some never received revelations) or that all prophets were apostles (not all had been commissioned as divinely authoritative messengers), but it does mean that some apostles at some times functioned as prophets. So there are no compelling reasons in Eph. 2.20 which require that it mean "the apostles and NT prophets," and the possibility must be left open that it means "the apostles who are also prophets."

Furthermore, there are substantial difficulties in understanding this to mean "the apostles and the NT prophets" in such a way that "prophets" is a separate group from the apostles.

(1) There does not appear to be a convincing reason why "prophets" should be included in this foundation. (i) If membership in the "foundation" implies early membership in the church (in fact, membership at the very beginning of the church), then the NT prophets (who are not apostles) have no right

to be included there. The apostles certainly were the charter members of the church, but in addition to the apostles no other group is distinctive enough to be designated as the foundation.[173] Certainly the prophets in Corinth or Ephesus or Thessalonica, for instance, were not a foundation in this sense. (And it should be noted that the notion of chronological development seems to be the most natural implication of this foundation and building metaphor.)

(ii) If those in the foundation are understood to be those with ruling or governing authority in the NT church, then the prophets should not be included. For nowhere in the NT is there clear evidence that NT prophets (who were not also apostles) had any leading or ruling functions in the church (cf. Chap. 4). On the other hand, if this foundation is one consisting of church leaders, we would perhaps expect elders (at least the Jerusalem elders of Ac. 15) to be included (cf. Ac. 15.2, 4, 6, 22, 23, 16.4, in a context which, incidentally, has much more to do with ruling authority in the church than does Eph. 2.20).

(iii) If the foundation consists of authoritative preachers and teachers in the NT church, once more prophets are an inappropriate group to be named here. Throughout the NT prophecy and teaching are kept quite distinct, and prophets (who are not also apostles) are never said to engage in any teaching activity.[174] Moreover, it would be strange to have included prophets but excluded teachers from such a "foundational" group.

(iv) If apostles and prophets in the role of itinerant church-planters (founders) are thought to be the foundation, similar objections apply. Prophets are nowhere seen to have such a task, while evangelists, who do have this task, are inexplicably absent from the verse.

(v) If those in the foundation are there because of their role as recipients and interpreters of

---

[173] Members of the Jerusalem church might conceivably be the foundation in this sense, but certainly not all of them were prophets.

[174] Cf. Chap. 2, pp.   and Chap. 3, pp.

"revelations,"[175] then apostles and NT prophets (who are not also apostles) are the two most obvious classes to be mentioned (cf. Chap. 2). But this possibility is unlikely for other reasons. First, it neglects the idea of chronological priority, the most significant idea in the "foundation" metaphor, and instead emphasizes almost exclusively the idea of "importance" to the building. Perhaps one could say that the foundation means the most important part of the building, but that, while probably true, is a distant and difficult connection to make. (Might not someone else think that the most prominent stones were the most important? Or, in view which is closer to the intent of Eph. 2 (and 1 Cor. 12), might it not be thought that all the stones are equally important?

So this view can only be maintained by emphasizing an uncertain interpretation of the foundation (= importance) in order to deny a very obvious interpretation (= chronological priority). Elsewhere in the NT the writers feel free to assume that the idea of chronological sequence will be evident when their readers read a foundation metaphor (Rom. 15.20, 1 Cor. 3.10ff, Heb. 6.1-2; cf. Herm. Sim 9.4.2-3, 9.12.2, 9.15.4). Especially here in Eph. 2.20, with explicit mention made that the Gentiles are added on (ἐποικοδομηθέντες), it seems clear that any interpretation would have to be consistent with the idea that the foundation was laid first and afterwards the superstructure was added. But this chronological sequence does not allow prophets as part of the foundation, since it cannot be said that apostles and prophets, and no one else, were the first members of the church.

Second, if we conclude that the "apostles and prophets" here are the same as in 3.5, then the kind of revelation which is said to come to them is not elsewhere said to come to NT prophets. For it is not just any kind of revelation which those apostles and prophets have received, but specifically the revelation of the Gentile inclusion in the church (3.5-6). Now the NT several times reports this revelation as coming to the apostles (cf. Mt. 28.19, Lk. 24.47, Ac. 1.8, 10.15, 34-35, 47-48, 11.9-18, 15.7, 14-20, 28, 22.21, 26.17-18, Gal. 1.16), but not once is there any indication that such a revelation was also made to NT

---

[175] So Caird, Paul's Letters, 61.

prophets who were not also apostles. So if NT prophets are included here it must be done by assuming something about these prophets for which there is no clear evidence elsewhere in the NT.

Third, the picture of a foundation which is already laid seems to suggest that its members are a distinct group with a fixed number of members: once the superstructure is begun, no stones can be added to or taken from the foundation. Now this image fits the apostles, but it fits other NT prophets less well if at all. Wherever a new church began to grow, there were more people with the ability to prophesy, so the prophets were a steadily expanding group.[176]

Fourth, to include NT prophets in this foundation metaphor would seem inconsistent with the purpose of vss. 14-22, which is to show the equal citizenship of Jews and Gentiles in the church. For while the NT apostles were all Jews, that was certainly not true of all the NT prophets. There were no doubt Gentile prophets in Corinth, in Thessalonica, in Rome, and even among the Gentile recipients of Ephesians. Now if they are made part of the foundation, it would be inconsistent to see them as also part of the superstructure which is added on. Nor would the metaphor have much force, for if Gentiles are already part of the foundation, there is no point in drawing attention to the fact that they are also part of the superstructure. It would be much more important to emphasize their membership in the very foundation. So there are several reasons which make interpretation (c) unacceptable. It neglects the concept of chronological priority which seems inherent in the foundation metaphor; it assumes without further NT support that there were non-apostolic prophets to whom the "mystery" of the Gentile inclusion was revealed in some initial or foundational way; it fits poorly with the idea of a fixed number of members (an idea which seems inherent to the metaphor of a foundation); it fits awkwardly or perhaps not at all with the purpose of this section of Ephesians (to show the equal membership of Jews and

---

[176]An indication that the apostles could be thought of both as a foundational group of God's people and as a unique group which included no other members is found in Rev. 21.14. (E. Best, One Body in Christ (London, 1955), 162-68, argues for a "growing" foundation, but only because interpretation (c) demands this.)

Gentiles in the church but not in the foundation).

Interpretation (d), "the apostles who are also prophets,"[177] has the following arguments in its favor:

(1) The absence of the second article in τῶν ἀποστόλων καὶ προφητῶν means that the writer views the apostles and prophets as a single group, and that we cannot immediately be sure whether that group has one or two components. But the grammatical structure clearly allows for the possibility that one group with one component is meant, for there are several instances in the NT where one definite article governs two or more nouns joined by καί and it is clear that one group with only one component (or one person) is implied. In Ephesians itself 4.11 is noteworthy: ἔδωκεν τοὺς μὲν ἀποστόλους, τοὺς δὲ προφήτας, τοὺς δὲ εὐαγγελιστάς, τοὺς δὲ ποιμένας καὶ διδασκάλους. The "pastors and teachers" are the same people but two different functions are named.[178] In what follows, I have listed most of the clear examples of this type of construction

---

[177] I have translated "the apostles who are also prophets" because this phrase, though cumbersome, most clearly reflects the force of καί in this idiom. "The apostle-prophets" or "the apostles, even prophets," would also be possible (but less clear and less readable) translations. "The apostles who are prophets" gives too little weight to the καί.
(Ac. 13.9 shows another possible way of expressing this idea: Σαῦλος δέ, ὁ καὶ Παῦλος.)
It must be admitted that one major barrier for native speakers of English in adopting this translation is the fact that the English word "and" does not exactly duplicate the force of καί in this Greek construction, and sometimes a paraphrase is necessary to bring out the sense more clearly.

[178] The last τοὺς δὲ functions for both ποιμένας and διδασκάλους (so Meyer, 218f; Hodge, 79; Hendricksen, 197; more cautiously, Abbott, 118). These pastor-teachers are most likely to be men who had both ruling and teaching responsibilities in the church, since the shepherding metaphor is appropriate to and closely connected with the function of rule (Ac. 20.28, 1 Pet. 5.2; cf. Jn. 21.16 with 1 Pet. 5.1; 1 Pet. 2.25), and since ruling and teaching functions are elsewhere connected together (1 Tim. 3.2, Tit. 1.9).

from the Pauline corpus, along with some scattered examples from elsewhere in the NT:

With reference to people, it is not unusual to describe the same person with two or more titles:

Rom. 16.7 Ἀνδρόνικον καὶ Ἰουνιᾶν τοὺς συγγενεῖς μου καὶ συναιχμαλώτους μου

Eph. 4.11 τοὺς δὲ ποιμένας καὶ διδασκάλους

6.21 Τυχικὸς ὁ ἀγαπητὸς ἀδελφὸς καὶ πιστὸς διάκονος

Phil. 2.25 Ἐπαφρόδιτον τὸν ἀδελφὸν καὶ συνεργὸν καὶ συστρατιώτην μου

Col. 1.2[179] τοῖς ἐν Κολοσσαῖς ἁγίοις καὶ πιστοῖς ἀδελφοῖς ἐν Χριστῷ

4.7 Τυχικὸς ὁ ἀγαπητὸς ἀδελφὸς καὶ πιστὸς διάκονος καὶ σύνδουλος ἐν Κυρίῳ

Phlm. 1 Φιλήμονι τῷ ἀγαπητῷ καὶ συνεργῷ ἡμῶν

Heb. 3.1 τὸν ἀπόστολον καὶ ἀρχιερέα τῆς ὁμολογίας ἡμῶν, Ἰησοῦν

1 Pet. 2.25 ἐπὶ τὸν ποιμένα καὶ ἐπίσκοπον τῶν ψυχῶν ὑμῶν

2 Pet. 3.18 γνώσει τοῦ κυρίου ἡμῶν καὶ σωτῆρος Ἰησοῦ Χριστοῦ

Phrases in which God is named commonly take a similar form:

Rom. 15.6 τὸν θεὸν καὶ πατέρα τοῦ κυρίου ἡμῶν Ἰησοῦ Χριστοῦ

2 Cor. 1.3 ὁ θεὸς καὶ πατὴρ τοῦ κυρίου ἡμῶν Ἰησοῦ Χριστοῦ

11.31 ὁ θεὸς καὶ πατὴρ τοῦ κυρίου Ἰησοῦ

Gal. 1.4 κατὰ τὸ θέλημα τοῦ θεοῦ καὶ πατρὸς ἡμῶν

---

[179]Cf. Lightfoot, *Colossians and Philemon*, 132.

Eph. 1.3   ὁ θεὸς καὶ πατὴρ τοῦ κυρίου ἡμῶν Ἰησοῦ Χριστοῦ

(ℵAB)   5.20   εὐχαριστοῦντες . . . τῷ θεῷ καὶ πατρί

(p^{46} D*)   . . . τῷ πατρὶ καὶ θεῷ

Phil. 4.20   τῷ δὲ θεῷ καὶ πατρὶ ἡμῶν ἡ δόξα

Col. 1.3   τῷ θεῷ καὶ πατρὶ τοῦ κυρίου ἡμῶν Ἰησοῦ Χριστοῦ

(ℵA P Ψ Byz, several Fathers)

3.17   εὐχαριστοῦντες τῷ θεῷ καὶ πατρί (D G Ψ Byz, several Father)

1 Th. 1.3   ἔμπροσθεν τοῦ θεοῦ καὶ πατρὸς ἡμῶν

3.11   ὁ θεὸς καὶ πατὴρ ἡμῶν

3.11   ἔμπροσθεν τοῦ θεοῦ καὶ πατρὸς ἡμῶν

6.15   ὁ βασιλεὺς τῶν βασιλευόντων καὶ κύριος τῶν κυριευόντων

Tit. 2.13 (?)   τῆς δόξης τοῦ μεγάλου θεοῦ καὶ σωτῆρος ἡμῶν Ἰησοῦ Χριστοῦ

2 Pet. 1.1 (?)   ἐν δικαιοσύνῃ τοῦ θεοῦ ἡμῶν καὶ σωτῆρος Ἰησοῦ Χριστοῦ

2 Pet. 1.11   εἰς τὴν αἰώνιον βασιλείαν τοῦ κυρίου ἡμῶν καὶ σωτῆρος Ἰησοῦ Χριστοῦ (cf. 2.20)

Non-personal objects occasionally are named in this way also:

1 Th. 3.7   ἐπὶ πάσῃ τῇ ἀνάγκῃ καὶ θλίψει ἡμῶν

Tit. 2.13   προσδεχόμενοι τὴν μακαρίαν ἐλπίδα καὶ ἐπιφάνειαν τῆς δόξης . . .

If constructions using participles and infinitives are included there are several more examples:

1 Cor. 11.29   ὁ γὰρ ἐσθίων καὶ πίνων

Gal. 1.7   οἱ ταράσσοντες ὑμᾶς καὶ θέλοντες μεταστρέψαι τὸ εὐαγγέλιον . . .

1 Th. 5.12 εἰδέναι τοὺς κοπιῶντας ἐν ὑμῖν καὶ προϊσταμένους ὑμῶν ἐν κυρίῳ νουθετοῦντας ὑμᾶς

(Cf. also 2 Cor. 1.21, 22, 5.15, 18, Gal. 1.15, 2.20, 3.5, Eph. 2.14, 3.12, 18, 4.6, 5.5, Phil. 1.7, 20, 23, 2.17, 3.3, Col. 2.3, 22. 1 Th. 3.2, 4.6, 2 Th. 2.4, 3.2, 1 Tim. 4.3, 6.20, 2 Tim. 1.8).

This does not imply that Eph. 2.20 <u>must</u> mean "the apostles who are also prophets," for there are many other examples which could be listed where one group with two distinct components is named (cf. Ac. 13.50, τὸν Παῦλον καὶ Βαρναβᾶν and Ac. 15.2, τοὺς ἀποστόλους καὶ πρεσβυτέρους, for example,[180] and in Paul, Rom. 1.20, 2 Cor. 6.7, 7.3, 13,11, Phil. 1.19, 25, 2 Th. 1.4, 2.2). Nevertheless, it must be noted that I was unable to find in the Pauline corpus even one clear

---

[180] The use or non-use of a second article in Luke does not appear to be entirely arbitrary, however. When only one article is used there is at least an idea of unity, if not of identity (cf. M. Zerwick, <u>Biblical Greek</u>, (ET Rome, 1963), § 184). So in Ac. 15.2 there is only one article because, seen from Antioch, "the apostles and elders" constitute one group of leaders. In Ac. 15.4, 6, and 22 there are two articles, because from a Jerusalem perspective "the apostles and the elders" were more clearly two groups. But in Ac. 16.4 we return to a distant perspective and to the use of a single article again. Of course in other cases other reasons than distance may cause two people or groups to be seen as one. The longest list of examples (though by no means complete) is in Robertson, <u>Grammar</u>, 785-89; cf. p. 1398 (but here the difference between Mt. 17.1 and Mk. 9.2 may be due to a Petrine influence on Mark).

There are also some examples in the <u>Didache</u> which might show that two separate groups could be meant: Did. 11.3 (περὶ δὲ τῶν ἀποστόλων καὶ προφητῶν), Did. 15.2 (τῶν προφητῶν καὶ διδασκάλων). But cf. Ign. Phld. 9.1, οἱ προφῆται καὶ οἱ ἀπόστολοι (misprinted in the Loeb text; cf. J. B. Lightfoot, <u>The Apostolic Fathers</u>, Part II, Vol. II, Sect. 1, 275, who gives Greek variants in full (ibid., p. 8) and Herm. <u>Sim</u>. 9.16.5 (οἱ ἀπόστολοι καὶ οἱ διδάσκαλοι). Furthermore, there is really nothing in the context of <u>Did</u>. 11.3 and 15.2 which would preclude a similar translation there ("the apostles who are also prophets" and then "the prophets [that is, apostle-prophets] who are also teachers"). So these two examples are ambiguous.

example analogous to Ac. 13.50 or 15.2, where two distinct <u>people</u> or classes of <u>people</u> (as opposed to things) are joined by καί and only one article is used.¹⁸¹ This may be more or less significant, depending in part on one's view of the authorship of Ephesians. But it should not be overlooked that when Paul wants to distinguish two people or groups he does not hesitate to use a second article (1 Cor. 3.8, 8.6 etc.; cf. Eph. 3.10). And I have listed above over twenty Pauline examples ¹⁸² where clearly only one person or group is implied by this type of construction.

So Eph. 2.20 views "the apostles and prophets" as one group. Grammatically, that group could have two distinct components, but such an interpretation would not be exactly in accord with Pauline usage.¹⁸³ If the author had meant to speak of a two-component group he certainly did not make this meaning very clear to his readers (as he could have done by adding another τῶν before προφητῶν).¹⁸⁴ On the other hand, the large number of NT parallels shows that "the apostles who are also prophets" would have been easily understood by the readers if other factors in the context allowed for or favored this interpretation.¹⁸⁵

---

¹⁸¹Eph. 1.1, 5.5, 2 Thess. 1.12 and Tit. 2.13 are ambiguous.

¹⁸²The exact number will depend on which epistles one counts as Pauline; within the total Pauline corpus there are 24 examples.

¹⁸³Within Ephesians itself, there is also a frequent preference for pairs of words where the second only makes the first more precise or adds a slightly different nuance (Cothenet, <u>DBS</u> 8, cols. 1306f).

¹⁸⁴The two would still have been seen as in some way unified since τῷ θεμελίῳ is singular, so the absence of the second article was not necessary to the purpose of showing one group with two components. If he had wanted to show one group with one component (the apostles), however, he would have had to omit the second article, just as he did.

¹⁸⁵If one rejects Pauline authorship of Ephesians, and especially if one sees stylistic similarities between Ephesians and Luke-Acts, this argument is less strong, but it still demonstrates the very clear possibility of interpretation (d).

(2) I argued above that NT prophets who were not also apostles would have been an inappropriate group to include in the foundation metaphor, no matter what kind of significance is attached to the idea of a foundation (pp. 93ff). The recipients of this epistle, having knowledge of the NT prophets who were in their own churches, would have immediately realized that. The phrase ἐποικοδομηθέντες ἐπὶ τῷ θεμελίῳ would have been a very clear signal to the readers that NT prophets were not intended: the readers knew that they had in no sense been "built up on a foundation" which consisted of their friends and neighbors who prophesied at the worship services. Their minds would have settled easily--indeed, without conscious effort--on the other possible interpretation, "the apostles who are also prophets."

(3) This interpretation is very appropriate to the overall argument being developed here by the author. He wants to convince his Gentile readers that they are totally equal with Jews in God's new house. Therefore, he emphasizes the fact that they are members of the same building as the apostles (cf. σύσσωμα, 3.6), the most important representatives of Jewish Christianity and the charter members of the church. If they are members of such an "apostolic" building, then certainly they have equal standing with all the other (Jewish) saints (συμπολῖται τῶν ἁγίων, vs. 19).

But the author goes even farther than that. He wants to emphasize one particular role of the apostles, namely, their role as recipients of revelations from God. As I argue in Chap. 2, the term προφήτης in the NT usually means a person who receives "revelations" from God and then reports them in public. The term itself says nothing about authority. It can refer either to those who have divinely autoritative messenger status or to those who do not. The term defines not authority but one's role as a recipient and reporter of revelation. Now in Eph. 2.20 the writer assumes for a moment that his readers have all heard the amazing news that the inclusion of the Gentiles in the church was made known to the apostles by revelation (then, in 3.2-6, he mentions this fact again for any who may not have heard). By adding the phrase καὶ προφητῶν he reassures the Gentiles of their equal status by reminding them that it was actually the <u>apostles</u>, not some unimportant fringe group in the church, to whom the revelation about the Gentile inclusion came. The Gentiles can be certain of their equality because those who are οἱ ἀπόστολοι, the divinely authoritative proclaimers of the true Gospel, are καὶ προφῆται the recipients of new directions from the Holy Spirit, and especially of directions about the inclusion of the Gentiles. Thus, the full inclusion of the Gentiles is not some weakly based idea; rather, it is a central concept which was first made known to and is now endorsed by the principal members and leaders of the church.[186]

(4) This understanding of the meaning of καὶ προφητῶν in 2.20 is reinforced by the more explicit statement in 3.5: the mystery of Christ (vs. 4), the Gentile inclusion (vs. 6), was not made known to the sons of men in former generations ὡς νῦν ἀπεκαλύφθη τοῖς ἁγίοις ἀποστόλοις αὐτοῦ καὶ προφήταις ἐν πνεύματι. This is a parenthetical section (cf. 3.2) in which the author expands on what he has been saying for those who may not be so familiar with it, and we would expect a similar topic to be covered. The same grammatical construction is used (one definite article governing two nouns joined by καί),[187] and "his holy apostles who are also prophets" makes sense in the context. OT prophets are not meant (see above, p. 92)

---

[186] I am not suggesting here that apostles belonged to the foundation only because they were recipients of revelation; rather the foundation metaphor was appropriate because they were chronologically the first members of the church, and also probably because they were a distinct class of authoritative rulers and teachers in the church. Once the readers understand this, then it is extremely significant to them to hear that these foundational members are also the ones to whom the revelation about the Gentiles came. This is, incidentally, the reason why the word order τῶν προφητῶν καὶ ἀποστόλων would have been less appropriate: the role of apostle is of primary importance, and the function of receiving revelations is simply the one aspect of that role which receives additional emphasis.

It should not be objected that καὶ προφητῶν is redundant because ἀποστόλων already carried the idea of a recipient of revelation. It is a matter of emphasizing one particular function of the apostles for the author's immediate purpose (cf. 1 Tim. 2.7).

[187] Τοῖς also governs προφήταις, since ἁγίοις and

but neither would it be appropriate to understand a separate group of NT prophets here. As I mentioned in connection with interpretation (c), nowhere in the NT is there clear evidence that the Gentile inclusion was revealed to any non-apostolic NT prophets, but several times we are told that this revelation did in fact come to those who were apostles (cf. Mt. 28.19, Lk. 24.47, Ac. 1.8, 10.15, 34-35, 47-48, 11.9-18, 15.7, 14-20, 28, 22.21, 26.17-18, Gal. 1.16, and in the immediate context Eph. 3.3-4).[188]

If one were to argue that there might have been some non-apostolic NT prophets (unknown to us) to whom this revelation also came, this would simply be an argument from silence, and would not be confirmed by other evidence about prophets from elsewhere in the NT.

(5) If the building metaphor suggests a chronological ordering (as it would naturally do to most readers), it is fitting that the apostles and no one else should constitute the first members, the foundation.[189]

(6) Apostles are elsewhere in the NT seen as performing prophetic functions, and it is not at all inappropriate that they should be called "prophets" (see above, p. 53f).

αὐτοῦ modify προφήταις and the following ἐν πνεύματι modifies ἀπεκαλύφθη. The αὐτοῦ does not make this reading difficult, since in this construction "the genitive may occur with either substantive and apply to both" (Robertson, Grammar, 785).
This verse is very different from Eph. 4.11, where προφήτας has its own article and a distinct group is clearly signified.

[188]The author can refer to the apostles as a group without necessarily implying that this revelation came to each one individually (see following note).

[189]It should not be objected that this excludes Paul the latecomer from the foundation, for the metaphor allows the author to speak in general terms without making pedantic qualifications. If one wanted to name one group who constituted the first members of the church, the only possible name would be "the apostles."

(7) The idea that apostles constitute the foundation of the church is consistent with other similar metaphors about the apostles in the NT (Rev. 21.14, Mt. 16.18).

So interpretation (d), "built upon the foundation of the apostles who are also prophets," seems to be the best solution. Understood this way, it is consistent with texts we have examined earlier indicating a prophetic role for NT apostles, and indicating the appropriateness of designating some or all of the NT apostles as "prophets." Eph. 2.20 therefore does not refer to the less authoritative type of prophecy indicated in 1 Corinthians, but refers rather to the type of prophecy exemplified, for example, by Paul and other NT apostles who claimed to speak with a divine authority of actual words.

J. 1 Th. 5.19-21

Even if the δέ in vs. 21 be omitted, the close conjunction of vs. 21 with vs. 20 means that "prophecies" are most naturally included in the "all things" of vs. 21.[190] But δέ is rightly included,[191] and thus it brings out the contrast more clearly: "Do not despise prophecies, <u>but</u> test all things; hold fast to what is good." This process of evaluating prophecies to sort the good from the bad is exactly parallel to what we found in 1 Cor. 14.29,[192] and provides additional

---

[190] No doubt the πάντα includes other things such as teaching as well, but because vs. 20 is so close the primary reference seems to be to prophecy (Cothenet, <u>DBS</u> 8, col. 1289).

[191] The external attestation is roughly equal. Δέ is included by Alexandrian (B P Ψ 1739 cop^{sa} Clement; ℵ^c ?), Byzantine (K goth eth), and strong Western (D G it^{c,d,e,g}vg) texts, but it is omitted in some Byzantine (arm Lect), two Western (88 it^f) and several Alexandrian (ℵ A 33 81 104 cop^{boh}) texts, as well as by syr^p, pal. Yet "δέ is almost necessary for the sense; and where omitted. . . , may have been absorbed in the following syllable" (Lightfoot, <u>Notes on Epistles of St. Paul</u> (London, 1895), 84.

[192] Note that the prophecies, not the prophets, are to be judged (Best, 240).

confirmation that in Thessalonica as well as in Corinth Paul did not think that the prophets spoke with a divine authority of actual words. Moreover, the bare fact that Paul would even have thought it necessary to warn a church not to despise prophecies is an indication that the Thessalonians themselves were far from regarding prophecies as absolutely authoritative actual words of the Lord.

K. The Book of Revelation

The entire Book of Revelation claims to be a prophecy (1.3, 22.7, 10, 19; cf. 10.11), and provides a clear example of a claim to divine authority of actual words.[193]

---

[193]David Hill, "Prophecy and Prophets in the Revelation of St. John," NTS 18 (1971-72), 414-15. G. Friedrich, TDNT VI, 849, says that the author of Revelation "claims for himself an authority which can be compared only with that of the apostles"; cf. A. T. Nikolainen, "Über die theologische Eigenart der Offenbarung des Johannes," TLZ 93 (1968), 162f.

M. Eugene Boring, "The Apocalypse as Christian Prophecy," SBL 1974 Seminar Papers, ed. Geo. MacRae (2 vols.; Cambridge, Mass., 1974), II, 56, says that many of Hill's arguments about the differences between John and other NT prophets can be accounted for (i) by the fact that John wrote his prophecy because of the geographical distance separating him from the churches, and (ii) by seeing that the difference between John and the other prophets is one of degree rather than kind. However, Rev. itself presents the writing not only or even primarily as a geographical necessity, but as a response to the commands by which John was commissioned as a divinely authoritative messenger (cf. Rev. 1.11, 19, 2.1, 8, etc.). Thus, the writing is not an incidental difference but one which is integrally related to John's unique messenger status, and one which is closely related to the writing activity of the OT prophets and NT apostles. With respect to authority, the difference between the possession and non-possession of absolute divine authority is certainly a difference in kind. Boring graciously admits that "we may learn from Hill's essay that we cannot too easily generalize from the Apocalypse to the other prophets in John's . . . churches," but maintains that Revelation is still a good example of one type, if not

John is commissioned as a messenger by the risen Christ who appears to him: "Write what you see in a book and send it to the seven churches" (1.11). Repeatedly, he is commanded, "Write what you see" (1.19) or simply, "Write": (2.1, 8, 12, 18, 3.1, 7, 14, 14.13, 19.9, 21.5). There are some things which are revealed to John which he has no authority to write (cf. 10.4); the implication is that he has written no more and no less than that for which he had a divine commission, and it is this commission which imparts authority to his words.

In fact, there is in Revelation an emphasis on the very words which were heard and then written by John. Some examples are Rev. 1.3, 19.9 (οὗτοι οἱ λόγοι ἀληθινοὶ τοῦ θεοῦ εἰσιν) 21.5 (Write this, for [ὅτι] these words are faithful and true"), 22.6, 7, 9, 10, 18, 19; also the repeated "He who has an ear, let him hear what the Spirit says to the churches" closing the dictated messages in 2.7, 11, 17, 29, 3.6, 13, 22.

So it is no surprise that the book claims for itself an absolute kind of divine authority. The author's words are beyond challenge or question (22.18-19), and obeying them brings great blessings (1.3, 22.7), while altering them at all brings direct punishment from God (22.18-19).

With regard to the other prophets mentioned in Revelation, very little can be said because the evidence is scarce. The two prophets in Rev. 11 appear to be special eschatological figures who function in the time immediately prior to the consummation (cf. 11.14, 15).[194]

None of the other seven uses of προφήτης in Rev. is very specific (10.7, 11.18, 16.6, 18.20, 24, 22.6).[195] In general, it is quite difficult to tell

---

all types of early Christian prophecy (with which Hill would of course agree).

[194] Cf. G. E. Ladd, Revelation 154. If, however, they are merely symbolic figures intended to represent the church, then they do not bear at all on our discussion of NT prophecy.

[195] It is difficult to find a satisfactory explanation for the use of προφητεία in Rev. 19.10, ἡ γὰρ μαρτυρία Ἰησοῦ ἐστιν τὸ πνεῦμα τῆς προφητείας. The easiest way out is to make πνεῦμα mean something like "central message," and then Ἰησοῦ can be an objective

whether OT prophets or NT prophets or both are in view (cf. Rev. 10.7 with Rom. 1.2 and 16.25-26, but also with Eph. 3.5).[196] Sometimes it seems as though οἱ προφῆται is used not to describe one specific class of Christians, but almost to refer to all Christians who bear any kind of "prophetic" witness in troubled times. So the term "prophets" is four times coupled with other terms which include all Christians:

> 11.18 your servants the prophets and the saints[197] and those who fear your name
>
> 16.6 the blood of saints and prophets

---

genitive: "The central message of prophecy is a testimony about Jesus" (therefore, John should worship Jesus and God, not the angel). However, no instance of πνεῦμα in this sense has been found, and "the Spirit of prophecy" is frequently used in the Targums as a name for the Holy Spirit (cf. T. O. on Gen. 41.38, Num. 11.25, 26, 29, 24.2, 27.18; T. Ps.-Jon. on Gen. 45.27, Num. 11.17, 25-19, etc.).

The next best option seems to be to say that "the spirit of prophecy" does refer to the Holy Spirit but that the verse means "the central concern of the Holy Spirit (who inspires prophecy) is to bear witness to Jesus" (cf. G. R. Beasley-Murray, 276). Admittedly this loads ἐστιν with much unusual baggage, but when it is used to connect a personal noun (πνεῦμα) with an impersonal noun referring to a message or to communication (μαρτυρία), some such step is necessary. In any case, the point of the sentence is clear: John should not worship the angel who conveys the prophecy, but God and Jesus with whom the prophecy is concerned and from whom it originates.

(It should be noted that ψευδοπροφήτης also occurs at 16.13, 19.20 and 20.10.)

[196]Ladd (p. 145) also mentions 1 Qp Hab. 7.4-5, where God makes known the mysteries (רזי) of the (OT) prophets to the Teacher of Righteousness; but we should realize that the context has the mysteries first being revealed to the OT prophets (1 Qp Hab. 7.1-2, 7-8).

[197]"Saints," ἅγιος, clearly refers to all believers in 5.8, 8.3, 4, 13.7, 10, 14.12, 19.8, 20.9, 22.11, 21, and probably also in 11.18, 16.6, 17.6, 18.20, 24. There is no case where it clearly refers to a special class of believers only.

18.24   the blood of prophets and saints and all
        those slain on the earth

22.9   I am a fellow servant[198] with you and your
        brothers the prophets[199] and those who
        keep the words of this book.

This leads David Hill to conclude that in Revelation
"all members of the church are, in principle or
potentially, prophets." Those who are called "prophets"
are those who "are carrying out a function which could
be--and ideally should be--served by all, that of
declaring the word of God and the witness of Jesus."[200]
In any case, there is not enough information about
these other prophets for us to draw any further implications about the type of authority they are thought
to possess.

L. Did. 11

Although it is very difficult to decide when the
Didache was written or how representative it is of
life in the early church,[201] the eleventh chapter has

---

[198]"Servant," δοῦλος, is not restricted to apply
only to prophets, but applies to all believers in
2.20, 7.3, 19.2, 5, 22.3, and (therefore) probably in
1.1 and 22.6. It applies only to prophets in 10.7 and
11.8.

[199]The fact that John's "brothers" are said to
be prophets does not mean that they share in his
unique authority, for all the readers of the book are
seen as John's "brothers" in 1.9 (cf. 19.10; Heb. 2.11).

[200]Hill, "Prophecy and Prophets," 413-14. We
should also recall that Rev. has very little interest
in church offices: ἀπόστολος occurs only at 2.2, 18.20
and 21.14, πρεσβύτερος is only used of the 24 elders
in heaven and never of church officers, and
διδάσκαλος, ἐπίσκοπος, διάκονος, ποιμήν, and εὐαγγελιστής
do not occur at all.

[201]J. A. T. Robinson, Redating the New Testament
(London, 1976), 322-37, provides a recent summary of
arguments about the date of the Didache, and places it
between 40 and 60 A.D. He sees little conclusive
proof that the author knew actual NT writings.

such an explicit discussion of prophecy that I mention it briefly here. Did. 11.7 says, "Do not test or examine any prophet who is speaking in the Spirit (καὶ πάντα προφήτην λαλοῦντα ἐν πωεύματι οὐ πειράσετε οὐδὲ διακρινεῖτε), for every sin shall be forgiven, but this sin shall not be forgiven." The reference to the sin against the Holy Spirit shows that these prophets were thought to be speaking with a divine authority of actual words. To evaluate (διακρίνω) anything they said ἐν πνεύματι was to sin against the Holy Spirit.[202] So this passage must be classified with the others which picture a type of prophecy with absolute divine authority.

(Incidentally, the use of διακρίνω here can be seen as a slight confirmation of our understanding of 1 Cor. 14.29. Here, to evaluate (διακρίνειν) a prophecy is to challenge its absolute divine authority. But in 1 Cor. 14.29 Paul's command to evaluate (διακρίνειν) prophecies indicates that he, unlike the author of the Didache, did not think that prophets spoke with absolute divine authority: prophecies could be and should be subjected to evaluation, challenge and questioning.)

M. Conclusion

An investigation of other passages in the NT has given further evidence of the existence of two types of prophecy in the NT. Belonging to the first type, that for which a divine authority of actual words is claimed or presupposed in the narrative, are Mt. 10. 19-20 (and parallels), Eph. 2.20 and 3.5, Revelation, Did. 11.7, and perhaps Ac. 13.2 (if it refers to prophecy).

Representing the second type, prophecy for which a lesser kind of authority than a divine authority of actual words is indicated, are (in addition to the

---

[202] Crone, ECP, 271 thinks Did. 11.7 only means not to judge the prophets while they are speaking. This view is not convincing, however. If the statement refers to spoken evaluation, it would have been an obvious courtesy hardly necessary to mention, while if it refers to silent evaluation it would have been "sinning against the Holy Spirit" (from the standpoint of the author) whenever it was done.

the Corinthians) the disciples at Tyre (Ac. 21.4), the Thessalonians (1 Th. 5.19-21), probably the disciples at Ephesus (Ac.19.6), and perhaps Agabus in Ac. 11.28 and Philip's four daughters (Ac. 2.9). Most difficult to classify is Agabus in Ac. 21.10-11, for the passage gives indications of both types.

N. Additional Note on Prophecy in Early Church History

This investigation has already taken us far beyond 1 Corinthians, and we must forego the inclusion of more material from other documents in the early history of the church.[203] But one general comment is in order. If we assume for a moment that this study is correct in seeing two types of NT prophecy, the one thought to have a divine authority of actual words, and the other only thought to have a (divine) authority of general content, it must still be admitted that such a distinction between types of authority is a fine one and one which might easily be blurred or forgotten. It would eventually be very easy for more and more Christian prophets, whether for good or ill motives, to begin to claim not only that they had received a "revelation" from God or Christ, but also that they spoke with a divine authority of actual words. This was in fact apparently what happened, at least in Montanism and probably in many other cases as well.[204] Of course, if these prophets began to promote heretical ideas, the reaction of the rest of the church would eventually be to drive them out altogether: someone who claims absolute divine authority would eventually be accepted or rejected; he could not be merely tolerated. But along with this rejection of prophets who misunderstood their status there

---

[203]C. Friedrich, TDNT VI, 859f; Cothenet, DBS 8, cols. 1331-36; von Campenhausen, Ecclesiastical Authority, 178-212; J. Reiling, Hermas and Christian Prophecy (Leiden, 1973).

[204]Cf. e.g., Od. Sol. 6.1-2, 8.8-19, 10.4-6, 42.6; perhaps Barn. 16.10, Ign. Phld. 7.1.

was also a rejection of prophecy altogether,[205] so that a failure on the part of the church itself to distinguish between these two types of prophecy might have been the cause of a total loss of prophecy in the church. This explanation is of course speculative, but I offer it here as a suggestion for further research.

VIII. SUMMARY OF CHAPTER ONE

The chapter begins by distinguishing different senses of the phrase "divine authority": the authority may be claimed by someone, or the claim may be evaluated as valid by someone else. Also, someone may claim a divine authority for the actual words he is speaking, or merely for the general content or main idea of his message. Examples of a claim to "divine authority of actual words" were found in the OT; examples of a lesser claim to a "divine authority of general content" were found in extra-Biblical Jewish literature. The Hebrew and Greek words for "prophet," prophecy, etc., were found to have a range of meaning broad enough to allow them to be used of both kinds of speech, that which claimed a divine authority of actual words and that which only claimed a divine authority of general content. The NT apostles are seen as close counterparts to the OT prophets in that they are viewed as messengers of the risen Christ who speak with a divine authority of actual words. They may occasionally be called "prophets" in order to emphasize their role in receiving and reporting revelations, but this is not their usual designation because the term "prophet" was too general to imply unambiguously the status of divinely authoritative messenger.

In 1 Corinthians, five different brief passages are found to indicate that, in Paul's view, Corinthian prophecy only possessed a divine authority of general content. This secondary type of prophecy also seems to have been found at Tyre (Ac. 21.4), Thessalonica (1 Th. 5.19-21), Ephesus (Ac. 19.6), and

---

[205] von Campenhausen, _Ecclesiastical Authority_, 191, observes, "In vain did Irenaeus warn his contemporaries against driving the true prophecy out of the church over concern for the false." Friedrich says, "With the repudiation of Montanism prophecy came to an end in the church," (TDNT VI, 860).

perhaps in other places (Ac. 11.28, 21.9, 21.10-11 [?]).
The primary type of prophecy, that which claimed a
divine authority of actual words, seems to be indicated in Mt. 10.19-20 (and parallels), Eph. 2.20 and
3.5, Revelation, Did. 11.7, and perhaps in other
places (Ac. 13.2, 21.10-11 [?]).

CHAPTER TWO

THE PSYCHOLOGICAL STATE OF THE PROPHET

In Chapter 1 we were concerned with the words spoken by a prophet. Now we must inquire into the source of a prophet's words. How does a prophet know what to say? What does he think or feel before and during the time that he speaks? Is he fully in control of himself or does he experience moments of near-ecstasy?

The important distinction which we discovered between the type of authority claimed for many OT prophets and the prophets at Corinth should warn us against too facile a jump from a description of the psychological state of the OT prophets to that of the NT prophets. Our primary source of information must be the text of 1 Corinthians itself. In this and the following chapters, therefore, I have focused most of my attention on 1 Corinthians, and then briefly on the rest of the NT, and have only brought in OT or extra-Biblical materials where they were especially relevant.

I. 1 CORINTHIANS 14.30: THE RELATIONSHIP BETWEEN PROPHECY AND "REVELATION"

A. The Situation

Paul begins his specific regulation of prophetic speech in the church meeting by saying, "Let two or three prophets speak, and let the others weigh what is said" (1 Cor. 14.29). Then, to insure against disorder, he continues, "If a revelation is made to another who is seated, let the first be silent. For you are all able to prophesy one by one . . ." (ἐὰν δὲ ἄλλῳ ἀποκαλυφθῇ καθημένῳ, ὁ πρῶτος σιγάτω. δύνασθε γὰρ καθ'ἕνα πάντες προφητεύειν . . . 1 Cor. 14.30-31). Apparently the first prophet (ὁ πρῶτος) was standing while he spoke (a common practice: cf. Lk. 4.16, Ac. 1.15, 5.34, 11.28, 13.16) and the rest of the congregation was sitting listening to him (cf. Ac. 20.9, Jas. 2.3). Then suddenly something would be revealed (ἀποκαλυφθῇ) to one of the seated listeners (ἄλλῳ καθημένῳ). He would somehow have to signal this fact to the speaker, perhaps by standing up also. Then the first speaker would be silent (σιγάτω)[1] and allow the second to speak his prophecy.

B. An Analysis of the "Revelation" to the Prophet

This glimpse of the procedure to be followed by prophets at Corinth allows us to make several observations about the psychological state of the prophet and the "revelation" which is said to come to him.[2]

---

[1] Robertson and Plummer observe, "The Apostle does not say σιγησάτω, 'let him at once be silent,' but σιγάτω, which need not mean that." Although such a distinction between aorist and present imperatives cannot always be relied upon (cf. Moule, pp. 20-21), it is interesting to note the aorist subjunctive of σιγάω in Lk.18.39 (ἵνα σιγήσῃ) with the nuance, "be silent at once," and the present imperatives of σιγάω in Am. 6.10 and Tob. 10.6, 7 with the meaning, "be silent and continue to be silent; do not speak any more." The present imperatives in 1 Cor. 14.28 and 34 also refer to continual silence (although in these verses and in vs. 30 the silence is of course not a permanent one). These examples make it probable that Paul does not envisage a resumption of speech by the first prophet.

[2] My argument in this section depends both on the specific evidence in the context of 1 Cor. 14.30 and on an analysis of the use of the terms ἀποκαλύπτω and ἀποκάλυψις in contrast to other terms related to the concept "revelation" throughout the NT. James Barr, "Revelation," (Hastings's) Dictionary of the Bible, (Edinburgh, 1963[2]), 849, includes the very diverse LXX uses of these terms, and concludes that "it is doubtful whether we can identify any 'Biblical concept of revelation' with which all cases would fit." Yet he admits that the NT usage is "more specialized in a theological direction" (p. 848). In fact, we find that these terms have become very specialized and restricted in the NT, so that their precise connotations can be determined with a reasonable degree of accuracy. The NT meaning is paralleled in the LXX when ἀποκαλύπτω appears in religious contexts (e.g., Is. 56.1, Am. 3.7), but the term also has a much broader use in the LXX.

1. Spontaneity

The thought that occurs to a prophet is pictured as coming to him quite spontaneously, for it comes while the first speaker is talking. (Furthermore, Paul's use of the aorist subjunctive ἀποκαλυφθῇ would normally imply an action viewed as a single event.) So this prophecy does not seem to be a sermon or lesson which had been prepared beforehand; it is much more spontaneous than that.

2. Individuality

This "revelation" is something that is seen as coming to an individual person (note the singular ἄλλῳ καθημένῳ), not to the entire congregation. Had Paul meant to speak of a public "revelation" of some fact or event, he would probably have used φανερόω, which in the NT always refers to an external, public

---

A study of the specifically Biblical usage of ἀποκαλύπτω and ἀποκάλυψις is especially important because, "When the Greek feels the need to speak of something analogous to revelation, he selects other terms. Our words are rare, and outside the Bible their theological usage dates only from a later period" (A. Oepke, TDNT III, 570).
Twentieth-century theologians have frequently claimed that the Bible presents "revelation" as occurring in historical events but not taking the form of "propositions." (So Alan Richardson, "Revelation," A Dictionary of Christian Theology (London, 1969), 294f; John Baillie, The Idea of Revelation in Recent Thought (New York, 1956), esp. pp. 27-40, 62-82; A. Oepke, TDNT III, p. 591.) Against this view see James Barr, "Revelation," HDB[2], 847ff ("All the Biblical evidence is for revelation as special and particular, with its own content of communication in each situation," p, 849); idem, "Revelation Through History," 193ff, where he defends the idea of "direct verbal communication between God and particular men on particular occasions" (p. 201). For a more philosophical analysis, see Paul Helm, "Religious Propositions and Timeless Truths," Relig. St. 8 (1972), 127ff.
Of course, "events" and "propositions" are not the only possibilities: one could also think of visions, dreams and perhaps vague feelings about some things.

disclosure or manifestation.³ Ἀποκαλύπτω, however, is often used to speak of a private, individual transmission of information which comes about through the working of God in a person's mind or heart (Mt. 11.25, 27, 16.17, Lk. 10.21, 22, Eph. 3.5; probably 1 Cor. 2.10, Phil. 3.15, 1 Pet. 1.12).⁴ Thus the prophecy seems to be not simply a comment on some new fact which had just been disclosed by the first speaker, but is rather thought by Paul to be based on something which has come privately to the mind of the second prophet, without the rest of the congregation having been aware of it.

3. Origin

The "revelation" which comes to the prophet is thought by Paul to be of <u>divine, not human origin</u>.⁵

---

³In the NT φανερόω (49X) and φανερός (18X) are never used of secret or private communication of information. The "manifestation" is always public, something to be seen and known by all observers (cf. Ac. 4. 16, Mt. 6.14, Phil. 1.13, 1 Tim. 4.15; Jn. 3.21, Rom. 1.19, Eph. 5.13, 1 Pet. 5.4). These words are never used of the internal working of God in a person's mind or heart. Cf. Burton, <u>Galatians</u>, 433ff. (The only possible exception is Mt. 1.20, but even here, within the context of the dream, the manifestation is external to Joseph and thereby "public"; it is not [in the dream] seen merely as an idea in his mind.)

D. Lührmann, <u>Das Offenbarungsverständis bei Paulus und in paulinischen Gemeinden</u> (Neukirchen-Vluyn, 1965), 38, fails to distinguish ἀποκαλύπτω from φανερόω and so wrongly sees 1 Cor. 14.30 as a reference to all gifts, after the pattern of 12.7.

⁴Ἀποκάλυψις is also used in this way: 2 Cor. 12.1, 7, 1 Cor. 14.26, Eph. 3.3; probably Gal. 2.2 Before the Parousia, the only clearly public "revelations" referred to in the NT with the terms ἀποκαλύπτω or ἀποκάλυψις are the revelation of the wrath of God from heaven (Rom. 1.18) and the revelations given by the basic Gospel message (Lk. 2.32, Rom. 1.17, Gal. 3. 23). After the Parousia, everything is "revealed" publicly (Lk. 17.30, Rom. 8.18-19, 1 Cor. 3.13, etc.).

⁵J. Lindblom, <u>Prophecy</u>, recognizes that prophets themselves speak of prophetic inspiration in terms of

this is evident from both the use of the term ἀποκαλύπτω and from the context.

a. The use of ἀποκαηύπτω

'Αποκαλύπτω occurs 26 times in the NT, and ἀποκάλυψις 18 times, and neither one is ever used of human activity or communication.[6] The "revelation" is always given by the activity of God (Mt. 11.25, 16.17, Gal. 1.16, Phil. 3.5), of Christ (Mt. 11.27, Gal. 1. 12), or of the Holy Spirit (1 Cor. 2.10, Eph. 3.5), or is a result of events brought about directly by them (especially the Parousia: Rom. 2.5, 8.9, 1 Cor. 1.7, 1 Pet. 1.7, etc.).[7]

---

its divine origin, but that the same experience might be described quite differently, without reference to any divine influence, in the technical language of psychology: "Certain ideas, images, emotions, impulses from the subconscious, subliminal, unconscious, co-conscious self (whichever term may be used) arise in the mind so spontaneously and so independently of reflection and meditation, that the inspired person feels as though his ideas were coming not from himself, but from another realm, and are given him by a power other than himself" (p. 34). Paul, of course, does not hesitate to speak of divine influence on the prophet, and neither does the OT. (For the OT, see pp. 11ff and n. 50 below.)

Such divine origin is also assumed in the Rabbinic literature: in M. Sanh. 11.5, the false prophet is "he that prophesies what he has not heard and what has not been told him." For similar material on Moses and the OT prophets, see b. Sanh. 99a, b. B.B. 15a, Ex.R. 28.6; however, see also b. Meg. 31b and Ex.R. 47.9 on Moses' own contributions to the Torah.

[6]The NT writers (and especially Paul) generally use γνωρίζω to speak of human activity in making something known (1 Cor. 12.3, 15.1, 2 Cor. 8.1, Gal. 1.11, etc.).

[7]Cf. 1 Cor. 2.8-9 and 10 where human means of gaining knowledge are contrasted with revelation from God.

b. 1 Cor. 14.32: The Spirits of the Prophets

Paul's method of argument in 1 Cor. 14.29-33 also shows that he has in mind a "revelation" which is divine in origin, and specifically one which comes from the Holy Spirit. In order to demonstrate this, it is necessary first to determine the meaning of πνεύματα προφητῶν προφήταις ὑποτάσσεται in vs. 32.

We shall examine three possible interpretations.

An unusual view is that of E. Ellis, who thinks these πνεύματα are angelic spirits.[8] The use of πνεύματα in relation to angels is found in the NT (Heb. 1.7 and 14, based on Ps. 104.4), but such a use is extremely rare, and never occurs in Paul.[9] Indeed, it would be totally out of place for Paul, who has been talking about the Holy Spirit and his gifts throughout 1 Cor. (12.3, 4, 7, 8, 9, 11, 13) to switch and mean "angelic spirits" here, with no indication to the reader. The Corinthians would never have understood that.[10]

---

[8] E. Earle Ellis, "Christ and Spirit in 1 Corinthians," CSNT, 275f.

[9] Even Heb. 1.7 and 14 are not instances where πνεῦμα means "angel." Πνεῦμα there simply means "non-physical being" (cf. Lk. 24.37, 39, Ac. 23.8, Mt. 12.43, etc.) or perhaps, in vs. 7, "wind" (cf. Jn. 3.8). So there is no NT instance where πνεύματα without further contextual qualification would be taken to mean "angels," and thus no NT precedent for Ellis's unusual proposal.

[10] Ellis has further arguments (pp. 275f):
(1) "Angelic mediation of Yahweh's word was a recognized form of prophetic experience." The only support he gives is 1 Kgs. 13.18. But this is a testimony of a false prophet, and a lie at that (cf. the false prophecy inspired by (presumably) an evil spirit, 1 Kgs. 22.20-23, and Paul's warning in Gal. 1.8).
(2) "Prophets were included in heavenly (angelic) councils." But the context of every example he quotes disproves his case, showing that God, not angels, inspires true prophets (1 Kgs. 22.19, 28, Isa. 6.9; Jer. 23.18: "to perceive and hear his word").

(3) The prophets "were conducted by interpreting angels and guarded by angelic armies." This is sometimes the case, but that says nothing about the inspiration of prophets, which is everywhere in the OT seen to be from God or from his Spirit.

(4) The Qumran material gives evidence, as follows:
    (a) Angels are often called "spirits."
    (b) "Spirits" have a special relationship to the wise" (משכילים) at Qumran.
    (c) "The wise" have a striking resemblance to Pauline pneumatics.
    (d) Therefore, there is a possible parallel between the angelic "spirits" at Qumran and πνεύματα in 1 Cor. 14.32.

Here Ellis's argument is admittedly indirect. The texts he quotes (such as 1 QS 4.21f, 1 QH 12.11f, 2.13f, 1 QS 3.13f, 9.14, 17) do speak of good and evil spirits working in the hearts of men, and of men who know God and his wisdom by "Thy Holy Spirit." But we find in these references no mention of inspired or prophetic speech, and no statement about angelic inspiration of prophetic speech.

(5) Paul associates angels with prophets and spiritual gifts in 1 Cor. 13.1 and 11.4, 10. But if "tongues of angels" in 13.1 implies inspiration by angels, then "tongues of men" in the same phrase must imply inspiration by (presumably) foreign men, clearly an impossible suggestion. 11.4 does not mention angels, and the obscure διὰ τοὺς ἀγγέλους in 11.10 with reference to veils as a symbol of authority can hardly be taken to prove angelic inspiration of prophecy.

(6) Other NT references associate angelic (and demonic) spirits with prophecy and spiritual gifts. Examining these references we find that Rev. 12.10, 10.9-10, and 22.6 do indeed describe angelic voices in heaven which are heard by John and which sometimes tell him what to write. This is as close as we can come to a reference to angelic "inspiration," but there remains an important distinction. This purports to be communication coming to the prophet from without; that is, John speaks of himself as being able to see and talk with the angel (19.9-10). One might call these examples of externally perceived "auditions," and they are set in the context of a translation to heaven. In fact, angelic intermediaries are not uncommon in apocalyptic revelations. But this is still somewhat different from the picture in 1 Cor. 14.29-33, where a prophet sitting in the midst of the congregation suddenly has something revealed to him. In such

A second possible interpretation is to regard πνεύματα as a reference to the individual human spirits of the prophets.[11] Four considerations might be adduced in favor of this position:

(i) The plural form πνεύματα cannot refer to the Holy Spirit, for there is only one Holy Spirit (1 Cor. 12.4, 9, 11, 13). But πνεῦμα is often used in the NT to refer to the individual spirit of a man (in 1 Cor. alone: 2.11, 5.3, 4, 7.34, 16.18), and we might expect the same meaning in 1 Cor. 14.32.

(ii) The OT speaks of God as "the God of the spirits of all flesh" (אֱלֹהֵי הָרוּחֹת לְכָל בָּשָׂר), Num. 16.22,

---

a case, it is very unlikely that Paul thinks the prophet would imagine himself to be in heaven, talking with angels (and that in every case, if 14.32 be understood as a general statement applicable to all who prophesied at Corinth). Much more likely is the idea that Paul pictured the prophet as suddenly preceiving an "inspiration" which he thought of as a rather quiet activity of the Holy Spirit working in his own mind.
1 Jn. 4.1-3 does speak of judging prophetic "spirits," but to assume (with regard to true prophecy) that this means angels is to beg the question.
In a subsequent article, "'Spiritual' Gifts in the Pauline Community" (NTS 20 [1973-74], 134-144), Ellis buttresses his arguments with more evidence of the same type. He includes a longer discussion of the multiplicity of evil spirits which inspire false prophecy, but that is an obvious fact which does not affect the clear Biblical opposition between the one true Spirit of prophecy and the many evil spirits associated with false prophecy.
So my objections to Ellis are primarily two: (a) Within the NT, there is no unambiguous instance where πνεύματα without further specific qualification from context must refer to angels; this simply was not a term which the NT writers commonly applied to angels. (b) Outside the NT, Ellis has not found even one instance of true prophetic speech which is ever said to be inspired by angels (and there is of course no clear case of this in the NT). Ellis has made an interesting suggestion, but I do not find it convincing. (Cf. Dunn, JS, 419, n. 170).

[11]So Meyer, 332; Lenski, 613; Bruce, "The Spirit in the Apocalypse," CSNT, 339.

27.16), and this may be echoed in Rev. 22.6, "the God of the spirits of the prophets" (ὁ Θεὸς τῶν πνευμάτων τῶν προφητῶν). So John equates the spirits of the prophets with human spirits.

(iii) In 1 Cor. 14.14 Paul says, "If I pray in a tongue, my spirit prays but my mind is unfruitful." Here, τὸ πνεῦμά μου might be understood to refer to Paul's own spirit,[12] as the parallel with "my mind" (ὁ νοῦς μου) suggests.

(iv) If Paul had meant πνεύματα as a reference to the Holy Spirit in 1 Cor. 14.32, it would have been inconsistent with the rest of his theology. For how could he say that the Holy Spirit is subject to men? Therefore, Paul must be speaking of a prophet's own human spirit, which he is able to control.

These four arguments fail to be convincing for the following reasons:

(i) It is true that Paul would not have used πνεύματα to refer to a multiplicity of "Holy Spirits." But to make this a reference to human spirits is not the only other option. As the one Holy Spirit dwells in various individuals (1 Cor. 12.8-11), it would have been possible for Paul to use πνεύματα to refer to the many different manifestations of the Holy Spirit present in different individuals. 1 Cor. 14.12, "Since you are zealous for spirits" (ἐπεὶ ζηλωταί ἐστε πνευμάτων), is probably to be understood this way. (Cf. RSV: "Since you are eager for manisfestations of the Spirit.") There is a similar willingness to talk about both the one Spirit of God and his plural manifestations in 1 Jn. 4.2: "By this you know the Spirit of God: every spirit which confesses that Jesus Christ has come in the flesh is of God."[13]

---

[12] See below, pp. 124f, for a discussion of the view that τὸ πωεῦμά μου means "my share of the apportioned Spirit of God."

[13] So in 1 Jn. 4.3-4, John can speak of "every spirit which does not confess Jesus," then say, "This is the spirit of antichrist of which you heard that it was coming," and then, "You are of God and have overcome them." Cf. 2 Th. 2.2, where πνεῦμα means "communication (and thus, more generally, 'manifestation') of the Spirit"; also perhaps 1 Cor. 12.10, 1 Jn. 4.1.

(ii) It is unlikely that Rev. 22.6 has Num. 16.22 and 27.16 in view. For one thing, the LXX has a completely different meaning, "the God of spirits and of all flesh" (ὁ θεὸς τῶν πνευμάτων καὶ πάσης σαρκός). Then also, John might well have hesitated to speak of human spirits of prophets in light of Ezk. 13.3, which defines false (foolish) prophets as "those who follow their own spirit."[14]

(iii) One cannot automatically assume in 1 Cor. 14.14 that τὸ πνεῦμά μου speaks of Paul's own human spirit. Robert Jewett argues that Paul is speaking here of the "apportioned spirit of God," and that "he speaks of the πνεῦμα in typical enthusiastic fashion as having entered his possesion."[15] If this

---

When Paul speaks of human spirits, he can also show unusual variation in the use of singular and plural, using the singular for a multiplicity of spirits in Gal. 6.18: Ἡ χάρις τοῦ κυρίου ἡμῶν Ἰησοῦ Χριστοῦ μετὰ τοῦ πνεύματος ὑμῶν, ἀδελφοί (so also Phil. 4.23; cf. Phlm. 25, 2 Tim. 4.22).

In the light of such wide variation with this word, we cannot put too much emphasis on the use of the plural πνεύματα in 1 Cor. 14.32.

Cf. also Zech. 6.5, where the angel says of the chariots, אֵלֶּה אַרְבַּע רוּחוֹת הַשָּׁמַיִם יוֹצְאוֹת מֵהִתְיַצֵּב עַל--אֲדוֹן כָּל--הָאָרֶץ, "These are the four spirits of heaven, going forth from standing before the Lord of all the earth." Although the LXX translates רוּחוֹת as ἄνεμοι "winds," the personal activity ascribed to them (vss. 6-8) and the fact that they depart from the Lord's presence to do his bidding (vss. 5, 7) argue for interpreting רוּחוֹת as "spirits," that is, as various manifestations of the Spirit of God (or perhaps as angels, as in Ps. 104.4, but this is made less likely by the specification of four only, and by the fact that רוּחַ without further specification would not normally be understood to mean "angel").

[14] This is especially relevant because of the heavy dependence on Ezekiel shown by the author of Revelation. (The LXX renders רוּחָם in Ezk. 13.3 as καρδίας αὐτῶν).

[15] Robert Jewett, *Paul's Anthropological Terms* (Leiden, 1971), 190-92. Jewett refers in this passage to Weiss, 327f.

interpretation be accepted. then 1 Cor. 14.14 cannot be used as evidence that vs. 32 refers to the human spirits of the prophets.

But even if someone did not accept Jewett's view, and in fact held that 1 Cor. 14.14 spoke of Paul's own human spirit, this verse would still be inadequate evidence with which to argue for "human spirits" in vs. 32. For if vs. 14 be thought to speak of Paul's own human spirit, vss. 2-3 would still explain how that situation differed from prophecy. "One who speaks in a tongue speaks not to men but to God" (vs. 2). In this case, the speech in tongues is a prayer, and it therefore can be seen to originate with man, with his own spirit.[16] The role of the Holy Spirit in this case is to give verbal expression to the emotions of the man's heart as he prays. But the situation is the opposite with prophecy: "On the other hand, he who prophesies speaks to men for their upbuilding . . ." vs. 3). Here the communication is from God to men, through the prophet. So the prophecy must have its origin with God. So on this view vs. 14, far from proving that πνεύματα in vs. 32 means human spirits, would provide a contrasting situation whereby we could still understand vs. 32 to refer to a working of the Holy Spirit.

(iv) To speak of the Holy Spirit as he works in a believer's life as being subject (ὑποτάσσεται) to the believer is not inconsistent with Pauline theology. Ὑποτάσσω is often used of voluntary submission which is not the necessary result of inferior power (Lk. 2.51 of Jesus to his parents, 1 Pet. 5.5 of the younger to the elder, 1 Cor. 15.28 of the Son to the Father). In fact, the word is most frequently used of a submission by choice, in order to make effective a pattern of order which God has established (Rom. 13.1, 1 Cor. 16.16, Eph. 5.21, 22, Tit. 2.9).[17] So also

---

[16] On this view, it would still be possible to think that Paul understands tongues as also having a God-to-man function (cf. vs. 5, "unless someone interprets"). But vs. 14, on this view, would clearly portray man-to-God communication ("my spirit prays").

[17] Thus ὑποτάσσεται is better understood as a middle ("spirits of prophets subject themselves to prophets"). In English, "spirits of prophets are made subject to prophets" conveys the voluntary aspect of

here, Paul is showing that the Holy Spirit will not force a prophet to speak, but allows the prophet himself to determine when he should speak. This is a voluntary submission in one particular function for the sake of order, and implies no theological statement about man as somehow superior to the Holy Spirit. So all four of the possible arguments in favor of the second interpretation are seen to be inconclusive.

The third possible interpretation is to understand πνεύματα as a reference to the workings of the Holy Spirit in various prophets.[18] Similar references are found in 1 Cor. 14.12 and 1 Jn. 4.2, which have been discussed above.[19] In addition to the reasons given above under the discussion of the other two interpretations, there are some contextual considerations which make this third interpretation virtually certain.

(i) Vs. 33, "For God is not (a God) of confusion but of peace," is the reason Paul gives to ground vss. 31-32 (cf. γάρ, vs. 33). Now this verse speaks about the character of God. As such, it makes very good sense if vs. 32 is describing the activities of the Holy Spirit. Paul would reason: the Holy Spirit will subject his inspiration to the prophet's own timing, and thus will never force a prophet to speak out of turn, because it is not in the nature of God to inspire confusion; it would contradict his own character. If, on the other hand vs. 32 is a reference to human spirits, it is hard to see how the description of God's character in vs. 33 could serve as the ground for vs. 32: a statement about God's character would

---

the middle voice well enough, while preserving the continual aspect of the present tense.

[18] Related to this view is the argument of Jewett that Paul can use πνεῦμα to mean "the apportioned spirit of God" (Paul's Anthropological Terms, 175-200). (Jewett does not apply this concept to 1 Cor. 14.32, however.)

[19] The ἑπτὰ πνεύματα τοῦ θεοῦ in Rev. 3.1, 4.5 and 5.6 (cf. 1.4) may also be a symbol for the various manifestations of the Holy Spirit, but it is also possible that πνεύματα here simply means "non-physical beings" (cf. Rev. 8.2).

not allow Paul to draw conclusions about the actual behavior of men.[20]

(ii) If we borrow a preliminary conclusion from the earlier part of this argument, we notice that ἀποκαλυφθῇ in vs. 30 carries the idea of divine activity in revelation. It could rightly be paraphrased, "If God reveals something to another who is seated, let the first be silent." So if vs. 32 is a reference to the working of the Holy Spirit, it continues to talk about the divine source of revelation and is totally consistent with Paul's train of thought.

(iii) It is understandable why Paul used πνεύματα here instead of τὸ πνεῦμα τὸ ἅγιον: it would have been misleading for Paul to say "the Holy Spirit is subject to prophets," for that is not true as a general statement, but only in the issue of deciding when a prophet should speak. Πνεύματα fits Paul's purposes better, since it has a more limited reference to the Spirit's specific manifestations.

(iv) As a fourth argument for this interpretation, and also by way of summary, it is now possible to

---

[20] It would be possible to avoid the force of this argument if one said that vs. 33 is not the ground for vs. 32, but rather for vs. 30. Thus, Paul would be saying that the first speaker should be silent (vs. 30) because God is not a God of confusion (vs. 33). Though it is not a false line of reasoning, I do not believe it is the one the apostle had in mind at this point (1) because it requires the insertion of an additional idea which is not expressed in this text, namely, that the Corinthian prophets should imitate God's character; (2) because the idea of imitating God's character, though certainly not foreign to Paul, is foreign to this paragraph (here, Paul is arguing for edification (vs. 26) and vs. 31 admirably fits his purpose as a ground for vs. 30, whereas to use vs. 33 as a ground for vs. 30 would introduce a new kind of reasoning); (3) because vs. 33 is so far removed from vs. 30 that some compelling reason is required before one can say that it does not ground vs. 32, which is so near at hand; and (4) because vss. 31 and 32 already provide two grounds for vs. 30 and are rightly connected by καί (vs. 32), so that vs. 33 would also have to be connected by καί to provide a third ground for vs. 30.

suggest the purpose vs. 32 has in its context. Vs. 30 gave a rule for the regulation of prophecy: if one person is prophesying, and then another receives a revelation, the first should be silent. Then Paul proceeds to give two reasons for this rule, vss. 31 and 32. That they are coordinate and both to be understood as reasons for vs. 30 is seen from the καί connecting them and from the way in which the two main verbs in the indicative (δύνασθε and ὑποτάσσεται) which open and close the sentence set themselves in marked contrast to the string of imperatival main clauses by which they are surrounded (γινέσθω, vs. 26; διερμηνευέτω, vs. 27; σιγάτω, λαλείτω, vs. 28; λαλείτωσαν, vs. διακρινέτωσαν, vs. 29; σιγάτω, vs. 30; σιγάτωσαν, ὑποτασσέσθωσαν, vs. 34, etc.).

There are two possible objections to Paul's rule in vs. 30 which would require vs. 32 as an answer. First, someone might argue that he was forced to prophesy. When the Holy Spirit came upon him with a revelation, he simply could not restrain himself. He had to speak. Paul's answer is that the Holy Spirit remains subject to the prophets; he will never force a prophet to speak. Second, someone might object that he could not wait his turn to speak; if he did, the message might be irrevocably lost. To this vs. 32 replies that the Holy Spirit is not so impetuous and uncontrollable as that. He is subject to the wise timing and oversight of the prophets.

The best solution, then, is to say that "spirits of prophets" in vs. 32 means "manifestations of the Holy Spirit at work in prophets,"[21]

If this is the proper understanding of vs. 32, and if the καί indicates that it is coordinate with vs. 31 as a ground for vs. 30, then we can paraphrase: "If a revelation is made to another sitting by, let the first be silent, for . . . the Holy Spirit working in the prophets subjects himself to the prophets, for God is not a God of confusion but of peace." So Paul is arguing that the first prophet should be silent because the Holy Spirit will not force him to continue

---

[21] RP, 323, Ellicott, 281; Godet, 307; Barrett, 329; Hodge, 170; Goudge, 131; Wendland, 115; Chrysostom, 219, Schlatter, 385. Also Greven, "Propheten," 12f, but with προφήταις referring to other prophets who want to speak, a view disproven by RP, 323.

speaking. This again assumes that the "revelation" which comes to the prophet comes from the Holy Spirit, and comes so directly that the manner in which it comes reflects both the character of God (οὐ . . . ἀκαταστασίας . . . ἀλλὰ εἰρήνης) and the personal volition of the Holy Spirit (ὑποτάσσεται).

4. Perspective

The "revelation" would enable the prophet to know something from a <u>divine or heavenly perspective</u>.[22] This observation is important for distinguishing NT prophecy from pagan fortune-telling or soothsaying, in which a person may have had special knowledge of hidden facts, but always used it for personal benefit or in the service of false religion (cf. Ac. 8.6ff, 16.16ff). The NT authors do not use ἀποκαλύπτω and ἀποκάλυψις in describing these pagan practices, but Luke in particular finds other terms: μαντεύομαι (only at Ac. 16.16,[23] πύθων (only at Ac. 16.16), μάγος (Ac. 13.6, 8), μαγεύω (only at Ac. 8.9), μαγεία (only at Ac. 8.11), περίεργος (Ac. 19.19). On the other hand, wherever ἀποκαλύπτω and ἀποκάλυψις are used in the NT, there is a definite eschatological emphasis: to "reveal" something is to make it known in the way in which it will be known in the consummation. This explains the frequent use of ἀποκαλύπτω in discussions of events of the Parousia. There, things which are now hidden from men's eyes will be clearly disclosed: Christ himself (Lk. 17.30), the true quality of men's works (1 Cor. 3.13), God's judgment (Rom. 2.5), everything (Mt. 10.26). But before Christ's return, ἀποκαλύπτω is used to refer to glimpses of things as they will then be seen. To have a "revelation" in this age is to be given a bit of the vision or knowledge which is appropriate to the age to come: it may

---

[22] This can be seen as a result of observation (3) above: since it is God who gives the "revelation," it is from his perspective that he causes the information to be seen.

[23] In the LXX μαντεία (14X), μαντεῖον (3X), μαντεύεσθαι (12X) and μάντις (5X) are all but once (Prov. 16.10) used only of pagan divination or to refer to evil or false prophets (Dt. 18.10, 14, 4 Kgs. 17.17, etc.). In Philo, <u>Spec. Leg.</u> 1.60, Moses forbids all different types of μαντική, "divination."

be called "kingdom-knowledge" or a "kingdom-perspective."

Thus, in contrast with "the wisdom of this age" (1 Cor. 2.6), Paul can speak of a glimpse of the age to come: "What no eye has seen, nor ear heard, nor the heart of man conceived, what God has prepared for those who love him, God has revealed (ἀπεκάλυψεν) to us through the Spirit" (1 Cor. 2.9-10). Paul himself claimed to have experienced an extended period of kingdom-vision. He was "caught up to the third heaven . . . into Paradise " and thereby experienced an "abundance of revelations" (2 Cor. 12.2, 3, 7). Of course, in Paul's thought the participation of believers in "the age to come" is not entirely in the chronological future.[24] So if we understand ἀποκαλύπτω to refer to kingdom-knowledge, we need not restrict it to knowledge of things in the future or of things in heaven. If one comes to know something in the way in which it will be known in the consummation, that is, from the perspective of the age to come, that could also be called an ἀποκάλυψις. Thus, if a believer's sinful disposition is made clear to him, he has come to see it from a kingdom-perspective; it has been "revealed" to him (Phil. 3.15). When Peter comes to understand who Jesus really is, he comes to see him in kingdom-perspective: this has been "revealed" to him (Mt. 16.17).

And so any time someone has an insight into God's plan of redemption through Christ, he abandons his old perspective, the perspective of this age which views God's plan as foolishness (1 Cor. 1.18, 20, 2.6-8). He comes to understand God's plan and Christ's work from the perspective of the age to come, and this can be called a "revelation" (Mt. 11.25, Rom. 1.17, Gal. 3.23 of initial faith; Eph. 3.3, 5, Gal. 1.12 of Paul's insight into God's plan; 1 Pet. 1.12 of the understanding given to OT prophets; Eph. 1.17 of growth in understanding in the life of a believer).

---

[24]Cf. Hermann Sasse, "αἰών, αἰώνιος," TDNT I, esp. 204-07. 1 Cor. 13.12, τότε δὲ ἐπιγνώσομαι καθὼς καὶ ἐπεγνώσθην, allows us to compare the kind of knowledge Paul thought he would have in the consummation with the kind of knowledge God has now. Thus, we can call this kind of knowledge either a "consummation perspective" or a "kingdom perspective" or a "divine perspective."

This uniformity in the NT use of ἀποκαλύπτω allows us to suppose with a fair degree of certainty that the prophets of whom Paul spoke in 1 Cor. 14:30 did not simply engage in fortune-telling and divination, announcing unrelated hidden facts to satisfy curiosity or avarice, knowing something only from the perspective of this age.[25] Rather, the "revelations" they were given enabled them to see facts in relation to God's purposes, and to report that information in such a way that the church might be built up, encouraged and consoled (1 Cor. 14.3).

5. Perceptibility

Our final observation concerns the force with which the "revelation" came to a prophet. It is possible to make two tentative statements. First, Paul seems to think of this revelation as a momentary and quite recognizable occurrence, for it happens spontaneously and with such force that it justifies the interruption of a man who is already speaking (1 Cor. 14.30). In fact, it sometimes came so forcefully that the Corinthians were in danger of thinking they could not resist the Holy Spirit; Paul had to reassure them that the Spirit subjects himself to them in this matter (14.32).

On the other hand, there are terms besides ἀποκαλύπτω and ἀποκάλυψις which the NT authors prefer when speaking of very direct or spectacular examples of "revelation."[26] χρηματίζω is used to refer to God's audible voice (Heb. 8.5 [burning bush], 11.7 [Noah], 12.25 [Sinai]; cf. χρηματισμός in Rom. 11.4 [Elijah]) or a speech from God or an angel in a dream

---

[25]Modern examples of phenomena which would not have been termed ἀποκαλύψεις by the NT authors include ESP, astrology, and various other occult practices, in so far as they claim to divulge hidden or future facts but do so without placing these facts in the perspective of the age to come; that is, without seeing them from the theological focus of the NT, but seeing them only from the perspective of this world, as isolated facts, unrelated to God and his purposes.

[26]Lindblom, Prophecy, 122-148 and 173-182 describes many different types of visions, auditions, etc., and distinguishes varieties of the "revelatory state of mind."

(Mt. 2.12, 22, Ac. 10.22).²⁷ Dreams themselves are referred to with the terms ὄναρ (only at Mt. 1.20, 2.12, 13, 19, 22, 27.19, always of "supernatural" communication), ἐνύπνιον and ἐνυπνιάζω (Ac. 2.17 and Jude 8), while a vision is a ὅραμα (Mt. 17.9 of the Transfiguration, and 11X in Acts, always of events which include communication from God or an angel: 7.31, 9.10, 12, 10.3. 17, 19, 11.5, 12.9, 16.9, 10, 18.9), a ὅρασις (Ac. 2.17 in this sense), or an ὀπτασία (only at Lk. 1.22, 24.23, Ac. 26.19, 2 Cor. 12.1, always including communication from God or an angel). In fact, communication from angels to men is quite frequent in the NT: excluding Revelation, there are 14 incidents of communication from an angel to men recorded in 19 places in the NT.²⁸ There are also five instances of a voice from heaven, a bath qol, which are reported in 13 places in the NT.²⁹ Finally, the term ἔκστασις sometimes refers to a "trance" in which God speaks to men (Peter in Ac. 10.10, 11.5; Paul in Ac. 22.17).³⁰

---

²⁷In the LXX, χρηματίζω also refers to audible speech, either from God (Jer. 37(30). 2, 43 (36). 2, 32 (25). 30) or a prophet (Jer. 33 (26). 2; false prophet: 36 (29). 23).

²⁸Mt. 1.20ff, 2.13, 2.19f (all Joseph), 28.5ff with Lk. 24.23 (the women at the tomb), Lk. 1.12ff (Zechariah), 1.26ff (Mary), 2.10ff (the shepherds), Jn. 20.13 (Mary Magdalene), Ac. 5.19ff (the apostles in prison), 7.38 with Gal. 3.19 and Heb. 2.2 (Sinai), Ac. 8.26 (Philip), 10.3ff with 10.22 and 11.13f (Cornelius), 12.7ff (Peter in prison), 27.23 (Paul on the ship). In addition, there are three general statements about angelic communication to men: Jn. 12.29, Ac. 23.9, Gal. 1.8.

²⁹Jesus' baptism (Mt. 3.17, Mk. 1.-1, Lk. 3.22), the Transfiguration (Mt. 17.5, Mk. 9.7, Lk. 9.35f, 2 Pet. 1.17f), the voice in Jerusalem (Jn. 12.28), Paul on the Damascus road, (Ac. 9.4ff, 27.7ff, 26.14), Peter and the sheet from heaven (Ac. 10.13ff, 11.7ff). Rev. 1.10 might be counted as a sixth instance, or might be considered part of John's vision.

³⁰The other four NT occurrences of ἔκστασις refer to "amazement, astonishment, fear" aroused by miracles: Mk. 5.42, 16.8, Lk. 5.26, Ac. 3.10.

Ἔκστασις occurs 29X in the LXX (and 13 times more in the versions), and usually means "great fear"

Two surprising facts ·merge from a study of this large number of revelation phenomena. First, these terms and reported incidents are almost never connected with prophecy.[31] In almost every case these more spectacular experiences were for the purpose of giving specific individual instruction to a single person who had a certain role to play in some significant

---

or "amazement" (Num. 13.33 [32], 1 Kgs. [Sam.] 11.7, etc.). Five times it means "deep sleep or trance" [Gen.2.21], 15.12, Th. Job 33.15, Th. 1 Kgs. [Sam.] 26. 12, Symm. and Th. Pr. 19.15, translating תַּרְדֵּמָה in every case). In no case does ἔκστασις refer to ecstatic worship or prophetic experience: in Ps. 30 (31), title, it means "fear" (cf. vs. 22); in Ps. 67 (68). 27 it is a mistranslation (רֹדֵם was thought to be from רָדַם, to sleep deeply, instead of רָדָה, to rule); in Dan. LXX 7.28 it means "fear" (it comes after the vision, not during it); and in Aq., Symm. Hos. 9.7 its significance is unclear but it certainly refers to all the people, not to the prophet.

Ἐξίστημι (17X in NT) usually means "to be amazed or fearful" (Mt. 12.23, Mk. 5.42, etc.). In Mk. 3.21 and 2 Cor. 5.13 it is sometimes taken to mean "to be mad" or even "to be in frenzy or delirium, to be out of control of oneself," but it may simply mean "to speak or act very foolishly, unreasonably" (cf. the contrast with σωφρονέω in 2 Cor. 5.13 and a similar contrast in Ac. 26.25).

Μαίνομαι (only at Jn. 10.20, Ac. 12.15, 26.24, 25, 1 Cor. 14.23; cf. μανία [Ac. 26.24 only]), probably also means "to speak foolishness," for it is always in the NT applied to people who speak perfectly coherent words but with unusual content.

[31]Rev. 1.1ff may be an exception. However, it speaks of the ἀποκάλυψις Ἰησοῦ Χριστοῦ ἣν ἔδωκεν αὐτῷ ὁ Θεός, which sounds as if Jesus, not John, is the recipient of the "revelation." Does this mean that Jesus is the prophet and John, at least for chapters 2-3, is simply the scribe who records the prophecy?

Ac. 2.17ff mentions several types of revelatory phenomena together (dreams, visions, prophecy, wonders and signs) without any attempt at distinction. (I have excluded the terms σημεῖον, τέρας and δύναμις from consideration here because they do not imply verbal communication.)

development in NT redemptive history.³² The recipients of these extraordinary communications were not messengers commissioned to deliver to other people the message which they received; rather, the message was intended only for the recipients themselves.

Second, with such a large number of revelatory experiences and such a large number of terms used to describe them, it is surprising that the term ἀπακαλύπτω is never associated with any of these, and the term ἀποκάλυψις only seldom.³³ The reason cannot be that the terms were unfamiliar, for ἀποκαλύπτω occurs 26 times and ἀποκάλυψις 18 times in the NT. It seems probable that ἀποκαλύπτω and ἀποκάλυψις were more general terms which could conceivably have applied to any type of revelatory experiences.³⁴ However, when discussing rather spectacular phenomena like dreams, visions, angelic appearances, trances and voices from heaven, the NT authors had more specific and precise terms available to them. Consequently, ἀποκαλύπτω and ἀποκάλυψις fell into disuse with regard to these specific kinds of experiences and were only used (1) to discuss "revelations" in general, without necessarily specifying any one type of experience (2 Cor. 12.1, Gal. 2.2; perhaps Rev. 1.1, 1 Cor. 14.6, 26), or (2) to discuss revelatory events which were not adequately described by the other specific terms

---

³²There are a few places where the communication came to a group, not an individual: the instances of the shepherds, the baptism of Jesus, the Transfiguration, the voice in Jerusalem, the women at the tomb, the diciples in prison, and the NT references to Sinai.

³³In 2 Col. 12.1 Paul uses ἀποκάλυψις to speak of his "visions and revelations of the Lord." The only other possible association of ἀποκάλυψις with these phenomena is Rev. 1.1.
It may be noted that the term "revelation" in traditional systematic theology has been used in a sense broader than that indicated by the use of ἀποκαλύπτω and ἀποκάλυψις in the NT.

³⁴Note that each of the four characteristics of an ἀποκάλυψις which we have defined so far fit these other phenomena very well; (1) spontaneity, (2) individuality (in most cases), (3) divine origin, (4) divine perspective.

available.³⁵ In this second category fall examples of less dramatic "revelations" where, for instance, a thought simply comes to mind and impresses itself forcefully on the consciousness of the recipient³⁶ (so probably Mt. 11.25, 27, 16.17, 1 Cor. 2.10, Eph. 1.17, 3.5, Phil. 3.15; perhaps 1 Cor. 14.6, 26).

If this is so, then ἀποκαλυφθῇ in 1 Cor. 14.30 is best understood in sense (2). While the prophet was sitting in a meeting, a thought would come more or less forcefully to mind. He would stand, and as soon as there was opportunity would begin to speak what he had received. Paul's words about the orderly and restrained character of the situation (14.30-33; cf. 11.33f, 14.27, 40) and the fact that everyone should be able to understand what is happening (14.2-25), plus the fact that more spectacular phenomena in the NT are never meant for anyone other than the original recipients, make it unlikely that the "revelation" in 14.30 took the form of a voice from heaven, a dream, a trance, a vision, or an angelic appearance.³⁷ It was

---

³⁵2 Cor. 12.7 and Rev. 1.1 might be explained on this basis.

³⁶Vos, BT, 236, defines "internal speech" as "an inner occurrence in which, apart from the bodily ear, the prophet perceives a divine voice addressing him, and that with such objectivity as to enable him clearly to distinguish its content from the content of his own thinking."

³⁷The failure of the NT authors ever to associate prophecy or the term ἀποκαλύπτω with these phenomena also confirms this view.
It is just possible, however, that the ἀποκάλυψις would occasionally take the form of a vision such as the one in Ac. 16.9 (the man of Macedonia): it would certainly come within the scope of ἀποκάλυψις as a general term (2 Cor. 12.1) and would not necessarily bring disruption to the meeting, especially if only one person were aware of it. Yet the experience of a vision is certainly not commonly implied by ἀποκαλύπτω in the NT, and 1 Cor. 14.32 would prevent us from thinking that the prophet ever lost his awareness of what was going on around him (see below on the question of ecstasy). I prefer to call a less forceful kind of "vision" a "mental picture" to avoid connotations of ecstasy. (But cf. Mart. Pol. 5.2 with 12.3)

rather thought to be a less dramatic but nonetheless recognizable communication perceived inwardly by the prophet in the form of words, thoughts or perhaps mental pictures coming to his mind.

C. Related Verses in 1 Corinthians

1. 1 Cor. 12.8-11: Is Prophecy "Miraculous"?

Here Paul confirms the conclusion we reached above concerning the divine origin of the revelation: prophecy (vs. 10) is one of the abilities which are empowered by the Holy Spirit (vs. 11: πάντα δὲ ταῦτα ἐνεργεῖ τὸ ἓν καὶ τὸ αὐτὸ πνεῦμα). But we should also observe that prophecy is not unique in this sense, for all the gifts Paul lists are included in the πάντα of vs. 11: λόγος σοφίας, λόγος γνώσεως, πίστις, χαρίσματα ἰαμάτων, ἐνεργήματα δυνάμεων, προφητεία, διακρίσεις πνευμάτων, γένη γλωσσῶν, ἑρμηνεία γλωσσῶν. This is significant because it means that prophecy cannot be accorded greater status or greater authority in the church simply because it is based on a "revelation" from the Holy Spirit. The fact that prophecy originates with the Holy Spirit only puts it on a par with the other gifts.

At this point it may be asked whether prophecy is a "miraculous" gift. The question requires different answers, depending on the sense in which "miracle" is used: (i) If a "miracle" is defined as "something which arouses awe and wonder in men because of its apparent contradiction of normal laws of natural human or physical behavior," then prophecy would be considered a miraculous gift on the basis of 1 Cor. 14. 22-25: prophecy is a "sign" (σημεῖον)[38] for believers (vs. 22), an evident demonstration that God is working among them, and also an amazing process that evokes wonder from an unbeliever (vs. 25). Because it is such an unusual way for God to work, it is more clearly seen as an indication of divine activity.

(ii) But if "miracle" is defined as "a direct intervention by God in history" in an attempt to distinguish prophecy from other gifts which are thought

---

[38] I understand 1 Cor. 14.22 to require an elliptical εἰς σημεῖον in the second half of the verse: see Chap. 3, pp. 192ff.

to be more "natural" or non-miraculous, then the answer must be that this definition is foreign to the context of 1 Corinthians and any attempt to separate miraculous from non-miraculous gifts in this way imposes on the text a distinction which it will not bear. This is clear for the following reasons: (a) Paul makes no distinction in the kinds of working of the Holy Spirit (such as "direct" and "indirect") in various gifts, but emphasizes that they all are brought about by the working of the Holy Spirit (πάντα δὲ ταῦτα ἐνεργεῖ τὸ ἕν καὶ τὸ αὐτὸ πνεῦμα, 1 Cor. 12.11).[39] Now Paul is arguing against the pride and jealousy concerning spiritual gifts which troubled the Corinthian church. He is trying to show how all the gifts are valuable because they all are from the Holy Spirit. It would destroy the force of his argument if it could be claimed that some gifts are "more directly" from the Holy Spirit or more a result of the Holy Spirit's own activity than others.

(b) Paul himself lists the various gifts and offices in different ways at different times, showing no awareness of any "miraculous versus non-miraculous" distinction in categories of gifts: faith, and words of wisdom and knowledge are listed alongside of gifts of healing and workings of acts of power (12.8-10); "helps" and "administrations" are mixed in between gifts of healing and kinds of tongues (12.28); hymns, lessons, revelations, tongues and interpretations can be mentioned in the same breath (14.26); revelation, knowledge, prophecy and teaching all come together (14.6).[40]

Thus if one wanted to argue that prophecy is a "miraculous" gift because it resulted from the direct activity of the Holy Spirit, then he would have to argue that all the gifts are "miraculous" in that sense. But this would void the term "miracle" of any value for distinguishing some kinds of activities from others.

---

[39] A similar emphasis is found in vs. 6, where Paul says of the diversities of gifts (or activities: ἐνεργήματα), that it is ὁ . . . αὐτὸς θεός, ὁ ἐνεργῶν τὰ πάντα ἐν πᾶσιν.

[40] Cf. Rom. 12.66ff, where prophecy is put with service, teaching, exhortation, etc.

So prophecy is at least sometimes a "miraculous" gift in terms of the response it elicits from men, but any attempt to classify it as "more directly" from God than some other gifts is exegetically invalid.[41]

This means that it is not acceptable to challenge the conclusions reached in our first chapter about the less authoritative nature of prophecy in 1 Corinthians with the argument that since the "revelation" comes from God, it must therefore impart to the actual words of the prophecy an absolute divine authority. For any such argument would have to apply equally to all the gifts Paul lists (including, for instance, administration and teaching), but this would be clearly an impossible suggestion.

2. 1 Cor. 14.6

In attempting to encourage the Corinthians to speak understandably when they met together, Paul uses his own visits as an example: "Now, brothers, if I come to you speaking in tongues, how shall I benefit you unless I speak to you with some revelation or knowledge or prophecy or teaching?" (ἐὰν μὴ ὑμῖν λαλήσω ἢ ἐν ἀποκαλύψει ἢ ἐν γνώσει ἢ ἐν προφητείᾳ ἢ ἐν διδαχῇ;). The catalogue "revelation, knowledge, prophecy, teaching" includes most or all of the possible kinds of intelligible speech with which Paul might have addressed a congregation, and is put in contrast to the unintelligible speech of tongues. When Paul says, "A revelation . . . or prophecy" one might at first think that he makes revelation a kind of speech act distinct from prophecy. But this is not necessarily so. The first two terms imply the reception or possession of information (it is in private that men "receive" or "have" revelations, and only God gives them: 1 Cor. 14.26, Gal. 1.12; cf. Mt. 11. 25, 27, 1 Cor. 2.10, Phil. 3.15; similarly, men "receive" or "have" knowledge: 1 Cor. 8.1, 10,

---

[41] One might argue that those gifts which arouse men's wonder do so because they exhibit a more unusual or uncommon result of the Holy Spirit's activity, but this does not imply that the activity is in any way more "direct" or conveys any more authority. (So our earlier argument that a "revelation" must come from God means that it comes from him in a manner distinct from the ordinary workings of human memory and reason.)

2 Cor. 4.6, Phil. 3.8). But the second two terms refer to the communication of information (a prophecy or teaching is publicly spoken or written by men to others: 1 Tim. 1.18, 2 Pet. 1.21, Rev. 1.3; Mk. 4.2, Ac. 5.28, Rom. 16.17, 2 Jn. 10).[42] So λαλεῖν ἐν ἀποκαλύψει and λαλεῖν ἐν γνώσει refer here to the content of Paul's speech, while λαλεῖν ἐν προφητείᾳ and λαλεῖν ἐν διδαχῇ refer to the form the speech would take: "How shall I benefit you unless I report to you a revelation or some knowledge, or unless I prophesy to you or teach you?" This means that there might be conscious "abab" parallelism in the structure of 1 Cor. 14.6: an ἀποκάλυψις is communicated by προφητεία while γνῶσις is communicated by διδαχή:[43] "How shall I benefit you unless I bring you a revelation or some knowledge by means of prophecy or teaching?" But this parallelism is not made explicit in the text, so we cannot reply too heavily upon it.

What is clear, however, is that an ἀποκάλυψις in 1 Cor. 14.6 need not be seen as a speech act distinct from prophecy, any more than knowledge need be seen as distinct from teaching.

D. The Essential Characteristics of Prophecy: The Difference Between Prophecy and Teaching

At this point we may ask: (1) Does every ἀποκάλυψις give rise to a prophecy? (2) Does every prophecy require an ἀποκάλυψις as its basis? In order to answer these questions, we can examine both the data in 1 Corinthians and some relevant information from the rest of the NT.

(1) The answer to the first question must be negative. There are many instances in the NT where a "revelation" is given for the private benefit of the individual recipient, and he does not subsequently

---

[42] This distinction does not always hold, for someone can "have" either a διδαχήν or an ἀποκάλυψιν to present to the congregation (1 Cor. 14.26). This is because διδαχή can refer either to the act of teaching (Mk. 4.2) or to the thing taught (Ac. 5.28, 1 Cor. 14.26). In 1 Cor. 14.6 it most likely refers to the act of teaching.

[43] So Conzelmann, 234, n. 20.

report it in a public proclamation (Mt. 11.25, 27, Jn. 12.38, Rom. 1.17, 18, Phil. 3.15, 1 Pet. 1.12; Gal. 2.2, Eph. 1.17). So the reception of a "revelation" alone would not constitute a man a prophet; only where the revelation is also proclaimed publicly, as in 1 Cor. 14.29-33, is a prophecy said to occur.

(2) The second question, whether every prophecy requires a "revelation" as its basis, requires an affirmative answer because of the following considerations:

(a) In 1 Cor. 14.29-33, Paul assumes that the person about to prophesy is the person who has received a "revelation" (vs. 30). No other valid reason is given for silencing the first prophet and allowing the second to speak. The probable (but not quite certain) implication is that nothing but a "revelation" could qualify the second man as a prophet.

Then also when Paul argues that the Holy Spirit at work in prophets is subject to the prophets themselves (vs. 32), he specifically has in mind the activity of the Holy Spirit in imparting a "revelation" (vs. 30).[44] Vs. 32 is a general statement which applies to all prophets, just as vs. 31 explicitly includes all who prophesy. It does not seem possible that some prophet at Corinth could have avoided Paul's instructions by claiming that vss. 30-33 did not apply to him, because he normally prophesied without ever having a "revelation." Rather, Paul assumes that his instructions apply to all the prophets, and thus that all prophesy on the basis of "revelations" imparted to them by the Holy Spirit.

(b) In 1 Cor. 14.24-25 those who prophesy make a public disclosure[45] of the secrets of a man's heart (vs. 25a). The visitor responds in a way that indicates that, at least in his view, only God could have made these things known to the prophets (vs. 25b). And apparently everyone who prophesies contributes to this act of conviction and investigation (ὑπὸ πάντων, vs. 24). So again Paul seems to assume that all who prophesy have received an ἀποκάλυψις.

---

[44] Cf. pp. 118ff.

[45] Cf. Chap. 3, pp. 200f.

(c) In the rest of the NT, all the examples of Christian prophecy about which we have enough information to make a decision also imply the prior reception of some kind of "revelation." In Ac. 11.28 and 21.10f, Agabus's predictions are presented as being descriptions of future events, and thus based on something that had been revealed to him. In Ac. 19.6 the disciples at Ephesus "began to speak with tongues and to prophesy" as soon as Paul had laid his hands on them and the Holy Spirit had come upon them. The spontaneity of the event and their ignorance of even the rudiments of Christian teaching (vs. 2) show that this prophesying (whatever form it took) was not intelligent Christian preaching but rather the result of some extraordinary working of the Holy Spirit, and thus probably the result of an ἀποκάλυψις. In Eph. 3.5 revelation by the Spirit is specifically said to be given to apostles and prophets.

Elsewhere the NT also speaks of pre-Pentecost prophecy. This material must be treated with more caution because we are not as certain that it represents what the NT authors thought of Christian prophecy, but it does give us an idea of the kinds of abilities which were thought to characterize those who could be designated προφῆται. In several cases, the distinguishing characteristic of a prophet is seen to be his possession of information which could only come through a "revelation." In Lk. 7.39, the Pharisee assumes that a prophet could know about the life of someone he had just met--presumably by receiving a "revelation." And in Jn. 4.19, when Jesus startles the woman at the well with knowledge of her previous life, she says, "Sir, I can see that you are a prophet." In Lk. 23.63f, the guards blindfold and beat Jesus, then cruelly demand of him, "Prophesy! Who hit you?," apparently employing a popular conception of a prophet as one who can know things through "revelations" and need not rely on ordinary means of acquiring information. In Ac. 2.30f, where David is said to have foreseen and therefore spoken of the resurrection, he is specifically designated as a prophet. In Jn. 11.51, Caiaphas is said to predict both the fact and the meaning of Jesus' death. "This he did not say of himself, but . . . he prophesied" (τοῦτο δὲ ἀφ'ἑαυτοῦ οὐκ εἶπεν, ἀλλὰ . . . ἐπροφήτευσεν, here prophesying is specifically contrasted to speaking "of oneself," from one's own knowledge).

In addition to these examples, there is the negative consideration that we find no example in the

NT of a prophet simply speaking on the basis of his own knowledge or ideas instead of on the basis of some kind of "revelation."

(d) Although the previous chapter has shown that one cannot always depend on the phenomena of OT prophecy to provide parallels with NT prophecy, at this point it is useful to recall that the possession of a revelation from God was what distinguished true from false prophecy in the OT. A false prophet was one who spoke when the Lord had given him nothing to speak (Dt. 18.20), who spoke from his own mind (Ezk. 13.3, Jer. 23.16ff), or who spoke by a lying spirit (1 Kgs. 22.23). But a true prophet was one to whom God had revealed his secret (Am. 3.7; LXX: ἀποκαλύψῃ).

In this connection it is interesting to note the way true and false prophets are distinguished in 1 Jn. 4.1-6. A false prophet (vs. 1) is one who speaks by a spirit which is not of God, the spirit of the antichrist (vs. 3). So even the false prophet speaks by a "revelation" of sorts, but it is from an evil spirit, not from "the Spirit of God" (vs. 2).

(e) Finally, there are strong indications that in the NT it is the presence or absence of an ἀποκάλυψις which distinguishes prophecy from teaching.[46] We have seen how NT prophecy always depends on a "revelation." But by contrast (i) no human speech act which is called a διδαχή or διδασκαλία, done by a διδάσκαλος, or described by the verb διδάσκω, is ever said to be based on an ἀποκάλυψις,[47] and (ii) no ἀποκάλυψις in the NT is ever said to give rise to a

---

[46] Cf. Best, "Prophets and Preachers." 147; contra E. Schweizer, "Observance of the Law and Charismatic Activity in Matthew," NTS 16 (1969-70), 228f.

[47] These same considerations apply to the terms κατηχέω, παιδεύω and παιδεία.
    The lack of connection between ἀποκάλυψις and διδαχή is quite significant because of the great frequency of occurrence of members of the διδαχή word group in the NT: διδαχή occurs 30 times; διδασκαλία, 21; διδάσκαλος, 59; διδάσκω, 95. And ἀποκαλύπτω occurs 26 times and ἀποκάλυψις, 18, yet members of the two word groups never once occur together in describing the same speech act.

"teaching" of one man by another.[48] Rather, "teaching" from men is put in contrast to a divine "revelation" (Gal. 1.12). Teaching is often simply an exposition or application of Scripture (Ac. 15.35, 18.11, 25, Rom. 2.20-21, Col. 3.16, Heb. 5.12) or a repetition and explanation of apostolic instructions (1 Cor. 41.17, Rom. 16.17, 2 Th. 2.15, 2 Tim. 2.2, 3.10).

So if a man in the congregation at Corinth suddenly received the kind of "revelation" we have described above, and stood and spoke about what had been revealed to him, then, in Paul's view, he would be prophesying.[49] But if a man stood and preached from some Scripture passage, explaining it and applying it to the lives of the hearers, Paul would have thought him to be engaged in teaching.[50] And if he simply thought of some word of exhortation or encouragement and delivered it to the congregation, he would be thought to be teaching.

(3) Summary: Prophecy not only in 1 Cor., but in the entire NT, seems to have two distinctive features. First, it must be based on an ἀποκάλυψις; if there is no ἀποκάλυψις, there is no prophecy. Second, it must include a public proclamation. The mere reception of an ἀποκάλυψις does not constitute a

---

[48] I have excluded here the several instances in which men are said to be "taught" by God (Jn. 6.45, 1 Cor. 2.13, Lk. 12.12, Jn. 14.26; cf. 1 Th. 4.9), because it is specifically human teaching which is under consideration.
The one exception to these conclusions might be Jn. 7.16f, where Jesus claims, "My teaching is not mine, but his who sent me." However, John never connects this with any specific ἀποκάλυψις from God to Jesus, and it would be precarious to draw too close a parallel between the teaching activity of Jesus and the gift of teaching in the NT church.

[49] In n. 63 below I discuss how a man could know whether he was receiving a revelation from the Holy Spirit or not.

[50] A similar distinction is maintained by David Hill, "Christian Prophets as Teachers or Instructors in the Church," in Prophetic Vocation in the New Testament and Today, ed. J. Panagopoulos (Leiden, 1977), pp. 122-123 and 127-128, although he would not distinguish prophecy from teaching as clearly as I have done here.
It is interesting that Chrysostom says, "He that prophesieth speaketh all things from the Spirit; but he that teacheth sometimes discourses also out of his own mind." (p. 186, on 1 Cor. 12.28).

prophecy until it is publicly proclaimed.[51]

II. 1 CORINTHIANS 13.8-12: CERTAINTY AND CLARITY OF PERCEPTION

In order to show the superiority of love Paul must demonstrate the temporal limitations of gifts

---

[51] Origen defines prophecy as "knowledge of unseen things that is signified through speech" (προφητεία ἐστὶν ἡ διὰ λόγου τῶν ἀφανῶν σημαντικὴ γνῶσις), but then makes the subject matter quite philosophical: ". . . the knowledge of the composition of the world and the activity of elements and times" (ἡ εἴδησις τῆς τοῦ κόσμου συστάσεως καὶ ἐνεργείας στοιχείων καὶ χρόνων). This he distinguishes from teaching, which is "the instructive word (διδασκαλικὸς λόγος) spread abroad to many." However, he goes on to explain "revelation," ἀποκάλυψις, as implying a much more ecstatic state "when the mind is outside of the earthly body" (τῶν γηΐνων). (Claude Jenkins, "Origen on 1 Corinthians," JTS o.s. 10 (1909), 36; cf. Conzelmann, 234, n. 20) It is interesting that after Lindblom has surveyed prophetic experiences in several religions and cultures he concludes, "Common to all representatives of the prophetic type here depicted is the consciousness of having access to information from the world above and experiences originating in the divine world" (Lindbom, Prophecy, p. 32).

In Philo, the definition of a prophet is "one who has the power to know things beyond sense perception" (Wolfson, Philo, II, 21).

Much OT prophecy is similar to NT prophecy with respect to these two essential characteristics. Although גלה (=ἀποκαλύπτω) is not used frequently to describe revelation from God to the prophet (but cf. Am. 3.7, 1 Sam. 3.21, Dan. 2.19ff), there is a repeated insistence that the prophet must have a word from the Lord before he can speak as a prophet (Dt. 18.18-20, Jer. 14.14, 23.16ff, 29.31-32, Ezk. 13.1ff; cf. Num. 16.28), and this word is often seen as mediated by the Spirit of God (Num. 24.2-3, 2 Chr. 15.1-2, Ezk. 11.5, Neh. 9.30). Indeed Jeremiah waited ten days before prophesying (Jer. 42.7), because before he could prophesy he first required a message from Yahweh. This "revelation" may have come in different forms at different times, but it is often pictured as a personal

such as prophecy and tongues. So in this section he says that prophecy will cease (13.8) <u>because</u> (γάρ) it is imperfect (vs. 9). It is imperfect <u>because</u>[52] (γάρ) we see in a mirror dimly (vs. 12: βλέπομεν γάρ ἄρτι δι'ἐσόπτρου ἐν αἰνίγματι, τότε δὲ πρόσωπον πρὸς πρόσωπον).

The phrase, "for now we see in a mirror dimly," seems to be an allusion to Num. 12.6-8.[53] "We" are now in the position of the prophets who see δι' αἰνιγμάτων (Num. 12.8) and perhaps בַּמַּרְאָה (Num. 12.6),

---

verbal address to an individual person in a particular circumstance (1 Sam. 3.1-14, 2 Sam. 7.4ff, 24.11-12, 1 Kgs. 14.5, 19.9, 22.14, 2 Kgs. 20.4, 2 Chr. 12.7, Is. 6.1ff, 7.3, 20.1-2, Jer. 1.1-3, 7.1-2, 13.1-7, 18. 1ff, 21.1-3, Ezk. 1.1-3, Hos. 1-3, Jon. 1-4, Hag. 1.1, 2.1, 10, 20, Zech. 1.1, 7, 7.1). On the other hand, a revelation alone does not constitute a prophecy (cf. Is. 7.10, 1 Kgs. 19.9). Rather, the prophecy occurs when the revelation is proclaimed publicly, and often the command to "prophesy" is thus a command to go and proclaim a message which has been received (Ezk. 11. 4-5, 13.2, 17, Am. 7.15, Jer. 25.30).

[52]V. 11 is an illustration of the general truth stated in vs. 10, and vss. 9-10 together support vs. 8b. Thus, the γάρ in vs. 12 must be taken to indicate that vs. 12 is an argument not for the parenthetical vs. 11, but for vss. 9-10.

[53]In addition to the fact that both contexts speak of prophecy, there are three other indications that Paul is alluding to Num 12. Only here in the LXX is αἴνιγμα used in a context of seeing or listening to God. (It usually refers simply to riddles, as in 3 Kgs. 10.1, Prov. 1.6). Second, although Num. 12.8 has στόμα κατὰ στόμα λαλήσω (פֶּה אֶל־פֶּה אֲדַבֶּר), the equivalent when referring to an experience of seeing God would almost certainly be πρόσωπον πρὸς πρόσωπον βλέπειν (cf. Dt. 34.10 where Moses is a man whom the Lord knew πρόσωπον κατὰ πρόσωπον, and the phrase πρόσωπον πρὸς πρόσωπον in Gen. 32.30 and Jud. 6.22, to refer to a theophany). A final possible parallel is seen in the phrase δι'ἐσόπτρου. Although the word ἔσοπτρον does not occur in Num. 12, the word מַרְאָה, "a vision," (which is used in Num. 12.6) is translated κάτοπτρον, "a mirror," in Ex. 38.8 (26), and means

"in a vision or mirror."⁵⁴ But "then" we shall see "face to face," a reference to seeing God at the

---

"mirror" elsewhere in Jewish literature (cf. Jastrow, 96). (In Num. 12.8, מַרְאֶה, "sight, physical appearance," should not be pointed מַרְאָה because it would then destroy the contrast with vs. 6, but it has sometimes been read that way in Jewish tradition; cf. T. N. and T. Ps.-Jon. to Num. 12.8, and Lev. R. 1.14, b. Yeb. 49b (the latter two with אספקלריא, not מראה, but both can mean "mirror" [Str.-B. III, 452].

Dautzenberg, UP, 159-255 argues that the use of Num. 12.6-8 in 1 Cor. 13.12 is similar to the use made of that passage in Jewish apocalyptic literature. He concludes that early Christian prophecy must therefore be understood largely in the light of Jewish apocalyptic. But such a conclusion is certainly unjustified: the similar use may only have been coincidental.

⁵⁴Although this phrase is not taken to mean "mirror" by the LXX, it is not impossible that Paul was making an allusion to a contemporary understanding of מַרְאֶה as "mirror," since it commonly came to mean that in later Hebrew (cf. Jastrow, 96). On the other hand, Paul may have been introducing an image from some other source than Num. 12 (for suggestions see Conzelmann, 226ff, and note his sensible conclusion: "A 'pure' pedigree of the figure is not to be postulated at all" [p. 228]).

The suggestion that Paul is referring to catoptromancy, a particular kind of divination using mirrors (first proposed by H. Achelis, "Katoptromantie bei Paulus," Theologische Festschrift für G. Nathaniel Bonwetsch (Leipzig, 1918), 56-63 [not available to me]; followed by Kittel, TDNT I, 179 and Héring, 142), is not very convincing. The repeated OT prohibitions against divination (cf. esp. Dt. 18.10-19 where various means of divination are contrasted with the true prophet like Moses; also Lev. 19.31, 20.27) make it very unlikely that Paul would have alluded to such a practice without condemning it. Cf. C. Spicq, Agapè dans le Nouveau Testament (3 vols.; Paris, 1959), II, 96ff; however, his objection based on Rabbinic prohibitions is a misreading of Tos. Shab. 12 (Zuckermandel p. 130, 1.16); cf. Str.-B. III, 452, with translation of the passage, and b. Shab. 149a: the

consummation.⁵⁵ The mirror imagery suggests both the
indirectness and the incompleteness (one does not see
everything, but only those things within the borders
of the mirror) of the revelation presently received by
those who prophesy,⁵⁶ but need not suggest that the
image is distorted.⁵⁷ If we apply this to prophecy, it
means that the prophet does not see God face to face
or speak with him directly, but only receives revelation from God in some kind of (here undefined) indirect
manner. It also means that what the prophet sees or
learns is only a glimpse of some reality, but not the
whole picture. The phrase ἐν αἰνίγματι indicates that
what the prophet sees or learns, or the implications
of what is "revealed," are often difficult to understand (cf. Jn. 11.50, 1 Pet. 1.11).

That this is the correct understanding of Paul's
metaphor is made more clear by an examination of vs. 9:
it is precisely the limitations of prophecy which are
in view, and thus it is the way in which a mirror lim-
its one's vision which Paul emphasizes. Furthermore,
in vs. 12b, it is present partial knowledge (ἄρτι
γινώσκω ἐκ μέρους) which is parallel is seeing in a mirror dimly in 12a, and this is contrasted with full knowledge in the consummation (τότε δὲ ἐπιγνώσομαι, 12b).

The imperfection of prophecy is described in
another way in vs. 9: ἐκ μέρους γὰρ γινώσκομεν καὶ ἐκ
μέρους προφητεύομεν, "For we know in part and we
prophesy in part."⁵⁸ The phrase ἐκ μέρους refers

---

prohibition simply is against work on the Sabbath.

⁵⁵In the LXX πρόσωπον πρός (or κατὰ)πρόσωπον
is clearly used to speak of seeing God personally, as
in a theophany (Gen. 32.30, Dt. 5.4, 34.10, Jud. 6.22,
Ezk. 20.35; cf. also Ex. 33.11). Contra E. Miguens,
"1 Cor. 13.8-13 Reconsidered," CBQ 37 (1975), 76-87.
    That "when the perfect is come" (vs. 10) refers
to the consummation is argued in Chap. 3, pp. 211ff.

⁵⁶Because vs. 12 is a ground for vs. 9; see n.
52 above.

⁵⁷Conzelmann, 227, n. 91 and Kittel, TDNT I, 179
n. 9 give references showing the clarity of mirrors in
antiquity.

⁵⁸The verse cannot mean, "We have knowledge
concerning many things, and we prophesy concerning

primarily to a quantitative imperfection in prophecy: it only gives partial knowledge of the subjects it treats.⁵⁹ Agabus might come to know something about

---

the rest," because vs. 9 argues for vs. 8, where Paul puts both knowledge and prophecy together as things to be rendered useless at the consummation. Thus, vs. 9 shows that both are imperfect, not that one complements the other.

⁵⁹The meaning of the phrase ἐκ μέρους is not decisive, but it is of some help in understanding the precise kind of imperfection implied. Although Robertson and Plummer say that the term is "fairly common in both LXX and NT" (p. 297n), it is in fact not at all common in this sense. All 21 occurrences in the LXX have a locative sense, "side" or "edge" (Ex. 26.4, Num. 20.16, 3 Kgs. 6.8, 23.26, etc.), and none is adverbial. In the NT, all five instances are in this passage (1 Cor. 12.27, 13.9 [2X], 10, 12). 12.27 has a different sense, perhaps "(each) for his part" (Bl.-D. §212), or perhaps "individually," as in Ep. Arist. 102. But that cannot be the sense in chapter 13, for then 13.9 could not support 13.8. So there is no exact parallel in the Bible.

However, the similar Pauline phrase ἀπὸ μέρους always has an adverbial force in the NT, and always implies quantitative rather than qualitative imperfection (Rom. 11.25, 15.15, 24, 2 Cor. 1.14, 2.5). In Philo, the phrase ἐκ μέρους can speak of quantitative deficiency also: he refers to Moses and "his partial (ἐκ μέρους) distribution of territories to the combatants," that is, to Reuben, Gad and Manasseh before crossing the Jordan (Mos. 2.1). Moses had not distributed the territories poorly; he had simply done it partially, and more was to be done later.

Thus Grosheide's remark is not accurate: "The words do not imply that we only know a part of that which is to be known, but rather that the knowing itself is imperfect (cf. we prophesy in part)" (p. 309).

Schlatter, 361, refers to a similar phrase רָאָה מִקְצָה in Eccl. R. 1.8: It is argued that although the prophets did not see all of the future, or all of God's secrets, "they surely did see a part (ראו מקצה)."

Amos 3.7 is adduced as proof: "For the Lord God does nothing, without revealing his secret to his servants the prophets." When asked how the prophets saw these things, R. Berekiah said, "As [one peeps] through a

the future (Ac 11.28, 21.11), but he cannot see all of it.⁶⁰ This is why prophecy will be rendered useless (καταργέω):⁶¹ it is only a temporary and partial substitute for the full and complete means of attaining knowledge which men will have in the consummation. When that perfect means of knowing comes, the imperfect ways will pass away (vs. 10).

To summarize this passage: prophecy is imperfect (i) because it gives only a glimpse of the subjects it treats (ἐκ μέρους, vs. 9); (ii) because the prophet himself only receives some kind of indirect revelation, and a limited one at that (βλέπομεν . . . δι'ἐσόπτρου vs. 12); and (iii) because what the prophet does receive is often difficult for him to understand or interpret (ἐν αἰνίγματι, vs. 12). We conclude from this that the prophet may not always understand with complete clarity just what has been revealed to him,⁶² and at times may not even know with complete certainity

---

crack in the door." This parallel is very close to the 1 Cor. 13 phrase and lends support to the idea that it implies quantitative imperfection.
The illustration of growing from childhood to adulthood (vs. 11) might suggest another contrast. Just as "baby talk" gives way to adult speech, perhaps imperfect and poorly done prophecy will give way in the consummation to perfect, full prophecy. However, this suggestion makes too much of an illustration. Prophecy need not be replaced with better prophecy; it can give way to a better mode of knowing altogether. Paul does not say that prophecy will become perfect; he says it will become useless.

⁶⁰Cf. 2 Kgs. 4.27, where God hides from Elisha the death of the Shunammite woman's son.

⁶¹Καταργέω is a favorite Pauline word (25 of 27X in the NT). It means to make powerless (ἀ-εργόν); hence, ineffective. useless. Often in Paul, and always in 1 and 2 Cor., it refers to things of this age which will be useless in the age to come. It clearly has this sense in 1 Cor. 13.

⁶²Ac 21.4 and 11, and Jn. 11.49-52, show that the prophet may sometimes have misunderstood or misinterpreted the revelation that came to him.

whether he has in fact received a revelation.[63]

III. 1 CORINTHIANS 14.29-33: THE QUESTION OF PROPHETIC ECSTASY

A. The Problem Defined

The English word "ecstasy" can be used to mean several different things. In investigating the psychological state of the NT prophet we are concerned with four specific questions within the general area of ecstatic experience:

(1) Was he forced to speak against his will?

(2) Did he lose his self control and begin to rave violently?

(3) Did he speak things which made no sense to him?

---

[63] It may be asked how the prophet can know that the "revelation" which he seems to be receiving at any moment is in fact from the Holy Spirit. It is interesting that Paul did not consider this a big enough problem to write specific instructions about: he apparently assumes that the prophet will know! Nonetheless, we can venture a guess that in practice such a decision would have included both an objective and a subjective element. Objectively, did the revelation conform with what the prophet knew of the OT Scriptures and with apostolic teaching which had already been received as authoritative? (Cf. 1 Cor. 12.3, 1 Jn. 4.2-3; Dt. 13.1-5.) But there was no doubt also a subjective element of personal judgment: did the revelation "feel like" something from the Holy Spirit; did it seem to the prophet to be similar to other experiences of the power of the Holy Spirit which he had known previously in worship? (Cf. 1 Jn. 4.5-6, Jn. 10.1-5, 27.) Apparently Paul thought that authentic NT prophets would have an above-average ability to determine what exactly did come from God (1 Cor. 14.37). (S. Mowinckel, "'The Spirit' and 'The Word' in the Pre-exilic Reforming Prophets," JBL 53 (1934), pp. 212ff, suggests a similar procedure for OT prophets.)

(4) Was he for a time unaware of his surroundings?

For the purpose of this investigation, I shall consider a prophet to be in an ecstatic state if any one of these four conditions is true of him.[64] But merely (i) prophesying in an excited state, or (ii) speaking with strong emotion, or (iii) having a high level of concentration or awareness of the meaning of his words, or (iv) having an unusually strong sense of the presence and the working of God in his mind, I shall not consider to be sufficiently abnormal states to warrant the use of the term "ecstasy."[65]

---

[64]Lindblom uses the term ecstasy "when the inspiration has grown so strong that the inspired person has lost full control of himself. The normal current of mental life is interrupted. The ordinary mental faculties, and sometimes the physical powers, are put out of function" (p. 35). He then describes many different degrees and types of ecstasy and of revelatory experience (pp. 35-46). Lindblom's "concentration ecstasy" is nearest to my meaning no. 4.

[65]Lindblom (p. 35) would use the term "inspiration," not "ecstasy," in these latter four cases, but recognizes that a precise distinction cannot be made in every instance.

I discussed in Chap. 1 (pp. 34ff.) some examples of OT prophecy which might be termed ecstatic. It is interesting to notice that among the more convincing examples of OT prophetic ecstasy (1 Sam. 10.5ff, 19. 19ff; perhaps Num. 11.25) there is no instance where a prophet is said to be speaking an intelligible message (the activity which would bear formal similarities to NT prophesying). One possible exception to this is 2 Kgs. 9.11, where the prophet who anointed Jehu king is called mad (מְשֻׁגָּע) by one of the servants, but this might well refer to his rude interruption and precipitate departure (vss. 5, 10) or to other strange mannerisms; it could not refer to the prophet's behavior during the reception or delivery of the message, neither of which the servant witnessed (vss. 1, 6). More to the point is 2 Chr. 25.16, where a prophet has enough self-control to break off his prophecy when commanded by Amaziah to stop. (See also n. 103).

On the other hand the common visions experienced by OT prophets (Is. 6.1ff, Jer. 1.11ff, Ezk. 1, Dan.

B. __1 Cor. 14.29-33__

Within this passage alone we find considerations which indicate that Paul thought none of the four

---

7-12, Zech. 1.7ff, etc.) can no doubt be termed "ecstatic" in sense 4: the prophet was unaware of his surroundings. These experiences had to do with the reception of revelation, not its delivery, which is always in a non-ecstatic state in the OT (Num. 24.4, 16 are possible exceptions, but then Balaam is not a typical OT prophet either).

The frequency with which the great classical prophets refer to visions (this brief list could be greatly expanded) makes it unlikely that this kind of ecstasy was depreciated in their eyes.

On ecstasy in the OT see Lindblom, __Prophecy__, 47-65 (the "primitive" OT prophets), 105-08 (similarities between the classical and primitive prophets), and 423f (ecstasy in the classical prophets); G. Vos, BT 230-52, esp. 244f; Eichrodt. __Theology of the OT__, I 340, n. 2; Young, __My Servants__, 83-92, 161-90. Kaufmann, __Religion__, has an interesting distinction between unintelligible (ecstatic) and intelligible prophecy, and claims that only the latter was regarded as containing divine words or messages, (p. 97). Leon J. Woods, "Ecstasy and Israel's Early Prophets," __BETS__ 9 (1966), 125ff, argues that the OT prophets experienced fervency and emotional excitement but not ecstasy. However, he cannot adequately account for the involuntary aspect of the instances in 1 Sam., and he fails to consider the frequent visions of the classical prophets.

Josephus seldom describes prophecy in terms which would suggest ecstasy, but does do so in his description of Balaam, who "was no longer his own master but was overruled by the divine spirit" (__A__. 4.118).

Philo has a well-developed theory of prophetic ecstasy, but his views are much influenced by a Platonic philosophy in which union with the immaterial was man's highest goal (__Quis Her__. 69-70; cf. E. R. Goodenough, __An Introduction to Philo Judaeus__, 134-60). So he does not reflect typical Jewish thinking of his day on this subject (Goodenough, 14).

The major texts in Philo which deal with prophetic ecstasy are __Quis Her__. 249ff (a description of four kinds of ecstasy), __259__ ("a prophet . . . has no utterance of his own, but all his utterance comes from elsewhere"), 266 ("his organs of speech . . . are

criteria of ecstasy to be true of the Corinthian prophets.

(1) That the prophet was not forced to speak against his will is shown by the fact that he could stop his prophecy to allow another to speak (vs. 30b), that the second prophet apparently did not suddenly burst into speech but rather signalled that he was ready to prophesy and then waited for the first prophet to stop (vs. 30a), that all prophets were able to prophesy in turn (καθ'ἕνα, vs. 31), and that the Holy Spirit subjected himself to the prophet in such a way that he could act in a restrained and orderly

---

wholly in the employ of Another'), Spec. Leg. 1.65, 4.49 ("knowing not what he does he is filled with inspiration, as the reason withdraws and surrenders the citadel of the soul to a new visitor and tenant, the Divine Spirit which plays on the vocal organism and dictates words"), Mos. 1.283, 2.250, Q. Gen. 3.9, 4.196, Mig. 35 (on Philo's own ecstatic experiences: "under the influence of the Divine possession I have been filled with corybantic frenzy and been unconscious of anything, place, persons present, myself, words spoken, lines written").

A similarly high estimate of ecstasy, by which Philo seems to have been influenced, is found in Plato: "Just as the Corybantian worshippers do not dance when in their senses, so the lyric poets do not indite those fine songs in their senses (ἔμφρονες), but when they have started on the melody and rhythm they begin to be frantic" (Ion 534A). "No man achieves true and inspired divination (μαντικῆς ἐνθέου καὶ ἀληθοῦς) when in his rational mind" (Tim. 71E). In Phaedrus 244A-245B Plato explains the advantages of various types of madness (μανία), including the type found in prophecy (244B), and argues that the most excellent kind of madness (249D) is one in which the soul of man rises upwards to behold the upper regions of heaven (246Dff).

The strange fire-colored water passage in 4 Ezra 14.37ff may not imply any involuntary ecstasy of the type we have defined, but emphasizes rather a miraculous gift of understanding and physical endurance.

manner (vs. 32).[66]

(2) That he did not lose his self control or begin to rave violently is made clear by Paul's argument in vs. 33 when he says that the result of the Spirit's working in a prophet is not disorder or frenzied disturbance (ἀκαταστασία) but peace (εἰρήνη), as well as by vs. 32 where it is made explicit that the prophet himself retains control of the situation, because the Holy Spirit is subject to him.

(3) Although there is no explicit statement that a prophet understood what he was saying, it is clear that the hearers understood, for they were to evaluate what was said (vs. 29), and they would all learn and be encouraged by the prophecies (vs. 31). If the hearers all understood and learned from the prophecy, then certainly the prophet himself understood what he was saying.[67]

(4) Since the first prophet was able to recognize from some clear signal that someone else had received a revelation and was ready to prophesy (vs. 30), it is clear that Paul assumed him to be well aware of his surroundings, not out of touch with reality at all. This was true not only while a man was prophesying, but also while he was receiving a revelation, for the second prophet knew enough to wait his turn while someone else was speaking, so that they

---

[66] One example of "forced" speech might be found in Mart. Pol. 7.2, where Polycarp, on the night he was captured, stood and prayed, and he was "so full of the grace of God, that for two hours he could not be silent" (μὴ δύνασθαι σιγῆσαι). However, the language need not be interpreted too strongly, for he was dependent on the permission of the soldiers to continue speaking.

[67] Jn. 12.49ff and 1 Pet. 1.10ff serve to caution us against saying that a prophet must have understood all the implications of what he said. Rather, I am arguing that a prophet's words were fully intelligible words and, at least on one level of meaning, made very good sense to him.

could prophesy "one by one" (vss. 30-31).

C. Related Verses in 1 Corinthians

1. 1 Cor. 14.3-4

Here we find more evidence for the intelligibility of the prophet's words, for he speaks "to men" and the result is that they are strengthened, encouraged and comforted (vs. 3). The contrast here is between speech in tongues which no one understands (vs. 2) and prophecy which is understood by the hearers.

2. 1 Cor. 14.23-25

Whereas an unbelieving visitor might level the charge of madness against the congregation if all spoke in tongues (vs. 23), this would not be true in the case of prophecy: even if <u>all</u> prophesied[68] (vs. 24), a situation which might well have been thought to give opportunity for some ecstatic outbreaks, the result would not be confusion but very understandable speech which would convince the visitor of his sin (vs. 25).

3. 1 Cor. 14.40

When Paul commands that all things (including prophecy, vs. 39) be done "in a fitting and orderly way" (NIV), he assumes that the prophets would behave not in an ecstatic manner but as men who were very much in control of themselves.

D. Objections

1. The Problem at Corinth

It might be argued that although Paul thought a prophet should behave in the way we have outlined, in fact the prophets at Corinth were engaged in some quite ecstatic behavior, and Paul was attempting to correct their disorder in this epistle.

---

[68] Presumably one by one (vs. 31).

However, before Paul gives the instruction in 14.29-33 he already assumes that prophecy at Corinth was commonly understood to be very intelligible and quite beneficial to the hearers (14.3-4, 23-25). The problem--if we can define it with any certainty--was simply that more than one prophet tried to speak at once (vss. 30-21), and perhaps that some claimed they could not refrain from speaking (vs. 32). Paul's reponse is that the Corinthians are able to control themselves, for this is the way the Holy Spirit <u>always</u> acts: he creates peace, not confusion, and is <u>subject</u> to the prophet (vss. 32-33). So the claim that some prophets were unable to exercise self-control was simply not true, according to Paul. His reply both corrects the Corinthian disorder and shows that Christian prophecy itself is by nature non-ecstatic.

2. 1 Cor. 12.1-3[69]

Three arguments designed to show that there was ecstatic prophecy at Corinth might be deduced from

---

[69]The syntax of vs. 2 is difficult. Westcott and Hort, followed by RP, suggested inserting a π to read ὅτι πότε, "You know that formerly you were heathen . . ." But there is no ready explanation for such a scribal error, and no textual evidence to support it. Further, it puts ἀπαγόμενοι in the same clause as ἔθνη and thereby makes the lack of agreement in gender more harsh (as does the weakly attested ὅτι alone [G, syr^P]).

Barrett suggests making the ὡς resume the clause begun by the ὅτι: "You know that, when you were Gentiles, how you were led away . . ." But he later acknowledges that Prof. Moule's objection is correct: to place an ἄν iterative before the verb, yet divorced from a (relative) ὡς, is to adopt a word order foreign to Greek (Barrett, 278, 399).

Héring, 123f, suggests that we delete the ὅτι, which was put there by a scribe who did not see the ὡς so far away and felt the need for a conjunction to follow οἴδατε. But it is difficult to accept that such a naive alteration which only made the sentence more awkward would have been made intentionally by a copyist.

The most probable solution is that we supply another ἦτε to go with the ἀπαγόμενοι. It is possible that Paul wrote the sentence as it stands, using an unusual anacoluthic construction (so Meyer, Godet). It is also possible, as Prof. Moule suggests (in Barrett, 399), that there was orginally a second ἦτε immediately

this section:

(a) In 12.1, where Paul introduces the section with περὶ δὲ τῶν πνευματικῶν, the term πνευματικῶν refers especially to the gifts of prophecy and tongues, and therefore shows that the wild cry in vs. 3 sometimes accompanied these gifts.

(b) Ἀπαγόμενοι in vs. 2 refers to moments when prophets are swept away in an ecstatic state.

(c) The cry, "Jesus be cursed" in vs. 3 is something uttered by prophets while in an ecstatic state.[70] These three arguments must now be examined in detail.

(a) In order to deal with the first argument, it is necessary to understand the meaning of πνευματικός in 1 Corinthians. Especially noteworthy is the great predominance of πνευματικός in this epistle compared to the rest of the NT (15X in 1 Cor., 19X in Pauline homologumena, 24X in total Pauline corpus, 26X in NT). One must also ask whether Paul and the Corinthians were using this word in the same way, or whether perhaps at points Paul was quoting the Corinthians in their special use of the term. Several points should be made with regard to these questions.

(i) The large number of times πνευματικός is used in 1 Corinthians does not necessarily imply that it was a favorite term at Corinth, or that it was used there in a specialized way which Paul was trying to correct. One might equally well suppose that, rather than attempting to correct the vocabulary of the Corinthians, Paul was concerned to correct their beliefs and practices with respect to the Holy Spirit. Since they were so concerned about the activity of the Spirit, Paul seizes every opportunity to show them directly or by implication what it really means to be "spiritual." Thus, the very subject matter of the epistle may account for the large number of occurrences of πνευματικός in 1 Corinthians (πνεῦμα

---

after the first, but it was lost through an early haplography. In either of these cases, the sense would be the same: "You know that when you were pagans you were led away to dumb idols, however you were led."

[70]So Robin Scorggs, "The Exaltation of the Spirit

is also used 40X in 1 Cor.--more than in any other
Pauline epistle, and Paul's only use of πνευματικῶς
is in 1 Cor. 2.14).

(ii) Paul uses πνευματικός to refer
to persons in 1 Cor. 2.15, 3.1, 14.37, Gal. 6.1, and
perhaps in 1 Cor. 12.1.[71] In Gal. 6.1 the word
quite clearly refers to those who are mature believers,
that is, those who well reflect the character of the
Holy Spirit: "You who are spiritual (οἱ πνευματικοί)
should restore him in a spirit of gentleness." In 1 Cor.
3.1 πνευματικός also has an ethical nuance and refers to
those who are spiritually mature,[72] because it is set
in contrast to those who are σαρκίνοι and νήπιοι ἐν
Χριστῷ. In 1 Cor. 2.15 the man who is πνευματικός has
sound and trustworthy judgment, so the context again
suggests a sense of "spiritually mature."

This leaves 1 Cor. 14.37 and perhaps 1 Cor. 12.1.
If one wanted to argue that πνευματικός in these
verses referred to those who were "spiritually gifted,"
he would have to say that Paul is here quoting the
Corinthians' special sense of πνευματικός, and is not
using it in the normal Pauline sense of "spiritually
mature" or "reflecting the character of the Spirit,"
when applied to persons. In this connection, it might
be argued that in 1 Cor. 3.1 Paul is intentionally
correcting the Corinthians.

However, this suggestion faces several difficulties. First, there is the problem of intelligibility.
If Paul knew that the Corinthians had a special sense
for πνευματικός, and that the word would cause disagreement between him and the Corinthians, is it
reasonable to think that he would have used it in his
own senses seven times in the epistle (2.13, 15, 3.1,
9.11, 10.3, 4, 4) before suddenly switching to use it
in the Corinthians' specialized sense, and then without
explicitly indicating the switch? Or can we suppose
that, knowing the specialized meaning which the
Corinthians attached to πνευματικός, he nevertheless

---

by Some Early Christians," <u>JBL</u> 84 (1965), 366.

[71] It may also refer to persons in the difficult passage 1 Cor. 2.13, but this is not immediately relevant to our inquiry here.

[72] Barrett, 79, "For spiritual men compare ii.14f;

proceeded to use it in a sense unlike theirs in all of these verses (or at least in 2.15 and 3.1 when applied to persons), expecting that somehow from the flow of argument they would understand and accept his meaning? One could hardly expect that the ordinary Corinthian Christian who heard the epistle would have grasped a semantic dispute carried on at such a subtle level.

And if we suppose that 3.1 is an attempt by Paul to correct the Corinthians' vocabulary, it is difficult to understand why he waited until 12.1 to apply the lesson, and said nothing about it in between.

Furthermore, if 12.1 means, "Concerning persons whom you call 'spiritually gifted,'" it makes a poor heading for chapters 12-14. In the following verses Paul argues that not some but all Christians have spiritual gifts (12.7, 11, 12, 13, 21, 27), so he could not have agreed to the Corinthians' restrction of the term to a special group. Now these verses could be seen as a corrective to the Corinthians' understanding of the term, except that (a) Paul does not in chaps. 12-14 talk about a special class of people whom the Corinthians called "spiritually gifted," but talks about gifts possessed by all believers (thus, 12.1 would be a misleading heading for these chapters); (b) there is no explicit indication by Paul that he is attempting to correct their understanding of the term πνευματικός, but he certainly could have put one in if he had wanted to be understood in this way; and (c) the overall concern of chaps. 12-14 is really not without certain types of people, and how the church should handle them, but with various types of gifts of the Spirit, and how they should be used in worship.

So the translation "spiritual men"[73] in 12.1 is unlikely, even if one supposes that it might be a

---

the meaning is the same as mature (ii.6). Compare also xiv. 37; Gal. vi. 1." Cf. also Bruce, 41f, and Dunn, JS, 287f.

[73]Hurd, Origin, 194 n. 1: Weiss, 194; Bruce, 116. Allo, Barrett, and Morris are undecided between "spiritual men" and "spiritual gifts."
Holtz, "Kennzeichen," 368f, argues that the Corinthians asked Paul about οἱ πνευματινοί, "gifted men," and he replied in terms of τὰ πνευματινά (cf. Chevallier, Esprit, 119f). But this fails to take account of Paul's earlier uses of πνευματικός to apply

quotation by Paul of a Corinthian understanding of πνευματικός to mean "spiritually gifted men."[74] Much to be preferred, and more suited to the context, is the translation, "concerning spiritual gifts."[75]

Similar arguments can be applied to 1 Cor. 14:37. If πνευματικός there refers to a sense in which the Corinthians thought themselves to be πνευματικοί, that is, "spiritually gifted," then (a) Paul's earlier use of πνευματικός in 1 Cor. betrays great insensitivity to this specialized use, (b) it would have been very confusing for the Corinthians to try to understand in each case whether Paul was using the word in his sense or theirs, and they could rightly have accused Paul in being a very poor communicator.

Furthermore, in 14.37 the meaning "spiritually gifted" allows the ἤ to have no real disjunctive force and προφήτης becomes redundant, for all prophets were "spiritually gifted." Paul could simply have said, "If anyone thinks himself to be spiritually gifted." But if we adopt the meaning "spiritually mature," the ἤ makes sense: some might have thought themselves to be mature, but no prophets.

Then in 14.37, the sense, "if anyone thinks himself to be spiritually gifted" would be somewhat confusing. After Paul's discussion in 12.4-31, all those who were persuaded by Paul's argument would have thought themselves to be "spiritually gifted." So was

---

to spiritually mature men (3.1), which would have been impossible if Paul had known of a special sense in which the Corinthians used the term.

[74]This definition is commonly assumed (cf., e.g., Conzelmann, 246), but it cannot be defended from analysis of the Pauline use of the term. Ellis, "'Spiritual' Gifts," 128-33, couples this definition with the view that τὰ πνευματικά refers only to speech gifts.

[75]This meaning is requied in 14.1 (ζηλοῦτε δὲ τὰ πνευματικά), a crucial summary verse. Paul uses πνευματικός to modify χάρισμα in Rom. 1.11, and uses χάρισμα interchangeably with πνευματικός in 12.4 (cf. 12.1) and 12.31 (cf. 14.1). "Gifts" is favored by Pearson, Terminology, 50; Calvin, 258; Conzelmann, 204, n. 1; Goudge, 109; Moffatt, 177; Evans, 332; Findlay, 885; Bittlinger, 13; Ellicott, 225f; RP, 259; Godet, II, 178f; Hodge, 136.

Paul using πνευματικός in the supposed old sense of the Corinthians (referring to a special group) or in yet another new sense (referring to all Christians)? It would have been very difficult to decide.

Finally, if Paul had used πνευματικός in 14.37 as a quotation of a specialized Corinthian meaning for the term, he would have undermined his entire purpose. At the very end of his discussion, after trying to show how there was no elite class of specially gifted Christians, he would have given acknowledgement to the fact that some Corinthians still considered themselves to be a special class of πνευματικοί, and would have given implicit acceptance of their right to continue to do so. But this would have nurtured more of the very factionalism which he was fighting.

(iii) It is also very unlikely that Paul in 1 Cor. 12.1 is using τῶν πνευματικῶν to refer to just prophecy and tongues, either as his own expression or as a quotation of the Corinthians. This verse introduces the entire section on spiritual gifts (chaps. 12-14),[76] and it is simply a misunderstanging of the overall structure of this section to say that Paul's dominant concern here is with prophecy and tongues. The section rather treats a wide variety of gifts and Paul's concern is that they all be understood and used correctly. This concern for much more than just prophecy and tongues is reflected in 12.4-11, in the entire body metaphor of 12.12-26, in the list of 12.27-30, in 13.1-3, 8, in 14.6, and in the crucial summary statements of 14.1, 12, and 26. Prophecy and tongues receive attention in chapter 14 simply because they are excellent examples of gifts which are more helpful and those which are less helpful to the assembled congregation. Therefore they help Paul's argument in 12-14, which can be summarized as follows: Concerning spiritual gifts (vs. 1): you all have useful gifts, and it is good to seek the greater gifts (12.2-31a). But it is even better to use the gifts in love (12.31b-13.13), which means speaking intelligibly and worshipping in an orderly way so that the church will be built up (14.1-40).

David Baker argues that ζηλοῦτε τὰ πνευματικά was a catch-phrase of the Corinthian church which Paul

---

[76]Compare περὶ δὲ in 12.1 with 7.1, 7.25, 8.1, 16.1, 16.12.

simply quotes, and that by τὰ πνευματικά the Corinthians meant primarily tongues and prophecy.[77] This suggestion is not possible because (a) Paul could not have used τὰ πνευματικά in such different ways in 1 Cor. if it had become at Corinth almost a technical term for only these two gifts (it would produce nonsense at 2.13, 3.1, 9.11); (b) since Paul founded and instructed the church at Corinth (cf. Ac. 18.1-18, esp. vs. 11), we would expect the Corinthians' use of this distinctive term to be roughly parallel to Paul's use, and Paul nowhere uses it this way; (c) even if Paul is quoting the Corinthians in 14.1 (which is certainly not obvious), he is still quoting them with approval. (The ζηλ- word group is not always negative in Paul: Rom. 10.2, 2 Cor. 11.2, Phil. 3.6, Gal. 1.14; its neutrality is clear in Gal. 4.18; cf. Tit. 2.14). Thus if τὰ πνευματικά meant "prophecy and tongues," Paul would be saying that the "more excellent way" (12.31) is to "seek after love, and earnestly desire prophecy and tongues, especially prophecy" (14.1). But this would contradict 12.28-31, where Paul puts tongues last, not second, and would destroy the force of chap. 14, which is an argument for intelligible speech.

(b) Thus even if ἀπαγόμενοι in 1 Cor. 12.2 did mean "carried away" in religious ecstasy,[78] it would not specifically refer to prophecy, for 12.1 includes all the gifts. But it is more likely that

---

[77] David Baker, "The Interpretation of 1 Cor. 12-14," EQ 46 (1974), 224ff. Baker largely follows Chevallier, Esprit, 148, n. 3 and 162f.
 D. W. B. Robinson, "Charismata vs. Pheumatika: Paul's Method of Discussion," RTR 31 (1972), 49ff, claims that τὰ πνευματικά was used by the Corinthians to refer just to tongues. Objections (a) and (b) above apply to this view as well, as does the fact that 12.1 introduces a discussion of all the gifts.

[78] Barrett (278) argues that it suggests moments of ecstasy in heathen religion, and quotes Hans Dieter Betz, Lukian von Samosata und das Neue Testament, TU 76 (Berlin, 1961), 40, n. 10. Betz speaks of "der offenbar technische Term. (ἀπ) ἀγεσθαι" in 1 Cor. 12.2 and lists six references in Lucian of Samosata to show that the term can refer to someone carried away by a demon in ecstasy. However, not one of these references

12.2 refers to actual travel to idol temples, because ἀπάγω in the NT (15X) and in the LXX (54X) always is used to refer to physical movement (frequently with an element of compulsion,[79] and usually in contexts of leading away to exile, destruction or death), and because there is a specified destination in this verse (πρὸς τὰ εἴδωλα τὰ ἄφωνα).

This means that several interpretations of 12.2 are quite unlikely. To say that ἀπαγόμενοι means "carried away" in an ecstatic experience finds no

---

uses the word ἀπάγω (they all have ἄγω), and in no case is there evidence of a technical religious significance to the term: it simply means "lead" or "bring." So in dial. mort. 19.1 Paris denies personal responsibility for falling in love with Helen by saying that a god (here, Eros) controls all men's lives and "leads us wherever he chooses"; similarly, a god (δαίμων) is said to have led a ship astray in ver. hist. I, 33; in Philops. 14 and 25 and dial. meretr. IV, 5 spiritual powers are said to lead men from one geographical location to another: in de Syr dea 36 an oracle prophet sits on the shoulders of some priests and he "leads" them backward and forward to signify "yes" or "no." Such examples (except the last) of "spiritual" leading can be paralleled in the NT (Rom. 8.14, Gal. 5.18; 1 Th. 4.14?), but in no case does even the term ἄγω imply that there is religious ecstasy of any kind experienced by those who are led.

Chrysostom, 169f, gives at 1 Cor. 12.2 several examples of ecstasy among heathen prophets, but contrasts this with the self-control of Christians at Corinth.

[79]The compulsion may have come from demonic influence (so Pearson, Terminology, 48f; Calvin, 259; Ellicott, 227; Godet, II, 181; Héring, 124; Meyer, 276; Evans, 332; cf. 1 Cor. 10.20, 1 Th. 2.18) or from intense social pressure at Corinth (RP, 260; cf. Ac. 8.9-10, 16.19-24, 19.23-41). Paul's ὡς ἂν ἤγεσθε, "however you were led," could allow for both, and perhaps too fine a distinction between human and divine influence should not be made here: Justin Martyr, Apology 1.58.3, uses ἀπάγω to speak of demons who "lead men away from God who made them" by working through men like Marcion.

("Whenever" is also a possible translation of ὡς ἄν; cf. Gen. 6.5, Ex. 33.9, 1 K. 2.13, 2 K. 14.26, Job 1.5).

support at all in the other uses of the word.⁸⁰ If Paul had meant that, he could easily have used a word like ἁρπάζω (2 Cor. 12.2, 4; cf. 1 Th. 4.17)⁸¹ Neither does it mean "to be deceived" and carried into doctrinal or moral error.⁸² For this, Paul would probably have used πλανάω (1 Cor. 6.9, 15.33, Gal. 6.7, etc.), ἀπατάω (Eph. 5.6, 1 Tim. 2.14), or ἐξαπατάω (Rom. 7.11, 1 Cor. 3.18). Nor does it imply that the Corinthians intentionally turned aside from the truth and became idolators (for which we would expect ἐκκλίνω, as in Rom. 3.12 and 16.17). It simply means that they were under strong compulsion to attend idol temples. We conclude that neither vs. 1 nor vs. 2 gives us reason to postulate the existence of any religious ecstasy at Corinth.

(c) The cry Ἀνάθεμα Ἰησοῦς in vs. 3 is unusual enough to have given rise to many fanciful explanations. The common fault with most of them is a neglect of the context of the verse, especially its close relationship with vss. 1 and 2, signified by διό, "therefore." It is <u>because</u> Paul does not want the Corinthians to be ignorant about spiritual gifts (vs. 1), and <u>because</u> their previous lives included attendance at the temples of dumb idols (vs. 2), that Paul writes

---

⁸⁰See above, n. 78, for this view. In a slight variation of this view Héring, 123f (also Heinrici, 341), reads ἀνήγεσθε instead of ἂν ἤγεσθε and says that ἀνάγω is a technical term for snatching away into the invisible world by supernatural powers. But ἀνάγω (23X in NT) does not suggest ecstatic experience (in Lk. 4.5 and Mt. 4.1 physical travel is in view), and to translate ἀνήγεσθε as "you were led up" would make no sense in 1 Cor. 12.2.

⁸¹Or perhaps ἀποφέρω (Rev. 17.3, 21.10).

⁸²This meaning is proposed by Edwards, 307, but poorly supported by reference to Tit. 3.3, which contains πλανάω, not ἀπάγω. He would have found slightly better support in the use of συναπάγω in Gal. 2.13 and 2 Pet. 3.17 (cf. Hodge, 137), but such evidence still is not strong enough to overthrow the very consistent use of ἀπάγω throughout the NT and LXX to refer to physical motion, and the fact that Paul specifies a destination in this verse. (Ἀπάγω does mean "lead astray" in Dg. 9.1, however.)

vs. 3. The first two verses emphasize nothing more complex than the sheer lack of experience with true "inspired" speech which the Corinthians had: the idols were ἄφωνα and so the Corinthians could not use their experience with idols as a guide in deciding questions concerning speech spoken under the influence of the Holy Spirit.[83]

There are three major ways of understanding vs. 3: (i) Paul wants to provide the Corinthians with a test for true and false prophecy. (i) Paul is dealing with incipient Gnosticism at Corinth. (iii) Paul simply wants to correct the ignorance of the Corinthians concerning spiritual gifts, an area which was unknown to them when they served dumb idols.[84]

---

[83] They may of course have experienced other kinds of "inspired" speech from what Paul would call demonic "inspiration" (cf. 1 Cor. 10, 20), but this would still have left them ignorant concerning "true" inspired speech from the Holy Spirit.

[84] Several other views have been proposed but not widely adopted. J. D. M. Derrett, "Cursing Jesus (1 Cor. 12.3): The Jews as Religious 'Persecutors'," NTS 21 (1974-75), 544ff, argues for the very early existence of Jewish attempts to force Christians out of the Jewish community, and supposes that some Jewish Christian may have uttered, "Jesus be cursed," in an attempt to remain in the synagogue. But in order to do this he must relate 12.2 not to the previous lives of the Corinthians but to God's judgment on Israel in the OT, which is quite difficult to reconcile with "when you were heathens . . . you were led away." Furthermore, the context deals with spiritual gifts (vs. 1), not primarily with any kind of persecution. Nor does a persecution theory offer a convincing explanation for vs. 3b which is grounded in vs. 2.
Grosheide, 280f, suggests that some Corinthians, not understanding what was spoken in tongues, were worried that tongues messages might contain blasphemy, perhaps unknown even to the speaker. So Paul reassures them, "No one speaking by the Spirit of God says 'Jesus be cursed.'" The interpretation fits 12.3a taken in isolation, but on this interpretation 12.3b has no real purpose and 12.2 is totally unrelated to the inquiry.
Hurd, 193, sees it as composed by Paul as a hypothetical opposite to the cry "Jesus is Lord."

(i) Vs. 3 as a test for true and false prophecy. On this interpretation, the Corinthians had simply asked Paul for a reliable means of

---

However, the διό in vs. 3 makes it seem to flow much more closely out of the Corinthians' earlier experience in vs. 2, and it would be awkward to have a hypothetical example come before the concrete example it is opposing.

W. F. Albright and C. S. Mann, "Two Texts in 1 Corinthians" (NTS 16 [1969-70], 271ff), propose a radical emendation of vs. 3 to make it an Aramaic liturgical formula. But they do this only because "it is hard to imagine any situation in which Paul would have wasted time explaining that, for Christians, cursing Jesus was not a work of the Spirit" (p. 273). I suggest however that several of the proposed solutions seem more plausible than a totally recast sentence with absolutely no manuscript evidence to support it.

Karl Maly, "1 Kor. 12.1-3, eine Regel zur Unterscheidung der Geister?," BZ n.s. 10 (1966), 82-95, suggests that Paul uses vss. 2 and 3 to show (1) that there is a contrast between the Corinthians' former slavery to idols and their current freedom in the Spirit, and (2) that although this freedom has certain obvious boundaries (vs. 3a), it does extend to the empowering of confessions of faith in Christ and thence (vss. 4-7) to all the gifts, not just to speech gifts. Although I am in agreement with Maly at several points, his emphasis on the freedom of life in the Spirit is a contrast which is not found even implicitly in the text. Further, there is some difficulty with γνωρίζω if we hold, with Maly, that vs. 3a is only an extreme boundary laid down by Paul because he knew it would gain immediate agreement from all at Corinth.

Holtz, "Kennzeichen," 365-76, argues that by employing the two antithetical expressions Paul intends his readers to understand that he is referring not just to speech but also to heart belief (cf. Rom. 10. 9) and thus to the whole of a person's life. While I agree that in Paul's mind a confession indicated heart belief, it is reading too much into the text to suppose that while Paul merely wrote about spoken confessions in fact he meant to talk about all of life. I do agree with Holtz, however, that the main purpose of vss. 2-3 is to exclude all those who have no part in the Spirit and to include all those who do (p. 371).

distinguishing true prophecy from false. So Paul wrote back and said if a prophet curses Jesus, he is false, but if he confesses Jesus as Lord, he is true.

This interpretation has much to commend it, and does represent part of what I understand to be the true situation behind vs. 3. False prophets were indeed a problem in the early church (Mt. 7.15, 24.11, Ac. 13.6, 1 Jn. 4.1).[85] But for several reasons this explanation does not exactly do justice to vs. 3 in its context. First, it completely neglects vs. 2. Being led astray to dumb idols might with the help of a vivid imagination be made to have some relation to false prophets, but that relationship certainly is not in the text itself.

Second, these words somehow seem to be quite a poor test for false prophets. There could have been many prophets at Corinth who fell in neither of the apostle's categories: they were careful never to utter the words "Jesus be cursed," but neither did they make a habit of prefacing each public pronouncement with the password, "Jesus is Lord." (Indeed, it is hard to imagine that Paul would expect this to happen). If a false prophet were asked to say, "Jesus is Lord," he might verbally comply in order to gain acceptance by the church. Or there might even be a true believer who would speak a heartfelt "Jesus is Lord," but who would then mistakenly "prophesy" false words without any empowering or approval from the Holy Spirit. How would vs. 3 be an adequate test for him?

G. de Broglie, "Le texte fondamental de Saint Paul contre la foi naturelle," RScR 39 (1951-52), 253-56, sees vs. 3b simply as doctrinal teaching by Paul in which he emphasizes that a true confession of Jesus as Lord must be made possible by the Holy Spirit. However, de Broglie is too hesitant (pp. 256f) to apply this to the situation of worship at Corinth.

Barrett, 279f, mentions other interpretations of vs. 3, but they are all precluded by arguments presented there by him. The view Barrett himself adopts (after Allo), namely that "Paul is referring to the cries of Christian ecstatics who were resisting the trance or ecstasy which they felt coming upon them," depends on his finding a reference to ecstasy in vs. 2. But, as I have argued above, such a view is not very convincing.

[85]Cf. Lampe, "Grievous Wolves," 253-68.

Third, Paul had another means for evaluating prophecies: "Let two or three prophets speak and let the others (the members of the congregation) weigh what is said" (1 Cor. 14.29). The evaluations were presumably done on the basis of conformity with received doctrine and with the Old Testament Scriptures (Gal. 1.8, 1 Cor. 14.37-38, 1 Jn. 4.2-3, 6, Ac. 17.11). Such a test was a much better means of sorting true prophecy from false and would have dealt effectively with even the true believer who mistakenly prophesied. So understanding 1 Cor. 12.3 as a test for true and false prophecy does not adequately explain the verse.

(ii) Vs. 3 as an indication of Gnosticism at Corinth: This is a more recent suggestion for understanding 1 Cor. 12.3, proposed by Walter Schmithals.[86] According to this theory, ἀνάθεμα Ἰησοῦς was shouted by early Gnostics who venerated the heavenly Christ but denied that he was the same as the earthly Jesus, and expressed this denial in the harsh words of this curse.[87]

B. A. Pearson[88] attempted to fault Schmithals's formulation of this theory by challenging his use of a "parallel" passage in Origen (Contra Celsum 6.28). Pearson doubts that the Ophite Gnostics mentioned by Origen really did curse Jesus; rather, Origen thought they cursed Jesus when they associated him with the serpent of Gen. 3 (p. 304). Pearson's analysis is open to question however. He must suppose that Origen misunderstood the Ophites on a point so important to them (the veneration of the serpent) that it had given them their particular name.[89] It is better to take

---

[86] Gnosticism in Corinth, 124-30.

[87] Ibid., 127.

[88] B. A. Pearson, "Did the Gnostics Curse Jesus?," JBL 86 (1967), 301-05.

[89] Origen does understand this point, for he clearly distinguishes between the anathemas an Ophite convert was to pronounce against Jesus and the praises the Ophites give to the serpent: the convert is not admitted εἰ μὴ ἀναθεματίσῃ τὸν Ἰησοῦν, but the Ophites are so named because of "the unlawful things they speak in praise of the serpent" (οὐ θεμιτὰ λέγουσιν εἰς ἐγκώμιον τοῦ ὄφεως) (text in Jenkins, "Origen," 30, 11.31-33).

Origen at face value and accept his statement that there were Ophites who required one to curse Jesus as a prerequisite for membership in their sect.[90]

Nevertheless, Schmithals's proposal is inadequate for another reason, namely, his failure to exegete 1 Cor. 12.3 in context. His proposal may explain vs. 3 if we examine the verse in isolation. But this explanation bears no relationship to vs. 2 and thereby cannot account for the διό in vs. 3 which connects it closely with the preceding verse: Paul is speaking in vs. 2 of some heathen experience in the lives of the Corinthians <u>before</u> they became Christians, not of Gnostics <u>presently</u> in the Corinthian church. For this reason we must reject the proposal of Schmithals.[91]

(iii) <u>Vs. 3 as an antidote for the ignorance of the Corinthians concerning spiritual gifts</u>. This interpretation commends itself as fitting in well with the entire context. Paul says, in effect, "I don't want you to be ignorant about spiritual gifts. You know that you formerly served gods who could not speak, and, therefore, gods from whom you could have learned nothing. So you are ignorant about spiritual gifts. Therefore, I make known to you that no one speaking by the Spirit of God says, 'Jesus be cursed,' and no one can say, 'Jesus is Lord,' except by the

---

[90] Nor is Pearson right in saying that Origen attributes the curse of 1 Cor. 12.3 to "Jews, not Gnostics" (p. 301, n. 2). Rather, <u>both</u> Jews and Ophites are mentioned as illustrations of those who curse Jesus.

[91] Brox, " ΑΝΑΘΕΜΑ ΙΗΣΟΥΣ (1 Kor. 12.3)," <u>BZ</u> n.s. 12 (1968), 103ff, also argues that the curse-phrase in vs. 3a is a Gnostic saying, one which exalts the heavenly Christ by denying the earthly Jesus. The same criticism applies: this is exegesis-in-isolation. Brox does not even consider vs. 2 or the διό of vs. 3, which, I feel, show his suggestion to be untenable.

On the general question of Gnosticism at Corinth, cf. Wilson, "How Gnostic?," 65-74 ; Bruce, <u>1-2 Corinthians</u>, 21; A. D. Nock, <u>Essays on Religion and the Ancient World</u>, ed. Z. Stewart (2 vols.; Oxford, 1972), II, 957f; S. Arai, "Die Gegner des Paulus im 1. Korintherbrief und das Problem der Gnosis," <u>NTS</u> 19 (1972-73), 430-37.

Holy Spirit."[92] Understood in this way, the verses provide a fitting introduction to chaps. 12-14, for here Paul can be seen to emphasize the fact that every Christian has within him the Spirit of God, enabling him to make such a statement.

(a) A suggested background for these verses. There are no doubt many possible reconstructions of the situation at Corinth which may be suggested as a background for these verses. It may be imagined, for example, that certain persons at Corinth were claiming an exclusive kind of possession of the Spirit, and Paul wanted to emphasize that every believer had the Spirit within him. Several other similar situations might also be proposed, and the evidence is slender enough that it would be difficult to choose between them. Nevertheless, I shall propose here one possible solution which, it seems to me, accounts for all of the factors in vss. 1-3 in a rather appealing way.

Perhaps the Corinthians had expressed to Paul a concern about the intermingling of idolatry and Christianity. There were several former idolaters in the church (cf. 1 Cor. 6.9-11, 8.7), and those who caused the most suspicion fell roughly into two categories. On the one hand, people who claimed to be inspired were coming to the worship services and giving a very impressive performance, perhaps prophesying with much emotion. Yet they were saying some very disturbing things, sometimes even blaspheming Christ.[93] Might the Holy Spirit nevertheless be

---

[92] So Ellicott, 227; Godet, II, 183; Meyer, 277; Morris, 167; RP, 260; Evans, 332; Findlay, 886.

[93] I understand ἀνάθεμα Ἰησοῦς to be a spoken curse on Jesus. W. C. van Unnik, "Jesus: Anathema or Kurios," CSNT, 113-26, suggests that the phrase means that Jesus was given over to complete destruction for sin (cf. γενόμενος ὑπὲρ ἡμῶν κατάρα in Gal. 3.13) in order to save men from God's wrath (p. 119). The deficiency in the statement would then be that it mentions only Jesus' death and in so doing implicitly denies his vindicatory resurrection and present Lordship (p. 124). The suggestion is interesting and the concepts of Christ's substitutionary sin-bearing and subsequent resurrection are not foreign to Pauline thought. However, we find that the biblical authors

empowering them, if not in the blasphemy,[94] at least in some of the other things they said? Paul answers, "No, these people are not speaking by the Spirit of God. If the Holy Spirit were at work in them, they simply would not say such a thing."

On the other hand, if the Corinthians were not to trust these people, it would be difficult for them to know whom to trust. A large segment of the church consisted of converted idolators, some of them with as yet only marginal Christian understanding. How could it be determined that any former idolator was speaking the truth--or even that any of his gifts, whether they be prophecy, teaching, healing, tongues, administration or whatever, were to be trusted in the church? To this Paul replies, "You must not be overly suspicious and exclude true believers from the work of the church. Anyone who makes a true, sincere Christian confession has made it by the power of the Holy Spirit and should be fully accepted in the church."[95]

We cannot of course understand 12.3 to refer to a simple repetition of some magic formula (cf. the false professions in Mt. 7.21-23 and 15.8). Rather, the confession "Jesus is Lord" to which Paul refers must be viewed as a profession of personal faith,

---

are quite careful in their use of this word: although ἀνάθεμα and ἀναθεματίζω occur often in the LXX and eight times in the NT, they are not once used to refer to persons or things who bear the sin of others. (Rom. 9.3, which van Unnik quotes, is difficult, but we cannot understand Paul to mean that some additional sacrifice besides that of Christ would somehow be necessary to atone for the sins of the Jews.) "The controlling thought here is that of delivering up to the judicial wrath of God of one who ought to be ἀνάθεμα because of his sin" (J. Behm, TDNT I, 354).

[94] R. Scroggs, "The Exaltation of the Spirit by Some Early Christians," JBL 84 (1965), 359-74, suggests that some Corinthians may even have thought that the blasphemy was justified because it was uttered "in the Spirit." This is hardly likely.

[95] Similarly Holtz, "Kennzeichen," 371; Crone, ECP, 224-26; von Campenhausen, Ecclesiastical Authority, 183, n. 25.

given credibility by some reasonable indication of accompanying sincerity and understanding. Similarly, the words "Jesus be cursed" do not by themselves necessarily indicate unbelief, for they would have been pronounced by anyone at Corinth who read Paul's letter aloud. But if they seemed to indicate the speaker's own sentiments, then Paul would consider them an indication of unbelief. Of course Paul was not proposing a 100% foolproof system, because it would not have been possible in every case for the Corinthians to tell if a man was sincere, especially with the confession of faith. But as a general rule, useful in most cases, Paul was saying that blasphemy indicated unbelief and a confession of faith indicated belief.

(b) <u>More than speech gifts are under consideration</u>. With this understanding of 12.3, we see that Paul does not have speech gifts alone in view in this section. Although the confession of faith and the blasphemy are speech activities, they function as indications of the presence or absence of the work of the Holy Spirit in a person's life. If someone confesses that "Jesus is Lord," it indicates that the Holy Spirit is at work within him (12.3) and thus that he is a member of the one body of Christ (12.13) and has gifts which are to be used for the benefit of that body (12.7, 11, 12-31). If a person blasphemes, it indicates that the Holy Spirit is not at work within him (12.3) and thus that he is not a member of Christ and does not at that time have gifts which benefit the church.[96]

So περὶ δὲ τῶν πνευματικῶν, "now concerning spiritual gifts," is an appropriate heading for 12.2-3 as well as for all of chapters 12-14. In a city full of idolatry, 12.2-3 distinguishes those who have spiritual gifts (believers) from those who do not (unbelievers).

(c) <u>Speaking ἐν πνεύματι θεοῦ</u>. I have suggested that 1 Cor. 12.3a be understood as blasphemy which gives away the actual spiritual state of a false

---

[96] 1 Jn. 4.1ff is similar to 1 Cor. 12.3 because in both cases it is the speech of a prophet which gives away the kind of spirit by which he is speaking.

believer in the church, and that 12.3b represents a confession of faith made possible only by the enabling work of the Holy Spirit. If this interpretation is accurate, we are now in a position to define more carefully what Paul had in mind when he wrote about someone speaking "under the influence of the Spirit of God"[97] (ἐν πνεύματι Θεοῦ or ἐν πνεύματι ἁγίῳ) in 1 Cor. 12.3.

(i) Paul did not envisage the speaker to be completely controlled by the Holy Spirit or to be speaking the Holy Spirit's words for him. If 12.3b is a confession of faith, then it is a _personal_ confession. If sincere, the speaker is speaking out of his own heart. So the words he speaks are his own and we should not suppose that they could be taken as the Holy Spirit's words: to preface "Thus says the Holy Spirit" (cf. Ac. 21.11, 1 Tim. 4.1) to this kind of speech would completely invalidate it as a credible profession of _personal_ faith. Indeed, if one were to argue that 1 Cor. 12.3b only refers to "fully inspired" speech, that is, speech in which the Holy Spirit himself is the speaker, he would have to argue that no one except the Holy Spirit could confess that Jesus is Lord. This is certainly an impossible position and would destroy Paul's argument in 1 Cor. 12.1-3.

(ii) Yet Paul did see speech ἐν πνεύματι as motivated or made possible in some way by the Holy Spirit. "No one is able (οὐδεὶς δύναται) to say, 'Jesus is Lord,' except by the Holy Spirit." If we understand this to refer to a confession of faith, then it was probably in the areas of understanding the Gospel (1 Cor. 1.18ff, 2.6ff) and willingness to believe that Paul envisaged an active influence of the Holy Spirit.

E. Related Verses in the NT

Very briefly we note other NT verses which might relate to the problem of prophetic ecstasy.

---

[97]The phrase ἐν πνεύματι (or πνεύματι alone) frequently signifies influence but not control by the Holy Spirit: for prayer: Eph. 6.18, Jude 20; 1 Cor. 14.2, 15; worship: Jn. 4.23-24; Phil. 3.3; other activities: Lk. 2.22; Rom. 8.13; Gal. 5.16, 25. (But cf. Mt. 22.43 for an apparently stronger sense.)

1. **Ac. 19.6**

Here speaking in tongues and prophesying are closely joined as if they might be a single experience. But the text itself gives no indication of any ecstatic experiences here. And with regard to precisely the one characteristic by which tongues might be termed "ecstatic" (its unintelligibility, my criterion [3]), Paul, in the more full discussion in 1 Corinthians, clearly differentiates tongues from prophecy (cf. 1 Cor. 12).[98] So we do not find NT evidence for tongues as ecstatic in any sense that would bear on the question of prophecy.[99]

2. **2 Cor. 12.1ff**

Paul says that he was "caught up to the third heaven" and experienced "visions and revelations of the Lord" (vss. 2, 1). The experience was "ecstatic" in sense (4): he was for a time so unaware of his surroundings that he did not know whether he was in the body or out of the body (vs. 2). Might this be an example of NT prophetic ecstasy?

This section is not really relevant to our investigation of the NT gift of prophecy because (a) the "revelations" Paul received were specifically not given in order that he might prophesy (that is, report them to others): he heard things which are not permitted for men to speak (vs. 4), and was so reticent about even mentioning the experience that he waited 14 years (vs. 2) and then spoke of it in the third person (vss. 2-5); and (b) such an experience seems to Paul to be extremely unusual, and not the normal experience of prophets or any other Christians, for he says the revelations were of an extraordinary character (τῇ ὑπερβολῇ τῶν ἀποκαλύψεων, vs. 7), and relates that

---

[98]That there is no convincing basis for considering tongues "ecstatic" on any of the other three grounds we list was argued convincingly by R. H. Gundry. "'Ecstatic Utterance' (N.E.B.)?" JTS n.s. 17 (1966), 299-307.

[99]Even if tongues had been ecstatic in some other sense (such as loss of self-control), Ac. 19.6 would still contain insufficient data to argue that such a psychological state would also carry over into prophecy.

experience only as a last-ditch attempt to show his superiority over the false apostles, and thus as something of which he "might" boast (vss. 5-6). So this experience cannot be taken as characteristic of NT prophecy.

3. 2 Pet. 1.21

We read here that "no prophecy of Scripture came by the will of man" (θελήματι ἀνθρώπου ἠνέχθη), "but men carried along by the Holy Spirit spoke from God" (ἀλλὰ ὑπὸ πνεύματος ἁγίου φερόμενοι ἐλάλησαν ἀπὸ Θεοῦ ἄνθρωποι). For two reasons this cannot be used as good evidence of NT prophetic ecstasy: (a) It is OT prophets who are in view here, for (i) the προφήτης word group is always used of OT prophets in the Petrine epistles; (ii) it is specifically the "prophecies of Scripture" (προφητεία γραφῆς, vs. 20) which are in view, and there is no group of NT writings to which this phrase is ever applied;[100] (iii) in 3.2, the "holy prophets" are OT prophets because they "spoke beforehand" words which the readers had heard before and could recall, and because they are clearly distinguished from the NT apostles through whom the Lord spoke his commandment (vs. 2b); (iv) the "false prophets among the people" in 2 Pet. 2.1 are no doubt false OT prophets who arose ἐν τῷ λαῷ,[101] and are with "false teachers" ἐν ὑμῖν, and if the false prophets in 2.1 are OT prophets, then so must the prophets in 1.21 be OT prophets. Thus, the verse has no direct bearing on our investigation of NT prophecy.

(b) The phrase ὑπὸ πνεύματος ἁγίου φερόμενοι need not necessarily imply prophetic ecstasy. The

---

[100] Γραφή in the NT always refers to the OT Scriptures (AG, 165), except in 2 Pet. 3.16, where by implication it refers also to Paul's writings, and perhaps in 1 Tim. 5.18, where it seems to refer to the statement of Jesus recorded in Lk. 10.7 (cf. Mt. 26.56).

[101] The aorist ἐγένοντο puts these prophets so clearly in the past that it must point to OT history, not to relatively recent events in the history of the early church (especially if the readers were to understand Peter as the author: 1.17, 3.1). Thus, "the people" are the OT people of God, and are distinguished from "you," the Christian readers of the epistle.

point under discussion is not the psychological state of the prophet but the origin (vs. 21a, "not by the will of man") of his writings and therefore their non-susceptibility to arbitrary and fanciful interpretations (vs. 20; cf. 3.16).[102] To make this point the author speaks in very strong terms of the control of the prophet by the Holy Spirit (φερόμενοι),[103] but the way in which he does this is so ambiguous that it need not imply that the prophet was forced to speak against his will or lost his own self control (note that ἐλάλησαν . . . ἄνθρωποι, and they may well have done so with full consent to the "bearing along" by the Holy Spirit). Because neither NT prophecy nor prophetic ecstasy are under consideration in this passage, it cannot bear directly on our inquiry.

F. Conclusion

An examination of data in 1 Corinthians and then elsewhere in the NT indicates that certainly at Corinth, and quite probably elsewhere in the NT church, prophets do not seem to have had ecstatic experiences while prophesying.

---

[102]Or perhaps the impossibility of interpreting them apart from the Holy Spirit (NEB: "No one can interpret any prophecy of Scripture by himself").
    M. Green, 2 Peter and Jude, 89ff argues that γίνεται in vs. 20 means "comes from," and that therefore vs. 20 also describes the origin of prophetic writings: "No prophecy of Scripture comes from the prophet's own understanding (ἐπίλυσις)."
    On any of these views, it is the origin of the writings, not the means by which they were produced, which is in view.

[103]Philo of course uses the term θεοφόρητος to speak of a prophet in full-fledged ecstasy (Mos. 2.246, cf. 250; Quis Her. 258), but we need not suppose that his ideas of ecstasy were shared by the NT authors, even though there is a formal similarity in language. (Cf. n. 65) (However, Hos. 9.7 [LXX] translates מְשֻׁגָּע אִישׁ הָרֹחַ with ἄνθρωπος ὁ πνευματοφόρος.)

IV. 1 CORINTHIANS 13.2: UNDERSTANDING MYSTERIES AND KNOWLEDGE: THE EFFECT OF LOVE

A. Mysteries and Knowledge

Paul writes, "If I have prophecy and know all mysteries and all knowledge . . . but have not love, I am nothing" (ἐὰν ἔχω προφητείαν καὶ εἰδῶ τὰ μυστήρια πάντα καὶ πᾶσαν τὴν γνῶσιν . . . ἀγάπην δὲ μὴ ἔχω, οὐδέν εἰμι.). This verse does not mean that every prophet has an understanding of "all mysteries and all knowledge," for Paul is using hypothetical superlatives in his argument. He takes several examples of gifts (prophecy, faith, self-sacrifice)[104] and argues that even if developed to their greatest possible degree, they would be worthless without love: "If I have all faith, so as to remove mountains . . . If I divide into fragments[105] all my possessions . . . if I deliver my body to be burned"[106] (the ultimate in self-sacrifice). So Paul is simply saying that the ultimate result of prophecy developed to its fullest possible extent would be a knowledge of all mysteries and all knowledge.[107] This is not now the case with any living prophet, according to Paul, for "we prophesy in part" (vs. 9) and so only at the consummation do we know fully, "even as we are known" (vs. 12).

---

[104] It is not clear that speaking in the "tongues of angels" is itself a superlative degree of speaking in tongues (as claimed by Gundry, "Ecstatic?," 301): Paul need not have used an unattainable superlative in every case to prove his point, for "tongues of men" is certainly not a superlative category of tongues. Paul may simply have meant, "No matter what language I speak, heavenly or earthly . . ."

[105] Ψωμίζω, perhaps to give away (RSV); perhaps to feed others (Barrett, 301).

[106] Καυθήσομαι or καυθήσωμαι, but καυχήσωμαι, "that I may boast," is also possible.

[107] That (a) having prophecy and (b) knowing all mysteries and all knowledge are to be taken as a unit and not as distinct gifts is clear from the fact that καὶ ἐάν (κἄν) sets off every new item in Paul's list but is not repeated before εἰδῶ τὰ μυστήρια πάντα καὶ πᾶσαν τὴν γνῶσιν.

Nevertheless, this passage does make clear by implication that knowing "mysteries and knowledge," even if only in part, is a normal component of the gift of prophecy. So there is an epistemological benefit which comes to the prophet as a result of his having the gift of prophecy: he understands and knows more than he would have otherwise.

Τὰ μυστήρια are "the secret thoughts, plans, and dispensations of God which are hidden from the human reason . . . and hence must be revealed to those for whom they are intended" (AG, 532), and so this verse corroborates our earlier understanding of "revelation" as an essential element of prophecy. But the verse will not allow us to go beyond this and define with much certainty the precise content of the "mysteries and knowledge," for, as Barrett says, "It is probable that Paul is here piling up words without too nice a regard for the distinctions between them. 'I may know everything there is to know, but if I have no love I am nothing'" (p. 301).

B. Love

To be "nothing" when one prophesies without love may refer either to the benefits to others or to the benefits to oneself. If the former, Paul would be saying that a prophet without love has no good effects (similar to the noisy gong or clanging cymbal in vs. 1, which are meaningless and disruptive), presumably because even though he prophesies he does not take care that his words are spoken with kindness (vs. 4), and without arrogance or disorderliness (vs. 5). This then would be another indication of the great degree of freedom enjoyed by NT prophets: apparently their own choice of words, of tone, and of attitude would determine the effectiveness of their prophecies. The prophecy would be a result both of the "revelation" received by the prophet and of the words which the prophet chose to report it.

But if the latter, then Paul would be saying that a loveless prophecy brings him no credit in the eyes of God, even though it may do some good for others (similar to giving away his goods in vs. 3). It is perhaps impossible to choose between these two interpretations.

While investigating the psychological state of a prophet, it is appropriate to mention the way in which this love in chap. 13 would affect the gift of prophecy in chap. 14. Paul sees the main result in this: the prophet who acts in love will take care that his speech always edifies his hearers. Thus, he will wait his turn (14.31, cf. οὐκ ἀσχημονεῖ in 13.5), will speak to men for their benefit and seek their good (14.3; cf. οὐ ζητεῖ τὰ ἑαυτῆς in 13.5), will willingly submit his prophecy to evaluation and scrutiny by others (14.29; cf. οὐ φυσιοῦται in 13.4), will gladly give way and allow another to prophesy instead of himself (14.30; cf. οὐ περπερεύεται . . . οὐ ζητεῖ τὰ ἑαυτῆς in 13.4-5), and even when speaking of the sins of others will presumably not do it in the kind of triumphant, haughty manner which would provoke alienation and withdrawal by the outsider, but rather with the kind of compassion which would evoke worship of God (14.24-25; cf. οὐ παροξύνεται . . . οὐ χαίρει ἐπὶ τῇ ἀδικίᾳ in 13.5-6). In short, the prophet prophesying in love would continually seek to use his gift to benefit others and not himself.[108] This could not be done mechanically, but must be the result of a "psychological state" or inward attitude of love for others in the congregation. Only then would prophecy be of greatest benefit to the church according to the "more excellent way."

V. SUMMARY OF CHAPTER TWO

The reception of a "revelation" and the public report of that revelation seem to be the two essential characteristics of prophecy, both at Corinth and in the rest of the NT. The Pauline terms for this revelation, ἀποκαλύπτω and ἀποκάλυψις, are both frequent enough and sufficiently restricted in use to enable us to say that, in Paul's view, the revelation came quite spontaneously (but privately) to an individual, was of divine origin, was seen from a divine perspective, and probably took the form of words, thoughts or mental pictures which suddenly impressed themselves forcefully on the mind of the prophet. However, it does not seem that the divine origin of the revelation can be used to demonstrate any divine authority in the prophet's words unless an extra-biblical concept of "miracle" be imposed on the text.

---

[108]Cf. Mic. 3.5-12 for a description of OT prophets who prophesy for wrong motives.

Since there are indications in 1 Corinthians that the prophet was not forced to speak against his will, did not lose his self-control or rave violently, did not speak things which made no sense to him, and was not unaware of his surroundings, he should not be termed "ecstatic." In 1 Cor. 12.1-3, Paul speaks of all the gifts and implies that anyone who curses Jesus is a false believer and should not use his "gifts" in worship, while anyone who sincerely confesses Christ is a true believer and should be allowed to use his gifts in worship. Speaking "under the influence of the Holy Spirit" refers to speech which is made possible by the Spirit without depriving the speaker of his individual volition in deciding what to say.

Because of the limitations of this present age, Paul thinks that both the revelation received by a prophet and the resulting prophecy will give only partial information about the subject, and will sometimes be difficult to understand or interpret.

The effect of love is to make a prophet use his gift for the benefit of others, not himself.

CHAPTER THREE

THE FUNCTION, CONTENT AND FORM OF PROPHECY

Our purpose in this chapter is to understand the way in which prophecy benefits the church. What is the purpose of prophecy? What kinds of things might a prophet say? Once again we shall study the relevant passages in 1 Corinthians first, and then examine in somewhat less detail the related passages elsewhere in the NT. The investigation is divided into three sections: (1) the functions of prophecy, or the purposes it served in the congregation; (2) the content or subject matter of prophecies; (3) the form of prophecy, or the distinctive phraseology which occurred in prophetic speeches.

I. THE FUNCTIONS OF PROPHECY

A. 1 Cor. 14.3: Upbuilding, Encouragement, Consolation

The basic text here is 1 Cor. 14.3: "But he who prophesies speaks to men for their upbuilding and encouragement and consolation" (ὁ δὲ προφητεύων ἀωθρώποις λαλεῖ οἰκοδομὴν καὶ παράκλησιν καὶ παραμυθίαν). Paul is arguing that the Corinthians should seek especially to prophesy (vs. 1). In vss. 2-5, he contrasts tongues and prophecy: no one understands the person speaking in tongues, so he is not speaking to men but to God (vs. 2). But by contrast (δὲ, vs. 3) he who prophesies is speaking to men so that they can understand, and by a prophet's words the hearers receive edification, encouragement and comfort (vs. 3). While the tongue-speaker edifies himself, the prophet edifies the church (vs. 4). This is the reason prophecy is superior to tongues: it brings more benefit to the church (vs. 5).

This context shows that Paul sees prophecy as an essentially public gift. There is no indication that a prophet would prophesy in private for his own personal benefit. If he did, his prophecy would be on the same level as the tongues in vs. 4 ("he who speaks in a tongue edifies himself"), and this would not be the kind of prophecy the Corinthians were to seek (vs. 1). So unless prophecy functions in the assembled meeting of the church, it loses its pre-eminence among the gifts.[1]

While the context of 1 Cor. 14.3 demonstrates the necessity for prophecy to function publicly, the three specific terms used by Paul in this verse define more precisely the wide range of functions that prophecy was thought to have.

Οἰκοδομή, "edification, upbuilding, strengthening," is said to be the result not just of prophesying but of many different human activities: church discipline (2 Cor. 10.8, 13.9), considerate eating habits (Rom. 14.19), self-denial for the benefit of others (Rom. 15.2), and acts of love (1 Cor. 8.1, with the verb οἰκοδομέω). Within the assembled congregation, any legitimate speech activity can result in edification: a psalm, a teaching, a revelation, a tongue, an interpretation (14.26). In fact, according to Eph. 4.29 ("Let no evil talk come out of your mouths, but only such as is good for edifying"), all Christian speech, even that of ordinary conversation, should bring about this kind of edification.

The term παράκλησις can mean "comfort" (from sorrow: Lk. 2.25, 6.24; 2 Cor. 1.3, 4, 5, 6, 7) or "encouragement" (to those who are discouraged: Rom. 15.4, 5, 2 Cor. 7.4, 13; cf. παρακαλέω in Eph. 6.22; Col. 2.22, 4.8, 1 Th. 3.2, 7, 4.18) or "exhortation or appeal" (that is, an urging of someone to do something: 2 Cor. 8.17, 1 Th. 2.4, Heb. 12.5, 13.22; in Paul,

---

[1]This confirms our conclusion in Chap. 2 that public proclamation of the revelation was an essential element of prophecy. It may be asked at this point if there was in the NT church anything equivalent to the function of "seer" in the OT, that is, a person to whom private individuals could go for specific information about the future or about facts inaccessible to ordinary means of perception (cf. 1 Sam. 9.6ff). Although we saw in Chap. 2 that there are instances of "revelation" which do not result in public prophecy (e.g., Phil. 3.15, Gal. 2.2), these always come spontaneously to individuals for their own benefit and are never said to be given to a "professional" of whom others may inquire as they need to. There is no positive evidence in the NT for the existence of any Christian "seers." (In fact, any prophet who answers questions put to him "in the Spirit" is condemned as a false prophet in Herm. Mand. 11.2, 3, 4, 6 and 8.)

this meaning is especially frequent with the verb
παρακαλέω: Rom. 12.1, 15.30, 1 Cor. 1.10, 4.16, 16.15,
etc.). Yet it has a weaker force than "command," for
Paul contrasts the verb παρακαλέω with ἐπιτάσσω in
Phl. 9-10: "I am bold enough in Christ to command
you . . . yet . . . I prefer to appeal to you." It is
probable that the range of meanings "comfort -
encouragement - exhortation" was not neatly divided in
the minds of Paul's readers, and so any NT use which
is not further defined by context (Ac. 9.31, 13.15,
Rom. 12.8, Phil. 2.1 and 1 Tim. 4.13, for instance)
might be thought to encompass a variety of speech
activities which could include any or all of these
elements. 1 Cor. 14.3 is also an example of an "undefined"
use of παράκλησις and could equally well mean
"comfort" or "encouragement" or "exhortation."

Concerning the last term, παραμυθία, G. Stählin
writes, "In Paul . . . παράκλησις is so central a concept
that παραμύθια (sic) always seems to be just
supplementary . . . It is natural to see a distinction
between παρακαλέω and παραμυθέομαι, but difficult to
find a convincing criterion by which to draw any sharp
line of demarcation. Both are characterized by the
twofoldness of admonition and comfort."[2]

This means that prophecy cannot be distinguished
from other speech activities simply by means of its
functions, for there is no one function that will serve
as a distinguishing characteristic.[3] Every function of
prophecy (edification, encouragement, exhortation, consolation)
is also a function of several other
activities, such as teaching, preaching, singing
"psalms, hymns and spiritual songs" (Col. 3.16), and
engaging in ordinary Christian conversation (Eph.
4.29). Thus, an analysis of the functions of prophecy
is a poor starting point for finding criteria which
would allow one to distinguish "prophetic" speech in
the Gospels, for instance. Nor is it accurate to say
that Paul (or any other NT writer) is speaking as a
prophet whenever he engages in some "paracletic"
acitivity. It is also interesting to notice that the
common conception of a prophet as one who predicts the

---

[2] G. Stählin, TDNT V, 820f.

[3] Crone, ECP, 212-26 and 90-96 has great difficulty
trying to find functions that are distinctive to
prophecy.

future plays no part in Paul's definition at this point. It is not, as we shall see later, that prediction was excluded from prophecy, but rather that prediction was not an end in itself; it was only valuable as it served the purposes outlined in 1 Cor. 14.3.[4]

How, then, is prophecy different from other speech activities in the NT church? What made prophecy so valuable that Paul wanted it to be sought above all the other gifts? The answer is found not in the function of prophecy but in the fact that prophecy is based on a divine "revelation" (see Chap. 2). Because of this revelation, the prophet would be able to speak to the specific needs of the moment when the congregation assembled. Whereas the teacher or preacher would only be able to obtain information about the specific spiritual concerns of the people from observation or conversation, the prophet would have in addition the ability to know about specific needs through "revelation." In many cases the things revealed might include the secrets of men's hearts (cf. 1 Cor. 14.25), their worries or fears (which need appropriate words of comfort and encouragement), or their refusal or hesitancy to do God's will (which need appropriate words of exhortation). Sometimes the prophet might have only the need revealed to him, and sometimes only the word of exhortation or comfort, for Paul does not restrict the content of revelation so closely as that, and either possibility would fulfill the purposes defined in 1 Cor. 14.3. Nor can we say that the prophet would always know to which person in the congregation his words applied. At times, that may have been revealed to him, while at other times he, like a preacher, may not have known who in the congregation was helped by his specific word of exhortation or encouragement. Indeed, many times the words of a prophet would perhaps have edified several people at once, or perhaps everyone present.

Prophecy, then, is superior to the other gifts because the revelation on which it depends allows it

---

[4]Fortune-telling like that usually done by the soothsaying girl in Ac. 16.16ff, which simply satisfied curiosity or advanced someone's financial status, would therefore not be included in the type of prophecy Paul defines in 1 Cor. 14.3.

to be suited to the specific needs of the moment,[5]
needs which may only be known to God (cf. 1 Cor. 14.
25; Rom. 8.26-27). In this way, prophecy is supremely
qualified to be speech which edifies, speech which
"fits the occasion, that it may impart grace to those
who hear" (Eph. 4.29).

B.   1 Cor. 14.31: Teaching?

Paul says that if a revelation is made to another
sitting by, the first (prophet) should be silent, "for
you are all able to prophsey one by one, in order that
all may learn and all may be encouraged" (ἵνα πάντες
μανθάνωσιν καὶ πάντες παρακαλῶνται, 1 Cor. 14.31).
Does the word μανθάνω here imply that prophecy also
had a teaching function, perhaps even one that included
rather standard kinds of doctrinal instruction? Not
necessarily, for the term μανθάνω can often mean "to
learn how to act, to learn knowledge that will affect
one's manner of life" (Mt. 11.29, Rom. 16.17, 1 Cor.
4.6, Eph. 4.20, Phil. 4.9, 11, 1 Tim. 5.4, Ti. 3.14,
Heb. 5.8). So Paul's use of μανθάνω in 1 Cor. 14.31 is
entirely appropriate to any prophecy in which the
hearers are edified, encouraged, exhorted or comforted.
In every case, the hearers would be "learning," and
though this process may have included the reception of
doctrinal material, it would always have been used in
order to bring about spiritual growth (οἰκοδομή). The
emphasis of the prophecy would have been on immediate
practical application to the hearers' lives. So 1 Cor.
14.31 does not mean that a prophet performed exactly
the same function as a teacher.

C.   1 Cor. 14.20-25: A Sign of God's Attitude

Paul writes, "In the law it is written, 'With
other tongues and with other lips I will speak to this
people, and even then they will not listen to me,' says
the Lord. So tongues are a sign not to believers but
to unbelievers, but prophecy (is a sign) not to
unbelievers but to believers." Before trying to understand the function of prophecy in this passage, it is
important to answer two preliminary questions: (1) What
was the meaning of the "other tongues" in Is. 28.11

---

[5]So Dunn, JS, 229.

(from which Paul is quoting), and (2) how does Paul's use of this OT passage relate to that original meaning?

1. Is. 28.9-13

The passage is notoriously difficult, but if we take the Masoretic Text as it stands[6] we can make several observations, beginning with the conclusion in vs. 13 and working backwards. The term לְמַעַן, "in order that," in vs. 13, makes it clear that when the word of the Lord comes to the Samaritans in the form "ṣaw laṣaw . . . qaw laqaw," it will be a word of judgment. "The word of the Lord will be to them ṣaw laṣaw, ṣaw laṣaw, qaw laqaw, qaw laqaw (צַו לָצָו צַו לָצָו קַו לָקָו קַו לָקָו) a little there, a little there, in order that (לְמַעַן)[7] they may go, and fall backward, and be broken, and snared, and taken" (Is. 28.13). That word of the Lord to them will lead to a certain result: they will start to go (יָלְכוּ) somewhere, but like a confused animal pursued by hunters they will fall and be taken. The word of the Lord thus functions as a word of judgment simply because it provides no clear guidance. With no one saying to them, "This is the way, walk in it" (Is. 30.21), the people will become easy prey for their adversaries.

But if לְמַעַן requires this sense in vs. 13, then the strange "ṣaw laṣaw . . . qaw laqaw" must be a set of sounds which give no coherent meaning to the hearers. Instead of being guided, they are confused by it. Now it might be a collection of nonsense syllables,[8] but

---

[6]Paul's quotation is much closer to the MT than to the LXX here (see below).

[7]"לְמַעַן is always 'in order that,' never merely 'so that'" (BDB, 775). (BDB point out that sometimes in rhetorical passages it refers ironically to an unintended result of some action as if it were intended (ibid.), but all of the examples they cite refer to the sinful actions of foolish men, not to the words or deeds of God.)

[8]BDB, 875, I. In this case "a little there, a little there" would mean that they only catch a distinct syllable once in a while, or that their learning of the language is extremely slow and comes a little

it is more probable that צַו and קַו are older names for successive letters of the Hebrew alphabet, צ and ק.⁹ In that case "a little there, a little there" refers to the step by step learning process undertaken by someone who begins to learn a new language, or to a schoolmaster teaching young children to read. In either case it is a slow process, and meaningful messages certainly cannot be communicated to those who have not learned the first day's lesson, the letters of the alphabet. The word of the Lord will come to the Samaritans as sounds without meaning, as alphabet letters in a language in which they yet understand no words.

The translation "precept upon precept . . . line upon line" (RSV, KJV; cf. NASB) is very unlikely because (i) a clear and simple repetition of God's precepts assuredly would not cause the people to "fall backward . . . and be taken" (vs. 13); (ii) צַו is simply an unknown word, and is never elsewhere used of God's command (in Hos. 5.11, its only other occurrence, following the צַו brings judgment); (iii) while קַו, which normally means a carpenter's measuring line, is used metaphorically to speak of God's building a kingdom according to righteousness and justice (Is. 28.17), it is never used to speak specifically of a standard by which men should guide their conduct; thus, it would also require an unprecedented sense here.

---

at a time. Against this view are (i) the symmetrical repetition of each phrase, which makes the passage seem like more than mere nonsense syllables, and (ii) the fact that צ and ק are successive letters of the Hebrew alphabet.

⁹Wm. W. Hallo, "Isaiah 28.9-13 and the Ugaritic Abecedaries," JBL 77 (1958), esp. pp. 337-8. Hallo notes very early evidence for an order of letters in the alphabet, but no corresponding evidence for an early and uniform set of letter names. The pattern consonant + (any) vowel would have provided an easy naming system for many letters, and is probably preserved in waw and taw, as well as in Is. 28.11, 13, צַו and קַו, which would then be vocalized ṣaw and qaw (Cf. F. Field, Hexapla (Oxford: 1875) II, 479-80, where later Greek transliteration shows σαυλασαυ and καυλακαυ).

187

Further evidence that צַו and קַו are not meaningful words is the fact that nowhere in Jewish written tradition has anyone hit on a correct interpretation of the terms. The LXX translators thought צַו was צַר, "tribulation, distress," and translated ϑλῖψις, and thought קַו was related to תִּקְוָה "hope," and so translated ἐλπίς. The Isaiah Targum takes צַו as "commandment," but then launches out into a discourse about the people who walk after the desire of their own soul and think that God's sanctuary is a small (cf. זְעֵיר) thing.[10] The Syriac Peshitta translates "filth upon filth, and filth upon filth (cf. Heb.√צֹאָה, "filth"), vomit upon vomit, and vomit upon vomit."[11] Symmachus translates ἐντολὴ οὐκ ἐντολή as if the text read צַו לֹא צַו, and Theodotion follows the Peshitta with δεισαλία εἰς δεισαλίαν . . . ἔμετός εἰς ἔμετόν, "filth to filth, vomit to vomit."[12] The Isaiah Scroll from Qumran (1 Q Is^a) has צִי לְצִי צִי לְצִי (changing ו to י) in both vs. 10 and vs. 13, indicating that the scribe apparently had no idea what the phrase meant.[13]

---

[10] J. F. Stenning, ed. and trans., The Targum of Isaiah (Oxford, 1949), 88.

[11] I am grateful to Dr. Vern Poythress for providing me with a translation from Syriac of Is. 28.9-13.

[12] Field, Hexapla, II, 479-80. Using standard indices I was unable to locate any reference to Is. 28.10 or 13 in Philo, Josephus, the Mishnah, the Babylonian Talmud, the Midrash Rabbah, or the (extra-Biblical) Dead Sea Scrolls.

[13] The scroll quite clearly has י not ו in all eight places (cf. M. Burrows, et al., The Dead Sea Scrolls of St. Mark's Monastery [New Haven, 1950], Vol. I, Plate XXII). The only known meanings of צִי, "ship" or "wild beast" (BDB, 850) do not fit the context, so the scribe apparently wrote without understanding the meaning. It is in fact probable that the scribe was simply copying an earlier manuscript which had צִי instead of צַו, for the exchange of י and ו does not seem to have been a common mistake in the Isaiah Scroll (it is not listed by M. Burrows in "Variant Readings in the Isaiah Manuscript," BASOR 113 [Feb., 1949], 25-26).

Whenever the mistake was made, it was intentional, because eight different waws had to be changed

So taking Is. 28.13 alone, we find two possible interpretations of "ṣaw" and "qaw." They might be old names for alphabet letters or they might possibly be meaningless syllables repeated in a mocking, singsong manner. It does not really matter which they are,[14] for in either case they function for the hearers as sounds which carry no meaning and thereby lead to judgment and destruction.

Now we can examine vss. 11-12 more closely: "For with stammering[15] lips and with other tongues he will speak to this people, to whom he said, 'This is rest, give rest to the weary, and this is repose," but they were not willing to hear" (כִּי בְּלַעֲגֵי שָׂפָה וּבְלָשׁוֹן אַחֶרֶת יְדַבֵּר אֶל-הָעָם הַזֶּה אֲשֶׁר אָמַר אֲלֵיהֶם זֹאת הַמְּנוּחָה הָנִיחוּ לֶעָיֵף שְׁמוֹעַ [or אָבֹא] וְזֹאת הַמַּרְגֵּעָה וְלֹא אָבוּא [אָבֹא]). Isaiah must be the speaker here, for "the people" are referred to in the 3rd person. Thus, the unspecified subject of "he will speak" and "he said" must be the Lord. In the past (note the perfects אָמַר and אָבוּא) the Lord had spoken clear and comforting words to the people. But they had stubbornly resisted his word. So as a result Isaiah says that in the future the Lord will speak unclear words "with stammering lips and other tongues," as a punishment for their hardness of heart. This future speech of punishment is thus the same as the word of the Lord in vs. 13, "ṣaw laṣaw . . . ," which brings the hearers to destruction. So the words "ṣaw laṣaw . . . qaw laqaw" are intended by Isaiah to represent the speech of foreigners whom Isaiah's Samaritan hearers cannot understand. This still does not tell us whether the words represent nonsense

---

for yods. Even if one צו was accidently changed to צי no scribe would insert an unknown word צי for צו in the other seven places, unless צו was also an unknown word and the scribe had no way of knowing which was correct. So at a very early date, a scribe copying Is. 28.10 and 13 did not know what צו meant.

(If Hallo is right, however (see n. 9), this could have been another early name for the letter, צ, after the pattern consonant + [any] vowel).

[14] In fact Paul himself probably did not know what the words meant, since Jewish tradition seems to have lost their meaning long before the first century A.D.

[15] Or "mocking, scornful" (לַעֲגֵי; LXX φαυλισμόν).

syllables or alphabet letters (the Samaritan hearers, like children, would only distinguish occasional letters, not meaningful words), but the intention to represent foreign speech is clear enough. The stammering lips" and "other tongues" are the lips and tongues of foreign (Assyrian) invaders, whom the Samaritans will not understand.

Verses 9 and 10 remain difficult. Do they represent the words of Isaiah's hearers, who scoff (cf. vs. 22) and mimic his messages as if they were lessons for young children? Or are they the rhetorical question asked and answered by Isaiah himself: "To whom will the Lord teach knowledge, and to whom will he interpret the message? To young children in the next generation, who must learn a foreign language from the beginning. For it will be ṣaw laṣaw . . ."? The former interpretation requires less to be read into the text, and is preferable. Such a view allows Derek Kidner to paraphrase 9-13, "Make nonsense of God's sense, and you will get your fill of it from Assyria."[16] But on either view, vss. 9-10 simply serve as a prologue to introduce vss. 11-13, whose meaning remains the same.

So the "other tongues" in Is. 28.11 are Isaiah's prediction of the foreign speech which the Lord would bring to the Samaritans by way of punishment[17] for their stubborn refusal to hear and obey his words.

2. Paul's use of Is. 28.11

Paul's quotation of this verse is quite free, but not foreign to the context. He writes, ἐν τῷ νόμῳ γέγραπται ὅτι ἐν ἑτερογλώσσοις καὶ ἐν χείλεσιν ἑτέρων λαλήσω τῷ λαῷ τούτῳ, καὶ οὐδ' οὕτως εἰσακούσονταί μου, λέλει κύριος. ὥστε αἱ γλῶσσαι εἰς σημεῖόν εἰσιν οὐ τοῖς πιστεύουσιν ἀλλὰ τοῖς ἀπίστοις, ἡ δὲ προφητεία οὐ τοῖς ἀπίστοις ἀλλὰ τοῖς πιστευουσιν. (1 Cor. 14.21-22). His λαλήσω τῷ λαῷ τούτῳ, "I will speak to this people,"

___

[16]Kidner, "Isaiah," 606.

[17]Invaders who speak a foreign language are seen as God's punishment to his disobedient people also in Dt. 28.49 ("The Lord will bring a nation against you . . . whose language (לָשׁוֹן) you do not understand")

aligns him with the MT (where the Lord is clearly the speaker), but not with the LXX (which has ὅτι λαλήσουσι τῷ λαῷ τούτῳ, "for they shall speak to this people").[18] He omits, "To whom he said, 'This is rest, give rest to the weary, and this is repose,'" and therefore changes the perfect "they would not hear" to a future, "they will not hear." Thus it has reference not to past stubbornness but to a future refusal to hear the speech in foreign tongues.[19] Paul further departs from the LXX, which used ἀκούειν for שׁמע, and uses εἰσακούσονται instead. The nuance is different, for εἰσακούω means "hear and respond; obey; heed."[20] Οὐδ' οὕτως here means "not even so," "not even in that case," or "not even then" (cf. Mk. 14.59; Bl.-D., §455, 2): not even when they hear foreign speech coming as punishment will they obey the Lord. We can translate, "'With other tongues and with other lips I will speak to this people, and not even then will they obey me,' says the Lord."[21] Paul understands very well that

---

and Jer. 5.15 ("I am bringing upon you . . . a nation whose language [לשׁוֹן] you do not know, nor can you understand what they say").

[18]"The apostles's knowledge of the original has enabled him to improve upon the faulty rendering of the LXX" (H. B. Swete, Introduction to the OT in Greek [Cambridge, 1902], 402).

[19]This might be a further application drawn by Paul himself, or it might simply be based on an inference from Is. 28.13 where the result of the foreign speech is not repentance and obedience but destruction.

[20]Εἰσακούω in the NT is used four times of God's answering prayer (Mt. 6.7, Lk. 1.13, Ac. 10.31, Heb. 5.7), and only here of men's obedience. But it commonly translates שׁמע in the OT with the sense "heed, obey" (Dt. 1.43, 9.23, etc.; cf. 1 Cl. 8.4).

[21]Paul's introductory formula ἐν τῷ νόμῳ γέγραπται ὅτι simply shows that it is an OT quotation, ans so λέγει κύριος is necessary to specify the speaker (contra Ellis, Paul's Use, 107-12).

Apparently Aquila produced a translation from the MT very similar to Paul's, for Origen says, "The prophecy of Isaiah is called 'law' by the Apostle, who tells us, 'In the law it is written, By men of strange

when God speaks to people in a language they cannot understand, it is a form of punishment for unbelief. Incomprehensible speech will not guide but confuse and lead to destruction. And it is one of the last in a series of divine rebukes, none of which have produced the desired repentance and obedience ("and not even then will they obey me"). So Derek Kidner, commenting on Is. 28, can say, "Paul's quotation of v. 11 in 1 Cor. 14.21 is thus a reminder, true to this context, that unknown tongues are not God's greeting to a believing congregation but His rebuke to an unbelieving one."[22]

3. Prophecy and tongues as signs

Paul interprets his quotation of Is. 28.11, "Therefore (ὥστε) tongues are a sign not for believers" (vs. 22). There is no need to translate αἱ γλῶσσαι εἰς σημεῖόν εἰσιν as "tongues are <u>for</u> a sign" (KJV, NASB), or even "tongues are <u>intended as</u> a sign" (NEB), because εἰς + accusative often can replace a predicate nominative with no real change in meaning.[23] Paul

---

tongues, and by the lips of strangers will I speak unto this people; and not even then will they hear me, saith the Lord'; and this is in effect what I found in Aquila's translation" (εὗρον γὰρ τὰ ἰσοδυναμοῦντα τῇ λέξει ταύτῃ ἐν τῇ τοῦ Ἀκύλου ἑρμηνείᾳ κείμενα). (Origen, <u>Philocalia</u> 9.2; text in J. A. Robinson, ed., <u>The Philocalia of Origen</u> (Cambridge, 1893), 55; ET in Geo. Lewis, <u>The Philocalia of Origen</u> (Edinburgh, 1911), 48-49.) The meaning seems to be, "This is indeed a quotation from Isaiah, <u>for</u> (γάρ) I found a reading with the same force in Aquila's translation."

[22]Kidner, "Isaiah," 606. Is. 28.11 is quoted at Qumran to apply to false prophets who apparently spoke another language (1 QH 4.16-17). Here also the speech in other tongues is not a blessing but a curse.

[23]Cf. AG 229, 8a. This use of εἰς + acc. is most common with εἰμί and γίνομαι. In Lk. 13.19, where the mustard seed grew and became a great tree, p^{45} p^{75} ℵ A B have ἐγένετο εἰς δένδρον but D has simply ἐγένετο δένδρον. The parallel in Mt. 13.32 reads γίνεται δένδρον. In 1 Cor. 15.45, the first man Adam ἐγένετο . . . εἰς ψυχὴν ζῶσαν, and the last Adam εἰς πνεῦμα ζῳοποιοῦν. In Lk. 3.5 (quoting Is. 40.4), the rough

simply says, "Tongues are a sign."

The second half of vs. 22 should be translated, "but prophecy is a sign, not to unbelievers but to believers," because of the following reasons. (i) The clear parallelism in the verse makes this the most natural reading, so that the reader automatically supplies ἐστίν. ὥστε αἱ γλῶσσαι εἰς σημεῖόν εἰσιν οὐ τοῖς πιστεύουσιν ἀλλὰ τοῖς ἀπίστοις ἡ δὲ προφητεία οὐ τοῖς ἀπίστοις ἀλλὰ τοῖς πιστεύουσιν.

(ii) On this view the δὲ has a very clear adversative function and the two clauses form a symmetrical balance of equal but contrasting ideas. With the major alternative view, understanding the datives as simple datives of advantage without an elliptical εἰς σημεῖον, the sentence deals with two quite distinct topics: in part one, Paul discusses signs, but in part two, he discusses the proper beneficiaries of a particular

---

places shall be smooth roads (ἔσονται αἱ τραχεῖαι εἰς ὁδοὺς λείας). Cf. also Heb. 1.5 and 2 Cor. 6.18 (2 Sam. [2 K.] 7.14), Heb. 8.10 (Jer. 31.32), Mt. 19.5, Eph. 5.31, 1 Cor. 6.16 (Gen. 2.24), 1 Jn. 5.8. Several of these are LXX quotations which reflect the Heb. לְ הָיָה (Gen. 2.7, etc.; BDB 226, 2 e-g.), and indeed the construction is very common in the LXX (Gen. 9.13, Wisd. 14.11, 1 Macc. 1.36, Judith 5.10, 21, 24, etc.). But the LXX can also translate לְ הָיָה as εἰμί without εἰς (Ex. 13.9, Dt. 28.46, Is. 8.18B) or put εἰς where there is no לְ (Is. 20.3B). So the translations "for a sign" and "intended as a sign," while grammatically acceptable as a use of εἰς (Mt. 21.46, Ac. 7.21, 13.22, 47, Wisd. 2.16; cf. Moule, Idiom Book, 70; but not usually (not ever?) with εἰμί or γίνομαι), are unnecessarily complicated for 1 Cor. 14.22, and are contrary to the other examples of εἰμί (or γίνομαι + accusative). (Bl. -D. §145(1) differ, but with no convincing examples.)
It is interesting that εἰς σημεῖον is not used in the LXX to refer to what might be called extraordinary or "miraculous" signs (except Num. 17.10 (25) A, Is. 55.13, perhaps Is. 8.18 א A). However, this is not an indication that εἰς σημεῖον means "non-miraculous sign" while σημεῖον alone means "miraculous sign" (σημεῖον and εἰς σημεῖον are used interchangeably of the same phenomenon in Gen. 9.12, 13, 17; cf. Num. 17.10 (25) where A has εἰς but א B omit it, similarly

gift. (So the KJV reads, "Wherefore tongues are for a sign, not to them that believe, but to them that believe not: but prophesying serveth not for them that believe not, but for them which believe," and the NEB has, "Clearly then these strange tongues are not intended as a sign for believers, but for unbelievers, whereas prophecy is designed not for unbelievers but for those who hold the faith.") It is necessary to import some idea into the second half of the verse on any reading, but the most natural one, and the one which provides the most clear contrast, is the idea of "sign" which lies so close at hand in the first half of the verse.

(iii) To say (with the KJV and NEB) that prophecy is designed for believers but not for unbelievers does not adequately explain the "therefore," with which Paul introduces vss. 23-25. In those verses Paul argues specifically that prophecy does have a positive function for unbelievers. But this reading would make Paul's argument become:

(a) Prophecy is designed not for unbelievers but for believers;

(b) therefore, you should prophesy to unbelievers. Such reasoning simply does not make sense, and a better solution is required.

(iv) The LXX meaning of σημεῖον fits exactly the idea that tongues are a sign to unbelievers but prophecy is a sign to believers, and such a view is confirmed by the meaning of vs. 25. In order to demonstrate that this is so, we now turn to an examination of the term σημεῖον in the LXX.

In the LXX, σημεῖον can often mean "an indication of God's attitude." These indications are either positive or negative: positive toward those who believe and obey God, but negative toward those who disbelieve

---

Is. 8.18, 20.3; also, σημεῖον alone is used of "non-miraculous" signs in Ex. 3.12, 13.19, 31.13, 17, Dt. 28.46, 1 K. (1 Sam.) 2.34, 10.1, 14.10, 4. K. (2 K.) 19.29, Is. 37.30, Jer. 51 [44].29). Rather, this is simply a function of the grammar: there usually is no need to say of an obvious miracle, "This is a sign," but it is often necessary to say that about some ordinary event which is to be a sign.

and disobey him. Many signs are entirely positive:
the rainbow (Gen. 9.12, 13, 14), the blood on the doorpost (Ex. 12.13), the invitation of the Philistines
(1 Kgs. [1 Sam.] 14.10), the mark on the forehead
(Ezk. 9.4, 6), or any other signs sought by people who
feel forsaken by God (Ps. 73 [74].9, 85 [86].17) (cf.
also Gen. 17.11, LXX Est. 10.3, 2 Macc. 6.13). Other
signs are entirely negative, since they show God's
disapproval and warn of judgment unless repentance is
quickly forthcoming: Korah, Dathan and Abiram (Num.
26.10), the bronze censers of these men (Num. 16.38
[17.3]; cf. vs. 40), Aaron's rod (Num. 17.10 [25]), the
fulfilled curses (Dt. 28.46), the defeat of Pharaoh
Hophra (Jer. 51 [44] .29), and Ezekiel's iron wall
(Ezk. 4.3) (cf. also Ps. 64 [65] .8, Is. 20.3 B, 2
Macc. 15.35). But sometimes the term can be used of
signs which are both positive and negative, indicating
God's approval and blessing on his people and his disapproval and warning of judgment toward those who are
disobeying him. This is especially true of the events
of the Exodus: when God sent a plague of flies on the
Egyptians but kept the flies out of the land of Goshen,
it was a sign (σημεῖον, Ex. 5.23 A; Heb. (vs. 19): אות)
of blessing to Israel but disapproval and warning to
the Egyptians. The same signs and wonders can be
negative signs to Pharaoh (Ex. 10.1-2, 11.9-10; Dt.
6.22, 11.3, Neh. 9.10) but positive signs to Israel
(Dt. 4.34-35, 6.22, 7.19, 26.8; cf. also Num 14.11,
Dt. 29.3 [2] on the refusal of Israel to believe these
positive signs) (cf. Ex. 7.3, Dt. 34.11, Josh. 24.5A,
Ps. 77 [78] .43, 104 [105] .27, 134 [135] .9, Jer. 39
[32] .20-21, Wisd. 10.16, Sir. 45.3, Bar. 2.11). So
σημεῖον, when used to mean "an indication of God's
attitude," can take either a positive or negative
sense.[24]

Also in the NT, σημεῖον can mean "an indication
of God's approval and blessing" (Ac. 2.22, 43, 4.30,
5.12, 6.8 (cf. vs. 8), 15.12, Lk. 2.34, Jn. 2.11, 4.54,
9.16; cf. Barn. 4.14, 1 Cl. 51.5) or "an indication of
God's disapproval and a warning of judgment" (Lk. 11.
30, 21.11, 25, Ac. 2.19; perhaps Mt. 12.39 (cf. vs. 41),
16.4; cf. 1 Cl. 11.2).

---

[24] אות as a divine warning also occurs at 1 QH 15.20.

So when Paul says "tongues are a sign not to believers but to unbelievers" he is using σημεῖον in a familiar and well-established sense. Toward those who disbelieve, signs as indications of God's attitude in the OT are always negative. They indicate God's disapproval and carry a warning of judgment. This was precisely the function of the "other tongues" in Is. 28.11 and Paul quite naturally applies the term σημεῖον to them.[25]

But signs for those who believe and obey God in the OT are generally positive. They indicate God's presence and power among his people to bless them. Thus Paul can quite easily apply the term to prophecy in a positive sense: prophecy is an indication of God's approval and blessing on the congregation because it shows that God is actively present in the assembled church.[26]

---

[25] Sweet, "Sign," 240-57, rightly understands Paul in vs. 22 to be saying that according to the OT the sign value of tongues is as a sign against unbelievers, not for believers (p. 244). I agree with his view that Paul did not oppose tongues completely, but only the Corinthians' overestimate of them. However, his suggestion that the Cephas party was responsible for the great demand for tongues at Corinth (p. 246f), while interesting, does not seem necessary: a more likely explanation is that the sinful pride of the Corinthian Christians (cf. 1 Cor. 1.30, 3.21, 4.7, 18-19, 5.6, 8.1-2, 12.21-24, 13.4) quite naturally found expression in the gift which was the most unusual and noticeable in public worship.

Dunn, JS, 231, also sees σημεῖον in 1 Cor. 14. 20-25 as a sign of God's attitude.

[26] In the OT it is a sign of God's judgment on the people when prophecy is taken away (Ps. 74.9, Is. 29. 10, Lam. 2.9, Mic. 3.6), whereas the gift of prophecy is counted such a blessing that in Am. 2.10-11 it is listed alongside the Exodus as an outstanding gift of God.

In the extra-biblical literature the presence of prophecy is also seen to indicate God's favor (both for the congregation and for the individual), but its absence his displeasure (especially on the people as a whole): cf. Mekilta, Pisha 1.165-66 (Lauterbach, I, 15; quoted in Davies, PRJ, 206), Jos. A. 8.296, T. Ps.-Jon. to Ex. 33.16, b. Sanh. 11a, Num. R. 20.2, b. Sanh. 39b,

This means that the οὖν, "therefore," in vs. 23 is quite natural. We can paraphrase Paul's thought as follows: "When God speaks to people in a language they cannot understand, it signifies his anger and results in their turning farther away from him. Therefore (οὖν, vs. 23), if outsiders[27] or unbelievers come in and you speak in a language they cannot understand, you will simply drive them away. This is the inevitable result of incomprehensible speech. Furthermore, in your childish way of acting (vs. 20)[28] you will be giving a "sign" to the unbelievers which is entirely wrong, because their hardness of heart has not reached the point where they deserve that severe sign of judment.[29] So when you come together (vs. 26), if anyone speaks in a tongue, be sure someone interprets (vs. 27); otherwise, the tongue-speaker should be quiet in the church (vs. 29)."

Similarly with prophecy, vss. 24-25 follow quite easily from the statement in vs. 22 that prophecy is a sign to believers. Once again we paraphrase: "Prophecy is an indication of God's presence among the congregation to bless it (vs. 22). Therefore (οὖν, vs. 23), if an outsider comes in and everyone prophesies (vs. 24), you will be speaking about the secrets of the outsider's heart which he thought no one knew. He will realize that these prophecies must be the result of God's working, and he will fall on his face and declare, 'Truly God is among you' (vs. 25). In this

---

b. Pes. 66b, b. Shab. 92a, b. Suk. 28a, b. B. B. 134a, b. Ned. 38a, Num. R. 13.9, Eccl. R. on 1.8, sec. 6, Philo, Quis Her. 249, Abelson, Immanence, pp. 243, 248-9.

[27] AG, p. 371 hold that the ἰδιώτης here is more than an unbeliever but less than a member, but the term is more likely simply a synonym for ἄπιστος; cf. H. Schlier, TDNT III, 217, and Conzelmann, 243.

[28] Cf. Jer. 4.22, where the Lord says his people are "stupid children. . . . skilled in doing evil."

[29] A similar mistaken eagerness to speak nonsense to unbelievers is demonstrated by the author of Hermas in Vis. 1.4.2, where the understandable part of the ancient lady's message was said to be for the righteous, but the earlier part which could not be understood was "for the heathen and the apostates."

way prophecy will be a sure sign to you that God really is at work in your midst."

It might be objected that this interpretation makes ἄπιστος mean "hardened unbeliever" in vs. 22 but "interested unbeliever" in vss. 23-24. This objection is not really accurate, because ἄπιστος must mean simply "unbeliever" (of whatever type) in both places. In fact, if it did not refer to all unbelievers in vs. 22, Paul's argument would not hold together. In vs. 21-22 Paul argues that when tongues have been used against unbelievers they have been a very severe and perhaps final indication of God's displeasure,[30] and they have resulted in further turning from God. On the basis of that historical example, Paul then cautions the Corinthians not to use tongues in the presence of unbelievers, lest the same thing happen (vs. 23). So Paul is saying that against even interested unbelievers, tongues would function as an indication of God's disapproval and would bring punishment. Tongues, according to vs. 23, would be a σημεῖον τοῖς ἀπίστοις not only for hardened unbelievers but also for visitors to the Corinthian church, and as such, it would be so wrong to use it that Paul must carefully caution against it. There, ἀπίστοις in vs. 22 must refer to unbelievers generally, even though the specific example in vs. 21 deals with hardened unbelievers in particular.

It should also be noted here that Paul's reaction to this recognition of the sign function of tongues is not to forbid tongues in public worship, but to regulate the use of tongues so that they will always be interpreted when spoken in public (vss. 27-28). This seems to be a very appropriate response, for it is only incomprehensible tongues which have this negative function toward unbelievers, both in Is. 28.11 and in 1 Cor. 14.23. But when a speech in tongues is interpreted, it is no longer incomprehensible and it no longer retains this ominous sign function.

---

[30]The "other tongues" in vs. 21 are seen by Paul as one of the last in a series of increasingly severe rebukes from God, as is clear from the context of Is. 28.11, where Isaiah speaks to those who had persistently rejected his message, and from the οὐδ' οὕτως, "not even then," of vs. 21, by which it is implied that other, earlier rebukes had also failed.

Therefore, it is important to realize that in 1 Cor. 14.20-23 Paul is not talking about the function of tongues in general but only about the negative result of one particular abuse of tongues,[31] namely, the abuse of speaking in public without an interpreter (and probably speaking more than one at a time [cf. vss. 23, 27]) so that it all became a scene of unedifying confusion. Concerning the proper public function of the use of tongues plus interpretation, or the proper private function of speaking in tongues, Paul is elsewhere quite positive (12.10-11, 21-22, 14.4, 5, 18, 26-28, 39). So to use Paul's discussion of an <u>abuse</u> of tongues in 14.20-23 as the basis for a general polemic against all other (acceptable) uses of tongues is quite contrary to the entire context in 1 Cor. 12-14.

Returning now to a consideration of prophecy, we are in a position to understand vss. 24-25 more clearly. "If you all prophesy" in vs. 24 is probably to be understood as a hypothetical situation which Paul need not have thought would ever actually occur (μὴ πάντες προφῆται; 12.29). Nevertheless, if several people prophesy the outsider is "convicted" (ἐλέγχεται) of sin and "called to account" (ἀνακρίνεται)[32] by several

---

[31]This crucial point is overlooked by O. Palmer Robertson, "Tongues: Sign of Covenantal Curse and Blessing," WTJ 38 (1975-76), 43-53. Neither Robertson nor Zane Hodges, "The Purpose of Tongues," Bib Sac 120 (1963), 226-33, adequately takes account of the fact that at Corinth any unbeliever who entered, whether Jew or Gentile, would not understand what was spoken in tongues (14.2, 9, 11, 14, 16, 19, 23, 28): Paul's whole concern in ch. 14 is to contrast intelligible with unintelligible speech.
Robertson argues that tongues were a sign of the transition between God's dealing with Israel and his dealing with all nations. That might possibly be true in some contexts (Ac. 2?), but it is totally foreign to the context of 1 Cor. 12-14, where Paul makes no mention of the Gentile inclusion or of judgment on the Jews. In the absence of any specific application of 1 Cor. 14.21 by Paul to Jews, it is much more likely that Paul is using Is. 28.11-12 not in a predictive sense (with reference to Jews) but in an illustrative sense (with reference to all unbelievers).

[32]AG, 56, 2.

different people (vs. 24), presumably in different ways or with respect to different matters. In this way the secret sins of his heart are "disclosed" (φανερὰ γίνεται, vs. 25). Although vs. 24 might simply mean that the outsider hears some general prophecy or preaching and is inwardly convicted of his sin, vs. 25 must mean that specific mention of one or more of his particular, individual sins is made in the prophecies[33] (although the prophets and the congregation may or may not know to whom their words apply; cf. 1 Pet. 1.11, Ac. 2.30, 21.11 ?). This is true because (i) φανερός (18 times) and φανερόω (49 times) in the NT always refer to a public, external manifestation, and are never used of private or secret communication of information or of the internal working of God in a person's mind or heart,[34] and (ii) the reaction of the outsider--"falling on his face he will worship God, declaring, 'Truly God is among you'"--is not normally one that accompanies even good preaching, but Paul seems quite sure that it will happen. Now Paul might have thought this would happen occasionally with a mention of general kinds of sins, but the statement as it applies to every situation like this is more understandable if he thought the prophecies would contain something very striking and unusual, such as specific mention of the visitor's sins. The visitor will think that these Christians know things that could only have been revealed to them by God: they know the secrets of his heart! It seems to be the fact of knowledge acquired by "supernatural" means, not merely the conviction of sin, which effectively convinces the outsider of God's presence.[35]

---

[33] Contra Müller, Prophetie und Predigt, 25, n. 25.

[34] Cf. Chap. 2, n. 3. To speak of an internal "illumination" by which only the visitor became aware of and felt a conviction for his sins, Paul would probably have used φωτίζω (or perhaps a general term like γινώσκω or ἐπιγινώσκω).

[35] 1 Cor. 14.25 provides a close parallel with Dan. 2.46-47, where Nebuchadnezzar falls on his face and confesses that Daniel's God is the true God because Daniel has been able to reveal the mystery of the king's dream. In Sir. 1.30 it is the Lord who will reveal the secrets of the arrogant man and cast him down "in the midst of the congregation." (Cf. also Jn. 4.19, Ac. 5.1-11; Best, "Prophets and Preachers," 146.)

This is why it is prophecy (rather than some other gift) which Paul calls a "sign to believers." The distinctiveness of prophecy is that it must be based on revelation, and revelation (ἀποκάλυψις) as it functions in prophecy is always something which, Paul thinks, comes spontaneously and comes only from God (see Chap. 2). Where there is prophecy, then, it is an unmistakable sign or indication of God's presence and blessing on the congregation--it is a "sign for believers"--and even an outsider who visits will be able to recognize this.

We can now summarize the function of prophecy in 1 Cor. 14.20-25. (i) Prophecy functions in evangelism to reveal the secrets of an unbeliever's heart and thereby both amaze him at the power of God at work and convict him of his sins. (ii) In doing this prophecy also serves as a certain indication (sign) that God is present and at work in the congregation to bless it and cause it to grow. (iii) By implication from Paul's example of the outsider we can further conclude that prophecy would also function from time to time to reveal the secrets of some believer's heart, convicting him of sin and calling him to repentance.[36] Although Paul does not cite this explicitly as a function of prophecy, it is certainly consistent with the picture of prophecy which we have found in these verses, and would fit perfectly well with Paul's view of prophecy as resulting in edification and exhortation in 14.3-5. Furthermore, it would allow prophecy to function in this way as a sign for believers not just when an outsider comes in, but at any time. Thus Paul's statement "but prophecy is a sign for believers" could be understood as a more general statement, not restricted to the specific application to which Paul puts it in vss. 24-25. Finally, we should note that each of these three functions depends on the fact which we discovered in Chapter 2, that the distinctiveness of the prophetic gift is that it must be based on a specific divine revelation from God to the prophet.

D. Functions Outside 1 Corinthians

1. Ac. 15.32

This verse confirms but does not add to what we

---

[36]So Dunn, JS, 232.

learned about the function of NT prophecy from 1 Cor. 14.3-5, since παρακαλέω occurs there also, and ἐπιστηρίζω, "strengthen," is a general term which serves here as a good synonym for οἰκοδομέω (1 Cor. 14.4).

2. Ac. 11.27-30 and 21.11

In both of these cases Luke shows Agabus predicting some future event. This is an indication that prediction of the future was one function of prophecy, but the other texts we have examined, both in 1 Cor. and in Acts, show that prediction should not be considered the only function of prophecy, and indeed not even its primary function. In both of these cases in Acts, Luke is careful to show how the predictions served to encourage, exhort or strengthen the church. In ch. 11, the prophecy seems to have led to preparation and perhaps even to some collection before the famine began (vs. 29), so that the church at Antioch was enabled by the prophecy to be of greater usefulness than they would have been without this special bit of "advance information." In ch. 21, the prophecy is said to allow the church at Antioch to know roughly what would happen to Paul, and thereby they are afforded an opportunity to see the strength of Paul's resolve to follow willingly in the steps of Jesus even when facing suffering and perhaps death. In seeing this, the church would no doubt have been encouraged and strengthened to imitate Paul's courage and obedience.

In each case the prophetic gift was necessary for a particular purpose. No other gift would have sufficed, for it was specifically knowledge of some future event which was needed in each case, and only prophecy, based as it was on revelation (see Chap. 2), could provide this knowledge.

In neither case, however, was prediction an end in itself. The NT always shows prophetic prediction as simply one of several kinds of means to a greater end, the encouragement and edification of the church.

3. <u>1 Tim. 1.18</u>

The verse reads, "This command I commit to you,

Timothy, my son, in accordance with the former[37] prophecies about you,[38] in order that by means of them you may fight the good fight." Here Timothy is given a command[39] which in some way corresponds to previous prophecies about him. Perhaps the command included tasks which required precisely the kinds of gifts that the prophecies had mentioned in connection with Timothy. Remembering these prophecies would encourage him: ". . . in order that by them (i.e., encouraged by them) you may fight the good fight." So in this case prophecy would have provided knowledge of a future type of ministry, or of a possession of abilities which hitherto may have been unrecognized. Thereby the prophecies would have encouraged Timothy to strive diligently toward the indicated goal, or perhaps would have brought to his attention gifts of which he was previously unaware, or of which he had thought himself unworthy because of youth or inexperience. In doing this the prophecies would have enabled him to develop and use gifts which would otherwise have remained dormant. Once again, then, the uniqueness of prophecy is found in its dependence on "revelations" (either about unknown facts or about future events), and its purpose is to strengthen the ministry of the church in some specific way.

4. 1 Tim. 4.14

In the midst of a string of personal instructions to Timothy (4.6-5.2) we read μὴ ἀμέλει τοῦ ἐν σοὶ χαρίσματος, ὃ ἐδόθη σοι διὰ προφητείας μετὰ ἐπιθέσεως τῶν χειρῶν τοῦ πρεσβυτερίου. There is not enough evidence in the context to decide with certainty what this gift was, and the word χάρισμα itself has an exceptionally

---

[37] The present participle of προάγω means "former" in Heb. 7.18, Mart. Pol. 1.1, and several times in the papyri (MM, 537); cf. AG, 709.

[38] Ἐπὶ σὲ here means "concerning you," as in Rev. 10.11 (but with dat.), Heb. 7.13, Mk. 9.12f; Ezr. 5.1, Ezk. 13.16, 37.4; cf. AG, 289 (ζ). προάγω in the sense "lead to, point to" would take εἰς (1 Tim. 5.24).

[39] Probably the command in vss. 3-4 (so Kelly, 57).

broad range of meanings.⁴⁰ But the phrase διὰ προφητείας suggests that the verse is talking about the same situation as that referred to in 1.18, "the former prophecies about you." In that case, it is possible that the gift mentioned here is a special ability in administration or church rule, in sound teaching, or in solving church disputes and silencing false teachers --in other words, a gift which would equip Timothy for the kind of work outlined in this epistle.

The phrase "through prophecy" (διὰ προφητείας) apparently indicates the means or instrument by which the gift was given. This is not at variance with the idea that gifts are given by God, because διὰ + genitive is often used to indicate a human or "natural" cause of a gift which at the same time is said to be divinely given (Ac. 7.25, 14.3; cf. Jn. 1.17, Ac. 8.18, 2 Tim. 1.6).⁴¹ So the verse need not imply that the prophetic words themselves were of such power that they created a gift in Timothy or somehow bestowed an

---

⁴⁰Of the 17 occurrences of χάρισμα 16 are in the Pauline corpus. It generally means "a gift given by God," and can be used of salvation (Rom. 5.15, 16, 6.23; prob. 11.29), deliverance from physical danger or death (2 Cor. 1.11), or a large number of different abilities which enable the Christian to serve more effectively in the church (celibacy in 1 Cor. 7.7, speaking or serving others in 1 Pet. 4.10, prophecy, teaching, exhorting, giving aid or money, etc. in Rom 12.6, wisdom, knowledge, faith, tongues, etc. in 1 Cor. 12. 8-10; cf. Did. 1.5 where it includes earthly goods). The word is several times connected with explicit statements that these gifts are from God and due to his grace (Rom. 12.6, 1 Cor. 1.5-7, 11, 1 Pet. 4.10). This exceptionally wide range of meanings indicates that the term could easily have been applied to any ability which helped a believer function more effectively in the church.

⁴¹With the verb δίδωμι we find that when a human agent is the sole actor, the normal ὑπό is used to express the subject of the passive verb (cf. Ac. 24.26). Διά is more loose and allows for more than one cause simultaneously. Thus, both the prophecies (1 Tim. 4. 14) and the laying on of Paul's hands (2 Tim. 1.6) can be seen as means by which the gift was bestowed, and the gift can nevertheless be called τὸ χάρισμα τοῦ θεοῦ (2 Tim. 1.6).

ability on him, any more than Ac. 8.18 implies that there was some magical power in the hands of the apostles which allowed them to bestow the Holy Spirit (as Simon falsely thought, vs. 19). Rather, the διά indicates a more loose connection, suggesting perhaps that prophecies were spoken at the same time the gift was given to Timothy.[42] They would thus have the function of making known to everyone present, including Timothy, what otherwise would have remained completely unknown until the gifts could be noticed in practice. Prophecy which functioned in this way would clearly benefit the church, for it would encourage Timothy to begin to use and develop his new abilities, and would encourage the other hearers to provide him opportunities where he could do so.

5. The Book of Revelation

The entire book claims to contain revelations of "what must soon take place" (1.1, 4.1, 22.6), and thus must be based on knowledge which could not be obtained by ordinary means. Even in the letters to the seven churches, where a disclosure of the future is not in view, John is given special information about the inward spiritual state of the churches (2.4, 23, 3.1, 9, 17), or at least an authoritative evaluation of the churches which required a divine revelation. But, as with other NT prophecy, attaining this special knowledge of the future or of hidden facts is not an end in itself. It is repeatedly made the basis for direct exhortation of the readers (2.5, 10, 16, 25, 3.2-5, 11, 18, 13.10, 14.7, 12, 27.17; cf. 1.3, 22.7). And the book frequently takes the opportunity to comfort believers who are undergoing trouble or persecution by proclaiming the sovereign rule of God in history, the certainty of his final triumph over evil, and the preservation and ultimate triumph of God's people with him (1.5, 2.26-27, 5.10, 6.10, 15-17, 11.15-18, 14.13, 17.14, 19.20-21, 20.6, 9-14, chapters 20-22, passim). Thus it is a prophecy whose function is to encourage, comfort and exhort those who read it.

---

[42]Cf. AG, 179, III. 1.b (διά of attendant circumstance).

6. Other possible functions

Several other possible functions for prophecy might be proposed, but for each one the evidence is so slight that only tentative conclusions are possible. Prophets might be seen to have a role in Gospel proclamation in Ign. Mg. 5.2, but this is more likely to be a reference to OT prophets.[43] E. Ellis[44] sees exposition and interpretation of Scripture as a function of Christian prophets in Acts, but he can adduce no examples where the person expounding Scripture is doing so specifically in his role as a prophet, and not in his role as a teacher or apostle or evangelist. This does not mean that prophecies could not include Scripture quotations and applications, of course. I only want to emphasize that where such exposition was based on preparation and reflection instead of on a spontaneous revelation, the NT writers would call it teaching (or perhaps παράκλησις) not prophecy.[45]

Finally, one might ask whether prophecies might sometimes include the man-to-God activities of prayer and praise.[46] In 1 Cor. 11.4-5 prophecy and prayer are mentioned together, but this might only mean that they are related yet distinct. In Lk. 1.67 Zechariah "prophesied" his song of praise, yet this may still be seen as primarily man-directed (the Lord God is spoken of in the third person: vss. 68ff). In 1 Cor. 14.15, praying and singing "with the mind" may refer to prophecy in contrast to tongues, but on the other hand it may simply refer to ordinary intelligible prayer and singing in contrast to unintelligible prayer and singing in tongues. The major difficulty for the idea that prayer and praise are prophetic functions is 1 Cor. 14.3: ὁ δὲ προφητεύων ἀνθρώποις λαλεῖ. Strictly interpreted, this would mean, "He who prophesies speaks only to men." However, Paul's concern here might simply be to emphasize that prophecy is able to

---

[43] See J. B. Lightfoot, The Apostolic Fathers (5 vols.; London, 1889-90), Part II, Vol. II, 260-62.

[44] "Role," 56-62.

[45] Cf. Chap. 2, pp. 139ff.

[46] Cf. Cothenet, "Prophétisme et ministère," 43f; Friedrich, TDNT VI, 852f.

be understood by men, or is primarily for their
benefit.⁴⁷ In that case, if prayer or praise was
prompted by revelation, and if it served also to
edify the hearers (because they silently participated
in it; cf. vs. 16), there would seem to be no reason
why it could not have been called "prophecy." Yet the
positive evidence for this is so slight that such a
conclusion cannot be given with much certainty.

E. Prophets as "Charismatic Leaders"?

In relation to this discussion of prophetic
functions it is appropriate to include a note about
the possibility that prophets exercised "charismatic
leadership" in early churches. One of the major arguments given in favor of the existence of this prophetic
function is the view that church offices such as elder
and deacon, especially in Pauline churches, were only
established at a later date.

Now it is not possible for us to discuss here
the very large question of "gift" and "office" and the
historical development of the relationship between
them. But with regard to ruling authority and prophecy
two brief comments can be made about the NT data itself.
First, it should not be thought completely certain that
any early churches lacked elders who had ruling authority. Several accounts in Acts purport to show elders
at a very early date: Ac. 14.23 (Derbe, Lystra,
Iconium, Pisidian Antioch--on Paul's first missionary
journey), 15.2ff (Jerusalem), and 20.17 (Ephesus; cf.
1 Tim. 1.3 with 5.17). These passages are of course
challenged as later interpolations (because they mention church offices), but one wonders if the argument
begins to show signs of circularity at this point.⁴⁸

---

⁴⁷This would require that ἀνθρώποις be seen somewhat as a dative or advantage, although the parallel
with Θεῷ in vs. 2 would not be exact. Yet one wonders
whether, with verbs of speaking, Paul or his readers
would have seen much distinction between a dative of
direct object and a dative of advantage.

⁴⁸Ernest Käsemann, "Ministry and Community in
the NT," in Essays on NT Themes, (ET London, 1964),
63-94, argues that there were no officially functioning
presbyteries in Paul's churches during Paul's lifetime
(p. 86). The fact that every Christian had the Spirit

Second, there does not seem to be much convincing evidence anywhere in the NT that anyone other than apostles (or "apostolic assistants" such as Timothy and Titus) and elders exercised ruling functions in the churches. The absence of any discussion of church offices in the major Pauline epistles is neutral evidence at best (and Phil. 1.1, 1 Thess. 5.12, and Eph.

---

and therefore had a charisma meant that there could be no specially privileged group (p. 78). The Pastorals and Acts reflect a later situation where formal offices have become established in order to combat heresies, especially Gnosticism (pp. 85-91).

But Käsemann fails to realize that the fact that all had gifts does not imply that all had gifts to rule. Nor does it imply that none had gifts to rule. Indeed, Paul distinguishes various kinds of gifts, and among them are gifts of administration, teaching, and the ability to judge wisely (1 Cor. 6.5). Those who had these gifts would no doubt have ruled in the church, and there seems to be nothing in the idea of a universal distribution of gifts which would preclude the early existence of formal offices. (The position of Dunn, JS, 180-82, 285-300, is similar to Käsemann's.)

To argue that the verses in Acts and the Pastorals which mention elders, overseers and deacons do not represent historical reality because they make such mention is circular argument: it assumes that such offices were a later development, and then arbitrarily makes the evidence fit the theory. (So Dunn, JS, 182; Haenchen, 436; cf. von Campenhausen, Ecclesiastical Authority, 76ff.)

On the other hand, it should be noted (1) that there is no evidence that the mere possession of a charismatic gift equipped one to rule (indeed, in 1 Cor. 14.26, 27 and 29 Paul distinctly addressed the congregation instead of those with the special gifts); and (2) that all the evidence we do have (whether one considers it late or not) does indicate that there were ruling offices from the beginning side by side with charismatic gifts. Cf. Cothenet, DBS 8, cols. 1284, 1288, 1291, 1301-03, 1312.

It is well to remember how thoroughly the evidence for ruling elders pervades the various strands of NT traditions: Ac. 14.23, 15.2ff, 20.17, Phil. 1.1, Eph. 4.11, 1 Thess. 5.12, 1 Tim. 5.17, Tit. 1.5, Heb. 13.17, Jas. 5.14, 1 Pet. 5.1-2. Such evidence cannot simply be brushed aside in favor of a theory about how one thinks the church "must" have developed.

4.11 cannot be ignored!), since what is needed is not to show that Paul simply fails to mention elders or overseers, but that he fails to mention them in contexts dealing with ecclesiastical leadership where such mention would have been appropriate.[49] On the other hand, the conclusions we have reached about the encouraging and edifying functions of prophecy, together with the absence of any NT verses to show that charismatic prophets did in fact perform leadership functions,[50] lead us at least to doubt whether there is

---

(Of course, one might object that many of these verses show early leadership but do not necessarily imply formally constituted "offices." This is possible but πρεσβύτερος in Acts does seem to speak of a formal office.)
    This theory underlies Käsemann's "Sentences of Holy Law," in which he claims that NT prophets "judged" primitive Christian communities until later formalized offices replaced them.

    [49]It is not sufficient to say that Paul would have addressed elders in Corinth, for instance, if there had been elders there (So Dun, JS, 285). Rather, the fact that Paul addresses the entire congregation shows that the entire congregation needed instruction and rebuke and that the elders had themselves been unable to deal with the problems. In fact, the elders were no doubt part of these problems. So for Paul to address the elders alone would not have been an adequate solution. 1 Cl. 42.4 and 44.3 must be taken as evidence (though not conclusive) that Paul himself appointed elders in Corinth and that many of the Corinthians alive in about 96 AD would remember that. In fact, some of the elders may have come from the household of Stephanas (1 Cor. 16.15-16; cf. ἀπαρχή here with a probable allusion to it in 1 Cl. 42.4).

    [50]Ac. 15.32 is evidence against any charismatic rule by prophets, since the ruling function of Judas and Silas was to deliver a decision to Antioch which had been reached by the apostles and elders (not the prophets) in Jerusalem in a decidedly non-"charismatic" way ("after there had been much debate," Ac. 15.7). They did this in their role as "leading men" among the brethren (15.22). (Indeed, the prophets in Antioch [Ac. 13.1] were manifestly unable to impose any "charismatic" solution on the community there.) But when Luke wishes to speak of the non-ruling functions

convincing NT evidence to support the view that prophets (as prophets) functioned as "charismatic leaders" in the early church.

F. 1 Cor. 13.8-13: The Time of the Cessation of Prophecy

1. The Purpose of 1 Cor. 13.8-13

Paul interrupts his discussion of spiritual gifts with Chapter 13 of 1 Corinthians, in which he intends to put the entire discussion of gifts in proper perspective. It is not enough simply to "seek the greater gifts" (12.31a). One must also "seek after love" (14.1), thus coupling proper goals with proper motives. Without love, the gifts are without value (13.1-3). In fact, Paul argues, love is superior to all the gifts and therefore it is more important to act in love than to have any of the gifts.

In order to show the superiority of love, Paul argues that it lasts forever, whereas the gifts are all temporary (13.8).[51] Vss. 9-12 further explain why the gifts are temporary. Our present knowledge and prophesying are partial and imperfect (vs. 9), but someday something perfect will come to replace them (vs. 10). This is explained by the analogy of a child who gives up childish thought and speech for the thought and speech of an adult (vs. 11). Paul then elaborates further on vss. 9-10 by explaining that our

---

of exhortations and strengthening (vs. 32), then he mentions that Judas and Silas were also prophets. Nowhere in the NT is any terminology related to ruling, leading or governing functions applied to someone because he has prophetic ability.
Did 15.1 may imply that bishops and deacons prophesied and taught; it does not imply that prophets and teachers ruled.

[51] I am distinguishing here love, (which is a motive or attitude) from "gifts" (which in 1 Cor. are always abilities for ministry). In view of the wide range of application Paul gives the term χάρισμα (cf. n. 40) it is not unlikely that he could have called love a "gift" as well. But for the purposes of this discussion I shall use the word "gift" to apply only to specific abilities for ministry.

present perception and knowledge are indirect and imperfect, but that someday they will be direct and perfect (vs. 12).

In this argument Paul connects the function of prophecy with the time of its cessation. It fills a certain need now, but does so only imperfectly. When "the perfect" comes, that function will be better fulfilled by something else, and prophecy will cease because it will be made obsolete (καταργηθήσεται, vs. 10).

It is appropriate for us at this point, having defined the function of prophecy, to examine this passage about the time of the cessation of prophecy. I suggest that vs. 10, "When the perfect is come, the imperfect will pass away," meant to Paul and his readers, "When the Lord returns, prophecy will cease."

2. 1 Cor. 13.10: The Cessation of Prophecy at the Parousia

Paul writes in vs. 10, ὅταν δὲ ἔλθῃ τὸ τέλειον, τὸ ἐκ μέρους καταργηθήσεται. The phrase τὸ ἐκ μέρους, "the imperfect, the incomplete," refers most clearly to knowing and prophesying, the two activities which are said to be done ἐκ μέρους, "partially, imperfectly," in vs. 9.[52]

No doubt Paul also intended tongues to be included here, since the omission of tongues in vs. 9 seems to be for stylistic convenience. Vs. 9 is the ground for vs. 8, as the γάρ shows. Thus vs. 9 must give the reason why tongues, as well as knowledge and prophecy, will cease. In fact, the repeated εἴτε . . . εἴτε . . . εἴτε in vs. 8 suggests that Paul could have listed more gifts here (wisdom, healing, interpretation?) if he had wished.[53] But for our purposes it

---

[52] Cf. Chap. 2, pp.147ff and n. 59.

[53] Εἴτε . . . εἴτε is used frequently by Paul when he wants to list several members of a set without necessarily implying that he has mentioned all the possible members: Rom. 12.6-8, 1 Cor. 3.22, 10.31, 12.13 (cf. Col. 3.11), (13.8), 14.17, Col. 1.16; cf. 1 Pet. 2.13-14. But it need not always be used this way: cf. 2 Cor. 8.23.

is sufficient that "the imperfect" in vs. 10 clearly includes the gift of prophecy.

As I argued in Chap. 2, Paul considers prophecy to be imperfect (ἐκ μέρους) because it gives only partial knowledge of the subjects it treats, because the revelation which a prophet receives is indirect and limited, and because the revelation is often difficult to understand or interpret.[54]

So 1 Cor. 13.10 means, "When the perfect is come, prophecy will cease." The only remaining problem is to determine what time is meant by ὅταν, "when." Several factors in the context argue that the time of the Lord's return is the time Paul has in mind.[55]

(a) Τότε, "then," in vs. 12 refers to the time "when the perfect is come" in vs. 10.[56] But the events of vs. 12, seeing face to face and knowing fully "even as I am known," are events which occur only in the consummation. Paul means, "Then we shall see the Lord face to face," as the LXX parallels to this phrase

---

[54]Cf. Chap. 2, pp. 145-150.

[55]So RP, 297, Morris, 187, and virtually all commentators. Calvin says, "It is stupid of people to make the whole of this discussion apply to the intervening time" (p. 281).
C. Shank, More of Christ (Cherry Hill, N.J., 1973), 22f, sees τὸ τέλειον both as "already" (at the first coming of Christ) and as "not yet" (not until the Lord's return). However, in 1 Cor. 13.8-13 the type of perfection Paul has in mind is entirely future (note "now" versus "then" in vs. 12).

[56]Τότε must refer to a future time because in vs. 12b τότε δὲ ἐπιγνώσομαι is future. The τότε in vs. 12a, τότε δὲ πρόσωπον πρὸς πρόσωπον, is future by analogy with 12b, by contrast with the ἄρτι in 12a, and by virtue of the consummational connotations of the phrase "face to face" (see below). But if τότε in vs. 12 refers to a future time, then there is only one other phrase in vss. 8-13 which could possibly have a future reference, and that is "when the perfect is come" in vs. 10.

make clear.57 "Now I know in part, then I shall understand fully (ἐπιγινώσκω), even as I have been fully understood," means not that Paul expects to know all things (he does not say ἐπιγνώσομαι τὸ πάντα), but that in the consummation he expects to be freed from the misconceptions and inabilities to understand (especially to understand God and his work) which are part of this present life. His knowledge will resemble God's present knowledge of him because it will contain no false impressions and will not be limited to what is able to be perceived in this age. Such language can only refer to the consummation. So "when the perfect is come" in vs. 10 must also refer to that time.

(b) The phrase τὸ τέλειον in vs. 10 must refer to a method of acquiring knowledge which is so superior to present knowledge and prophecy that it makes these two obsolete. For when this "perfect" comes it renders the imperfect useless (τὸ ἐκ μέρους καταργηθήσεται, vs. 10). But only the kind of knowledge Paul expected in the consummation could be so qualitatively different from present knowledge that it could provide this kind of contrast and be called τέλειος as opposed to ἐκ μέρους.58

57The phrase πρόσωπον πρὸς (or κατὰ) πρόσωπον does not occur in the NT, but it is clearly used to speak of seeing God personally, as in a theophany, in the LXX: Gen. 32.30, Dt. 5.4, 34.10, Jud. 6.22, Ezek. 20.35; cf. Ex. 33.11. These are the only occurrences of the phrase in the LXX

In this present age Paul can speak of Christians "with unveiled face beholding as in a mirror the glory of the Lord" (2 Cor. 3.18), but does not speak of seeing the Lord face to face (2 Cor. 4.6 refers not to literal vision but metaphorically to inward or heart (cf. καρδίαις) knowledge at conversation). To see someone's face is to see him in person in 1 Th. 2.17, and 3.10.

58Elsewhere in Paul τέλειος is used to refer to persons, and is used in contexts which speak of degrees of progress in the Christian life. In these contexts its means "mature" (1 Cor. 2.6, 14.20, Eph. 4.13, Phil. 3.15, Col. 1.28, 4.12). These examples are not relevant to 1 Cor. 13.10, however, since here it refers not to persons but to a means of acquiring knowledge which contrasts with present knowledge and prophecy.

(c) In 1 Cor. 1.7 Paul ties the possession
of spiritual gifts (χαρίσματα) to waiting for the
Parousia: "You are not lacking in any spiritual gift
as you await the revelation of our Lord Jesus Christ."
This suggests that Paul saw the gifts as a temporary
provision made to equip believers for ministry until
the Lord returned. So this verse provides a close
parallel to the thought of 1 Cor. 13.8-13, where
prophecy and knowledge (and no doubt tongues) are seen
in the same way as necessary until the Parousia but
unnecessary beyond that time.

(d) It is interesting that Paul uses
καταργέω several times in 1 Cor. to refer to the things
of this age which will pass away or will be made powerless or useless at the Parousia: the outwardly important things of this world (1.28), the rulers of this
age (2.6), the stomach and food (6.13), every rule and
authority and power (15.24), and death (15.26).[59]
These things will all be made powerless, ineffective
or idle (ἀ-ἔργον) when the Lord returns. It is not of
course necessary that the term have the same implications in 13.8-13, but such a meaning does fit the
context well and, in light of usage elsewhere in the
letter, would be very clear to Paul's readers.

1 Cor. 13.10, therefore, refers to the consummation and says that prophecy will cease when the Lord
returns.

3. Objections

Various other interpretations of this section
have been proposed, and any one of them would nullify
this conclusion about the time of the cessation of
prophecy.

Paul does use τελειόω (Phil. 3.12) and τέλος (1 Cor.
1.8, 15.24) to refer to the consummation.
The contrast with ἐκ μέρους indicates that here
Paul is not comparing the less mature with the more
mature but the partial with the complete or perfect.

[59] These are the only instances of καταργέω in
1 Cor. except for the four in 13.8-11. Elsewhere in
Paul the term has a wider range of usage.

(a) "When the perfect is come" refers to something other than the consummation, such as individual Christian maturity, the maturity of the church,60 the inclusion of the Gentiles in the church, or the completion of all the writings of the apostles.

Such views all break down at vs. 12, where Paul says that believers will see God "face to face" "when the perfect is come." This could not have been said about the time suggested in any of these other proposals. And since Paul considers prophecy the most useful gift (1 Cor. 12.28), it is likely that he would have expected a mature Christian or a mature church to use it more, not less.

The last proposal also depends on the supposition that the function of prophecy was to provide the church with divinely authoritative guidance until such guidance could be derived from a collection of apostolic writings. But I have argued that the NT does not indicate that that was a function of NT prophecy, at least not at Corinth. Rather, the function was to provide information which was needed for the edification of the church and which could only be acquired through a revelation. In many of the examples we have looked at this consisted of very specific, localized information. Access to the major doctrinal teachings contained in the apostolic writings would not make prophecy obsolete or useless.61

60Robt. L. Thomas, "Tongues . . . Will Cease," JETS 17 (1974), 81-89, argues that Paul did not know which would come first, the maturity of the church (vs. 11) or the Parousia (vs. 12). Therefore, he allowed for both and thought that this cessation would accompany whichever one came first. This view fails to recognize that vs. 11, which speaks of Paul in the first person and in the past, is merely an illustration, and our understanding of what it illustrates must conform to vs. 12, which speaks of believers generally ("we") and in the future ("shall know"). And only vs. 12 has a τότε which links it clearly to the ὅταν in vs. 10. Vs. 11 illustrates not the maturity of the church (an idea which is nowhere discussed in this context) but the fact that something complete or perfect replaces something incomplete or imperfect.

61If one wanted a proper provisional counterpart for the possession of a collection of apostolic

Finally, these suggestions trivialize the whole
passage in an unconvincing way. For Paul to make so
much of the obvious fact that love will last beyond a
certain date in the near future of the church does not
seem realistic. To demonstrate that love <u>never</u> fails
(οὐδέποτε πίπτει, vs. 8), it is most appropriate for
Paul to show that it lasts beyond the evident turning-
point between the present and eternity, the Parousia.[62]
Elsewhere in 1 Cor. when Paul wants to demonstrate the
eternal value of something, he does this by arguing
that it will last beyond the day of the Lord's return
(3.13-15, 15.51-58). By contrast, prophecy and other
gifts will not last beyond that day.

(b) Ἔλθῃ is a gnomic aorist. Paul has
no specific time in mind but is just asserting the
general truth that whenever something perfect comes,
something imperfect is no longer useful.

Such an interpretation artificially isolates vs.
10 from its context. Even if ἔλθῃ be considered a
gnomic aorist, it still expresses a general truth which
is applied by Paul to prophecy and the Parousia. The
τότε in vs. 12 shows that Paul had a specific time in
mind. The repetition in vs. 10 of the ἐκ μέρους from
vs. 9, plus the contrast between τὸ τέλειον and τὸ ἐκ
μέρους in vs. 10, show that Paul applies vs. 10 to
prophecy. So vs. 10 is not only true in general; it
is also true of prophecy and the Parousia in specific.

(c) Καταργηθήσεται means that prophecy
will be "made useless" but not that it will "cease" at
the Parousia. Therefore, Paul was not writing about
the time of the cessation of prophecy and, as far as
Paul was concerned (in this passage), prophecy might
well cease at any time before or after the Parousia.

It is true that καταργέω can mean "make useless,
powerless, ineffective" (Lk. 13.7, Rom. 3.3, Gal. 3.17)
as well as "abolish, bring to an end" or (as passive)

---

writings in the church it would be the existence of
live apostles in the church, not live prophets. Once
the apostles died they could no longer exercise active
rule over the churches. It was natural then that the
church should turn to the preserved writings of the
apostles for guidance.

[62]Cf. 1 Cor. 15.24, 51-57, 1 Th. 4.17 (πάντοτε).

"cease, pass away" (1 Cor. 6.13, 15.24, 2 Thess. 2.8, 2 Tim. 1.10; Ga. 5.11, 2 Cor. 3.7; Barn. 15.5; Ign. Eph. 13.2).[63] But the context here makes "cease, pass away" a better translation. Paul is arguing that love will continue forever, and the contrast is with the gifts which will not continue.

Yet even if we translate "will be made useless," it does not affect the argument very much. For in neither case is it possible to translate, "(prophecy) will be useless" (a state of affairs), since καταργέω implies an activity: something makes something else useless. So it is precisely the event of the beginning of the consummation which makes prophecy useless. That means for Paul prophecy would remain useful, powerful, or effective until the consummation. But if Paul was willing to say that prophecy would remain effective and useful until the consummation, he certainly would have thought that it would continue to be operative until that time.

(d) By "prophecy" Paul means only divinely authoritative prophecies, or prophecies contained in writings that are accepted as Scripture. Thus, Paul means that "written Scripture" will pass away at the consummation.[64]

This objection also ignores the context of 1 Cor. 13. Paul is talking about spiritual gifts and is showing how love is superior to them. In 1 Cor., προφητεία certainly does not refer to "written Scripture" but to a gift of prophecy which was not divinely authoritative.

(e) Prophecy is a miraculous sign-gift, and these were only associated with the apostles. Therefore, when the apostles died these miraculous gifts ceased.

This is not an exegetical but a dogmatic objection.[65] Unless it can be shown on exegetical

---

[63] AG, 418.

[64] S. D. Toussaint, "First Corinthians Thirteen and the Tongues Question," Bib Sac 120 (1963), 314.

[65] It can also take the form of a historical objection (see below). This is the view of B. B.

grounds to provide a possible explanation of the meaning of the text in question, it cannot help us determine what Paul actually said or meant here.[66]

(f) It is a historical fact that prophecy did cease early in the history of the church. Therefore, either Paul was wrong or he meant something else.

However, such an objection is again not sufficient from an exegetical standpoint. Whether or not Paul was wrong does not affect the question of what exactly he meant when he wrote 1 Cor. 13.10. On the other hand, simply to say that he must have meant something else is insufficient unless one can show from evidence in the text another plausible meaning.

Furthermore, I do not suggest that Paul was expressing an opinion on the relative frequency of prophesying in the history of the church. That would be subject to much variation depending on the spiritual maturity and vitality of the church in various periods, the degree to which prophecy was sought as a blessing or rejected as a heresy, the frequency with which public worship normally made provision for the exercise of this gift, and the degree to which the nature of NT prophecy was correctly understood.

What Paul is speaking about, however, is the total and final abolition of prophecy which is to be brought about by divine initiative at the Parousia. And he is saying that he thinks that until the time of the Parousia the gift of prophecy will at least to some

---

Warfield, Counterfeit Miracles (repr. London, 1972), although he sees this cessation as a gradual occurrence during a roughly-defined "apostolic age." Cf. W. Chantry, Signs of the Apostles (Edinburgh, 1973).

[66]This view is usually accompanied by the observation that all the miracles reported in the NT are closely connected with the apostles and function to confirm the truth of their message. Such an observation is interesting, but it should be accompanied by the observation that almost everything in the NT (including evangelism and the founding of churches, for instance) is closely connected with the apostles. This tells us nothing about whether miracles could occur in relation to other Christians to confirm the truth of the Gospel they proclaim or to serve some other purpose.

extent remain available for use, and God will continue to give men the revelations which make prophecy possible.

With particular reference to prophecy, Calvin (p. 305) notes the abundance of spiritual gifts in Paul's day and comments (on 1 Cor. 14.32):

> Today we see our own slendor resources, our poverty in fact; but this is undoubtedly the punishment we deserve, as the reward for our ingratitude. For God's riches are not exhausted, nor has His liberality grown less; but we are not worthy of His largess, or capable of receiving all that He generously gives.

4. Conclusion

In 1 Cor. 13.8-13 Paul tells the Corinthians that prophecy will continue until but not beyond the time the Lord returns. Thus, it is acceptable to paraphrase 1 Cor. 13.10, "When the Lord returns, the gift of prophecy will cease."

II. THE CONTENT OF PROPHECY

The types of subjects prophesied about in the examples we have seen are so varied that we might at first wonder whether it is possible to restrict at all the kinds of things a prophet might say. But we have now reached a point where each of our three chapters can provide its own type of restriction on the content of NT church prophecy. When those three restrictions are made explicit, we shall have a very broad but nevertheless useful description of the content of prophecy, and we shall be able to give several more examples of the types of things a prophet in the Corinthian church, for example, might say.

(1) <u>Prophecy of the type found in 1 Corinthians will not include any claims to be speaking with a divine authority of actual words.</u> This restriction is derived from the discussion in Chap. 1, where I argued that prophecy in 1 Corinthians is not seen by Paul as having a divine authority of actual words. This means that even if a prophecy contained words of ethical instruction ("You shouldn't go to Jerusalem" or "You

should leave your job and devote all your time to preaching" or "You should marry Philip"), these instructions would not be considered divine obligations (i.e. to disobey them would not be thought the same as disobeying God), but they would be viewed as the prophet's own fairly accurate (but not infallible) report of something he thinks (though not with absolute certainty) has been revealed to him by God. The person or persons to whom the prophecy is directed would therefore respond to the prophecy in much the same way they would respond to preaching or to personal advice: they would weigh it (cf. 1 Cor. 14.29) for conformity to Scripture, to received teaching, and to facts which from their own experience they know to be true.

For the other type of prophecy, that which claimed a divine authority of actual words, such a restriction of course would not apply.

(2) The prophecy will include material which seems to have come through a "revelation" from God. Generally, this will consist of claims to speak facts which could not be known by ordinary means. It may include prediction of the future (Ac. 11.27-30, 21.11), the disclosure of the secret sins or anxieties or problems hidden in a man's heart (1 Cor. 14.24-25), or the disclosure of certain gifts for ministry possessed by someone in the congregation (1 Tim. 1.18, 4.14). But very often we can suppose that the prophecy would also include not such spectacular revelations, but perhaps simply the statement of a known fact or verse of Scripture which needed to be called to the attention of the congregation at that particular moment. So perhaps someone would stand and say, "God has brought to my mind a verse of Scripture and I feel I must say it: 'Honor your father and mother, that your days may be long in the land which the Lord your God gives you.'" Then someone else might stand and admit that the prophecy called to his mind a Scriptural principle which he had not thought about in relation to his particular situation, but that upon hearing it again he was encouraged to make a particular decision with regard to his own life which he might not otherwise have made. Or again, someone might stand and say, "The Lord has put on my mind a tremendous concern for the Christians in Rome. I think we should pray for them now." Then later it might be learned that that day a new onslaught of persecution had begun in Rome.

In both of these cases the information contained in the prophecy was not hidden information which could only have been known by revelation. The members of the congregation, if they had been asked, would have agreed that it was good to honor one's father and mother and to pray for Christians in other cities. In these cases the revelation to the prophet was indispensable because it allowed those particular items of information (rather than some others) to be called to the attention of the congregation at those particular times (rather than at some other times). And the fact that these thoughts came spontaneously and forcefully to mind caused the prophet to think that they came from God and were not the product of his own reflection on and evaluation of the situation at hand (in which case it would have been a "teaching" or "exhortation").

(3) The prophecy will edify other members of the congregation.

Here I am using "edify" in an extremely broad sense, to include anything which contributes to the spiritual growth of anyone present, or anything implied by οἰκοδομή, παράκλησις and παραμυθία in 1 Cor. 14.3. This means that the prophecy will not include abstruse doctrinal discourses which the hearers are unable to apply to their own lives, or bits of "revealed" factual information (even true information, 1 Cor. 8.1) which have no usefulness for the hearers' lives. Rather, the prophecy must affect the lives of the hearers in a positive way. In order to be edifying, it must suit the needs of the moment.

This means that a prophecy may or may not include Scripture quotations, or exposition and application of Scripture. Certainly prophecy cannot be restricted to "midrashic" interpretations of Scripture (few of the examples we have looked at contain this). On the other hand, in order to be edifying, a prophecy would have to conform to (or at least not contradict) the ethical and doctrinal outlook of Scripture itself, or else it would be rejected as not actually having been revealed by God.

In summary, the type of prophecy in 1 Corinthians will not claim a divine authority of actual words, will be based on revelation, and will edify the hearers. Within these bounds, a prophecy could apparently speak to any subject and contain any kind of material which would contribute to its purpose.

III. THE FORM OF PROPHECY

The NT examples of church prophecy are so varied that it is not possible for us to isolate any specific formulas in which these prophecies would occur. The only clear example of a prophetic formula is found in the letters to the seven churches in Rev. 2-3 (each oracle begins with τάδε λέγει . . . and ends with "he who has an ear, let him hear what the Spirit says to the churches").[67] But this prophecy is claimed to be of the first type (with a divine authority of actual words), and is thus unlike the prophecy in 1 Cor. at least with respect to authority. So it is uncertain whether any specific formulas would occur in the second type of prophecy, like that in 1 Cor. Furthermore, the tremendous variety in subject matter, plus the fact that each prophet expresses his prophecy in his own words, make it highly unlikely that any one item, or any one pattern of expression, would repeat itself with unusual frequency in church prophecies.

We can say, however, that the requirement that prophecies edify the congregation means that these prophecies had to be intelligible to the congregation. On first reading 1 Cor. 14, one might think, for instance, that a prayer to God spoken in tongues ("he speaks not to men but to God," 1 Cor. 14.2) could have "built up" or "strengthened" the church, especially if it was a prayer for the church. But Paul thinks otherwise: "He who speaks in a tongue edifies himself" (1 Cor. 14.4), and the contrast is with the one who "prophesies" and thereby "edifies the church." In order for the church to be edified in public assembly, the members have to hear and understand something that is spoken. Again in vss. 16-17, Paul says that if a person "does not know" what is spoken in a

---

[67] W. C. van Unnik, "A Formula Describing Prophecy," NTS 9 (1962-63), 86-94, adduces many examples to show that "that which was, is and shall be" (cf. Rev. 1.19) was a common prophetic formula, even among pagan prophets. However, his examples show a great degree of variety and may just indicate an obvious fact: much prophecy claimed to be a specially revealed interpretation of past and present history, and a means of gaining insight into future history.

prayer, he is not edified by that prayer (vs. 17)[68]
So prophecy does not benefit the church in a mysterious, indiscernible way. Rather, people are helped by prophecies specifically as they gain new understanding and encouragement from what the prophet says.

Thus NT prophecy at Corinth was far removed from the frenzied, unintelligible utterances of the Pythia at Delphi.[69] Furthermore, it is unlikely that NT prophecy would often have been couched in the notoriously ambiguous phraseology of the prophets who "interpreted" the Pythia's response.[70] According to Paul, speech which could not be understood simply did not edify.[71]

---

[68]However, a prayer spoken in tongues does appear to benefit the speaker, even though he may not understand what he is saying. He "edifies himself" (vs. 4) and "gives thanks well" (vs. 17). Although this edification does not come through his understanding, it comes somehow through his active involvement and participation in the prayer ("my spirit prays," vs. 14). In the case of one who listens to a message he does not understand, however, even the element of participation is lacking, and so no edification occurs.

[69]At Delphi the Pythia was the woman who acted as immediate spokesman for Apollo. Her answers "would vary in . . . degree of coherence and intelligibility," but would regularly have to be interpreted by one of the nearby male prophets who assisted her. It was the prophet who then dictated the response to the inquirer (Parke and Wormell, Oracle, I, 33). On the ecstatic state of the Pythia, cf. pp. 37-40 (with notes). Parke and Wormell admit that "the confused and disjointed remarks of a hypnotized woman must have needed considerable exercise of imagination to reduce them to the form of a response" (p. 39).

[70]On this ambiguity, see Parke and Wormell, Oracle, 40, and 44, n. 99.

[71]This section further confirms the discussion in Chap. 2, pp. 154ff, on the intelligibility of prophecy.

IV. ADDITIONAL NOTE: PROPHETIC CONTRIBUTIONS TO THE GOSPEL TRADITION

A common idea in NT scholarship in this century has been that NT prophets, under the influence of the Holy Spirit, received actual words from the risen Lord which they then uttered in the congregation. These words were taken as authoritative sayings of Jesus and, with the passage of time, some of them found their way into the Gospel traditions about the earthly life of Jesus. Eventually they came to be presented in the Gospels as words spoken by the earthly Jesus, but that really was not a serious mistake, because they were words of Jesus anyway, even if not words spoken during Jesus' earthly life.

This theory has come under severe criticism, however, and most of the opposing arguments are summarized in David Hill's article, "On the Evidence for the Creative Role of Christian Prophets" (NTS 20 [1973-74], 262-274). Repeating especially the earlier criticisms of F. Neugebauer,[72] Hill lists several objections which remain unanswered: (i) There is no similar transformation of logia from inspired prophetic speech to historical narrative in any of the available NT or Jewish writings.[73] (ii) The theory ignores the difference in method of composition and literary genre between a gospel and an apocalypse. (iii) If the words only gradually became part of the historical tradition, then at first the church clearly distinguished between recent charismatic sayings and "authentic" historical words, and there is no reason why that distinction should not have been maintained throughout the early years of the church until the Gospels attained their final form. (iv) If sayings of the risen Lord through the prophets were thought just as valuable as historical sayings of Jesus, then there would have been no reason for projecting them back into the context of Jesus' earthly life. (v) The theory neglects the concern of the early church, and especially the

---

[72] F. Neugebauer, "Geistsprüche und Jesuslogien," ZNW 53 (1962) 218-28.

[73] Related to this criticism is Colin Brown's observation, "Prophecies in the Bible were never anonymous, but were always ascribed to the human agent through whom they were uttered" ("Bultmann Revisited," The Churchman 88:3 (July-Sept., 1974, 180).

apostles, to safeguard the traditions about Jesus and prevent unwarranted corruption (cf. 1 Cor. 7.10, 12, 25). (vi) The theory must attribute to early Christian prophets essentially the same role as that played by Gnostic authors of apocryphal Gospels, in which the risen Lord conveyed special revelations to this or that privileged disciple, but the idea that such practices were common so early in the life of the church is itself a position open to serious doubt.

Hill's unique contribution, however, is not to rework these previous objections, but rather to examine closely the actual evidence in primary sources about early Christian prophets which has been proposed to support the position that there were in fact such prophetic contributions to the Gospel tradition. He begins with the principal modern statement of this theory, by R. Bultmann: "It would only be gradually that such sayings would come to be regarded as prophecies by the Jesus of history. The church drew no distinction between such utterances by Christian prophets and the sayings of Jesus in the tradition, for the reason that even the dominical sayings in the tradition were not the pronouncements of a past authority, but sayings of the risen Lord, who is always a contemporary for the Church."[74] Bultmann gives as evidence (i) the prophecies in Revelation, (ii) Odes of Solomon 42.6 (Christ says, "Then I arose and am with them, and will speak by their mouths"),[75] (iii) references to the works of von Soden (whose primary evidence is Revelation) and Gunkel (who refers to the first-person speech for Christ in the Odes of Solomon). Thus, the only primary documents used as evidence are Revelation and the Odes of Solomon.

Hill then argues that the Odes of Solomon are probably 2nd century Gnostic hymns, and thus of little value for studying early 1st century Christian prophecy. But even if they are early,[76] they do not

---

[74] R. Bultmann, The History of the Synoptic Tradition (ET Oxford, 1972; from second German edn., 1931), 127-28.

[75] H. Charlesworth, The Odes of Solomon (Oxford, 1973), 145.

[76] In view of the powerful arguments of Charlesworth ("The Odes of Solomon--Not Gnostic," CBQ 31

talk about Christ speaking through prophets but rather through believers generally. We should note that there is certainly no evidence in them of a transformation of contemporary prophetic sayings into alleged historical traditions.

Concerning Revelation, Hill notes that the author is certainly not typical of other NT prophets, and also that each prophetic saying is carefully preserved in a context which makes explicit that the words come from the risen Lord and through a particular prophet who is clearly identified. In sum, primary evidence which clearly supports the theory has simply not been found. There is no proven instance where a prophetic oracle became a part of a historical narrative.[77]

Now it is not my purpose at this point to examine the entire form-critical approach to the Gospels, but it is interesting to notice that wherever this approach depends in part at least on the view that NT prophets did contribute to the Gospel tradition, the weakness of evidence to support the alleged creative role of Christian prophets becomes more and more apparent. We cannot look at all of the modern examples, but a small selection will demonstrate this point. Philipp Vielhauer[78] mentions Revelation and Od. Sol. 42.6. Norman

---

(1969), I feel that it is much more likely that the Odes are 1st century Jewish Christian hymns, as he suggests. Nevertheless, Hill's point is valid: early Christian prophets are not discussed.

[77] If it be objected that no such case could be found because once the <u>logia</u> are embedded in a historical narrative they become isolated from their original prophetic context, the answer must be that this then becomes argument by assertion, not evidence, and must be recognized for what it is.
John 14.26, "The Holy Spirit . . . will bring to your remembrance all that I have said to you," might be mentioned as evidence, but as it stands it is unconvincing, both because the context does not talk about prophets but about the apostles and because remembrance of historical statements is exactly what critics of this view put in opposition to prophetic reception of new statments from the risen Lord.

[78] "Prophecy," 605-07.

Perrin[79] does not even go that far; on the first page of his book he simply tells us, without any footnotes or supporting evidence, "The early church made no attempt to distinguish between the words the earthly Jesus had spoken and those spoken by the risen Lord through a prophet in the community."

M. Eugene Boring[80] attempts to eliminate the *a priori* approach to this problem by first drawing a picture of the work of NT prophets from the NT iself, but in his brief analysis he sees Revelation and Paul as primary examples of early Christian prophetism (p. 504), then uses Paul and Revelation to justify other conclusions about prophetic form and function (pp. 514, 515, 516-17). On p. 516 he claims, "All our secondary sources indicate that not only Jesus, but early Christian prophets spoke with authority, and not as the scribes. . . . space will not be taken here to elaborate this easily-documented assertion" (p. 516).[81]

Earnst Käsemann's well-known essay, "Sentences of Holy Law in the NT,"[82] has been criticized from many sides,[83] and Hill rightly notes Käsemann's lack of primary evidence about the activity of NT prophets.[84] Once more with respect to Käsemann, we must call attention to the methodological impropriety of using Pauline material as a primary example of early Christian prophecy (he builds his case largely on 1 Cor.

---

[79] *Rediscovering the Teaching of Jesus* (London, 1967), 15

[80] M. Eugene Boring, "How May We Identify Oracles of Christian Prophets in the Synoptic Tradition?" *JBL* 91 (1972), 501-21.

[81] Boring subsequently acknowledged the validity of many of the criticisms by David Hill, "Prophecy and Prophets," 401-18; see Chap. 1, n. 193. Since Paul only classifies himself as a prophet in a very indirect way (1 Cor. 13.9, 14.6), one may wonder how valid it is to use Paul as a starting point to investigate NT prophecy.

[82] In Ernst Käsemann, *New Testament Questions of Today* (Et, London, 1969), 66-81 (=[Germ] *NTS* 1 [1954-55], 248-60.

[83] A summary of the discussion is given in Hill, "Creative Role," 270-72.

[84] *Ibid.*

3.17, 1 Cor. 14.38, Gal. 1.19, and other Pauline texts).

To summarize: There are several arguments against the creative role of Christian prophets in relation to the Gospels from what we know of the history and activity of the early church, and Hill has now shown that there are no convincing data in the primary sources to support such a role. In addition to these two major kinds of objection, it is now possible to offer another observation, based on our analysis of prophecy in 1 Corinthians. We have found that it was not the task of prophets at Corinth and in some other churches to create actual "words of the risen Lord." Far from being interchangeable with the historical words of Jesus to which the community was subject, these prophecies were themselves subject to the community (1 Cor. 14.29, 1 Th. 5.20-21).[85] This observation does not constitute an entirely new objection to the theory under consideration, but it does show that the number of prophets who could have been expected to produce these new sayings of Jesus is not as large as the number of prophets in all the churches at the time of the NT; in fact, it may have been quite small.

With regard to the alleged ability to discover such prophetic sayings in the Gospels by recognizing their distinctive form or function (or both), we have seen that no function of prophecy is unique to that gift, and that the only unique formulas are those of Rev. 2-3--but few if any parallels to those formulas have been discovered. So any attempt to distinguish prophetic contributions in the Gospels by form or function faces almost insurmountable difficulties: alone or in combination, the forms and functions of prophecy are shared by teaching, preaching, counselling

---

[85] G. F. Hawthorne, "Christian Prophecy and the Sayings of Jesus: Evidence of and Criteria for," SBL 1975 Seminar Papers, ed. G. MacRae (Cambridge, Mass., 1975), 105-29, lists eleven pieces of "cumulative" evidence for the possibility that some sayings of Christian prophets may have been intermingled with sayings of Jesus in the Gospel tradition. However, his argument is based on the view that NT prophets spoke with divine authority (pp. 105-09). He also is unable to produce one certain example, but must make an entirely speculative step at the end of each of his crucial points (points 5-11, pp. 112-17).

and other types of Christian speech.[86]

On the other hand, the one unique feature of prophecy, its basis in a "revelation" from God, does not provide a criterion for distinguishing any prophetic sayings in the Gospels, for even if we could find a saying which presupposed a "revelation," it is hard to see how we could insist that this revelation be attributed to an early Christian prophet instead of to Jesus.

So I find that I must conclude with Hill and others that the theory of prophetic contributions to the Gospel tradition both lacks sufficient convincing evidence and seems to be contrary to much of what we do know about early Christian prophets and the churches in which they lived.

V. SUMMARY OF CHAPTER THREE

Paul defines the function of prophecy very broadly in 1 Cor. 14.3: its functions could include any kind of speech activity which would be helpful to the hearers. In 1 Cor. 14.20-25 prophecy and (uninterpreted) tongues function as signs of God's attitude, indicating favor for believers and warning of judgment for unbelievers. Paul says in 1 Cor. 13.10 that prophecy will continue until the Lord returns.

In content, prophecy of the type found in 1 Corinthians will not include any claims to divine authority (such as "Thus says the Lord"), but will include material which would be thought to have come through a revelation and which will edify the congregation.

---

[86] A good example of the inadequacy of formal and functional criteria combined is seen in Walter J. Houston, New Testament Prophecy and the Gospel Tradition (unpublished D. Phil. thesis, Oxford, 1973). He uses both functional and formal criteria to distinguish prophetic sayings: they must (i) have a paracletic purpose, (ii) be based on an apocalyptic midrash on OT words or words of Jesus; (iii) use eschatological language (p. 21). Just why an evangelist or apostle or Jesus himself, rather than a NT prophet, could not have spoken the passages Houston isolates, is never made clear to the reader.

The NT does not lead us to expect to find any distinctive speech forms for prophecy. The common idea that prophets contributed to the Gospel tradition has not yet been adequately substantiated by the NT data, nor does there seem to be convincing evidence that prophets as _prophets_ had regular leadership roles in the NT church.

CHAPTER FOUR

THE QUALIFICATIONS FOR BEING A PROPHET

I. INFORMAL RECOGNITION: THOSE WHO PROPHESY ARE PROPHETS

I now wish to define more precisely who the NT prophets were. Did the prophets in each church constitute a well-defined, distinct group? Did believers require some kind of formal recognition (such as a public announcement or a vote of approval from the congregation or an ordination ceremony) before they could be called "prophets" in the NT? In other words, was there in some sense an "office" of prophet in the NT? Or was the term "prophet" only used in a descriptive way, so that anyone who prophesied might be called a prophet?

It is important to recognize in this connection that even if someone had not received any kind of formal recognition a descriptive noun still might be applied to him. Thus, someone who helps others might be called a "helper," someone who assists with administrative work might be called an "administrator," someone who interprets tongues might be called an "interpreter," and someone who teaches (without formal public recognition) might be called a "teacher." When nouns are used in a merely descriptive way such as this, I shall refer to them as functional uses of nouns (since they simply describe functions which people perform), in order to distinguish them from nouns which are used as technical terms to describe some church office or some position which required more formal recognition.

There are several considerations which argue that "prophet" is used in such a functional sense in 1 Corinthians. First, even if one argued for an office of "prophet" in 1 Cor., he would have to admit that there were some who did not hold that office but who nevertheless prophesied occasionally. This would be inevitable in a church where everyone is encouraged to prophesy (12.31, 14.1, 5, 39). Some would hesitantly be trying to use the gift for the first time, while others would receive a revelation (14.30) only very infrequently. In any given congregation there would be all sorts of varying degrees of prophetic ability. Now these people who prophesy infrequently are still called "prophets" by Paul, for in 1 Cor. 14.32 he says "the spirits of prophets are subject to prophets." By this he cannot mean only that those who are formally recognized as prophets are able to control themselves when they prophesy, for then his instructions would have no relevance for the novices (who no doubt needed instruction as much as anyone). Nor would his statement be valid as a general truth applicable to all who prophesy because of a revelation of the Holy Spirit--and if it is not a general truth, then his argument against prophetic disorder will not hold. So it seems clear Paul calls anyone who prophesies a προφήτης in 14.32.

Then in 1 Cor. 14.29, "Let two or three prophets speak, and let the others weigh what is said," Paul cannot simply be giving instructions concerning a special, formally recognized group, for then he would be excluding from congregational participation those who had prophetic gifts but were not formally recognized--something contrary to Paul's express desire that all who have gifts be able to use them for the benefit of all (12.7, 21, 26, 14.5, 12; cf. Rom. 12.6). So once again, Paul means by προφήτης here anyone who has the ability to prophesy, or simply anyone who received a revelation and prophesied.

In 14.37, "If anyone thinks himself to be a prophet, or spiritual," there is an implicit element of subjective evaluation. Someone might think that he is a prophet, while someone else might differ with that opinion. If prophets were formally recognized, no such difference of opinion could occur, for everyone would know who was a prophet and who was not. Thus προφήτης here must mean someone who has the ability to prophesy or who prophesies frequently.

This leaves only 1 Cor. 12.28, which must be considered a neutral use of the term. The connection with "apostles" might suggest that church officers are named here, but that is not certain. "Teachers" might simply be a functional description of those who teach (as in 1 Tim. 2.7, 2 Tim. 1.11, Heb. 5.12, perhaps Eph. 4.11, Jas. 3.1; cf. Tit. 2.13, Col. 3.16). In the parallel gift list in Rom. 12.7, Paul simply uses the participle ὁ διδάσκων.[1] And it seems that Paul

---

[1] If 1 Cor. 12.28 had said, "First apostles, second prophets, third elders (or bishops) and deacons,"

would like all the Corinthians to strive to be "prophets" in the sense of 12.28,[2] a wish which would be extremely hypothetical if by "prophet" he meant some formally recognized function or office.

Elsewhere in the NT προφήτης is generally used in cases which are ambiguous enough to prevent us from deciding whether any kind of office or formally recognized position is in view (Ac. 11.27, 13.1, 15.32, 21.10, Eph. 2.20, 3.5, 4.11, Rev., passim).

Then there are some minor considerations. There is no hint in the NT about any ceremony of recognizing or installing someone in a prophetic office or to perform some specific prophetic tasks (as in Ac. 1.23-26, 6.6, 13.1-3, 14.23, 1 Tim. 4.14, 5.22, Tit. 1.5, etc.). Furthermore, there does not seem to have been any need for clear public recognition of those who were prophets, for anyone who received a revelation could prophesy (1 Cor. 14.31).

So προφήτης is usually, and perhaps always, a functional term when used of NT prophets. Nevertheless, as such, the term can have a more broad or more narrow meaning depending on the context in which it is used. 1 Cor. 14.32, "the spirits of prophets are subject to prophets." must use προφήτης to apply to anyone who prophesies even once. This is a very broad meaning, and the context makes it clear to the reader.

But in 1 Cor. 14.37, "If someone thinks himself to be a prophet, or spiritual," a more narrow meaning of the term is required. As I argued above, an element of subjective personal evaluation is suggested by the verb. Some people would consider a certain person a prophet, others would not. In such a case, whether or not the term "prophet" would be applied to a particular person would depend on at least three variable factors:

(i) The frequency and scope of that person's prophetic activity: someone who prophsied before the entire congregation very frequently and at great length would certainly be called a "prophet," while someone who

---

the situation would of course be different. But (for whatever reasons) it does not say that.

[2] Cf. Chap. 1, pp. 56ff and 1 Cor. 12.31 with 14.1, 5, 39.

prophesied less frequently and more briefly (and perhaps before a smaller group of believers) might not be so called.

(ii) The situation in that particular congregation: in a church where no one had prophesied for several months or years even a novice in prophetic activity would be called a prophet, but in a church where many prophets were active, people would not call the beginner a prophet until he began to prophesy more often.

(iii) The individual speech habits of believers in the congregation: some would enthusiastically want to label any novice a prophet, but others would be more restrictive in their use of the term.

Both the broad and the narrow use here described comprise what may be called an <u>informal</u> recognition that certain people are prophets and others (at least for the present) are not. There seems to have been no congregational vote to determine who could be called prophets, nor do we see evidence of any public announcement that certain designated people could be called prophets. Rather, it probably was generally recognized by the believers that προφήτης simply meant "someone who prophesies." Such a non-technical definition fits well with all the NT data.[3]

II. <u>CAN ALL BELIEVERS PROPHESY?</u>

In order to answer this question we must distinguish several specific meanings and answer the individual senses of the question one at a time:

---

[3] Similarly, Dunn, <u>JS</u>, 170f, 281. Ellis, <u>Luke</u>, 171f, says that prophets were "a distinct order in the early church," but gives little supporting evidence. Greeven, "Propheten," 8, suggests that the picture of prophecy in 1 Cor. is not a unified one: we have merely a glimpse of one point in the process by which prophecy as a universal possession was becoming limited to a certain group (followed by Best, "Prophets and Preachers," 142). J. Reiling, <u>Hermas</u>, 10, sees three types of prophecy in the early church: itinerant (as defined by Harnack), official (as defined by Greevan) and congregational (evident in Paul's epistles). He thinks the congregational type is still dominant at the time of Hermas (pp. 143-54, 175).

A. Are all believers permitted to prophesy?

B. Does every believer have a potential ability to prophesy?

C. Does every believer have an actual ability to prophesy?

D. Does every believer have the ability to prophesy at will?

A. Permission to Prophesy

Paul places certain restrictions on the permission to prophesy: no one can prophesy when someone else is speaking (14.30-31), and the limitations of time would not seem to allow every single person in the congregation to prophesy at one meeting (14.29).[4] But other than those restrictions there are no limitations on the permission to prophesy.[5] There was no special prophetic office such that only those who held that office could prophesy in church. Rather, anyone who received a revelation and waited his turn had permission to prophesy.

B. Potential Ability

By this we mean to ask whether every believer might someday prophesy, or, negatively, if there were any believers who for some reason were disqualified from ever being able to prophesy. Here the answer must be that such potential ability was possessed by everyone in whom the Holy Spirit worked. The gifts are given, Paul says, to each person (ἑκάστῳ 12.7, 11) by the Holy Spirit, and it is only the free volition of the Spirit (καθὼς βούλεται, 12.11) which determines who received which gift. Any Christian might possibly receive the gift of prophecy. Furthermore,

---

[4] This is not contradicted by 14.24, "if all prophesy," because 12.29, "not all are prophets," shows 14.24 to be a hypothetical situation which Paul did not think would ever actually exist.

[5] It has been argued that 14.34-35 forbids women to prophesy. However, I do not adopt that position (see below, pp. 239ff).

Paul urges all the Corinthians to seek to prophesy (14.1, 39), implying that there was for every one of them at least the possibility that they would receive this prophetic gift.

C. Actual Ability

In this case we are asking whether every believer (at least at Corinth) did in fact receive the ability to prophesy. Here the answer must be negative. Although Paul wants every Christian in Corinth to seek after prophecy and other useful gifts, he still is very clear that there is no one gift which will be possessed by every believer (12.8-10, 12, 14, 17, 19-20, 29-30) and even specifies prophecy as a function not possessed by all (μὺ πάντες προφῆται; 12.29). It should not be objected that 12.29 only means that not all hold a prophetic office, because προφήτης in 1 Cor. does not refer to a prophetic office, and because in the other verses just mentioned in 1 Cor. 12 Paul clearly denies that any single gift or ability will be possessed by all.

Nor is it inconsistent for Paul to say that not all will be able to prophesy while at the same time telling them all to seek to do so. Paul did not know which of the Corinthians would be given the prophetic gift. He could not have singled out some one group, such as adults, or leaders, or mature Christians, and told only these people to seek to prophesy, for then he would have arbitrarily excluded some potential prophets. His only alternative was to do exactly what he did: encourage all to seek the gift while at the same time exhorting those who do not attain it to be content and trust in God's wisdom concerning what is best for the church (12.11, 15-16, 18, 28 with 31).

Another objection might stem from Ac. 19.6, where a dozen Ephesian believers "spoke with tongues and prophesied." Although this prophecy is probably similar in many respects to the type of prophecy we find in 1 Cor., the fact that they all seem to have spoken in tongues and prophesied at once makes it quite different from the orderly congregational speech in 1 Cor. It appears rather as a dramatic and unique event confirming the giving of the Holy Spirit to the Gentiles similar to the events in Ac. 2.4 and 10.46, and need not have been repeated either in the founding of other churches or in the subsequent lives of these twelve at Ephesus.

A final objection can arise from 1 Cor. 14.31, where Paul says, "For you can all prophesy one by one, in order that all may learn and all may be encouraged" (δύνασθε γὰρ καθ' ἕνα πάντες προφητεύειν, ἵνα πάντες μανθάνωσιν καὶ πάντες παρακαλῶνται). One might argue that Paul is saying here that all believers can prophesy. But this is not the case. He says rather that all can prophesy <u>one by one</u>; in other words, that all are able to[6] control themselves and act in an orderly manner. The καθ' ἕνα comes early in the sentence for emphasis and intrudes between δύνασθε and προφητεύειν thus guaranteeing that the reader will understand that it is not the ability to prophesy but the ability to prophesy one by one which is in view. The subject of δύνασθε ("you") and the people included in πάντες are most naturally understood to be the entire congregation.[7] This does not mean that all actually can prophesy, but just that everyone in the congregation is able to control himself if he ever does prophesy. The ἵνα clause, "in order that all may learn and all may be encouraged," shows the result of prophesying one by one. The other situation, where several would prophesy at once, would allow few or none to learn and be encouraged, because no one would be able to hear or understand what was said.[8] But if

---

[6]Δύναμαι (209X in NT) means "to be able to," not "to be permitted to," so Paul must be talking about some kind of actual ability. For permission Paul uses ἐπιτρέπω as in vs. 34.

[7]But it would not make much difference if someone wanted to restrict the first πάντες to all those who prophesy, for the sense of the passages would be the same.

[8]We cannot be certain whether Paul is writing to correct or simply to prevent abuses of the gift of prophecy at Corinth. If he is writing to correct the problem of many prophets speaking at once, we may suppose that the Corinthians might have justified their behavior by appeal to the fact that they all possessed the Spirit and to examples such as Num. 11.25, 29, 1 Sam. 10.5 10, 19.20-22, Joel 2.28-32 and (perhaps) the events at Pentecost (cf. Ac. 2.4, 16.18; also Ac. 10.44-46 and 19.6).

Why does Paul insist on a different procedure than that represented in these examples? He seems to have thought that the purpose of the phenomena was

everyone who prophesies does so one by one, everyone will hear and understand the words, and everyone will thereby be encouraged and strengthened.

Vs. 32, "and (καί) the spirits of prophets are subject to prophets," does not exactly say the same thing as vs. 31. In vs. 31 Paul affirms the ability of the prophet to control himself while he prophesies, while in vs. 32 he is concerned to show that the Holy Spirit will not forcefully override that ability.[9] Both verses establish the same point, both are governed by the γάρ in vs. 31, and both are coordinate reasons (joined by καί), but vs. 31 emphasizes the ability of the prophet and vs. 32 the activity of the Holy Spirit. The γάρ in vs. 31 then does not strictly introduce the logical reason for Paul's command (although the ἵνα clause in vs. 31 is the reason), but signals more of an explanation of what has just been said.[10] So 1 Cor. 14.31 does not mean that all believers could prophesy.

Therefore, 1 Cor. 12-14 shows quite clearly that not all believers had an actual ability to prophesy.

D. Ability to Prophesy at Will

In the earlier investigation of 1 Cor. 14.30 (Chap. 2), we found that a "revelation" was thought to be something which came quite spontaneously to a prophet, that it came from God, and that without a "revelation" there could be no prophecy. Thus, no prophet could conjure up a revelation of his own accord and then begin to prophesy. He had to wait until

---

different. In each of the examples mentioned, the context makes it very clear that the writer understands the fact that everyone prophesied or spoke in tongues to signify that every person in the group had received the Spirit in a remarkable new way. If only one or few had spoken, this particular fact would not have been signified. But for Paul, the continuing purpose of prophecy (and tongues) in the church is edification. This can only be achieved when one person speaks at a time.

[9]Cf. Chap. 2, pp. 120ff.

[10]Cf. AG, 151, 2 (explanatory γάρ).

something was revealed to him.[11]

At this point there is a difference between prophecy and some of the other gifts mentioned by Paul. Gifts such as administration, teaching, helping, giving aid and (probably) speaking in tongues (1 Cor. 14.15, 18, 28) could be used at will. The believer who had one of these gifts could put it to use at any time. But prophecy was more spontaneous and could only be used when the prophet received a revelation.[12]

E. Summary

The evidence we have examined indicates that all believers had permission to prophesy, and all had a potential ability. But only some were given an actual ability to prophesy, and no one could prophesy at will.

III. 1 COR. 14.33b-35: COULD WOMEN PROPHESY IN CHURCH?

A. Statement of the Problem

Paul writes, "As in all the churches of the saints,[13] let the women keep silence in the churches.

---

[11] Cf. Jer. 42.7, Hab. 2.3; Herm. Mand. 11.2, 3, 5, 6, 8.

[12] A distinction related to this one was made in Chap. 2, pp. 136ff, where we called prophecy "miraculous," not because it depended on a more direct kind of divine activity, but because it depended on a less common one. Something like this distinction probably accounts for the fact that many people intuitively feel that prophecy is "miraculous" while teaching, for instance, is not.

[13] This first phrase goes with what follows, not with what precedes. It is common for Paul to reinforce some instruction by pointing out that it represents common ecclesiastical practice (1 Cor. 4.17, 7.17, 11.16, 16.1) and this is what vs. 33b does when linked with vs. 34. But when linked with vs. 33a (as KJV), the phrase is artificially made to restrict a general statement about God's character, so that it only says God is a God of peace "in the churches of the saints." But this kind of restriction would not help Paul's

For it is not permitted for them to speak, but they are to be subordinate, even as the law says. If they want to know something, let them ask their own husbands at home. For it is shameful for a woman to speak in church. Or did the word of God go forth from you, or to you only has it come?" The problem of interpretation arises in connection with 1 Cor. 11.4-16, and especially vs. 5, where Paul seems to allow women to pray and prophesy in the church meeting: "Any woman who prays or prophesies with her head unveiled dishonors her head." This passage itself is difficult, and we cannot enter into a discussion of all the problems involved. But it is clear that public worship is in view: I have already argued that Paul sees prophecy as a gift for public use (Chap. 3, p. 181), and surely the instruction about prayer could not apply to private prayer. (Could a man never pray with his head covered, even when alone outdoors in cold weather? Could a woman never pray with her head uncovered, even when alone in the privacy of her own home?) So in 11.5 Paul gives instructions concerning the way in which women should pray and prophesy in public worship, and thereby implies that such praying and prophesying is legitimate.[14] But then what can it mean in 14.34 for Paul to say, "Let the women be silent in the churches?"

B. The Possibility of a Post-Pauline Interpolation

The passage 1 Cor. 14.34-35 (and sometimes also vss. 36-38) is seen as a post-Pauline interpolation (along the lines of 1 Tim. 2.12) by several commentators, including Bittlinger (110f), Dautzenberg (UP,

---

argument at all, and it might suggest that God is a God of confusion outside the churches.

[14]To say that 11.5 only applies to small, informal worship is simply special pleading. There is no such restriction indicated in the context. W. J. Martin, "1 Cor. 11.2-16: An Interpretation," AHG, 231-41, suggests that the prayer in 11.5 may have been inaudible (p. 240). But certainly the prophecy was audible, and by giving instructions about prophecy Paul certainly assumes that it is practiced and gives tacit approval.

257-73) and E. Schweizer.[15] In fact, some early scribes thought that vss. 34-35 were out of place and transposed them to follow vs. 40. Even though their action cannot be accepted on text-critical grounds,[16] it does point to an early uneasiness about these verses which extends even to the present day.

Because this view is so widespread, it must not be lightly dismissed. The major argument in its favor is that it so easily solves a very difficult problem with what seems to many to be a very un-Pauline idea. We must admit that in view of the complexity of other proposed solutions, this advantage must be seriously considered. In fact, the reader may find it persuasive enough that all other proposed solutions seem quite evidently inferior. In that case, the following argument will be rejected, but its loss will not materially affect the rest of this investigation.

Nevertheless, the idea that vss. 34-35 (or 33b-36, etc.) are a later interpolation depends on the conviction that they seriously conflict with 11.5 and other passages in Paul. Therefore, an exegetical approach which claims to remove that conflict must be considered possible. It is that type of approach which I am about to suggest. I shall first examine the terms σιγάω and λαλέω, then analyze the structure of 1 Cor. 14.26-36, and finally propose a solution to the problem.[17]

---

[15]"The Service of Worship: An Exposition of 1 Cor. 14," Interp. 13 (1959), 402f.

[16]The textual support for such a change is poor (D G 88* it^{ar,d,e,f,g} Ambrosiaster, all Western texts with the earliest reading [Ambrosiaster] ca. 375), and the reason for wanting to find a "better" location for the verses is clearly the initial difficulty in seeing how they fit after vs. 33.

[17]Related to the possibility of considering the passage a gloss is the possibility of giving up hope of finding a reasonable solution and attributing inconsistency to Paul. But if a reasonable solution can be found such action is not necessary.

C. Contextual Limitations on Σιγάω and Λαλέω

An examination of the use of σιγάω in the NT shows that it never implies a total, unrestricted silence on all kinds of speech at all times, but that the context always specifies a restriction on the kind of silence intended. Quite often this is a temporal restriction: someone is to be silent while another person is speaking (e.g. Ac. 12.17, 15.2, 13). This kind of restriction is found in 1 Cor. 14.30, "If a revelation is made to another sitting by, let the first be silent" (σιγάτω). The first prophet is not expected to be silent on all topics for the entire worship service; rather, he is simply to be silent while the other prophet is speaking. And Paul does not need to spell out the explicit type of silence intended (he does not say, "Let the first be silent while the second is speaking"), because the context makes clear to the reader that this is what he has in mind.

Other kinds of restriction might be called topical or modal restrictions. The one who is "silent" does not speak about certain topics, or use certain forms of speech, but he can speak in other ways and about other topics. Such a modally restricted use of σιγάω is also found in the immediate context of Paul's instructions about worship at Corinth. In 1 Cor. 14.28 Paul says of the tongue-speaker, "If there is no one to interpret, let him keep silence (σιγάτω) in the church, and speak to himself and to God." Now this does not mean the tongue-speaker had to maintain total silence throughout the worship service. He could participate in the singing, in praying, in reading the Scriptures, and in discussion of concerns for prayer and thanksgiving. The command to be silent (σιγάτω) just meant to be silent with respect to the particular mode of speech under discussion, namely, speaking in tongues. The context makes this modal limitation clear.

Some other examples are found in Luke. In Lk. 9.36, after the transfiguration, Peter, James and John "were silent and told no one in those days anything of what they had seen" (καὶ αὐτοὶ ἐσίγησαν καὶ οὐδενὶ ἀπήγγειλαν ἐν ἐκείναις ταῖς ἡμέραις οὐδὲν ὧν ἑώρακαν). Here the silence is seen as lasting over a period of time, since "they were silent" is parallel to "they told no one in those days." Yet Luke does not mean that they said nothing at all in those days, but simply that they were silent concerning the particular topic defined by the context--in this case, the transfiguration. In Lk. 18.39, the people in the crowd rebuke the blind man, telling him to be silent (ἵνα σιγήσῃ). They did not demand a total silence (for it was a noisy crowd, and no one would care if the blind man talked with those near him, vss. 36-37), but they wanted him to stop shouting so loudly to attract Jesus' attention. Again, the context puts a restriction on the range of meaning Luke intends by the term σιγάω.[18]

In none of these cases does the writer feel any need to make pedantic qualifications in order to specify the particular kind of silence he means. The reader is expected to understand that it refers to silence concerning the matter currently being discussed.

This tendency to assume a contextually restricted meaning is of course not a special characteristic of the word σιγάω. It is simply a function of the fact that people in ordinary life talk to one another. So whenever someone uses words to describe human silence, those words will naturally have a contextual restriction similar to the ones we have described. This is evident when other terms such as ἡσυχάζω, ἡσυχία, σιωπάω and φιμόω are used to describe verbal silence in the NT. Luke writes that when Paul would not be persuaded, "We were silent, saying (ἡσυχάσαμεν εἰπόντες!) 'The will of the Lord be done'" (Ac. 21.14). The "silence" only pertained to their argument with Paul. Similarly, when Peter had reported his vision to those in Jerusalem, "They were silent, and (simultaneously, it seems)[19] they glorified God, saying, 'Then to the Gentiles also God has granted repentance unto life'" (ἡσύχασαν καὶ ἐδόξασαν τὸν Θεὸν λέγοντες . . . Ac. 11.18). Only their objections stopped, not

---

[18] Similar contextually restricted uses of σιγάω are found in Ps. 31 (32).3, 49 (50).21, 1 Macc. 11.5, Tob. 10.6, 7.

[19] Grammatically ἡσύχασαν and ἐδόξασαν might be either simultaneous or sequential, but what Luke must mean by ἡσυχασαν is that their criticism stopped (ingressive aorist). He cannot mean that they stopped speaking, because he says they became silent after they had heard Peter (ἀκούσαντες δὲ ταῦτα ἡσύχασαν). But surely Luke does not mean that they were talking during Peter's speech and only stopped talking when Peter was finished.

all their speech. In 1 Tim. 2.12 there is a context very similar to that of 1 Cor. 14.34-35. We read, "I do not permit a woman to teach or to have authority over a man; rather, she is to be silent" (διδάσκειν δὲ γυναικὶ οὐκ ἐπιτρέπω οὐδὲ αὐθεντεῖν ἀνδρός, ἀλλ'εἶναι ἐν ἡσυχίᾳ). The silence is not absolute, but applies only to speech which involves teaching or exercising authority over men (as the ἀλλά makes clear).

Examples with φιμόω, "to put to silence," are found in Mt. 22.34 (the Sadducees stopped challenging Jesus, but certainly did not stop talking completely) and Mk. 1.25 (the unclean spirit said no more about Jesus but did cry with a loud voice). Σιωπάω, "to be silent," is used in a similar contextually restricted sense in Mt. 20.31, Mk. 10.48, Lk. 19.40 (to be silent means not to praise Jesus) and Ac. 18.9 (to be silent means not to preach the Gospel).

Finally, when we come to negative statements with verbs of speaking such as λαλέω the same kind of topical or modal restriction is sometimes supplied by the context. I list here five NT examples with λαλέω, since that verb also occurs in 1 Cor. 14.34-35. In Mt. 13.34 and Mk. 4.34, "Without a parable Jesus did not speak to them" means that he did not give them any important teaching without illustrating it with a parable. John 18.20 says, "I have said nothing (that is, no major teaching) in secret." In Rom. 15.18 Paul says, "I will not dare to speak of anything except what Christ has done through me," but the context implies that he will not say anything else <u>when discussing the Gentile mission</u>. And in 1 Thess. 1.8, when Paul says, "We have no need to say anything," it is clear that he means, "We have no need to say anything <u>about you</u>."

This frequent contextual restriction on the meanings of terms for silence and speech means that when we attempt to understand σιγάω and λαλέω in 1 Cor. 14.34-35 we must realize that they will almost certainly have temporal, modal or topical restrictions derived from the context in which they occur. They will not refer to all speech at all times but only to certain kinds of speech at certain times. Now it is necessary to examine the structure of 1 Cor. 14.26-36 in order to understand exactly what the context is and what type of silence Paul intends.

D. The Structure of 1 Cor. 14.26-36

In vs. 26 Paul begins a new section in which he applies the principles reached in the previous discussion.[20] Here for the first time he tells the Corinthians the actual procedure they should follow in conducting their worship service.[21] Until we reach vs. 33b the structure of the section is quite clear. Vs. 26 is a general statement of the situation ("When you come together each one has a psalm, a teaching, a revelation, a tongue, an interpretation") and the main principle to be followed ("Let all things be done for edification"). Vss. 27-28 give more specific instructions about one particular mode of speaking (tongues) and vss. 29-33a about another (prophecy). Thus far we can outline the section as follows:

vs. 26   I. GENERAL STATEMENT: When you come together.
            . . . let all be done for edification.

vs. 27   A. SPECIFIC EXAMPLE 1: If anyone speaks in tongues
               1. Let it be two or at most three
               2. And let one interpret
vs. 28   3. If there is no interpreter
                  a. Let him keep silence in the church
                  b. And let him speak to himself and to God

vs. 29   B. SPECIFIC EXAMPLE 2: Let two or three prophets speak and let the others weigh what is said

---

[20] The new section is signaled by the phrase τί οὖν, which Paul often uses as a transition to another section, especially one flowing out or applying the preceding argument (cf. Rom. 3.1, 9, 4.1, 6.1, 15, 7.7, 9.14, 30, 11.7, 1 Cor. 3.5, 10.19, 14.15, Gal. 3.19).

[21] Vss. 20-25 have implications for the corporate worship service, but the point Paul is trying to make (it is more important to seek prophecy than tongues) is directed to individuals, and his example is highly hypothetical.

vs. 30	1. If a revelation is made to another. . . . let the first be silent
vs. 31	a. For you can all prophesy one by one
	(1) in order that all may learn and be encouraged
vs. 32	b. And the spirits of prophets are subject to prophets
vs. 33	(1) for God is not a God of confusion but of peace.

Now the problem is where to put vss. 33b-36. Several options might be proposed. One might think that this passage introduces an entirely new topic unrelated to vss. 26-33a. In that case it would be outlined as:

vs. 34   II. NEW TOPIC: Let the women keep silence in the churches.

The problem with this proposal, however, is that vss. 33b-36 do include instructions about the worship service (in vs. 35 there is a clear contrast between "in church" and "at home," and therefore the subject being discussed is public worship; cf. "when you come together" in vs. 26).[22] Thus, this passage is more closely related to vss. 26-33a than to any other section of 1 Cor. 12-14.[23] So it must be a passage in some way subordinate to the general statement in vs. 26.

Another option is to consider vss. 33b-36 as Paul's third specific example about the conduct of worship. It would be put in our outline as:

vs. 34   C. SPECIFIC EXAMPLE 3: Let the women keep silence in the churches.

---

[22] The plural ἐν ταῖς ἐκκλησίαις in vs. 34 must mean "in the church meetings." Paul can use ἐκκλησία to mean "church meeting," as in 1 Cor. 11.18, 14.19, 28, 35.

[23] An even more drastic measure would be to say that vss. 33b-36 are unrelated to any part of 1 Cor. 12-14. But this is impossible, both because the verses themselves talk about procedure in public worship and because Paul's summary for 12-14 is yet to come in vss. 39-40.

This would then be yet another modification of the general statement in vs. 26 and the implication would be that women could say nothing whatever in the worship service. For vs. 26 is a comprehensive statement in which Paul, by listing a few important examples, intends to speak of all (cf. πάντα) the things which might happen when the church met for worship. And if vss. 33b-36 referred to this general statement, it would mean that Paul allowed no women to speak in any way in church.

But the objections to this option are so strong that they make it impossible: (i) Paul clearly allows women to pray and prophesy in public worship in 11.5. Thus, it would be inconsistent for him to forbid all speech by women in 14.34-35. (ii) Such a major modification of Paul's teaching in these chapters would not come as a minor note in two short verses just before his conclusion. From the very beginning Paul has been speaking of the ability of every member of the congregation to use some gift for the common good (12.7, 11). As recently as 14.26 he reinforced that position (cf. ἕκαστος) with respect to public worship. But for him now suddently to add a postscript revealing that he really had meant to talk only about one half of the congregation (the men) would make 12.1-14.33a deceptive and misleading in the extreme. (iii) Although Paul's general summary in vs. 26 forewarns us that prophecy and tongues might be discussed (ἀποκάλυψιν ἔχει, γλῶσσαν ἔχει), there is no hint here at all that a separate third topic will be the prohibition of women's speech in church. This would make its introduction quite unusual. (iv) Such a prohibition would be entirely arbitrary and unreasonable for Paul. It would neither be required by his central concern in this passage (the promotion of edification in worship, vs. 26b) nor by any elements in what we know of Paul's thought from his other writings.[24]

---

[24] A slight modification of this position would be to argue that αἱ γυναῖκες means "the wives," not "the women." Support for this view might be sought in the phrase τοὺς ἰδίους ἄνδρας (vs. 35), "their own husbands." Then Paul's instructions would forbid married women to speak in church but allow it for single women.

All the objections to this position when γυναῖκες means "women" would also apply to this modification, however. With regard to objection (i), Paul clearly

Yet another option would be to make vss. 33b-36 an additional instruction about the use of tongues.

---

includes married women in 11.5 (cf. 11.3). Objection (iv) would still hold, for not all speech would challenge the authority structure Paul saw in marriage (11.3; cf. also Col. 3.18, Eph. 5.22-24): prayer, for instance, would not do so.

In addition, this modification has a further problem of making Paul's command nonsensical. For it would allow very young and immature girls to speak in church while denying that privilege to all married women, even those who were much older and wiser and thereby much more qualified to speak.

Τοὺς ἰδίους ἄνδρας is best taken as an example given by Paul to cover most cases. He does not need to add pedantic qualifications about single girls and widows because the procedure to be followed could be inferred by the readers from this main example (they could ask their fathers or other men in the congregation). A similar brief statement is found in 1 Tim. 3.2 (no doubt a bachelor or widower could also be an overseer). Cf. J. M. Ford, "Corinthians or Hebrews," 414, who thinks Paul's instructions apply only to wives.

Another modifcation of this view has been the suggestion that Paul is simply trying to combat a particular problem at Corinth, the problem of women who were behaving in a noisy and disorderly way in church, perhaps rudely shouting questions to one another, etc. (Cf. Cothenet, DBS 8, col. 1297). Such a speculative explanation is inadequate from several perspectives: (i) Paul's remedy is inconsistent with the offense. Where there are problems of disorder (as with tongues or prophecy) Paul simply prescribes order (cf. vss. 27, 29, 31). So here Paul would have forbidden noisy or disorderly speech, but not all speech. (ii) It cannot be argued that Paul only forbids disorderly speech, for there is nothing in the context that would restrict the meaning of σιγάτωσαν in this way. (iii) There is nothing in vss. 33b-36 or in the rest of the letter which indicates that disorder among the women was a problem at Corinth (vs. 33a is connected by the γάρ to vs. 32, and that in turn by the καί to vs. 31). (iv) Paul's remedy would be inequitable, for he would be punishing all women for the deeds of some (he does say, "Let the disorderly women be silent in the churches"). (v) Paul would also be unfair to punish women and not men. Surely not all the people behaving in a

When Paul finished speaking about tongues in vs. 28, one might argue, he neglected to say that women should not speak in tongues in public worship. Now he comes back to tongues in 33b and adds a postscript to his previous instructions. Such a proposal would appear in the outline as:

        C. POSTSCRIPT TO A: Let the women not speak (in tongues) in the church.

But this proposal must be rejected because it does great violence to the context and structure of the passage. Paul has finished discussing tongues in vs. 28, and has gone on to the subject of prophecy. No reader would ever think that he had gone back to the subject of tongues unless he had given explicit indication of this. And such a directive would also be unjustified by anything Paul says elsewhere. For if women are allowed to pray or prophesy in church (11.5), and if speech in tongues has a function similar to prayer (14.2), or perhaps to prophecy (14.5), then Paul would also have allowed women to speak in tongues in church.

A final option is that vss. 33b-36 contain more instructions about prophecy. The passage would fit in the outline as:

vs. 34   2. Let the women keep silence in the churches

This would make the section Paul's second modification of the general statement, "Let two or three prophets speak and the others weigh what is said" (vs. 29). Vss. 30-33 dealt with the problem of prophets who wanted to speak while someone else was speaking. Now vss. 33b-36 deal with women.

There are two possible ways in which this passage might modify vs. 29. If it pertained to the first half of the verse, it would forbid women to prophesy in church: "Let two or three prophets speak . . . (but)

---

disorderly way were women. But if there were also noisy men, why does Paul not forbid men to speak in church? So this suggestion has numerous difficulties and no clear supporting evidence. (But cf. Orr and Walther, 312f, who favor both of these views.)

249

let the women keep silence in the churches." But 11.5 makes this solution impossible. On the other hand, if it modified the second half of vs. 29, it would forbid women to give spoken evaluation of the prophecies: "Let the others weigh what is said . . . (but) let the women keep silence in the churches." This would not prevent them from silently evaluating the prophecies in their own minds, but it would mean that they could not voice their criticisms and opinions about the value of the prophecies.[25]

Structurally this is in fact the most attractive solution available. It means that Paul followed a very logical procedure. First he gave a specific example (B: Let two or three prophets speak and let the others weigh what is said). Then he gave additional instructions about the first half of the verse (vss. 30-33a), and then he gave additional instructions about the second half of the verse (vss. 33b-36). In fact, there was no earlier opportunity for him to have introduced this section about women, for vss. 30-33a are a unified whole, no part of which can be removed. This is most clearly seen if we reproduce this section of the outline:

vs. 29	B.	SPECIFIC EXAMPLE 2: Let two or three prophets speak and let the others weigh what is said
vs. 30		1. If a revelation is made to another . . . let the first be silent
vs. 31		a. For you can all prophesy one by one
		(1) in order that all may learn and be encouraged
vs. 32		b. And the spirits of prophets are subject to prophets
vs. 33a		(1) for God is not a God of confusion but of peace

---

[25] It was Dr. James B. Hurley who first suggested to me that vss. 33b-36 dealt with the evaluation of prophecies. See his unpublished Ph.D. dissertation, Man and Woman in 1 Corinthians (Cambridge, 1973), 71-75, and his article, "Did Paul Require Veils or the Silence of Women?" WTJ 35:2 (1973), 216-18. Cf. Héring, 154; Moffatt, 232f.

vs. 33b-34a	2. As in all the churches of the saints, let the women keep silence in the churches
vs. 34b	a. For they are not permitted to speak but they should be subordinate (1) even as the law says
vs. 35	b. If there is something they want to know, let them ask their own husbands at home, (1) for it is shameful for a woman to speak in church.
vs. 36	c. Or from you did the word of God go forth, or to you only has it come?[26]

Thus seen, this option seems to be a quite natural and straightforward interpretation of the passage. Although it would no doubt have been clearer if Paul had said in vs. 34, "Let the women keep silent in the churches <u>during the evaluation of prophecies</u>," we have seen above how the NT authors often fail to make explicit the contextual restrictions on σιγάω which they think will be clear to their readers. That seems to be exactly what Paul did here. This contextual restriction is more difficult to see at first glance because the section which comes between vss. 29b and 33a grew quite long as Paul wrote. But when the structure and subject matter are examined more closely it becomes clear that what Paul meant by σιγάτωσαν was "let them be silent when you are evaluating a prophecy."

E. <u>Reasons Why Vs. 34 Refers to the Evaluation of Prophecies</u>

At this point it is possible to examine vs. 34 in terms of an ever-widening context, first at the level of words, then the sentence, the paragraph, this section of the epistle, the rest of 1 Cor., and Pauline

---

[26] Vs. 36 probably is connected with vs. 33b, "As in all the churches of the saints." In vs. 36 Paul reminds the Corinthians that they are not the source of the (or: any) word of God, nor are they the sole possessors of it (cf. Chap. 1, pp. 71ff). Therefore, they should follow what is standard practice in all the churches.

thought as expressed outside 1 Cor. In each case there are considerations in favor of the interpretation that σιγάτωσαν means "let them be silent during the evaluation of prophecies." This list will include some repetition of arguments which have already been made and also some additional considerations.

1. <u>This interpretation is consistent with the NT usage of σιγάω and λαλέω</u>. We have seen several other examples of implicit contextual restrictions on the topics or modes of speech comprehended by these terms. Now an analysis of the structure of vss. 26-36 has shown vs. 29b to be both the phrase most closely related to the section on women and the phrase which provides the most--perhaps the only-- acceptable contextual restriction.[27] It is also significant that very close at hand, in vs. 28, Paul has given clear examples of contextual restrictions of σιγάω and λαλέω which are very similar to this one. For there σιγάω just means "let him keep silent <u>with respect to speaking in tongues</u>," and λαλείτω means "<u>let him speak in tongues</u> to himself and to God." But other speech by the tongue-speaker is clearly allowed.

2. <u>It is consistent with the meaning of vs. 34</u>. The ἀλλά in vs. 34 shows a strong contrast between speaking and being subordinate: οὐ γὰρ

---

[27] It might be objected that there is already an explicit restriction on σιγάτωσαν in the phrase ἐν ταῖς ἐκκλησίαις and so no further restriction should be sought. The verse then simply means that women should be silent in church (a temporal and locative restriction). However, this is equivalent to the proposal above to treat vss. 33b-36 as Paul's third specific example (pp. 246f), which proposal was shown to be inadequate.

Ἐν ταῖς ἐκκλησίαις is necessary for another reason, however. Paul does not want to say that women can never say anything by way of evaluation of prophecies (they can do it at home, vs. 35). He simply wants to prevent women from doing this <u>in church</u>, and so the phrase is necessary.

ἐπιτρέπεται αὐταῖς λαλεῖν· ἀλλὰ ὑποτασσέσθωσαν.[28]
Thus, the kind of speaking Paul has in mind is specifically speaking which involves not being subordinate. Now not every mode of speech would fit this description, but evaluating prophecies certainly would. It would often involve assuming the possession of superior authority in matters of doctrinal or ethical instruction, especially when it included criticism of the prophecy. Thus the women who criticized a prophecy would be assuming something other than a subordinate or non-authoritative role vis-a-vis the rest of the congregation, and particularly the men in the congregation.

In the phrase "but they are to be subordinate" we also have an additional argument for the contextual restriction of σιγάτωσαν and οὐ . . . ἐπιτρέπεται αὐταῖς λαλεῖν to only those speech activities which involved judging prophecies. This phrase shows Paul's readers that it is not an unlimited silence which he intends. And this contextual restriction is so close at hand--it is in the same sentence--that it is quite readily seen.

If this is the correct meaning of vs. 34, then vs. 35 is understandable. Suppose that some women in Corinth had wanted to evade the force of Paul's directive. The easy way to do this would be to say, "We'll do just as Paul says. We won't speak up and criticize prophecies. But surely no one would mind if we asked a few questions! We just want to learn more about what these prophets are saying." Then such questioning could be used as a platform for expressing in a none-too-veiled form the very criticisms Paul forbids. Paul anticipates this possible evasion and writes, "If they want to know something, let them ask their own husbands at home. For it is shameful for a woman to speak in church."

    3. **It is consistent with Paul's appeal to the OT.** Paul claims support for this regulation from the OT, for he adds in 1 Cor. 14.34, καθὼς καὶ ὁ νόμος λέγει. The apparent source (for there is no explicit OT parallel) is Gen. 3.16 where God says to Eve,

---

[28]Such contrast would be heightened by the infinitive ὑποτάσσεσθαι (D G K L syr^h), because it would be more clearly parallel to λαλεῖν.

"Your desire shall be for your husband, and he shall rule over you," probably in conjunction with Gen. 2.18ff, where Eve is made as a "helper fit for Adam" (cf. 1 Cor. 11.9). 1 Pet. 3.5-6 makes a similar appeal to the OT, this time using Sarah as an example. It is very significant that a principle of subordination in authority can be derived from certain OT passages, but a general principle of silence for women in worship certainly cannot be so derived (cf. Ex. 15.20, 2 Sam. 6.15, 19, Ps. 148.12).[29]

4. **It is consistent with the structure of of the paragraph.** I have argued above how vss. 33b-36 must modify vs. 29b. There is no other phrase in the entire chapter which these verses could suitably modify.

5. **It is consistent with the rest of 1 Cor. 12-14.** If this interpretation is correct Paul is still discussing the subject of prophecy in vss. 33b-36. His argument is logical and unified, and it progresses in an orderly way. But on any other interpretation vss. 33b-36 become a random element suddenly inserted into the argument for no apparent reason. They discuss matters unrelated to anything Paul has said before. This section becomes disorganized and hard to follow.

6. **It is consistent with 1 Cor. 11.5.** On this interpretation Paul becomes quite consistent in his directions in this epistle. He readily allowed women to pray and to prophesy in church (11.5) because these activities did not involve women in assuming a position of authority over the men in the congregation. We have seen that prophesying at Corinth was simply reporting to the congregation what God has revealed. It did not involve the assumption of any authoritative position or function. But evaluating and criticizing prophecies involved one in implicit or explicit

---

[29] S. Aalen, "A Rabbinic Formula in 1 Cor. 14.34," *Studia Evangelica II: I*, ed. F. L. Cross (Berlin, 1964), 513-25, sees vs. 37 as a reference to this OT "command." However, 14.37 occupies a position where it seems to include all of 12-14, and Paul's phrase "a command of the Lord" suggests that he means the Lord Jesus, not the OT Scriptures.

doctrinal or moral instruction of the congregation. It is understandable then why Paul, if we assume that he was opposed to having women in authority over men in the church, would allow women to prophesy in 11.5 but forbid them to judge prophecies in 14.34.

7. <u>It is consistent with the rest of the Pauline corpus and with the rest of the NT</u>. Elsewhere in the writings attributed to Paul, and in the rest of the NT, we find a concern for the maintenance of an authority structure in the church or in the family in which men may have authority over both women and other men, but women may not have authority over men. Even in 1 Cor. we read,"the head of a woman is her husband," (11.3) and,"Neither was man created for woman, but woman for man" (11.9). Elsewhere we read, "Wives be subject to your husbands, as to the Lord" (Eph. 5.22) and "Wives be subject to your husbands, as is fitting in the Lord" (Col. 3.18). Most striking is a passage in 1 Tim. 2.11-12 (in a context which discusses public worship, cf. vs. 8): "Let a woman learn in silence with all submissiveness. I permit no woman to teach or to have authority over men, but she is to be silent." Just as in 1 Cor. 14.34, there is an ἀλλά which makes clear the type of contextual restriction the author intends, because it puts the silence of women in strong contrast with certain types of activity (teaching and having authority over men) which involve the question of male-female authority relationships: διδάσκειν δὲ γυναικὶ οὐκ ἐπιτρέπω, οὐδὲ αὐθεντεῖν ἀνδρός, <u>ἀλλ</u>' εἶναι ἐν ἡσυχίᾳ. Then in Tit. 2.5, women are to be "submissive to their husbands," while in 1 Pet. 3.1 we read, "Likewise you wives be submissive to your husbands."

This means that for Paul to deny to women an authoritative speech function in 1 Cor. 14.33b-36 would not at all be unusual. It would be completely consistent with what we find elsewhere in the NT writings.

F. <u>Conclusion</u>

In 1 Cor. 11.5 Paul clearly allows women to prophesy in church, while in 1 Cor. 14.33b-36 it seems possible to think that he denies to them the right to give spoken evaluations of prophecies in the assembled congregation (unless the passage be seen as a post-Pauline interpolation).

IV. THE ABILITY TO PROPHESY

A. Was Prophecy a Temporary or a Permanent Gift?

There are two minor senses in which prophecy could be considered a temporary gift. In the first place no prophet could prophesy at will (see above, p. 238f). He could only prophesy when he received a revelation. Even if he prophesied quite often, one might say that he did not really "possess" the gift, since he had to wait until the moment the Spirit gave him a revelation.

In the second place Paul clearly recognizes the absolute sovereignty of the Holy Spirit in the distribution of gifts. All the gifts are "empowered by the same Spirit while he is distributing to each one as he wills" (πάντα δὲ ταῦτα ἐνεργεῖ τὸ ἓν καὶ τὸ αὐτὸ πνεῦμα, διαιροῦν ἰδίᾳ ἑκάστῳ καθὼς βούλεται, 12.11). So it is indeed possible that the Spirit would give someone a special ability--for healing or prophecy, say--for only a few moments and then never give it to that person again.

But in spite of these two valid points, it is possible to speak of prophecy generally as a permanent or at least semi-permanent gift. While admitting that no prophet can prophesy at will, we nevertheless find indications in 1 Cor. 12-14 that there were people who were able to prophesy frequently over an extended period of time. This fact need not contradict Paul's insistence on the sovereignty of the Spirit in distributing gifts. It may only mean that Paul recognized that the Spirit acted in an orderly and regular way, not in one that was totally haphazard and unpredictable.

In 1 Cor. 14.37, "If someone thinks himself to be a prophet" (προφήτης εἶναι), the reference is not to the time at which the person is prophesying but to the time at which Paul's letter is being read. This implies that some people prophesied frequently enough to be considered prophets all the time, not just when they were prophesying. Similarly, in 1 Cor. 13.2, the phrase "if I have prophecy" (ἔχω προφητείαν) suggests a continuous possession of the gift. Then in 12.29, "not all are prophets" implies that some are; that is, that some people prophesy with enough regularity to be thought of as prophets.

The same seems to be the case with other gifts. Apparently when someone had the ability to interpret tongues that fact was known to the entire congregation, because the tongue-speaker is supposed to know whether an interpreter (διερμηνευτής) is present, and, if not, to refrain from speaking in tongues in church (14.28). And in the body metaphor in 12.12-26, if members of the church are like parts of the body, the picture is one of retention of functions over a period of time.

So the pattern seems to have been that prophecy was normally a permanent gift,[30] even though no one could prophesy at will and there may have been some people who prophesied once and never again.

B. Degrees of Prophetic Ability

With many of the gifts Paul lists it is evident that various people possessed different degrees of ability in any specific gift. With gifts like teaching and administration, even among those who were recognized as "teachers" and "administrators" there was no absolute equivalence in ability. Some were better teachers than others. Then among those who did no public teaching or administrative work there were nevertheless lesser degrees of teaching ability, or administrative ability; even if these abilities were only exercised in one's own family or toward one's own children. So it is not exactly accurate to think of these gifts in the NT church in terms of absolute possession and absolute non-possession. It is more accurate to think in terms of a progression along a scale of increasing intensity.

When Paul says, "Not all are teachers" (12.29), he means that not all have significant enough teaching abilities to function as teachers in the congregation.

---

[30] There are no clear NT instances of someone losing a gift completely, but we may suppose that someone could have so neglected or misused the gift of prophecy that the Holy Spirit would no longer be willing (βούλομαι, 1 Cor. 12.11) to impart revelations to him. I am using "permanent" in a relative, not an absolute, sense. (Rom. 11.29 of course refers to access to covenant blessings given to a particular nation, not to specific abilities for ministries given to individuals. Thus it is not relevant here.)

But even this is a relative comparison: someone who had only a small degree of teaching ability might nevertheless be recognized as a "teacher" in a new congregation where everyone else had even less ability than he did.

Paul also recognizes degrees of ability (or frequency of use) with respect to tongues, saying, "I speak in tongues more than you all" (14.18). And other gifts such as faith or the ability to speak words of knowledge or wisdom would naturally vary in degree.

In the Pastoral Epistles there are indications that an individual himself may increase or decrease at least some of his abilities for ministry, for Timothy is told not to neglect the gift that is in him (1 Tim. 4.14) but to practice using it (vs. 15, where ταῦτα μελέτα includes at least vs. 14 and probably vss. 12-14) and to rekindle it (ἀναζωπυρέω, 2 Tim. 1.6).

These are all texts which deal with gifts other than prophecy, so it is not possible to be certain that prophecy itself follows the same pattern. But it seems likely that it would.[31] If so, there would be greater and lesser degrees of prophetic ability, ranged all along a wide spectrum, in any given congregation. Prophets would differ in ability among themselves, and would also see changes in the extent of their own prophetic abilities over a period of time. Those with a high degree of prophetic ability would prophesy more frequently, at greater length, from more clear and forceful revelations, about more important subjects, and over a wider range of topics.[32]

---

[31] Rom. 12.6 should be mentioned here. If it means, "Let us use prophecy in proportion to the measured quantity of faith which we have been given," then it would indicate degrees of prophetic ability which varied according to the amount of faith one had (so Sanday and Headlam, 356f; Leenhardt, 310f; Dunn, JS, 211f, with "faith" as "the believer's confidence that God's Spirit is speaking in the very words he is then uttering").

[32] I have now departed from the evidence in 1 Cor. and indulged in some speculation. It is interesting to speculate further and ask what form the prophetic gift (or something similar to the prophetic gift) would take at a very low degree of intensity. It might

C. Seeking the Prophetic Gift

There are certain statements of Paul's which so clearly emphasize the sovereignty of the Holy Spirit in bestowing gifts that if they were read in isolation they might cause one to adopt a fatalistic attitude toward the acquisition of the gift of prophecy. The Spirit "distributes to each one as he wills" (1 Cor. 12.11). God "has placed the parts in the body, even as he willed" (12.18). "God has put" people with various gifts in the church (12.28). A believer reading only those verses might decide that there was absolutely nothing he could do to acquire the gift of prophecy except sit and wait, hoping that someday the Holy Spirit might see fit to give this gift to him.

However, there are other verses in Paul which show that he expected the Corinthians to take some positive steps to seek out the gift of prophecy for themselves. "Seek earnestly (ζηλοῦτε) the greater gifts" (12.31). "Seek earnestly the spiritual gifts, especially that you may prophesy" (14.1). "Seek earnestly to prophesy" (14.39). Apparently Paul thought the Corinthians would understand how to do this, for he never gives a clear explanation of what this seeking involves. But there are various hints in the text which help us know that at least some of the steps he expected the Corinthians to take.[33]

1. *Pray*. A person could pray for the ability to interpret tongues (14.13), and so could no doubt also pray for the gift of prophecy.

---

include lightly perceived flashes of intuition, hunches, or vague feelings about certain events or courses of action--not strong enough to be called revelations or reported as prophecies, but too uncommon to ignore. (Cf. b. Ber. 55b, 57b: "If one rises early and a Scriptural verse comes to his mouth, this is a small prophecy." Dreams are called an "inferior variety" of prophecy in Gen. R. 17.5, 44.7.) Of course, this speculation also raises another difficulty: do not unbelievers also experience something similar to this? Perhaps Paul would not call this a "gift" at all.

[33]Once again these suggestions are speculative, but not, I think, foreign to Paul's argument in 1 Cor. 12-14.

2. *Be content with present gifts.* A believer should certainly not wrongly evaluate the gifts he does have by being puffed up with pride (12.20-24) or full of jealousy over gifts he does not have (12.14-19). He should rest content that the present distribution of gifts has been made by God and should be thought good and right (12.18, 27-30). Therefore, he should make up his mind to be content if he does not receive the gift he asks for.

3. *Be mature.* Paul links prophecy with general Christian maturity in 14.37 ("If anyone thinks he is a prophet or spiritually mature").[34] In 1 Cor. 2.6 it is the mature to whom Paul imparts a wisdom, and in 2.14 the immature (ψυχικός) man does not receive (an understanding of) the things of the Spirit of God. As it is with wisdom and understanding, so it may well be with prophecy: it is more often given to those who are mature.

4. *Have right motives.* In 14.1 Paul combines seeking the gift (prophecy) with maintaining the right motive (love). He reminds the Corinthians that they should strive to excel in building up the church (14.12), and in 12.31 he tells them to seek the "greater" gifts, that is, those of most value to the church.[35] Thus he implies that their overriding motive in seeking gifts should not be personal glory but the edification of the church.

5. *Use present gifts.* If the Corinthians did have a proper motive for seeking prophecy and sincerely wanted to have that gift for the benefit of the church, then Paul would quite fairly expect to see that high motive manifested in the use of gifts which were presently possessed for the benefit of the church (14.12, 26). If someone failed to use his present gift for the benefit of all, or misused it so that it attracted attention to himself but did the

---

[34] Cf. Chap. 2, pp. 157ff, where I argue that πνευματικός in 1 Cor. 14.37 means "spiritually mature."

[35] Cf. Chap. 1, pp. 56f.

church no good (as in 14.17), then it would be evident that his motives for seeking prophecy were not right.

6. <u>Try to prophesy</u>? Would Paul have encouraged a potential prophet simply to try to prophesy, perhaps opening his mouth and speaking whatever came to mind? Because of the OT background which defined false prophecy as something one did "from his own heart" without having a revelation from God (Jer. 23.16, 21-22, cf. Jn. 11.51), I would expect Paul to be very cautious here. Unless someone thought he had a revelation (14.30), such a practice would no doubt have been discouraged. On the other hand, Paul would probably have encouraged a person who was timid and who thought he had received a revelation but was not quite sure. In such a case, the presence of good judges in the congregation (14.29; cf. 1 Th. 5.19-20) would be a sufficient safeguard against harm to the welfare and stability of the congregation.

V. SUMMARY OF CHAPTER FOUR

The word "prophet" does not appear to describe a formally recognized "office" or position in 1 Corinthians, and probably not in the rest of the NT. Rather, it is a functional term: those who prophesy regularly are "prophets." All believers have a potential ability to prophesy, but not all have an actual ability. No one can prophesy at will. Women can prophesy in church (1 Cor. 11.5) but are to remain silent during the oral evaluation of prophecies (I Cor. 14.34-35), because the latter involves an exercise of ruling authority in the local congregation while the former does not. Prophetic abilities vary greatly in degree, and Paul gives some slight indications of the way in which a believer could seek to increase his prophetic ability.

CONCLUSION

This book began by calling attention to several indications in 1 Corinthians of a distinctive type of prophecy which claimed a lesser kind of authroity than that claimed by many OT prophets and some other NT prophets. This secondary type of prophecy was also seen to be suggested by NT verses dealing with prophecy at Tyre, Thessalonica, Ephesus, and perhaps in other places.

The remaining sections of the study were concerned with analyzing in detail various aspects of the kind of prophecy in 1 Corinthians, and comparing the conclusions at each point with data from other parts of the NT. The evidence was sufficient to allow us to define quite precisely the psychological state of the prophet, the function, content and form of prophecy, and the qualifications for being a prophet.

In the clear delineation of a secondary type of prophecy with diminished authority, and in the exegetical detail with which that type of prophecy was then analyzed, this book has attempted to contribute significantly to our understanding of prophecy at the time of the New Testament.

APPENDIX

GERHARD DAUTZENBERG ON 1 COR. 12.10[1]

In his brief study, "Zum religionsgeschichtlichen Hintergrund der διάκρισις πνευμάτων (1 Kor 12, 10),"[2] and later in his book, Urchristliche Prophetie (Stuttgart, 1975, pp. 122-148), Gerhard Dautzenberg argues that 1 Cor. 12.10 speaks not of "distinguishing between spirits" but of "interpreting the revelations of the Spirit" (which are spoken through prophecy). Οἱ ἄλλοι διακρινέτωσαν in 1 Cor. 14.29 then means, "let the others interpret" (what each prophet says). Professor Dautzenberg has done valuable work in challenging some of our uncritically-held assumptions about the meaning of διακρίσεις πνευμάτων in 1 Cor. 12.10, and has also called to our attention many lexical and historical data useful for understanding oracle and dream interpretation in the ancient world. But it may be questioned whether he has established a convincing argument for translating 1 Cor. 12.10, "interpreting the revelations of the Spirit." It is possible to summarize his argument in five points:

1. The gift of διάκρισις πνευμάτων is connected with prophecy in 1 Cor. 12.10 and 14.29.[3]

2. Διακρίνω and διάκρισις mean "interpret" and "interpretation" in these verses, for several reasons.

   a. Διάκρισις and διακρίνω belong to Greek interpretation terminology. As such, they are used interchangeably with συγκρίνω/σύγκρισις to translate Hebrew/Aramaic פשר/פתר.[4]

---

[1] This appendix was originally part of my Ph.D. dissertation but has also now been reprinted in BZ 22:2 (1978), pp. 253-270.

[2] BZ 15 (1971), 93-104.

[3] UP, 122f.

[4] UP, 125; "Hintergrund," 94-102.

b. Since there is often a connection between revelation and interpretation in post-biblical Judaism, a reference to such interpretative activity would have been understood by the Corinthians.[5]

c. This position would allow διακρίνω and διάκρισις to be translated with the same sense (something not normally possible with other positions).[6]

d. The other proposed meanings for 12.10 and 14.29, "distinguish," "judge," and "test," are all unacceptable.[7]

3. The history of religions argument in favor of the translation, "distinguishing between spirits," is inadequate, for neither 1 Th. 5.19-21 nor 1 Jn. 4.1-6 nor Did. 11 provides an adequate parallel.[8]

4. Πνευμάτων in 12.10 means "revelations of the Spirit."[9]

5. The context of 1 Cor. 12-14 requires this position:

a. If 1 Cor. 12.3 provides a test for distinguishing between spirits, then that same interpretation is excluded for 12.10.[10]

b. We have no evidence of a problem of false prophecy at Corinth at this point, but to translate "distinguishing between spirits," one would have to assume that.[11]

---

[5] UP, 125.

[6] UP, 123f, 126.

[7] UP, 126-29.

[8] UP, 129-35.

[9] UP, 135-42.

[10] UP, 143-46; "Hintergrund," 93.

[11] UP, 147.

c. In 1 Cor. 12-14 the gift of διάκρισις πνευμάτων is no "super-charisma" set over the others, but if it were a gift of distinguishing between spirits, it would certainly have come to assume such superior status.[12]

It now remains to subject each of these five arguments to rigorous scrutiny, to see whether they compel our acceptance.

AN ANALYSIS OF DAUTZENBERG'S ARGUMENTS

1. <u>Διάκρισις πνευμάτων is connected with prophecy in 1 Cor. 12.10 and 14.29.</u>

Dautzenberg's argument in 12.10 depends on his ability to divide the list of nine gifts in vss. 8-10 into four unequal groups, namely (i) λόγος σοφίας and λόγος γνώσεως: (ii) πίστις, χαρίσματα ἰαμάτων and ἐνεργήματα δυνάμεων; (iii) προφητεία and διακρίσεις πνευμάτων; (iv) γένη γλωσσῶν and ἑρμηνεία γλωσσῶν. He says, "Wenn man jedoch die sachliche Zusammengehörigkeit von <u>pistis</u>, <u>charismata iamaton</u> (12,9) und <u>energemata dynameon</u> anerkennt, wird das folgende Nebeneinander von Prophetie und diakriseis am besten durch ihr Nebenbzw. Nacheinander in der Gemeindeversammlung erklärt (14,29)."[13] Yet there are several different difficult questions which must be answered before this classification can be accepted.

(a) <u>Is the connection between members of the first three groups the same kind of connection which exists between tongues and interpretation?</u> The answer must be no. The connection which exists between tongues and interpretation is unique because they necessarily function together in the congregation. Interpretation cannot be exercised without tongues, and, according to Paul, tongues should not be exercised publicly without interpretation (1 Cor. 14.5, 13, 27-28). But that is not the case with the other groups which Dautzenberg suggests. A word of wisdom can certainly be spoken apart from a word of knowledge. A miracle can be performed separately from a

---

[12] Ibid.

[13] <u>UP</u>, 122.

healing. Consequently, even if we were to admit some
kind of relationship between prophecy and διακρίσεις
πνευμάτων in 12.10, it would not need to be the kind
of relationship which Dautzenberg seeks to establish,
a relationship of functional interdependence. Even if
these two gifts were related in some way, we could
still follow the analogy of Dautzenberg's first two
groups and conclude that διάκρισις πνευμάτων is a gift
that could function apart from prophecy.

(b) <u>Are there grammatical or stylistic
indications that would enable Paul's readers to recognize these four groups</u>? Again the answer is no. There
is no explicit division made by Paul at any point in
the long sentence. Moreover, if there is any stylistic
alteration at all it is found between χαρίσματα ἰαμάτων
and ἐνεργήματα δυνάμεων, where Paul ceases to mention
the Spirit with each gift. But that change, if one
thought it significant, would put works of miracles
with prophecy and διακρίσεις πνευμάτων, a classification different from the one Dautzenberg needs in
order to establish his case.

Dautzenberg also suggests that there is a conscious arrangement by Paul so that the gifts which the
Corinthians most overvalued are place last, and also
those which they would already have recognized as
"pneumatika."[14] But on neither ground could one
explain why prophecy is fourth from the end. Certainly
Paul was not concerned that the Corinthians would
overvalue prophecy--quite the opposite (14.1, 5, 39).
And since gifts of healing or miracles, which would
certainly have been acknowledged as "pneumatika," are
placed only fourth and fifth in the list, it is
difficult to think that there is any conscious arrangement from "less acknowledged" to "more acknowledged"
gifts. Indeed, such an arrangement would mean that
interpretation, the last gift in the list, was the one
"most acknowledged" by the Corinthians! It seems
much easier to think that tongues, the problem gift
at Corinth, was consciously reserved for last, and
interpretation was joined to it, while the other gifts
were listed with no conscious order intended.

(c) <u>Do other Pauline passages indicate
additional relationships between any two gifts such as
the special relationship between tongues and</u>

---

[14]<u>UP</u>, 123.

interpretation? Here also the answer must be no. The
only special relationships which might be suggested
are found in Rom. 12.6, where prophecy is connected
with faith (εἴτε προφητείαν κατὰ τὴν ἀναλογίαν τῆς
πίστεως), and in 1 Cor. 13.2, where prophecy is connected with knowledge. But these connections argue
against Dautzenberg's supposed groupings in 1 Cor.
12.8-10, since there prophecy is separated from both
faith and knowledge. And even these are not functionally interdependent relationships of the tongues-
interpretation type, for one might have a gift of faith
or knowledge without the gift of prophecy, and one
might prophesy without having a special "charisma" of
faith or knowledge. In 1 Cor. 14.29 one might say that
there is a special relationship between prophecy and
διάκρισις πνευμάτων, but that contention depends on an
assumption that 14.29 refers to the gift of διάκρισις
πνευμάτων, an assumption which will be challenged in
some detail below.

Whereas tongues and interpretation are explicitly
grouped together by Paul again and again in a way that
his readers could not miss (12.10 [where it is
ἑρμηνεία γλωσσῶν], 12.30, 14.5, 13, 26, 27, 28), Paul
can discuss prophecy in several places without any
mention of διακρίσεις πνευμάτων (Rom. 12.6, 1 Cor. 12.
29, 14.5, 24-25).[15] In these contexts, if διάκρισις
πνευμάτων had been essential to the proper functioning
or understandability of prophecy, we might have
expected it to be mentioned. So it is doubtful
whether 1 Cor. 12.8-10 implies any special relationships between two or more gifts, other than the special
relationship between tongues and interpretation.

(d) Is "faith, healings, miracles" really a
convincing group? Can one perceive, as Dautzenberg
suggests, a "sachliche Zusammengehörigkeit" among
these three gifts? Once again, it is necessary to
express some doubt. Of course, this is not to deny
that faith is in some way related to the gifts of
healing and working of miracles. But because of its
fundamental nature faith can be said to be related to
several of the gifts, such as prophecy in Rom. 12.6.
The question, rather, is whether there is such an
evident unity among faith, healings and miracles that
we are compelled to say that Paul intentionally grouped
them together. Neither stylistic evidence, nor

---

[15] I discuss 1 Cor. 14.29 below.

discussion elsewhere, nor the intrinsic nature of the
gifts, makes one sure that the group "faith, healings,
miracles" indicates an intentional assembling by
Paul of gifts which by nature belonged together. And
if we have serious doubts about whether these three
are intentionally juxtaposed, then can we entertain
any certainty about whether there is in 1 Cor. 12.10
an intentional relationship between prophecy and
διακρίσεις πνευμάτων?

(e) <u>Might Paul have simply listed several
gifts in 1 Cor. 12.8-10 as they came to mind, without
intending to imply any special interrelationships
among them?</u> In view of the preceding considerations,
this certainly must be considered a strong possibility.
Of course Paul must have consciously reserved tongues,
the problem gift at Corinth, until the end, and with
it its necessary concomitant, interpretation of
tongues. But except for that special pair, one wonders
if Paul had any other pairs or groups in mind. When
he began to compile a list of gifts to show the
diversity of the Spirit's working he may well have
mentioned individual gifts as he tought of them.
λόγος σοφίας perhaps reminded him of λόγος γνώσεως,
and from there many gifts came not in groups but
individually to mind.

One probably cannot reach complete certainty on
this question. But at least it can be said that the
supposed connection between prophecy and διακρίσεις
πνευμάτων in 1 Cor. 12.10 is certainly not an obvious
one. Indeed, one may well question whether Paul
intends to indicate any special relationship at all.

In 1 Cor. 14.29 the question is different. Here
Paul clearly relates prophecy and the activity indicated by the verb διακρίνω: προφῆται δὲ δύο ἢ τρεῖς
λαλείτωσαν, καὶ οἱ ἄλλοι διακρινέτωσαν. But it may
not be so readily assumed, as Dautzenberg does,[16] that
the activity designated here by the verb διακρίνω is

---

[16]On p. 123 he refers to general recognition of
this connection in the literature on 1 Cor. But such
a connection is surely not as generally recognized as
Dautzenberg implies. Note the following commentators
who hold that οἱ ἄλλοι διακρινέτωσαν in 14.29 refers
not to those who have the gift of "distinguishing
between spirits" but to the entire congregation:

the same as that designated by the phrase διακρίσεις πνευμάτων in 12.10.

In favor of such a connection are two factors, the proximity to a mention of prophecy in both 12.10 and 14.29, and the fact that διακρίνω in 14.29 is the verb which corresponds to the noun διάκρισις in 12.10. As for the first factor, I have argued above that it is very difficult to show that the juxtaposition of prophecy and διακρίσεις πνευμάτων in 12.10 is anything other than fortuitous. And to use 14.29 as evidence for a special relationship between the two gifts in 12.10, while using the relationship between the two gifts in 12.10 to show that the same gift is discussed in 14.29, would simply be to argue in a circle. Dautzenberg's case for one verse must be firmly established on independent grounds before he can use it to argue his case for the other verse.

Concerning[17] the use of διάκρισις in 12.10 and διακρίνω in 14.29, it must be noted that both the noun and verb have an extremely wide range of meaning.[18] It is not at all impossible that Paul would have used διάκρισις in 12.10 to mean "distinguishing" (among different kinds of spirits) while using διακρίνω in 14.29 to mean something quite different, such as "evaluate" or "judge" (prophetic utterances). In fact, in 1 Cor. alone Paul uses διακρίνω in several senses: in 11.31 it means "evaluate," in 1 Cor. 11.29, "distinguish" (or "evaluate"), in 6.5 "give a legal judgment," and 4.7, "distinguish." In Rom. 14.1 he apparently means "arguments" or "disputes" by διακρίσεις. In view of this wide range of Pauline meaning, it would be overly bold to assume that διάκρισις in 12.10 must have the same sense as διακρίνω in 14.29, and must refer to the same kind of activity or gift.

Barrett, 328; Bruce, 134; Godet, II, 303f; Lietzmann, 74; Cothenet, DBS 8, col. 1296.

[17]The following paragraph is repeated from Chapter 1, pp. 58f, for the sake of continuity in the argument of this appendix.

[18]Barrett, 274, says, "It is impossible to find a consistent rendering of the word distinguish (διακρίνειν), because Paul did not use it consistently.

So if we are asking whether οἱ ἄλλοι διακρινέτωαν in 14.29 refers to the gift of διακρίσεις πνευμάτων in 12.10, the only two positive arguments, an alleged connection between prophecy and διακρίσεις πνευμάτων in 12.10, and a somewhat parallel form of expression, both turn out on examination to be quite weak.

At this point it must be recognized that only by assuming the correctness of his view of 12.10 can Dautzenberg conclude that the same gift is in view in 12.10 and 14.29. If we assume that 12.10 means "interpreting the revelations of the Spirit which are spoken by prophets," then of course we could conclude that 14.29 means, "let the others interpret what the prophets say." But it is hardly fair to assume the conclusion in order to support one of the arguments in its favor. Again, this would be circular reasoning.

If we disallow such circular reasoning here, and if instead we accept for a moment the more common views of 12.10 and 14.29, then there are strong reasons why 14.29 does not refer to the gift of διάκρισις πνευμάτων. First, the objects are different. In 14.29 it is the speeches of the prophets which are evaluated or judged. Dautzenberg himself admits that the prophetic speeches, not the prophets themselves or the spirits by which they speak, are the objects of διακρίνω in 14.29.[19] But in 12.10, if we do not assume Dautzenberg's conclusion, it is spirits that are distinguished.

Second, there are different groups of people mentioned. In 12.10 only a limited number of people in the congregation have this gift, as with any other gift Paul mentions (ἄλλῳ δὲ διακρίσεις πνευμάτων, and cf. 12.29-30). But in 14.29, if διακρίνω means "evaluate," then there would seem to be no reason for thinking that only those with the gift of "distinguishing between spirits" could evaluate prophecies. Could not teachers, administrators, apostles, other prophets, and indeed all believers at least silently evaluate (διακρίνω) a prophecy as they heard it?[20] Where judgment of speech before the church is mentioned elsewhere in Paul's writings, it seems that all the congregation

---

[19] UP, 127f.

[20] I discuss the phrase οἱ ἄλλοι in 1 Cor. 14.29 in more detail above (pp. 60ff).

is involved (1 Cor. 12.3, 1 Th. 5:21; cf. 1 Jn. 4.1-6, Ac. 17.1). So in 14.29, in contrast to 12.10, διακρίνω refers to an activity carried out by the entire congregation. Thus, on the more common view of 12.10 and 14.29, both different people and different objects are involved.

These two considerations make it very unlikely that the gift of διάκρισις πνευμάτων is referred to by the phrase οἱ ἄλλοι διακρινέτωσαν in 14.29. Of course, if Dautzenberg could establish his view of 12.10 as "interpreting the revelations of the Spirit" on other grounds, then 14.29 could be made consistent with that interpretation. But until that view of 12.10 is established on other grounds, he should not be allowed to claim 14.29 in support of his case, as if it obviously contained a reference to διάκρισις πνευμάτων.

In conclusion, Dautzenberg claims that the gift of διάκρισις πνευμάτων is connected with prophecy in both 1 Cor. 12.10 and 14.29. But on closer examination it appears that we must retain serious doubt about the connection in both verses. In 12.10 it seems unlikely that there is any intentional or meaningful connection between the two gifts, and in 14.29, unless Dautzenberg can prove his view of 12.10 on independent grounds, it is very improbable that there is any reference to the gift of διάκρισις πνευμάτων.

2. Διακρίνω and διάκρισις mean "interpret, interpretation" here.

Dautzenberg has correctly pointed out that διάκρισις and διακρίνω can be used as technical terms for the interpretation of dreams in Philo,[21] in Symmachus's translation of Gen. 40.8,[22] and in Pausanias and Artemidorus (both 2nd c. AD.).[23] To his list

---

[21]"Hintergrund," 99f. Dautzenberg lists διακρίνω in Jos. 90, 104 and 143, and διάκρισις in Som. 2.7 and Jos. 93, 110, 125, 269. To this list should be added διακρίνω in Som. 2.4 and Jos. 248, and διάκρισις in Som. 2.110 and Jos. 98 and 116.

[22]"Hintergrund," 99 (διακρίνω and διάκρισις once each).

[23]"Hintergrund," 94f (Artemid. Oneirocriticon, 4, Prooem; 4, 1; Paus. 1.34.5).

should be added the two instances in T. Abr. (A) 4.[24]

He also notes that διακρίνω is used in Jos A.8. 148 (=Ap. 1.114) to speak of "solving" riddles,[25] and at least once in Greek literature is used of the interpretation of signs.[26] Finally, there is one instance of διακρίνω to mean "explain, interpret" spoken oracles (μαντεῖα). This is Stobaeus, Eklogai 4.50.95 (5th c. A.D.), where he is quoting Juncus (a philosopher, perhaps from the 2nd c. A.D., known only through the writings of Stobaeus).[27] Dautzenberg's one example of διακρίνω from the Apostolic Fathers, Herm. Sim. 2.1,[28] can be omitted here, for it simply means "consider, ponder" (a vine and an elm).

These instances of διάκρισις and διακρίνω can be summarized as follows:

Meaning	Number of Instances	Dates
Interpretation of dreams	20	1st-2nd c. A.D. (Philo, Symmachus, T.Abr., Paus., Artemid.)
Solving riddles	2	1st c. A.D. (Josephus)
Interpretation of signs	1	1st c. B.C. (Diod. Sic.)
Interpretation of oracles	1	5th c. A.D. (Stobaeus), or perhaps 2nd c. A.D. (Juncus)

It is certainly safe to conclude from this evidence that διακρίνω and διάκρισις could be used as technical terms to refer to the interpretation of

---

[24]This text is of uncertain date, but perhaps may be placed in 1st century A.D. (IDB I, 21).

[25]Intergrund," 101.

[26]"Hintergrund," 95. He lists only Diodorus Siculus 17.10.15 (1st c. B.C.). Cf. also (perhaps) Mt. 16.3.

[27]LS, xxvii, xxxvi.

[28]"Hintergrund," 102.

dreams, at least from the 1st c. A.D. Whether they could also have been used to interpret prophecies is still difficult to say. The single example from Stobaeus is the closest parallel, but it is very late, and it is not yet clear how similar this oracle was to early Christian prophecy. A better decision can be made after taking into account more information about the functions of διάκρισις, διακρίνω, and other words used for interpreting obscure oracles or prophecies in the time of the New Testament. In this regard, several observations can be made.

(a) Διακρίων and διάκρισις are not generally used to translate פשר and פתר. This contention is contrary to Dautzenberg's implication in UP, 125 and "Hintergrund," 100, 103, but it is clearly seen if all the data are examined. The following list gives the total number of times each Hebrew or Aramaic word is translated by the Greek words listed. This list includes every available example of direct translation of these words from the LXX, Aquila, Symmachus and Theodotion.[29]

	LXX	Aq., Sm., Th.
Aramaic		
פְּשַׁר (verb)	συγκρίνω 2	
פְּשַׁר (noun)	σύγκρισις 8	σύγιρισις 25 (all Th.)
	σύγκριμα 4	σύγκριμα 4 (all Th.)
	κρίσις 4	κρίμα 1 (Th. Dan. 5.16)
	κρίνω 2	ἐπίλυσις 1 (Sm. Dan. 2.25)
Hebrew		
פֵּשֶׁר	λύσις 1 (Eccl. 7.30)	

---

[29] These are the only examples of direct translation which are relevant for our purposes. Dautzenberg also mentions Philo's recounting of the Joseph story, but Philo often wanders so far from the Hebrew text in his discourse that, unless there are specific indications that he is attempting a translation at some point, his language can scarcely be counted as evidence for determining which Greek words were acceptable translations of a Hebrew word.

פָּתַר   συγκρίνω 7 ἐπιλύω 3 (all Aq.)
     ἀπαγγέλλω 1 διακρίνω 1 (Sm. Gen. 40.
                8)

פִּתְרוֹן σύγκρισις 2 ἐπίλυσις 1 (Aq. Gen. 40.8)
     διασάφησις 1 διάκρισις 1 (Sm. Gen.
                40.8)

Totals of all instances: συγκρίνω, etc. 52
            κρίνω, etc.   7
            ἐπιλύω, ἐπίλυσις 5
            διακρίνω, διάκρισις 2 (both
                         Sm.
                         Gen.
                         40.8)
                other   3
                TOTAL   69

  The most remarkable result of this compilation is to show that out of 51 examples of a Greek translation of the Aramaic פשׁר, it was not translated once by διακρίνω or διάκρισις. One may well question, therefore, whether Dautzenberg is justified in considering many examples of פשׁר-exegesis from Qumran as legitimate background material for understanding διάκρισις in 1 Cor. 12.10.[30]

  With the Hebrew פָּתַר, פִּתְרוֹן, and the loanword פֵּשֶׁר, out of 18 examples we find two instances of translation with διακρίνω and διάκρισις. These are both in Symmachus's 2nd-century A.D. translation and can be taken as further evidence of the fact that διακρίνω and διάκρσις could serve as technical terms to refer to the interpretation of dreams. But that does not necessarily imply that they could be used to translate פתר in other contexts.

  Moreover, when members of the פשׁר and פתר word groups are translated 52 times by συγκρίνω and related words and only twice by διάκρισις or διακρίνω, it seems to be an unjustified blurring of the evidence for Dautzenberg to make such general statements as, "συγκρίνω und διακρίνω haben ihr Gewicht als

---

(These lists were made by me by comparing a Hebrew concordance with Hatch-Redpath, with Field's *Hexapla*, and with the LXX text.)

[30]"Hintergrund," 100f.

Deuteausdruke gerade durch das grieschisch sprechende Judentum erhalten,"[31] or, "In jüdischen Texten begegnen συγκρίνω und διακρίνω als Übersetzungsvarianten für פשׁר/פתר."[32] The evidence is not nearly as strong as those statements would suggest.

(b) <u>In Jewish and Christian literature, διάκρισις and διακρίνω are not generally interchangeable with other κριν- words in interpretation contexts</u>. Dautzenberg correctly points out that Philo in <u>Mig</u>. 19 and <u>Jos</u>. 158 uses σύγκρισις instead of his usual διάκρισις to speak of Joseph's interpretation of dreams. This does not show that διάκρισις and σύγκρισις are precise synonyms, but simply that at this particular point--the interpretation of dreams-- the range of meaning of σύγκρισις came to overlap with that of διάκρισις (at least in Philo's usage). One can understand how this might have been so, when "combine" and "compare" were common meanings for συγκρίνω, and "evaluate," "understand correctly" and "separate" were acceptable meanings for διακρίνω. Each of those activities played a part in interpreting dreams, and each term could have come to have the general sense "interpret" when applied to dreams.

Now this semantic overlap might or might not have occurred with διακρίνω and συγκρίνω in other contexts, such as interpreting prophecies, or writings, or parables, etc. We cannot predict in advance whether that would happen or not. It is possible that one word group or both would remain as a technical term for interpreting dreams and would not be used in any other contexts to mean "interpret." In fact, in some contexts συγκρίνω as "combine" and διακρίνω as "separate" (or διάκρισις, "separation") are used as exact antonyms: Philo speaks of death as the <u>separation</u> (διάκρισις) of things that had been in <u>combination</u> (τῶν συγκριθέντων) (<u>Leg. All</u>. 106; cf. <u>Quod Deus</u> 82), namely, soul and body.

What we do find throughout Jewish and Christian literature is that members of the συγκρίνω and διακρίνω groups are never interchangeable and never have overlapping meanings outside of the particular context of dream interpretation (Philo, <u>Mig</u>. 19, <u>Jos</u>.

---

[31]"Hintergrund," 100.

[32]"Hintergrund," 103; cf. <u>UP</u>, 125, 138.

158, and Symm. Gen. 40.8). Dintinct meanings are maintained in all other contexts throughout the NT, the LXX, the Apostolic Fathers,[33] Josephus,[34] Aquila, Symmachus, Theodotion, the major Greek Pseudepigrapha,[35] and rest of Philo. This is true for the 161 extant examples of the συγκρίνω word group and the 215 extant examples of the διακρίνω word group.[36] It is hardly legitimate, therefore, for Dautzenberg to adduce non-dream instances of συγκρίνω (such as the notoriously difficult 1 Cor. 2.13)[37] as examples of places where it is synonomous with διακρίνω.

Nor can other κριν- words simply be exchanged with διακρίνω. Dautzenberg lists many instances where κρίνω or κρίσις can mean "interpret," and it is true that κρίνω in Classical Greek had a range of meanings very similar to that of διακρίνω.[38] However, by the NT period the meanings of κρίνω and διακρίνω seem to have become distinct enough that there are no instances where κρίνω means "separate, distinguish,"[39] whereas that is the most common meaning of διακρίνω. When Dautzenberg says, ". . . sachlich gibt es keinen Unterschied zwischen κρίνω und διακρίνω,"[40] he is

---

[33] 1-2 Clem., Did., Barn., Ign., Polycarp, Hermas.

[34] The concordance is not yet available for the συγκρίνω word group, however.

[35] Works checked were those for which a concordance was avilable to me: 4 Maccabees, the Testaments of the Twelve Patriarchs, the Life of Adam and Eve, the Greek Apocalypse of Baruch, 1 Enoch, the Apocalypse of Ezra, the Paralipomena of Jeremiah, the Apocalypse of Sedrach, the Psalms of Solomon, the Testament of Solomon, and the Letter of Aristeas.

[36] The total for the συγκρίνω group will be increased when that volume of the Josephus concordance becomes available.

[37] "Hintergrund," 103f; UP, 138-40.

[38] Cf. LS, 399, 996.

[39] AG, 452; Lampe, 778.

[40] "Hintergrund," 95.

simply not giving adequate attention to actual usage in the NT. The differences in ranges of meanings are even more pronounced with other words using the root κρίν-. Dautzenberg himself notes that ὑποκρίνομαι[41] and ἀνακρίνω[42] have meanings different from διακρίνω in Biblical usage, and one could think of other clearly different examples such as ἀποκρίνομαι, ἐγκρίνω or κατακρίνω.

So once again the precise nature of the kind of evidence we are seeking with respect to διάκρισις in 1 Cor. 12.10 and διακρίνω in 1 Cor. 14.29 must be defined more carefully than Dautzenberg has done. It is not enough to show that some words based on the root κρίν- can mean "interpret, explain." It must rather be shown that διάκρισις and διακρίνω can themselves mean "interpret, explain" when used in connection with prophecy.

(c) Διάκρισις and διακρίνω are never used in Jewish or Christian literature to refer to the interpretation or explanation of prophecies or other obscure words. When we come to seek precise and specific parallels to Dautzenberg's suggested meaning for διάκρισις and διακρίνω in 1 Cor. 12.10 and 14.29, we find not one example in all of Jewish and Christian literature: nowhere in more than 200 occurrences are these words used to speak of interpreting prophecies or other kinds of obscure words.[43] Indeed, in all of Greek literature, Dautzenberg has produced no examples of διάκρισις or διακρίνω used in this way except the

---

[41]"Hintergrund," 100.

[42]UP, 123, n. 7; 248-50.

[43]Probably the closest instance would be Jos. A. 8. 148 (= Ap. 1.114), where it is said that Solomon sent riddles to Hiram of Tyre, proposing that "τὸν δὲ μὴ δυνηθέντα διακρῖναι τῷ λύσαντι χρήματα ἀποτίνειν." (Josephus gives this as a quotation from an otherwise unknown Phoenician historian, Dios.) Διακρῖναι here may mean "to understand" (the riddles) or "to discern, to distinguish" (the solutions), for λύω is used both here and a few lines later to mean "solve." Διακρίνω might also be taken to mean "solve," as a synonym for λύω, but this would certainly not be a clear example. When not quoting someone else, Josephus himself chooses ἐπιλύω to speak of solving riddles and hard questions in A. 8. 167.

one late quotation in Stobaeus.[44] So the sense he proposes for διάκρισις in 1 Cor. 12.10 would be unique and unprecedented for its time.

(d) **Jewish and Christian authors prefer other terms when speaking of the interpretation or explanation of prophecies and other obscure words.**

This is a highly significant factor. Since διάκρισις and διακρίνω are used of interpreting dreams (and perhaps also of "solving" riddles), we should realize that they <u>might</u> have come to be used of interpreting prophecies or other obscure words as well. But when we examine the actual data, it becomes clear that Jewish and Christian writers consistently prefer to use other terms when they have occasion to talk about the interpretation of utterances or writings which are difficult to understand. The following list includes a large number of instances where Jewish or early Christian authors use a Greek term to refer to the interpretation or explanation of any spoken or written words. (Terms used to refer to "translation" from one known language to another are not included here.)

WORDS USED TO MEAN "INTERPRET, INTERPRETATION, INTERPRETER"

Interpretation or explanation of Scripture passages (or Mosaic laws)

διερμηνεύω	Lk. 24.27 (of OT prophecies, at least in part); Philo, <u>Sob.</u> 33
ἐξηγέομαι	Jos. <u>A.</u> 18.81, <u>B.</u> 2.162; Philo <u>Hyp.</u> 7.13
ἐξήγησις	Jos. <u>A.</u> 1.12; Philo <u>Vit. Cont.</u> 78
ἐξηγητής	Jos. <u>A.</u> 17.149, 214, 216; Philo, <u>Spec. Leg.</u> 2.159
ἐπίλυσις	2 Pet. 1.20 (of prophecies)

---

[44] There is one other problem with the quotation from Stobaeus: it refers not to interpreting a προφητεία but to interpreting a μαντεία, a term which often refers to mantic ecstasy among the pagans, and a term which Jewish and Christian authors never use of their own prophecies.

ἐπιλύω   Philo, Vit. Cont. 75

ἑρμηνεύω   Lk. 24.27 (D); Jos. A. 20.264

κρίσις   Jos. B. 6.312[45]

Interpretation or explanation of obscure sayings, or words difficult to understand

ἐξηγέομαι   Jos. A. 19.196

ἑρμηνεία   Aq. Prov. 1.6, Th. Prov. 1.6; of writing on wall: LXX Dan. 5.1

σύγκριμα   (of writing on wall): LXX Dan. 5.7, 7, 7, 8, 9, 12, 16, 30; Th. Dan. 5.26.

συγκρίνω   (of writing on wall): LXX Dan. 5.7; Th. Dan. 5.16

σύγκρισις   (of writing on wall): LXX Dan. 5.17; Th. Dan. 5.7, 8, 12, 15, 16, 17

Interpretation or explanation of parables which were enigmatic

διασαφέω   Mt. 13.36

ἐπίλυσις   Herm. Sim. 5.5.1, 5.6.8, 5.7.1

ἐπιλύω   Mk. 4.34, Herm. Sim. 5.3.1, 5.3.2, 5.6.3, 5.5.1

ἑρμηνεία   Sir. 47.17

Interpretation of tongues

διερμηνευτής   1 Cor. 14.28

διερμηνεύω   1 Cor. 12.30, 14.5, 13, 27

ἑρμηνεία   1 Cor. 12.10, 14.26

ἑρμηνευτής   1 Cor. 14.28 (B,D*)

---

[45] I have not attempted to compile a complete list of the times κρίσις and κρίνω are used to mean "interpret." AG, 452-54, give no instances for early Christian literature.

This list shows 58 instances where Jewish or early Christian authors had occasion to speak about the interpretation or explanation of difficult or obscure words or sayings. The kinds of interpretation included here are conceptually the closest possible parallels to prophecy: they all have to do with spoken or written material, and they refer to Scriptural prophecies, to other types of Scripture, to enigmatic sayings (often of divine origin), to parables, and to tongues.[46] It is significant therefore that not even one instance was found where διάκρισις or διακρίνω referred to this kind of interpretation.

This evidence implies that if Paul had wanted to speak of the <u>interpretation</u> of prophecies in 1 Cor. 12.10 and 14.29 he would almost certainly have used one of these terms which were commonly used to speak of the interpretation of prophecies and other kinds of speech similar to prophecy. He would not have used διάκρισις or διακρίνω.

The other two positive arguments Dautzenberg proposes, the connection between revelation and interpretation in post-biblical Judaism and the possibility of translating διάκρισις and διακρίνω in the same sense, do not retain much force in light of the preceding evidence. There could also be revelation which needed no interpretation,[47] and words with such broad ranges of meaning as διάκρισις and διακρίνω could certainly take different senses in different contexts.[48]

(e) <u>"Distinguishing between spirits" is a much more likely meaning for 1 Cor. 12.10.</u> Here Dautzenberg objects that in all other proposed examples where διάκρισις means "distinguishing between," the two classes of things to be distinguished are always

---

[46] I have included tongues here because this kind of speech might possibly be considered similar to prophecy in that it was considered a speech gift empowered by the Holy Spirit. If someone should prefer to count these instances as "translation" and therefore dissimilar to prophecy, the total number of instances would be reduced to 50.

[47] See the examples on pp. 286ff, below.

[48] Cf. pp. 269, above.

explicitly named (for example, Heb. 5.14: πρὸς διάκρισιν καλοῦ τε καὶ κακοῦ).49 So if διάκρισις were to mean "distinguishing" in 1 Cor. 12.10, the verse would have to say something like διάκρισις καλῶν καὶ κακῶν πνευμάτων.

Dautzenberg's objection is inadequate here because he only examines the examples given in Bauer's lexicon (Bauer, 367 = AG, 184). When other examples of διάκρισις are examined, it is clear that there are instances when the whole class of things among which distinctions are to be made is named (as in 1 Cor. 12.10, if it means "distinguishing between spirits"). Philo, Som. 2.39, speaks of the man who "aims at analysis and distinctions of things" (ὁ δὲ τομῆς καὶ διακρίσεως πραγμάτων ζηλωτής).50 In Som. 2.35, Dan is the symbol of distinguishing and analyzing matters (διακρίσεως δὲ καὶ τομῆς πραγμάτων). Plant. 45 says that God placed man's mind in the universe to distinguish between forces (ἐπὶ τὴν διάκρισίν τε αὐτῶν).51 1 Cl. 48.5, which speaks of a man σοφὸς ἐν διακρίσει λόγων, should probably be translated "wise in the distinguishing of words (or arguments)": Dautzenberg's objection that good and bad words are not specified[52] sounds again like circular reasoning: (a) διάκρισις can only mean "distinguishing" when both items are named, because (b) it does not mean "distinguishing" in 1 Cl. 48.5 or in other similar places; (c) it does not mean "distinguishing" in 1 Cl. 48.5 because (d) both items are not named.53

---

[49] UP, 126f, 128.

[50] The immediately following context requires that διακρίσεως means "distinctions" and not "interpretations," and so does the passage in Som. 2.35 to which this refers.

[51] "Making decisions" is a less likely translation here, because διάκρισις generally has that sense only as a technical term for judicial decisions (LS, 399).

[52] UP, 127.

[53] Other examples grammatically similar to 1 Cor. 12.10 but with different meanings for διάκρισις, are Rom. 14.1, Philo, Op. 136, Leg. All. 1.206, Mos. 1.212, Job 37.16 (AB). In none of these cases are both items mentioned; rather, the whole class of things

Far from being linguistically unprecedented, as Dautzenberg claims, the interpretation "distinguishing between spirits" has several good stylistic parallels in Jewish and early Christian literature and should be considered a very likely meaning for 1 Cor. 12.10.

To summarize this linguistic investigation: the translation "interpreting the revelations of the Spirits" in 1 Cor. 12.10 uses a meaning of διάκρισις which was unprecedented at the time of the New Testament. Furthermore, there were several other terms which Jewish and Christian authors regularly used to speak of the interpretation of prophecies or other obscure words. If Paul had meant "interpreting" in 1 Cor. 12.10, he would almost certainly have used one of these other words, not διάκρισις. By contrast, "distinguishing between spirits" uses a common and widely-understood meaning for διάκρισις, and the stylistic construction has several good parallels.

3. The history of religions argument. Dautzenberg in this section attempts to show that neither 1 Th. 5.19-21 nor 1 Jn. 4.1-6 nor Did. 11.7 is sufficiently similar to the situation one would have to suppose in 1 Cor. 12.10 if it meant "distinguishing between spirits." It is interesting that these are the three texts he chooses to analyze, for only one of them--1 Jn. 4.1-6--has any mention of evil spirits. He is of course correct in deciding that the other two texts have little to do with 1 Cor. 12.10.

Yet the fact that Dautzenberg chose to deal only with these texts, all three of which mention prophecy, shows that he has made an entirely unwarranted assumption. He has assumed that διάκρισις πνευμάτων in 1 Cor. 12.10, even if it deals with "distinguishing between spirits," only deals with distinguishing between spirits of the prophets. But 1 Cor. 12.10

---

among which separations or divisions are to be made is named.
Other texts which use διάκρισις to mean "distinguishing" are Jos. B. 2.303, 4.654; Philo, Cher. 127, Som. 2.24, Spec. Leg. 1.00, 340; perhaps T. Naph. 2.8.

does not say διακρίσεις πνευμάτων προφητῶν: it simply says διακρίσεις πνευμάτων. It[54] is not legitimate to presuppose that 1 Cor. 12.10 is restricted to the testing of prophets and prophecies. Bittlinger, for instance, mentions as examples of διακρίσεις πνευμάτων some of the exorcisms of Jesus where he knew there was a demon present, and the cases of Elymas (Ac. 13. 8ff) and the soothsaying girl (Ac. 16.16-18).[55] Robertson and Plummer define the ability as, "The gift of discerning in various cases (hence the plur.) whether extraordinary spiritual manifestations were from above or not."[56] If we resist the temptation to read into the text a limitation to the testing of prophecies, then a more general definition, like the one just mentioned by Robertson and Plummer, is in order. Something like "the ability to recognize the influence of the Holy Spirit or of demonic spirits in a person," might be suggested.

This means that any situation in which first century Christians would have seen demonic influence was a potential opportunity for the use of the gift of διάκρισις πνευμάτων. Was some sickness the result of demonic influence (cf. Mt. 12.22, Mt. 9.32-34)? Then the person with this gift could recognize it, and the demon could be cast out. Was an evil spirit causing someone to interrupt preaching or teaching or worship services (cf. Ac. 16.16-18)? Then the person with this gift could recognize the source of the trouble. Was someone prophesying by the power of an evil spirit (1 Jn. 4.1-6)? Then the person with this gift could call attention to it. Since it was thought that demons were involved in pagan worship in Corinth (cf. 1 Cor. 10.20f), one can imagine a large number of

---

[54] The next 1 1/2 pages are repeated from Chap. 1, pp. 59f, for the sake of continuity in the argument of this excursus.

[55] Bittlinger, Gifts and Graces, 46. Other commentators who see "distinguishing between sprits" as applying to more than just prophecy include Calvin, 263, Grosheide, 287f, Findlay, 889, and Lenski, 503f. Those who do restrict it to prophecy generally refer to 1 Jn. 4.1-6 and Did. 11, but give no further arguments.

[56] RP, 267. They soon say, "Perhaps the expression chiefly refers to the prophetic gift," but they do not restrict it to that.

cases where this gift would have been thought useful. Once διακρίσεις πνευμάτων is understood in this way, Dautzenberg's third objection loses its force.

4. <u>The meaning of πνευμάτων in 1 Cor. 12.10.</u>
Dautzenberg rightly points to 1 Cor. 14.12, where πνεύματα means "manifestations of the Spirit,"[57] and 2 Th. 2.2, where πνεῦμα apparently means "revelation of the Spirit."[58] He concludes that "revelations of the Spirit" is a possible rendering of πνευμάτων, whereas "spirits" is unlikely, because Paul never used πνεύματα to refer to both good and evil spirits.

This argument is unsatisfying on both counts, however. The major problem with it is that there was a much better and less ambiguous word which Paul could have used if he had meant to speak of "revelations of the Spirit spoken by prophets," namely, προφητεῖαι (1 Cor. 13.8, 14.6, 1 Th. 5.20). In 1 Cor. 14.12 and 2 Th. 2.2, the use of πνεῦμα to mean "manifestation of the Spirit" allows for a much broader reference, including several kinds of gifts in 1 Cor. 14.12, and perhaps any kind of "spiritual" communication in 2 Th. 2.2, such as a vision, a dream or a <u>bath qol</u>, as well as a prophecy: by the use of a general term, the reference in both cases is left as broad as possible.

But in 1 Cor. 12.10, according to Dautzenberg, the reference is not to many kinds of spiritual manifestations, but simply to the interpretation of prophecies. It is even a different gift from the interpretation of tongues. In this case, Paul would not have used a general word like πνευμάτων which would have been ambiguous to his readers. He would rather have written προφητειῶν.

With regard to the second objection, one need not have a specific Pauline example to show that πνεύματα could easily be used and understood by first century Christians to refer both to evil spirits and to the Holy Spirit. 1 Jn. 4.1 (δοκιμάζετε τὰ πνεύματα) is one clear example. And πνεῦμα could certainly be used to refer to an evil spirit (Mt. 8.16, 12.45, Ac. 19.12, 23.8, 9, 2 Cor. 11.4, Eph. 2.2, 2 Th. 2.2, 1 Tim. 4.1, Rev. 16.14, etc.). In fact, in all of

---

[57] <u>UP</u>, 137.

[58] <u>UP</u>, 140f.

early Christian literature, the meaning "manifestations of the Spirit" is quite uncommon for πνεύματα, and the meaning "spirits" (of whatever kind) is of course very common.

So the meaning "revelations or utterances of the Spirit through prophets," while possible, is unlikely in 1 Cor. 12.10. It is doubtful whether Paul's readers would have understood πνευμάτων in that sense when another word, "prophecies," would have expressed it so clearly. It is much more likely that the Corinthians would have understood πνευμάτων in its common sense, "spirits."

5. <u>The argument from the context of 1 Cor. 12-14</u>. Dautzenberg's primary argument here is that 1 Cor. 12.3 already provides a test for distinguishing evil spirits, and one which anyone could apply. Therefore, 1 Cor. 12.10 cannot speak of some similar ability which is limited only to a few individuals.[59]

The weakness of this argument is that it fails to recognize the differences which could exist between 12.3 and 12.10. First, it fails to recognize that several of the gifts Paul mentions are simply <u>special</u> or "highly developed" abilities which correspond to <u>general</u> abilities possessed by all believers. Faith, words of wisdom and knowledge, teaching, administration and "helps" (1 Cor. 12.28) are a few examples; more are found in Rom. 12.7-8. So 1 Cor. 12.3 might provide a general test for distinguishing those who are speaking under the influence of an evil spirit, and 1 Cor. 12.10 could speak of a special ability possessed by those who were very proficient in evaluating speakers who were supposedly under some "spiritual" influence.

Second, there may be a difference in the type of evaluation done. While 12.3 speaks of an objective test which could be applied to determine whether spoken words conformed to a certain explicit standard, 12.10 may describe a more subjective or internal kind of evaluation. Robertson and Plummer say, "An intuitive discernment is implied, without the application of tests."[60]

---

[59] <u>UP</u>, 143-46.

[60] RP, 267.

Third, the test in 12.3 seems to be applicable primarily to those who speak before the congregation, while 12.10 may speak of an ability to evaluate many other people as well, such as those who are ill, those who perform miracles, etc.

These suggested differences are enough to show that the existence of one kind of test for evil spirits in 1 Cor. 12.3 does not necessarily preclude the mention of a related but different ability in 1 Cor. 12.10.

The other two arguments which Dautzenberg raises from the context of 1 Cor. 12-14 also make certain unjustified assumptions. The objection that there is no evidence of a problem with false prophecy at Corinth is based on an assumption that 1 Cor. 12.10 would have to deal only with "distinguishing between the spirits of the prophets," an assumption which has been seriously challenged above. The objection that "distinguishing between spirits" would become a "super-charisma" if it existed, fails to recognize that distinguishing between spirits, like other gifts (such as words of wisdom, words of knowledge, teaching or administration), may well have been subject to confirmation or reevaluation by other members of the congregation.

So Dautzenberg's last argument, the argument from the context of 1 Cor. 12-14, does not raise any unanswerable objections against the view that 1 Cor. 12.10 speaks of the ability to distinguish between spirits.

FURTHER OBJECTIONS TO DAUTZENBERG'S POSITION

Each of Dautzenberg's five arguments has now been examined in some detail, and each one has been found to have serious deficiencies. However, there remain some additional weighty objections to Dautzenberg's position which should be mentioned.

1. <u>Dautzenberg's view lacks historical confirmation</u>. We must realize that there is simply no evidence that early Christian prophets ever actually spoke with the aid of an interpreter. When there are examples of prophets in Acts, for example, no interpreter is ever mentioned (cf. Ac. 11.28, 19.6, 21.4, 21.9, 21.10-11). Furthermore, these prophecies at least seem to have needed no interpretation: they were apparently immediately understandable to the hearers

(cf. Ac. 11.28, 21.4, 21.10-11). Yet 1 Cor. 14.29 certainly seems to be a general procedural rule which Paul expected to be followed for every prophecy. And at least two, and perhaps several or all of the members of the congregation are comprehended in οἱ ἄλλοι διακρινέτωσαν. So if Dautzenberg is correct, should we not suppose that every prophecy would have to have been interpreted, and by two or more people in every case? This would make "interpreting the revelations of the Spirit" a very prominent activity, and it would be difficult to understand why we have no other mention of it.

2. <u>Οἱ ἄλλοι in 1 Cor. 14.29 implies evaluation, not interpretation.</u> It must be noticed that Paul's instructions for the interpretation of tongues are general enough to allow the tongue-speaker himself to interpret his own utterance: καὶ εἷς διερμηνευέτω. (14.27). The εἷς who interprets could be the one who speaks (cf. 1 Cor. 14.13). This is acceptable where no evaluation or judgment is in view. But Paul's instructions with respect to prophets are different: καὶ οἱ ἄλλοι διακρινέτωσαν. Now if only interpretation or explanation of the prophecies was intended, there would seem to be no good reason to forbid the prophet himself from being his own interpreter by saying, "Let the others interpret." But if evaluation or judgment of the prophecies was intended, then the prophet himself would not be sufficiently impartial to pass judgment on his own prophecy. Then the phrase οἱ ἄλλοι would become very understandable: <u>others</u> must evaluate the prophecy, for the prophet himself cannot do it.

3. <u>Dautzenberg's position is foreign to Paul's emphasis on the understandable nature of Christian prophecy.</u> Throughout 1 Cor. 14 Paul emphasizes the contrast between the gift of tongues, which are unintelligible and therefore require an interpreter, and the gift of prophecy, which is intelligible. If someone speaks in a tongue, no one understands him (14.2), but one who prophesies speaks to men (14.3). The tongue speaker needs an interpreter in order to edify the church, but the prophet apparently does not (14.5). Tongues are unintelligible (14.9), and drive unbelievers away (14.23). But prophecy calls unbelievers to account and convicts them of sin (14.24-25), presumably with words which they could understand.[61]

---

[61]Dautzenberg realizes the force of this objection and tries to make 14.24-25 speak of a special

Now it is true that the revelation to the prophet may not always be completely clear to him, and may in fact sometimes be obscure in parts.62 But there is a great difference between an understandable prophecy with a few obscure details, and a prophecy which is so obscure that it needs an interpreter in order to edify others.

It is not enough, then, for Dautzenberg to object that, unlike tongues, prophecies are <u>intelligible</u> (that is, they are spoken in words which the congregation can understand), but they are not <u>understandable</u> (that is, their meaning is obscure). This position still does not explain how apparently uninterpreted prophecies can benefit the congregation.

CONCLUSION

Professor Dautzenberg's proposal that διάκρισις πνευμάτων in 1 Cor. 12.10 means "interpreting the revelations of the Spirit" (which are spoken by prophets) is supported by five major arguments. Each of these arguments, upon careful analysis, turns out to be unconvincing. In particular, it was found that many different words are used by Jewish and Christian authors to refer to the interpretation of prophecies and other inspired or obscure speech, but διάκρισις is not one of them. Nor was πνευμάτων a clear word to apply to "revelations of the Spirit" spoken through the prophets: προφητειῶν would have been much better. Dautzenberg's view also lacks historical confirmation and seems to conflict with Paul's emphasis on the understandable nature of prophecy and his desire that <u>others</u> respond to the prophecy (1 Cor. 14.29). So the more common translation, "distinguishing between spirits," is still to be preferred.

---

function of prophecy, that of Überführung (<u>UP</u>, 123, n. 7; 247f). But this is simply special pleading: 1 Cor. 14.24-25 is part of Paul's overall argument for the use of prophecy instead of uninterpreted tongues in the worship service.

62See above, pp. 79f, for example.

BIBLIOGRAPHY

Only works cited in the text have been included here. Standard reference works such as concordances and lexicons have been omitted. Only articles from TDNT of special importance to this study have been included.

Aalen, S. "A Rabbinic Formula in 1 Cor. 14.34." Studia Evangelica II: I Edited by F. L. Cross. Berlin: Akademie--Verlag, 1964.

Abbott, T. K. A Critical and Exegetical Commentary on the Epistles to the Ephesians and to the Colossians. ICC. Edinburgh: Clark, 1897.

Abelson, J. The Immanence of God in Rabbinical Literature. London: Macmillan, 1912.

Abrahams, I. Studies in Pharisaism and the Gospels: Second Series. Cambridge: University Press, 1924.

Achelis, H. "Katoptromantie bei Paulus." Theologische Festschrift für G. Nathaniel Bonwetsch. Leipzig, 1918. (Not available to me.)

Albright, W. F. From the Stone Age to Christianity. New York: Doubleday, 1957².

Albright, W. F. and C. S. Mann, "Two Texts in 1 Corinthians." NTS 16 (1969-70), 271-76.

Allo, E. B. Saint Paul: Première épître aux Corinthiens. Paris: Gabalda, 1956².

Anderson, Hugh. The Gospel of Mark. NCB. London: Oliphants, 1976.

Arai, Sasagu. "Die Gegner des Paulus im 1. Korintherbrief und das Problem der Gnosis." NTS 19 (1972-73), 430-37.

Baillie, John. The Idea of Revelation in Recent Thought. New York: Columbia University Press, 1956.

Baker, David. "The Interpretation of 1 Cor. 12-14," EQ 46 (1974), 224-34.

Barr, James. "The Interpretation of Scripture, II. Revelation Through History in the OT and in Modern Theology." Interp. 17 (1963), 193-205.

Barr, James. "Revelation." (Hastings's) Dictionary of the Bible. Edinburgh: Clark, 1963², 847-49.

Barrett, C. K. "The Apostles in and after the NT." SEÅ 21 (1956), 30-49.

Barrett, C. K. "Cephas and Corinth." Abraham unser Vater. (Fs. O. Michel). Edited by Otto Betz et al. Leiden: Brill, 1963.

Barrett, C. K. "Christianity at Corinth." BJRL 46:2 (March, 1964), 269-97.

Barrett, C. K. A Commentary on the First Epistle to the Corinthians. BNTC. London: Black 1971.²

Barrett, C. K. The Holy Spirit and the Gospel Tradition. London: SPCK, 1966².

Barrett, C. K. The Signs of an Apostle. London: Epworth, 1970.

Barth, Markus. Ephesians. The Anchor Bible. 2 vols. Garden City, N.Y.: Doubleday, 1974.

Beare, F. W. "Sayings of the Risen Jesus in the Synoptic Tradition." Christian History and Interpretation. (Fs. John Knox). Edited by W. R. Farmer, C. F. D. Moule and R. R. Niebuhr. Cambridge: University Press, 1967.

Beasley-Murray, G. R. The Book of Revelation. NCB. London: Oliphants, 1974.

Best, Ernest. A Commentary on the First and Second Epistles to the Thessalonians. BNTC. London: Black, 1972.

Best, Ernest. One Body in Christ. London: SPCK, 1955.

Best, Ernest. 1 Peter. NCB. London: Oliphants, 1971.

Best, Ernest. "Prophets and Preachers." SJT 12 (1959), 129-50.

Betz, Hans Dieter. Lukian von Samosata und das Neue Testament. TU 76. Berlin: Akademie-Verlag, 1961.

Bittlinger, Arnold. Gifts and Graces: A Commentary on 1 Corinthians 12-14. Translated by Herbert Klassen. ET London: Hodder and Stoughton, 1967.

Blank, Sheldon. "'Of a Truth the Lord Hath Sent Me': An Inquiry into the Source of the Prophet's Authority." Interpreting the Prophetic Tradition. Introduction by Harry M. Orlinsky. Cincinnati: Hebrew Union College Press, 1969.

Blau, Ludwig. "Bat Ḳol." The Jewish Encyclopedia. Edited by Isidore Singer et al. 12 vols. New York and London: Funk and Wagnalls, 1901-06. II, 588-92.

Blenkinsopp, Joseph. "Prophecy and Priesthood in Josephus." JJS 25 (1974), 239-62.

Boring, M. Eugene. "The Apocalypse as Christian Prophecy." Society of Biblical Literature 1974 Seminar Papers. Edited by George MacRae 2 vols. Cambridge, Mass., 1974.

Boring, M. Eugene. "How May We Identify Oracles of Christian Prophets in the Synoptic Tradition? Mark 3.28-29 as a Test Case." JBL 91 (1972), 501-21.

Bowker, John W. "'Merkabah' Visions and the Visions of Paul," JSS 16 (1971), 157-73.

Bowman, John. "Prophets and Prophecy in Talmud and Midrash." EQ 22 (1950), 107-114, 205-220, 255-275.

Broglie, G. de. "Le texte fondamental de Saint Paul contre la foi naturelle." RScR (1951-52), 253-66.

Brown, Colin. "Bultmann Revisited." The Churchman 88 (1974), 167-87.

Brox, Norbert. "ΑΝΑΘΕΜΑ ΙΗΣΟΥΣ (1 Kor. 12.3)." BZ n.s. 12 (1968), 103-11.

Bruce, F. F. 1 and 2 Corinthians. NCB. London: Oliphants, 1971.

Bruce, F. F. "The Spirit in the Apocalypse." Christ and Spirit in the New Testament. (Fs. C. F. D. Moule). Edited by Barnabas Lindars and Stephen Smalley. Cambridge: University Press, 1973.

Bruner, Frederick Dale. A Theology of the Holy Spirit: The Pentecostal Experience and the New Testament Witness. Grand Rapids: Eerdmans, 1970.

Bultmann, Rudolf. The History of the Synoptic Tradition. Translated by John Marsh. ET Oxford: Blackwell, 1968.^{2}

Burrows, Millar, ed. The Dead Sea Scrolls of St. Mark's Monastery, Vol. I: The Isaiah Manuscript and the Habakkuk Commentary. New Haven: The American Schools of Oriental Research, 1950.

Burrows, Millar. "Variant Readings in the Isaiah Manuscript," BASOR 111 (1948), 16-24 and 113 (1949), 24-32.

Burton, Ernest de Witt. A Critical and Exegetical Commentary on the Epistle to the Galatians. ICC. Edinburgh: Clark, 1921.

Caird, G. B. Paul's Letters from Prison. NC1B. Oxford: University Press, 1976.

Calvin, John. Commentaries on the Epistles of Paul to the Galatians and Ephesians. Translated by Wm. Pringle. Edinburgh: Calvin Translation Society, 1854.

Calvin, John. The First Epistle of Paul the Apostle to the Corinthians. Translated by John W. Fraser. Edited by David W. Torrance and Thomas F. Torrance. ET Grand Rapids: Eerdmans, 1960.

Campenhausen, Hans von. Ecclesiastical Authority and Spiritual Power in the Church of the First Three Centuries. Translated by J. A. Baker. ET London: Black, 1969.

Carrington, Philip. According to Mark. Cambridge: University Press, 1960.

Chantry, Walter. Signs of the Apostles. Edinburgh: Banner of Truth, 1973.

Charles, R. H. Eschatology: A Critical History of the Doctrine of a Future Life. London: Black, 1913².

Charles, R. H. Religious Development Between the Old and New Testaments. London: Butterworth, 1914.

Charlesworth, James H. The Odes of Solomon. Oxford: Clarendon Press, 1973.

Charlesworth, James H. "The Odes of Solomon--Not Gnostic." CBQ 31 (1969), 357-69.

Chevallier, Max-Alain. Esprit de Dieu, paroles d'hommes: Le rôle de l'esprit dans les ministères de la parole selon l'apôtre Paul. Neuchâtel: Delachaux et Niestlé, 1966.

Chrysostom, John. Homilies on the Epistles of Paul to the Corinthians. Translated by T. W. Chambers. Edited by Philip Schaff. NPNF 12. ET Grand Rapids: Eerdmans, 1969 (repr.).

Clements, R. E. Prophecy and Covenant. SBT 43. London: SCM, 1965.

Conybeare, F. C. "The Testament of Solomon," JQR 9 (1898-99), 1-45.

Conzelmann, Hans. Der Brief an die Epheser. Die kleineren Briefe des Apostels Paulus. By Hermann W. Beyer et al. NTD 8. Göttingen: Vandenhoeck and Ruprecht, 1965.

Conzelmann, Hans. 1 Corinthians. Translated by James W. Leitch. Hermeneia. ET Philadelphia: Fortress, 1975.

Cothenet, Éd. "Prophétisme dans le Nouveau Testament." Dictionnaire de la Bible, Supplement 8. Edited by L. Pirot et al. Paris: Letouzey et Ané, 1972.

Cothenet, Éd. "Prophétisme et ministère d'après le Nouveau Testament." La Maison-Dieu 107 (1971), 29-50.

Craghan, John F. "Mari and Its Prophets." BTB 5 (1975), 32-55.

Creed, John Martin. The Gospel According to St. Luke. London: Macmillan, 1930.

Crone, Theodore M. Early Christian Prophecy: A Study of Its Origin and Function. (Doctoral dissertation, Tübingen, 1973). Baltimore, Md., USA: St. Mary's University Press, 1973.

Dahl, Nils A. "Paul and the Church at Corinth according to 1 Corinthians 1.10-4.21." Christian History and Interpretation. (Fs. John Knox). Edited by W. R. Farmer, C. F. D. Moule and R. R. Niebuhr. Cambridge: University Press, 1967.

Dautzenberg, Gerhard. Urchristliche Prophetie: Ihre Erforschung, ihre Voraussetzungen im Judentum und ihre Struktur im ersten Korintherbrief, BWANT 6th series, no. 4. Stuttgart: Kohlhammer, 1975.

Dautzenberg, Gerhard. "Zum religionsgeschichtlichen Hintergrund der διάκρισις πνευμάτων (Kor. 12.10)." BZ 15 (1971), 93-104.

Davies W. D. Paul and Rabbinic Judaism: Some Rabbinic Elements in Pauline Theology. London: SPCK. 1970³.

Delling, Gerhard. "Die biblische Prophetie bei Josephus." Josephus-Studien. Edited by Otto Betz, Klaus Haacker and Martin Hengel. Göttingen: Vandenhoeck and Ruprecht, 1974.

Derrett, J. D. M. "Cursing Jesus (1 Cor. 12.3): The Jews as Religious 'Persecutors.'" NTS 21 (1974-75), 544-554.

Dibelius, Martin. An die Kolosser, Epheser, an Philemon. HNT 12. Third edition, revised by Heinrich Greeven. Tübingen: Mohr, 1953.

Dibelius, Martin, and Hans Conzelmann. The Pastoral Epistles. Translated by Philip Buttolf and Adela Yarbro. Hermeneia Series. ET Philadelphia: Fortress Press, 1972.

Dodd, C. H. The Authority of the Bible. London: Nisbet, 1928.

Dunn, James D. G. *Jesus and the Spirit: A Study of the Religious and Charismatic Experience of Jesus and the First Christians as Reflected in the New Testament*. London: SCM, 1975.

Dunn, James D. G. "New Wine in Old Wine-Skins: VI. Prophet." *ExpT* 85 (1973-74), 4-8.

Dupont-Sommer, A. *The Essene Writings from Qumran*. Translated by G. Vermes. ET Oxford: Blackwell, 1961.

Edwards, Thomas Charles. *A Commentary on the First Epistle to the Corinthians*. London: Hodder and Stoughton, 1903[4].

Eichrodt, Walter. *Theology of the Old Testament*. Translated by J. A. Baker. 2 vols. ET London: SCM, 1961-67.

Eissfeldt, Otto. *The Old Testament: An Introduction*. Translated by Peter R. Ackroyd. Oxford: Blackwell, 1965.

Ellicott, Charles J. *St. Paul's Epistle to the Ephesians*. London: Longmans, Green & Co., 1884[5].

Ellicott, Charles J. *St. Paul's First Epistle to the Corinthians*. London: Longmans, Green & Co., 1887.

Ellis, E. Earle. "Christ and Spirit in 1 Corinthians." *Christ and Spirit in the New Testament*. (Fs. C. F. D. Moule). Edited by Barnabas Lindars and Stephen Smalley. Cambridge: University Press, 1973.

Ellis, E. Earle. *The Gospel of Luke*. NCB. London: Nelson, 1966.

Ellis, E. Earle. *Paul's Use of the Old Testament*. Edinburgh: Oliver and Boyd, 1957.

Ellis, E. Earle. "The Role of the Christian Prophet in Acts." *Apostolic History and the Gospel*. Edited by W. Ward Gasque and R. P. Martin. Exeter: Paternoster, 1970.

Ellis, E. Earle. "'Spiritual' Gifts in the Pauline Community." *NTS* 20 (1973-74), 128-44.

Evans, T. S. 1 Corinthians. The Holy Bible ... with an Explanatory and Critical Commentary ... New Testament, Vol. III. Edited by F. C. Cook. London: John Murray, 1881.

Fascher, Erich. ΠΡΟΦΗΤΗΣ: Eine sprach-und religionsgeschichtliche Untersuchung. Giessen: Töpelmann, 1927.

Field, F. Origenis Hexaplorum quae supersunt ... Fragmenta. Oxford: Clarendon, 1875.

Filson, Floyd V. A Commentary on the Gospel according to St. Matthew. BNTC. London: Black, 1960.

Findlay, G. G. St. Paul's First Epistle to the Corinthians. The Expositor's Greek Testament. Edited by W. Robertson Nicoll. Vol. II. London: Hodder and Stoughton, 1900.

Ford, J. Massingberd. "The First Epistle to the Corinthians or the First Epistle to the Hebrews?" CBQ 28 (1966), 402-16.

Friedrich, Gerhard. "προφήτης: D. Prophets and Prophecies in the New Testament. E. Prophets in the Early Church." TDNT VI, 828-61.

Furnish, Victor P. "Prophets, Apostles, and Preachers: A Study of the Biblical Concept of Preaching." Interp. 17 (1963), 48-60.

Geldenhuys, J. Norval. Supreme Authority: The Authority of the Lord, His Apostles, and the New Testament. London: Marshall, Morgan & Scott, 1953.

Gerhardsson, Birger. "Die Boten Gottes und die Apostel Christi." SEÅ 27 (1963), 89-131.

Gnilka, Joachim. Der Epheserbrief. HTKNT X: 2. Freiburg, Basel, Vienna: Herder, 1971.

Godet, F. Commentary on St. Paul's Epistle to the Romans. Translated by A. Cusin. 2 vols. ET Edinburgh, 1892.

Godet, F. Commentary on St. Paul's First Epistle to the Corinthians. Translated by A. Cusin. 2 vols. ET Edinburgh: Clark, 1898.

Goodenough, E. R. An Introduction to Philo Judaeus. Oxford: Blackwell, 1962².

Goudge, H. L. The First Epistle to the Corinthians. WC. London: Methuen, 1926⁵.

Green, Michael. 2 Peter and Jude. TNTC. London: Tyndale, 1968.

Greeven, H. "Propheten, Lehrer, Vorsteher bei Paulus." ZNW 44 (1952-53), 1-43.

Grosheide, F. W. Commentary on the First Epistle to the Corinthians. NIC. Grand Rapids: Eerdmans, 1953.

Grundmann, Walter. Das Evangelium nach Markus. THNT 2. Berlin: Evangelische Verlagsanstalt 1968².

Guillaume, Alfred. Prophecy and Divination among the Hebrews and Other Semites. London: Hodder and Stoughton, 1938.

Gundry, Robert H. "'Ecstatic Utterance' (N.E.B.)?" JTS n.s. 17 (1966), 299-307.

Guttmann, A. "The Significance of Miracles for Talmudic Judaism." HUCA 20 (1947), 363-406.

Guy, H. A. New Testament Prophecy: Its Origin and Significance. London: Epworth, 1947.

Haenchen, Ernst. The Acts of the Apostles. Meyer Series. Translated by Bernard Noble, G. Shinn and R. Mc L. Wilson. ET Oxford: Blackwell, 1971.

Hahn, Ferdinand. "Der Apostolat im Urchristentum: Seine Eigenart und seine Voraussetzungen." KD 20 (1974), 54-77.

Hallo, Wm. W. "Isaiah 28.9-13 and the Ugaritic Abecedaries." JBL 77 (1958), 324-38.

Harless, G. C. A. von. Commentar über den Brief Pauli an die Epheser. Stuttgart: Liesching, 1858².

Harnack, Adolf. The Mission and Expansion of Christianity in the First Three Centuries. Translated by James Moffatt. 2 vols. ET London: Williams and Norgate, 1908².

Hawthorne, Gerald F. "Christian Prophecy and the Sayings of Jesus: Evidence of and Criteria for." SBL 1975 Seminar Papers. Edited by George MacRae. 2 vols. Cambridge, Mass.: Society of Biblical Literature, 1975.

Heinrici, Georg. Kritisch-exegetisches Handbuch über den esrsten Brief an die Korinther. Meyer Series. Göttingen: Vandenhoeck and Ruprecht, 1888.

Helm, Paul. "Revealed Propositions and Timeless Truths." Relig. St. 8 (1972), 127-36.

Hendriksen, William. Ephesians. London: Banner of Truth, 1972.

Héring, Jean. The First Epistle of St. Paul to the Corinthians. Translated by A. W. Heathcote and P. J. Allcock. ET London: Epworth, 1962.

Heschel, Abraham J. The Prophets. New York: Harper and Row, 1962.

Hill, David. "Christian Prophets as Teachers or Instructors in the Church." Prophetic Vocation in the New Testament and Today. Edited by J. Panagopoulos. SNovT 45. Leiden: Brill, 1977, 108-130.

Hill, David. The Gospel of Matthew. NCB London: Oliphants, 1972.

Hill, David. "On the Evidence for the Creative Role of Christian Prophets." NTS 20 (1973-74), 262-74.

Hill, David. "Prophecy and Prophets in the Revelation of St. John." NTS 18 (1971-72), 401-418.

Hindley, J. C. "Towards a Date for the Similitudes of Enoch: An Historical Approach." NTS 14 (1967-68), 551-65.

Hodge, Charles. A Commentary on the Epistle to the Ephesians. Grand Rapids: Eerdmans, 1954.

Hodge, Charles. An Exposition of 1 and 2 Corinthians. Wilmington, Del., USA: Sovereign Grace Publishers, 1972 (repr.).

Hodges, Zane. "The Purpose of Tongues." Bib Sac 120 (1963), 226-33.

Holladay, John S., Jr. "Assyrian Statecraft and the Prophets of Israel." HTR 63 (1970), 29-51.

Holtz, Traugott. "Das Kennzeichen des Geistes (1 Kor. 12.1-3)." NTS 18 (1971-72), 365-76.

Hort, Fenton John Anthony. The Christian Ecclesia. London: Macmillan, 1898.

Hort, F. J. A. Prolegomena to St. Paul's Epistles to the Romans and the Ephesians. London: Macmillan, 1895.

Houston, Walter J. New Testament Prophecy and the Gospel Tradition. Unpublished D. Phil. thesis. Oxford, 1973.

Huffmon, Herbert B. "The Covenant Lawsuit in the Prophets." JBL 78 (1959), 285-95.

Hurd, John Coolidge. The Origin of 1 Corinthians. London: SPCK, 1965.

Hurley, James B. "Did Paul Require Veils or the Silence of Women?" A Consideration of 1 Cor. 11.2-16 and 1 Cor. 14.33b-36." WTJ 35 (1972-73), 190-220.

Hurley, James B. Man and Woman in 1 Corinthians. Unpublished Ph.D. dissertation. Cambridge, 1973.

Jackson, F. J. Foakes and Kirsopp Lake. The Beginnings of Christianity, Part I. 5 vols. London: Macmillan, 1920-33.

Jenkins, Claude. "Origen on 1 Corinthians." JTS 10 (1909), 29-51.

Jepsen, Alfred. Nabi: Soziologische Studien zur alttestamentlichen Literatur und Religionsgeschichte. Munich: C. H. Beck, 1934.

Jeremias, Gert. Der Lehrer der Gerechtigkeit. SUNT 2. Göttingen: Vandenhoeck und Ruprecht, 1963.

Jeremias, Joachim. "ἀκρογωνιαῖος." TDNT I, 792.

Jeremias, Joachim. "Der Eckstein," ΑΓΓΕΛΟΣ 1 (1925), 65-70, 85.

Jeremias, Joachim. "Eckstein - Schlusstein," ZNW 36 (1937).

Jeremias, Joachim. "Κεφαλὴ γωνίας - Ἀκρογωνιαῖος," ZNW 29 (1930), 264-80.

Jeremias, Jörg. "Die Vollmacht des Propheten im Alten Testament." EvTh 31 (1971), 305-22.

Jewett, Robert. Paul's Anthropological Terms. Leiden: Brill, 1971.

Johnson, Aubrey R. The Cultic Prophet in Ancient Israel. Cardiff: Univ. of Wales Press, 1962².

Jones, Peter R. The Apostle Paul: A Second Moses According to 2 Cor. 2.14-4.7. Unpublished Ph.D. dissertation. Princeton, N.J.: 1973.

Joüon, Paul. "Notes de Philologie Paulinienne," RScR 15 (1925), 531-35.

Käsemann, Ernst. "Ministry and Community in the New Testament." Essays on New Testament Themes. SBT 41. Translated by W. J. Montague. ET London: SCM, 1964.

Käsemann, Ernst. "Sentences of Holy Law in the New Testament." New Testament Questions of Today. Translated by W. J. Montague. ET London: SCM, 1969.

Kaufmann, Yehezkel. The Religion of Israel. Translated and abridged by Moshe Greenberg. ET London, 1961.

Kelly, J. N. D. The Pastoral Epistles. BNTC London: Black, 1963.

Kidner, Derek. "Isaiah." The New Bible Commentary, Revised. London: Inter-Varsity, 1970.

Kirk, J. Andrew. "Apostleship Since Rengstorf: Towards a Synthesis." NTS 21 (1974-75), 249-264.

Kline, Meredith G. The Structure of Biblical Authority. Grand Rapids: Eerdmans, 1972.

Knight, Harold. The Hebrew Prophetic Consciousness. London: Lutterworth, 1947.

Koch, Klaus. The Rediscovery of Apocalyptic. SBT Second Series, 22. London: SCM, 1972.

Krämer, Helmut. "προφήτης: A. The Word Group in Profane Greek." TDNT VI, 783-96.

Kümmel, Werner Georg. Introduction to the New Testament: Revised Edition. Translated by Howard Clark Kee. ET London: SCM, 1975.

Ladd, G. E. Revelation. Grand Rapids: Eerdmans, 1972.

Lampe, G. W. H. "'Grievous Wolves' (Acts 20.29)." Christ and Spirit in the New Testament. (Fs. C. F. D. Moule). Edited by Barnabas Lindars and Stephen S. Smalley. Cambrdige: University Press, 1973.

Lane, William L. The Gospel according to Mark. NIC Grand Rapids: Eerdmans, 1974.

Lauterbach, Jacob Z. Mekilta de Rabbi Ishmael. 3 vols. Philadelphia: Jewish Publication Society, 1933-35.

Leaney, A. R. C. The Gospel According to St. Luke. BNTC. London: Black, 1966^2.

Leenhardt, Franz J. The Epistle to the Romans. Translated by Harold Knight. ET London: Lutterworth, 1961.

Leivestad, Ragnar. "Das Dogma von der prophetenlosen Zeit." NTS 19 (1972-73), 288-99.

Lenski, R. C. H. The Interpretation of St. Paul's First and Second Epistles to the Corinthians. Minneapolis: Augsburg, 1937.

Lewis, George. The Philocalia of Origen. Edinburgh: Clark, 1911.

Lietzmann, Hans. An die Korinther I-II. Revised by W. G. Kümmel. HNT 9. Tübingen: Mohr, 1949^4.

Lightfoot, J. B. The Apostolic Fathers. 5 vols. London: Macmillan, 1889-90.

Lightfoot, J. B. Notes on Epistles of St. Paul. London: Macmillan, 1895.

Lightfoot, J. B. St. Paul's Epistle to the Galatians. London: Macmillan, 1896^{10}.

Lindblom, Johannes. "Altchristlicher Prophetismus." Gesichte und Offenbarung. Lund: Gleerup, 1968, 162-205.

Lindblom, Johannes. Prophecy in Ancient Israel. Oxford: Blackwell, 1962.

Lührmann, Dieter. Das Offenbarungsverständnis bei Paulus und in paulinischen Gemeinden. WMANT 16. Neukirchen-Vluyn: Neukirchener Verlag, 1965.

McCown, Chester Charles. The Testament of Solomon. Leipzig: Hinrichs, 1922.

McKelvey, R. J. "Christ the Cornerstone." NTS 8 (1961-62), 352-59.

McKelvey, R. J. The New Temple. The Church in the New Testament. Oxford Theological Monographs. Oxford: University Press, 1969.

Maly, K. "1 Kor. 12.1-3, eine Regel zur Unterscheidung der Geister?" BZ n.s. 10 (1966), 82-95.

Maly, Karl. Mündige Gemeinde: Untersuchungen zur pastoralen Führung des Apostels Paulus im 1. Korintherbrief. SBM 2. Stuttgart: Katholisches Bibelwerk, 1967.

Manson, T. W. "The Corinthian Correspondence (1)." Studies in the Gospels and Epistles. Edited by Matthew Black. Manchester: University Press, 1962.

Mare, W. H. "Prophet and Teacher in the New Testament Period." BETS 9 (1966), 139-48.

Martin, William J. "1 Cor. 11.2-16: An Interpretation." Apostolic History and the Gospel. (Fs. F. F. Bruce). Edited by W. Ward Gasque and R. P. Martin. Exeter: Paternoster, 1970.

Masson, Charles. L'Épître de Saint Paul aux Éphésiens. In L'Épître de Saint Paul aux Galates; L'Épître de Saint Paul aux Éphésiens. By Pierre Bonnard and Charles Masson. CNT IX. Neuchâtel: Delachaux and Niestlé, 1953.

Metzger, Bruce. A Textual Commentary on the Greek New Testament. London and New York: United Bible Societies, 1971.

Meuzelaar, J. J. Der Leib des Messias. Aasen: van Gorcum, 1961.

Meyer, Heinrich August Wilhelm. Critical and Exegetical Handbook to the Acts of the Apostles. Translated by Paton J. Gloag and William P. Dickson. 2 vols. ET Edinburgh: Clark, 1877.

Meyer, Heinrich August Wilhelm. Critical and Exegetical Handbook to the Epistle to the Ephesians and the Epistle to Philemon. Translated by M. J. Evans. Edinburgh: Clark, 1895.

Meyer, Heinrich August Wilhelm. Critical and Exegetical Handbook to the Epistles to the Corinthians. Translated by D. Douglas Bannerman and William P. Dickson. ET New York: Funk and Wagnalls, 1884.

Meyer, Rudolf. Der Prophet aus Galiläa: Studie zum Jesusbild der drei ersten Evangelien. Darmstadt: Wissenschaftliche Buchgesellschaft, 1970^2.

Meyer, Rudolf. "προφήτης: C. Prophecy & Prophets in the Judaism of the Hellenistic-Roman Period." TDNT VI, 812-28.

Michel, Otto. "Spätjüdisches Prophetentum." Neutestamentliche Studien für Rudolf Bultmann. BZNW 21. Edited by Walter Eltester. Berlin: Töpelmann, 1957.

Miguens, Emanuel. "1 Cor. 13:8-13 Reconsidered." CBQ 37 (1975), 76-97.

Minear, Paul S. "False Prophecy and Hypocrisy in the Gospel of Matthew." Neues Testament und Kirche. (Fs. R. Schnackenburg). Edited by J. Gnilka. Freiburg, Basel, Vienna: Herder, 1974.

Mitton, C. Leslie. The Epistle to the Ephesians: Its Authorship, Origin and Purpose. Oxford: Clarendon Press, 1951.

Moffatt, James. The First Epistle of Paul to the Corinthians. MNTC. London: Hodder and Stoughton, 1938.

Monod, Adolphe. Explication de l'Épître de Saint Paul aux Éphésians. Paris: Meyrueis, 1867.

Moore, George Foot. *Judaism in the First Centuries of the Christian Era.* 3 vols. Cambridge, Mass.: Harvard University Press, 1927-30.

Moran, W. L. "New Evidence from Mari on the History of Prophecy." *Biblica* 50 (1969), 15-56.

Morris, Leon. *Apocalyptic.* London: Inter-Varsity, 1973.

Morris, Leon. *The First Epistle of Paul to the Corinthians.* TNTC London: Tyndale, 1958.

Mosbech, Holger. "Apostolos in the NT." *ST* 2 (1948), 166-200.

Moule, C. F. D. *The Epistles of Paul the Apostle to the Colossians and to Philemon.* CGT. Cambridge: University Press, 1957.

Mowinckel, Sigmund. *The Old Testament as the Word of God.* Translated by Reidar B. Bjornard. ET Oxford: Blackwell, 1960.

Mowinckel, Sigmund. "'The Spirit' and 'The Word' in the Pre-Exilic Reforming Prophets." *JBL* 53 (1934), 199-227.

Müller, Ulrich B. *Prophetie und Predigt im Neuen Testament: Formgeschichtliche Untersuchungen zur urchristlichen Prophetie.* Gütersloh: Mohn, 1975.

Munck, Johannes. *Paul and the Salvation of Mankind.* Translated by Frank Clarke. ET London: SCM, 1959.

Munck, Johannes. "Paul, the Apostles, and the Twelve." *ST* 3 (1950), 96-110.

Mussner, Franz. "Contributions made by Qumran to the understanding of the Epistle to the Ephesians " [sic]. *Paul and Qumran.* Edited by J. Murphy O'Connor. London: Chapman, 1968.

Myers, Jacob M. and Edwin D. Freed. "Is Paul Also Among the Prophets?" *Interp.* 20 (1966), 40-53.

Neugebauer, F. "Geistsprüche und Jesuslogien." *ZNW* 53 (1962), 218-28.

Nikolainen, Aimo T. "Über die theologische Eigenart der Offenbarung des Johannes." *TLZ* 93 (1968), 161-70.

Nineham, D. E. The Gospel of St. Mark. Pelican Gospel Commentaries. London: Black, 1968².

Nock, Arthur Darby. "Gnosticism." Essays on Religion and the Ancient World. Edited by Zeph Stewart. 2 vols. Oxford: Clarendon Press, 1972. (=HTR 57 [1964], 255-79).

Orr, William F., and James A. Walther. 1 Corinthians. Anchor Bible. Garden City, N.Y.: Doubleday, 1976.

Parke, H. W., and D. E. W. Wormell. The Delphic Oracle. 2 vols. Oxford: Blackwell, 1956².

Patsch, Hermann. "Die Prophetie des Agabus." ThZ 28 (1972), 228-232.

Pearson, Birger A. "Did the Gnostics Curse Jesus?" JBL 86 (1967), 301-305.

Pearson, Birger A. The Pneumatikos-Psychikos Terminology in 1 Corinthians: A Study of the Theology of the Corinthian Opponents of Paul and Its Relation to Gnosticism. SBLDS 12. Missoula, Mt., USA: Society of Biblical Literature, 1973.

Perrin, Norman. Rediscovering the Teaching of Jesus. London: SCM, 1967.

Pfammatter, J. Die Kirche als Bau. Analecta Gregoriana 110. Rome: Libreria Editrice dell' Università Gregoriana, 1960.

Plummer, Alfred. A Critical and Exegetical Commentary on the Gospel According to S. Luke. ICC. Edinburgh: Clark, 1922⁵.

Pritchard, James B. Ancient Near Eastern Texts Relating to the Old Testament. Princeton, N.J.: Princeton University Press, 1950.

Rad, Gerhard von. Old Testament Theology. Translated by D. M. G. Stalker. 2 vols. London: Oliver and Boyd, 1962-65.

Reiling, J. Hermas and Christian Prophecy: A Study of the Eleventh Mandate. SNovT 37. Leiden: Brill, 1973.

Rendtorff, Rolf. "נָבִיא in the Old Testament." TDNT VI, 796-812.

Rengstorf, Karl Heinrich. "ἀποστέλλω." TDNT I, 398-447.

Richardson, Alan. "Revelation." A Dictionary of Christian Theology. London: SPCK, 1969.

Robeck, Cecil M., Jr. "Th Gift of Prophecy in Acts and Paul." SBET 4 (1974), 15-35 and 5 (1975), 37-54.

Robertson, Archibald and Alfred Plummer. A Critical and Exegetical Commentary on the First Epistle of St. Paul to the Corinthians - ICC Edinburgh: Clark, 1914².

Robertson, O. Palmer. "Tongues: Sign of Covenantal Curse and Blessing." WTJ 38 (1975-76), 43-53.

Robinson, D. W. B. "Charismata Versus Pneumatika: Paul's Method of Discussion." RTR 31 (1972), 49-55.

Robinson, H. Wheeler, Inspiration and Revelation in the OT. Oxford: Clarendon Press, 1946.

Robinson, J. Armitage. The Philocalia of Origen. Cambridge: University Press, 1893.

Robinson, J. Armitage. St. Paul's Epistle to the Ephesians. London: Macmillan, 1909².

Robinson, John A. T. Redating the New Testament. London: SCM, 1976.

Roon, A. van. The Authenticity of Ephesians. SNovT 39. Leiden: Brill, 1974.

Ross, James F. "The Prophet as Yahweh's Messenger." Israel's Prophetic Heritage. (Fs. J. Muilenberg). Edited by Bernhard W. Anderson and Walter Harrelson. London: SCM, 1962.

Rowley, H. H. "The Nature of OT Prophecy in the Light of Recent Study." The Servant of the Lord and and Other Essays on the Old Testament. London: Lutterworth, 1952. (=HTR 38 [1945], 1-38).

Russell, D. S. The Method and Message of Jewish Apocalyptic. OTL. London: SCM, 1964.

Sanday, W. and A. C. Headlam. A Critical and Exegetical Commentary on the Epistle to the Romans. ICC. Edinburgh: Clark, 1902⁵.

Sanders, Jack T. "First Corinthians 13: Its Interpretation Since the First World War." Interp. 20 (1966), 159-87.

Sasse, H. "Apostles, Prophets, Teachers." RTR 27:1 (Jan.-Apr., 1968), 11-21.

Schlatter, Adolf. Paulus der Bote Jesu: Eine Deutung seiner Briefe an die Korinther. Stuttgart: Calwer, 1969⁴.

Schlier, Heinrich. Der Brief an die Epheser. Düsseldorf: Patmos, 1957⁵.

Schmithals, Walter. Gnosticism in Corinth. Translated by John E. Steely. ET Nashville, Tenn.: Abingdon, 1971.

Schmithals, Walter. The Office of Apostle in the Early Church. Translated by J. Steely. ET London: SPCK, 1971.

Schnackenburg, Rudolf. "Apostles Before and During Paul's Time." Translated by Manfred Kwiran and W. Ward Gasque. Apostolic History and the Gospel. Edited by W. Ward Gasque and R. P. Martin. Exeter: Peternoster, 1970.

Schütz, John Howard. Paul and the Anatomy of Apostolic Authority. SNTSMS 26. Cambridge: University Press, 1975.

Schweizer, Eduard. "Observance of the Law and Charismatic Activity in Matthew." NTS 16 (1969-70), 213-30.

Schweizer, Eduard. "The Service of Worship: An Exposition of 1 Cor. 14." Interp. 13 (1959), 400-08.

Scott, R. B. Y. "Is Preaching Prophecy?" CJT 1 (1955), 11-18.

Scroggs, Robin. "The Exaltation of the Spirit by Some Early Christians." JBL 84 (1965), 359-73.

Seitz, O. J. F. "The Commission of Prophets and 'Apostles': A Re-examination of Mt. 23.34 with Lk. 11.49." Studia Evangelica Iv. TU 102. Edited by F. L. Cross. Berlin: Akademie-Verlag, 1968, 236-40.

Selwyn, Edward C. The Christian Prophets and the Prophetic Apocalypse. London: Macmillan, 1900.

Selwyn, Edward Gordon. The First Epistle of St. Peter. London: Macmillan, 1946.

Shank, H. Carl. More of Christ. Cherry Hill, N.J.: Mack, 1973.

Spicq, C. Agapè dans le Nouveau Testament. 3 vols. Paris: Gabalda, 1959.

Stenning, J. F. The Targum of Isaiah. Oxford: Clarendon, 1949.

Stone, Michael E., tr. The Testament of Abraham. Missoula, Mt.: SBL, 1972.

Sweet, J. P. M. "A Sign for Unbelievers: Paul's Attitude to Glossolalia." NTS 13 (1966-67), 240-57.

Swete, Henry Barclay. The Holy Spirit in the New Testament. London: Macmillan, 1910^2.

Swete, H. B. An Introduction to the Old Testament in Greek. Cambridge: University Press, 1902.

Thomas, Robert L. "Tongues ... Will Cease." JETS 17 (1974), 81-89.

Toussaint, S. D. "First Corinthians Thirteen and the Tongues Question." BibSac 120 (1963), 311-16.

Unnik, W. C. van. "A Formula Describing Prophecy," NTS 9 (1962-63), 86-94.

Unnik, W. C. van. "Jesus: Anathema or Kurios (1 Cor. 12.3)." Christ and Spirit in the New Testament. (Fs. C. F. D. Moule). Edited by Barnabas Lindars and Stephen Smalley. Cambridge: University Press, 1973.

Vermes, G. The Dead Sea Scrolls in English. Harmondsworth, Middx: Pelican, 1968^3.

Vielhauer, Philipp. "Apocalyptic." New Testament Apocrypha. Edited by E. Hennecke, W. Schneemelcher, R. McL. Wilson, 2 vols. ET London: SCM, 1963-65. Vol. II, pp. 581-600.

Vielhauer, Philipp. Oikodome. Wiesbaden: Harrassowitz, 1940.

Vielhauer, Philipp. "Prophecy." New Testament Apocrypha. Edited by E. Hennecke, W. Schneemelcher, R. McL. Wilson. 2 vols. ET London: SCM, 1963-65. Vol. II, pp. 601-07.

Vos, Geerhardus. Biblical Theology. Grand Rapids, Mich.: Eerdmans, 1948.

Vriezen, Th. C. An Outline of Old Testament Theology. Translated by S. Neuijen. ET Oxford: Blackwell, 1970^2.

Warfield, Benjamin B. Counterfeit Miracles. Reprinted London: Banner of Truth, 1972.

Weiss, Johannes. Der erste Korintherbrief. Meyer Series. Göttingen: Vandenhoeck and Ruprecht, 1925^{10}.

Wendland, Heinz Dietrich. Die Briefe an die Korinther. NTD. Göttingen: Vandenhoeck and Ruprecht, 1965.

Westcott, Brooke Foss. St. Paul's Epistle to the Ephesians. London: Macmillan, 1906.

Westermann, Claus. Basic Forms of Prophetic Speech. Translated by Hugh Clayton White. ET London: Lutterworth, 1967.

Wilson, R. McL. "How Gnostic were the Corinthians?" NTS 19 (1972-73), 65-74.

Wolfson, Harry Austryn. Philo. 2 vols. Cambridge, Mass.: Harvard Univ. Press, 1947.

Wood, Leon J. "Ecstasy and Israel's Early Prophets." BETS 9 (1966), 125ff.

Young, Edward J. My Servants the Prophets. Grand Rapids: Eerdmans, 1952.

Zuntz, G. The Text of the Epistles: A Disquisition upon the Corpus Paulinum. London: British Academy, 1953.

Index of Authors Cited

Aalen, S., 254

Abbott, T. K., 83, 85, 97

Abelson, J., 25, 26, 197

Abrahams, I., 21

Achelis, H., 146

Albright, W. F., 18, 166

Allo, E. B., 58, 159, 167

Anderson, H., 76

Arai, S., 169

Baillie, J., 117

Baker, D., 161, 162

Barr, J., 17, 18, 116, 117

Barrett, C. K., 26, 44, 52, 55, 56, 57, 58, 62, 128, 156, 158, 159, 162, 167, 177, 178, 269

Barth, M., 83, 86

Beare, F. W., 2

Beasley-Murray, G.R., 108

Best, E., 1, 4, 5, 53, 75, 96, 105, 142, 200, 234

Betz, H. D., 162

Bittlinger, A., 59, 160, 240, 283

Blank, S. H., 13

Blau, L., 29

Blenkinsopp, J., 23, 27

Boring, M. E., 2, 106, 227

Bowker, J. W., 28

Bowman, J., 22

Broglie, G. de, 167

Brown, C., 224

Brox, N., 169

Bruce, F. F., 52, 57, 62, 122, 159, 169, 269

Bultmann, R., 2, 225

Burrows, M., 24, 188

Burton, E. D., 46, 118

Caird, G. B., 83, 95

Calvin, J., 59, 60, 83, 160, 163, 212, 219, 283

Campenhausen, H.von, 44, 111, 112, 171, 208

Carrington, P., 76

Chantry, W., 218

Charles, R. H., 31

Charlesworth, J. H., 225

Chevallier, M., 1, 60, 159, 162

Chrysostom, J., 128, 143, 163

311

Clements, R. E., 12, 13

Conybeare, F. C., 42, 86

Conzelmann, H., 42, 52, 55, 57, 83, 139, 144, 146, 147, 160, 197

Cothenet, É., 1, 2, 3, 4, 31, 46, 62, 80, 84, 101, 105, 111, 206, 208, 248, 269

Craghan, J. F., 12

Creed, J. M., 45

Crone, T. M., 1, 4, 23, 28, 40, 80, 110, 171, 183

Dahl, N. A., 55

Dautzenberg, G., 1, 52, 58, 146, 240, 263-288.

Davies, W. D., 21, 22, 25, 29, 31, 196

Delling, G., 21

Derrett, J. D. M., 165

Dibelius, M., 42, 83

Dodd, C. H., 17

Dunn, J. D. G., 1, 2, 21, 58, 122, 159, 185, 196, 201, 208, 209, 234, 258

Dupont-Sommer, A., 23

Edwards, T. C., 52, 164

Eichrodt, W., 16, 152

Eissfeldt, O., 14

Ellicott, C. J., 52, 56, 60, 83, 128, 160, 163, 170

Ellis, E. E., 2, 3, 45, 49, 76, 120, 122, 160, 191, 206, 234

Evans, T. S., 160, 163, 170

Fascher, E., 22, 34, 40

Field, F., 187, 188, 274

Filson, F. V., 75

Findlay, G. G., 59, 160, 170, 283

Ford, J. M., 55, 248

Friedrich, G., 1, 2, 3, 106, 111, 112, 206

Furnish, V. P., 44

Geldenhuys, J. N., 44

Gerhardsson, B., 14, 44, 47

Gnilka, J., 83

Godet, F., 53, 56, 61, 62, 128, 156, 160, 163, 170, 269

Goodenough, E. R., 152

Goudge, H. L., 128, 160

Green, M., 176

Greeven, H., 1, 5, 57, 60, 128, 234

Grosheide, F. W., 59, 60, 148, 165, 283

Grundmann, W., 76

Guillaume, A., 2
Gundry, R. H., 174, 177
Guttmann, A., 27, 29
Guy, H. A., 1, 2, 53

Haenchen, E., 208
Hahn, F., 44
Hallo, W. W., 187, 189
Harless, G. C. A., 84
Harnack, A., 24, 44, 234
Hawthorne, G. F., 228
Heinrici, G., 164
Helm, P., 117
Hendriksen, W., 83, 97
Héring, J., 52, 57, 62, 146, 156, 163, 164, 250
Heschel, A. J., 2, 18
Hill, D., 75, 106, 107, 109, 143, 224, 225, 226, 227, 228, 229
Hindley, J. C., 32
Hodge, C., 60, 83, 97, 128, 160, 164
Hodges, Z., 199
Holladay, J. S., 12, 16, 18
Holtz, T., 56, 159, 166, 171
Hort, F. J. A., 84

Houston, W. J., 229
Huffmon, H. B., 13
Hurd, J. C., 55, 159, 165
Hurley, J. B., 250

Jackson, F. J. F., 77, 79
Jenkins, C., 144, 168
Jepsen, A., 35
Jeremias, G., 23
Jeremias, Joachim, 85
Jeremias, Jörg, 12, 13
Jewett, R., 124, 125, 126
Johnson, A. R., 18, 36
Jones, P. R., 23, 44, 45
Jouon, P., 84
Käsemann, E., 2, 51, 52, 207, 208, 209, 227
Kaufmann, Y., 31, 46, 152
Kelly, J. N. D., 203
Kidner, D., 190, 192
Kirk, J. A., 13, 44, 47
Kline, M. G., 13, 44
Knight, H., 17
Koch, K., 31
Krämer, H., 40, 41
Kümmel, W. G., 55

Ladd, G. E., 107, 108

Lake, K., 77, 79

Lampe, G. W., xvi, 3, 52, 53, 65, 167

Lane, W. L., 42

Lauterbach, J. Z., 25, 196

Leaney, A. R. C., 45

Leenhardt, F. J., 258

Leivestad, R., 21, 22, 23, 25

Lenski, R. C. H., 59, 60, 122, 283

Lewis, G., 192

Lietzmann, H., 51, 52, 62, 269

Lightfoot, J. B., 43, 98, 100, 105, 206

Lindblom, J., 1, 2, 3, 7, 12, 14, 15, 18, 19, 118, 131, 144, 151, 152

Lührmann, D., 118

McCown, C. C., 42, 86

McKelvey, R. J., 83, 86, 87

Maly, K., 1, 60, 166

Mann, C. S., 166

Manson, T. W., 55

Mare, W. H., 53

Martin, W. J., 240

Masson, C., 83

Metzger, B., 50

Meuzelaar, J. J., 83

Meyer, H. A. W., 51, 58, 80, 83, 84, 97, 122, 156, 163, 170

Meyer, R., 24, 25, 27

Michel, O., 24.

Miguens, E., 147

Minear, P. S., 53

Mitton, C. L., 84

Moffatt, J., 160, 250

Monod, A., 84

Moore, G. F., 21, 29

Morris, L., 31, 159, 170, 212

Mosbech, H., 44, 47

Moule, C. F. D., xvi, 45, 156

Mowinckel, S., 17, 150

Müller, U. B., 1, 2, 3, 200

Munck, J., 55

Murray, G. R., 108

Mussner, F., 85

Myers, J. M., 46, 48

Neugebauer, F., 224

Nikolainen, A. T., 106
Nineham, D. E., 76
Nock, A. D., 169

Oepke, A., 117
Orr, W. F., 56, 249

Parke, H. W., 41, 223
Patsch, H., 81
Pearson, B. A., 52, 160, 163, 168, 169
Perrin, N., 227
Pfammatter, J., 84
Plummer, A., 45
Poythress, V. S., xvi, 188
Pritchard, J. B., 13
Proksch, O., 18

Rad, G. von, 17
Reiling, J., 2, 111, 234
Rendtorff, R., 12
Rengstorf, K. H., 13, 44, 48, 83
Richardson, A., 117
Robeck, C. M., 1
Robertson, A., 51, 56, 59, 116, 128, 148, 160, 163, 170, 212, 283, 285
Robertson, O. F., 199

Robinson, D. W. B., 162
Robinson, J. A., 83, 85, 86, 192
Robinson, J. A. T., 109
Roon, A. van, 84
Ross, J. F., 12, 13, 14
Rowling, H. H., 15
Russell, D. S., 31

Sanday, W., 258
Sanders, J. T., 57
Sasse, H., 1, 2, 130
Schlatter, A., 128, 148
Schlier, H., 83, 197
Schmithals, W., 13, 44, 46, 47, 55, 168, 169
Schnackenburg, R., 44
Schütz, J. H., 44
Schweizer, E., 142, 241
Scroggs, R., 157, 171
Seitz, O. J. F., 45
Selwyn, E. C., 1, 75
Shank, H. C., 212
Spicq, C., 146
Stenning, J. F., 188
Sweet, J. P. M., 55, 196
Swete, H. B., 67, 191

Thomas, R. L., 215

Toussaint, S. D., 217

Unnik, W. C. van, 170, 171, 222

Vermes, G., 24, 30

Vielhauer, P., 3, 24, 31, 83, 226

Vos, G., 15, 18, 135, 152

Vriezen, T. C., 12

Warfield, B. B., 218

Wedderburn, A. J. M., xvi

Weiss, J., 52, 57, 60, 124, 159

Wendland, H. D., 128

Westcott, B. F., 83

Westermann, C., 12, 18, 47

Wilson, R. M., 55, 169

Wolfson, H. A., 21, 23, 26, 27, 41, 144

Wood, L. J., 152

Wormell, D. E. W., 41, 223

Young, E. J., 18, 35, 37, 152

Zuntz, G., 50

Index of Subjects

Agabus, 76, 79-82, 202

Angels
    communicating with
        men, 120-122, 132

Apocalyptic literature,
    31-33

Apostles (NT):
    and Old Testament
        prophets, 43-53

    as messengers of Christ
        43-53

    as prophets, 53-54

    authority of, 48-52

    claims to authority,
        48-52

    in writings of early
        church, 46

    qualifications, 44

    speaking without divine
        authority, 49

Authority of prophecy:
    authority of actual
        words, 9-10, 11-20

    authority of general
        content, 9-10

    different types, 7-10

    Old Testament, 11-20

Bath qol (in NT), 132

Cessation of NT prophecy,
    210-219

Cessation of OT prophecy
    21-33

Corinth:
    problems at, 54-56,
        155-156, 237

1 Corinthians:
    background to, 55

1 Corinthians 12-14:
    purpose of, 54-57

    structure of, 54-56

1 Corinthians 13:8-13
    purpose of, 210

Delphi, Oracle of, 41, 223

Discerning of spirits, 58-60
    280-284

Distinguishing between
    spirits, 58-60, 280-284

Dreams, 132, 259

Ecstasy, definition of, 150-151

Ecstasy, prophetic, 150-176,
    173-177, 180

    in extra-Biblical literature, 152-153

    in OT prophets, 152

Elders, 207, 208-209

Functions of prophecy, 181-2

Gifts (spiritual),

    given through prophecy, 204-205

    greater, 56

    relative importance of, 56-57

Gnosticism at Corinth, 168-169

Gospel tradition,

    prophetic contributions to, 224-229

Interpretation,

    of obscure sayings, 279

    of prophecies, 280

    of riddles, 279

    of Scripture, 278

    of tongues, 279, 287

Love

    distinct from gifts, 210

    in prophesying, 178-179

Montanism, 111

Prophecies (NT),

    could be lost, 67-69

    intended recipient not always known to the speaker, 184

Prophecy,

    and angels, 120-122

    at Mari, 12-13

    false, 10, 37

    in early church history, 111-112

    in extra-biblical literature, 21-33, 196

    in extra-biblical literature as sign of God's favor, 196

    in history of religions, 4

    in Josephus, 23

    in Philo, 23

    intertestamental Jewish views, 21-33

    rabbinic views, 22

    two types, 3

Prophecy (NT),

    ability to prophesy, 234-239, 256-258, 261

    and bestowing of gifts, 203-205

    and contributions to Gospel tradition, 224-229

    and exposition of Scripture, 206

    as sign of God's attitude, 185-205

    content of, 219-221, 229

degrees of prophetic ability, 257-258, 261

different from preaching, 139-144

different from teaching, 139-144, 185

disobeyed by Paul, 78

edification as result, 182

encouragement as result, 182

essential characteristics of, 139-144

evaluation of, 62-67, 105-106, 250-255

forms of, 222, 230

functions of, 181-219, 228-229

imperfection of, 149-150, 180

inaccuracies in, 79-82

intelligible, 154, 223, 287-288

judging of, 62-67, 105-106, 250-255

lightly esteemed, 67-69, 105-106

must function publically, 140, 143, 181-182

need for evaluation of, 62-67, 105-106

no distinctive functions, 183-184

not merely prediction, 183-184

prayer for gift of, 259-260

prediction as a function of, 202

reason for great value, 184-185

revealing heart secrets 197-201

revelation required for, 140-144, 203

seeking the gift of prophecy, 259-261

whether ecstatic, 155, 173-177

whether miraculous or not, 136

whether praise included in, 206-207

whether prayer included in, 206

whether temporary or permanent gift, 256-258

with divine authority of actual words, 1-3, 53-54, 75, 81-82, 105, 106-109, 110, 112-113 without divine authority of actual words, 54-74, 76, 77-79, 82, 105-106, 110-111, 112-113

Prophets (NT),

and Gospel proclamation, 206

as charismatic leaders, 207-210

in book of revelation, 107-109

in foundation of church, 82-105

informal recognition of, 231-234

knowing mysteries, 177-178

not forced to speak, 153-154

not unaware of surroundings, 154-155

psychological state of, 115-180

qualifications for, 231-261

speaking in love, 178-179

subject to Paul's authority, 72

unable to speak God's words, 71

whether a recognized office, 231-234, 261

whether ecstatic, 150-176, 180

Revelation,

in apocalyptic literature, 31-33

in dead-sea scrolls, 30

in extra-biblical Jewish literature, 24-33

in inter-testamental literature, 24-33

in Josephus, 30

in Philo, 30

in rabbinic litature, 27-29

Revelation, book of

as prophecy, 106-109, 205

Revelation,

NT terms for, 131-132

of divine origin, 119

to NT prophet, 116-136

which does not result in prophecy, 139-140

without divine authroity of actual words, 69-70

Revelation to NT prophets,

clarity of, 147-149

how to know whether from Holy Spirit, 150

nature of, 135-136, 179

Seers, 182

Soothsaying,

    pagan, 129

Speaking in tongues, 174, 192-201, 211, 222-223

    interpretation of, 279-280, 287

    purpose of, 198-199

Teaching (NT)

    difference between teaching and prophecy, 139-144, 185

Trances, 132

Visions, 132, 174

Women as prophets, 72-73, 78-79, 239-255, 261

Index of Hebrew and Greek Words Discussed

Hebrew

הִתְנַבֵּא, 35

כֹּה אָמַד יהוה, 16

לְמַעַן, 186

מַרְאָה, 145-146

נָבִיא, 33-43

פֵּשֶׁר, 273-275

פֵּשֶׁר, 273-275

פָּתַר, 274-275

פִּתָרוֹן, 274-275

צוּ, 186-189

קוּ, 186-189

Greek

ἅγιος, 108

ἀκρογωνιαῖος, 85-86

ἀνάθεμα Ἰησοῦς, 164-172

ἀπάγω, 162-164

ἀποκαλύπτω, ἀποκάλυψις, 69-70, 116-117, 118, 119, 129-131, 134-135, 142-144, 179

ἀπόστολος, 47-48, 109

αὐξάνων, 92

βλέπων, 48

γραφή, 175

δέω, 79

διὰ τοῦ πνεύματος, 76, 78

διάκονος, 109

διακρίνω, 58, 64-66, 110, 271-282

διακρίσεις πνευμάτων, 58-60 263-288

διάκρισις, 58, 271-282

διδασκαλία, 142

διδάσκαλος, 109, 142

διδάσκω, 142

διδαχή, 142

δοκιμάζω, 65-66
δύναμις, 133
εἰς + accusative, 192-194
εἰσακούω, 191
εἴτε . . . εἴτε, 211
ἐκ μέρους, 211
ἔκστασις, 132-133
ἐν πνεύματι, 172-173
ἐνύπνιον, 132
ἐξῆλθεν (1 Cor. 14:36), 71
ἐξίστημι, 133
ἐπιγινώσκω, 213
ἐπίσκοπος, 109
θεμέλιος, 82-105
θεσπίζω, 48
θεσπιστής, 48
ἰδιώτης, 197
καταργέω, 149, 214, 216-217
κατηχέω, 142
κρίνω, 65-66, 276, 279
κρίσις, 276, 279
λαλέω, 242-244, 252
λέγει κύριος, 49
μαίνομαι, 133
μανθάνω, 185

μανία, 133
μαντεία, 129
μείζων, 56
οἱ ἄλλοι (1 Cor. 14:29), 60-62, 287
οἰκοδομή, 182
ὄναρ, 132
ὀπτασία, 132
ὅραμα, 132
ὅρασις, 132
παιδεία, 142
παιδεύω, 142
παραδίδωμι, 79
παράκλησις, 182
παραμυθία, 183
περὶ δέ, 161
πνεῦμα, 284
πνεύματα, 120-129, 284-285
πνευματικός, 157-161
ποιμήν, 109
πρεσβύτερος, 109
πρόσωπον, 147-149, 213
προφήτης, 107, 232, 234
σημαίνω, 76

σημεῖον, 133, 193-196

σιγάω, 242-244, 252

σιωπάω, 244

συγκρίνω, 276

σύγκρισις, 275

τάδε λέγει, 79, 82

τέλειος,]12-]13

τέρας, 133

τί οὖν, 245

ὑποτάσσω, 125

φανερός, 118, 200

φανερόω, 118, 200

φιμόω, 244

χάρισμα, 204

χρηματίζω, 131-132

ὡς ἄν, 163

Index of Biblical and Extra-biblical Passages Discussed

Old Testament

Numbers

11:24-30   36
11:29   46
12:6-8   145

Deuteronomy

18:15-22   19
18:20   66
18:22   66
34:10   145

I Samuel

10:5-13   36
18:10-11   34
19:20-24   34

I Chronicles

25:1-7   35

Isaiah

28:9-13   186-190
28:11   190-192

Joel

2:28   46

New Testament

Matthew

10:19-20   75
11:27   70
13:34   244

Mark

4:34   244

Luke

7:39   141

9:36   242
11:49 45, 75
18:39 242
22:64 42
23:63f 141

John
4:19   42, 141
11:49-52 149
11:51 141
14:26 226
18:20 244

Acts
2:17-18 75
2:30f 141
8:18   205
11:18 243
11:27-30 202
11:28 76, 141
13:2   77
13:8   59, 283
15:22 53
15:32 53, 201-202, 209-210
16:6-7 74
16:16-18 59, 282
19:6   77-78, 141, 174, 236

20:23 74
21:4   78, 149
21:9   78-79
21:10-11 79-82, 141
21:11 149, 202
21:14 243
28:17 80

Romans
1:18   70
11:29 257
12:6   258
15:18 244
16:26 53, 75

I Corinthians
1:7   214
2:14   260
11:5   72, 240, 254-255
11:31 64
12-14 54-58
12:1-3 156-173
12:1   157-161, 172
12:2   156, 162-164
12:3   164-169, 172-173
12:8-10 265-268
12:8-11 136-138

12:10	58, 263-288	14:33	126-127
12:11	256	14:33b	239
12:28	55, 56, 232	14:34	73, 252-254
12:29	236, 256	14:34-35	239-255
12:31	56, 259	14:36	70, 61, 251
13	57	14:37	50, 51, 160-161, 23 233, 256
13:1-13	56	14:37-38	50-53
13:2	177-179, 256	14:39	259
13:8-12	144-150	14:40	155
13:8-13	210-219		
13:10	211-219		
13:12	212-213		

II Corinthians

12:1ff   174-175

14:1-35   56

14:1   259

Galatians

1:11-12   48-49

14:3   181-185, 206-207

14:3-4   155

Ephesians

14:6   138-139

1:17   70

14:20-25   185-201

2:14-18   90

14:23-25   155

2:20   82-105

14:26-36   245-251

3:5   92, 103-104, 141

14:28   242, 258

4:11   97

14:29   58-67, 231-234, 287

5:22   255

14:29-33   152-155

Philippians

14:30   67-70, 115-136, 242

3:15   70

14:31   185

14:32   120-129, 232, 233

Colossians

3:18   255

I Thessalonians

1:8   244

4:19-21   63, 105, 282

II Thessalonians

2:2   74

I Timothy

1:18   202-203

2:11-12   255

2:12   244

4:1   74

4:14   203-205, 258

II Timothy

1:6   258

Titus

1:12   42

2:5   255

Hebrews

3:1   45

I Peter

1:10   75

3:11   255

4:11   75

II Peter

1:20-21   75

1:21   175

3:2   45

I John

4:1   66, 75

4:1-6   63, 282, 283

Revelation

1:1ff   133

1:3   107

2:3   222

3:1   126

4:5   126

5:6   126

11   107

19:9   107

19:10   107-108

21:5   107

Extra-biblical Literature
(see also pp. 21-33, passim)

INTERTESTAMENTAL LITERATURE

2 Baruch
85:3 22

1 Maccabees
4:45-46 21
9:27 22
14:41 22

Prayer of Azariah
15 22

Testament of Solomon
15:8 42

Wisdom
7:27 39

JOSEPHUS

Contra Apionem
1:114 277

Antiquitates Judaica
8:148 277

RABBINIC LITERATURE

b. Ber.
57b 259
55b 259

Gen. R.
17:5 259
44:7 259

M. Sanh.
11:5 119

THE DEAD SEA SCROLLS

1 QS
9:11 23

EARLY CHRISTIAN LITERATURE

1 Clement
42:4 209
44:3 209

Didache
11 109
11:3-12 62

11:7	110, 282	_Martyrdom of Polycarp_	
12:1	66	12:3	42
15:1	210		

Ignatius: Epistle to the Magnesians

Odes of Solomon

42:6   225-226

5:2   206